Thinking
Directed, undirected and creative

Thinking

Directed, undirected and creative

Third edition

K.J. GILHOOLY

*Department of Psychology, University of
Aberdeen, Aberdeen, Scotland*

ACADEMIC PRESS

Harcourt Brace & Company, Publishers
London   San Diego   New York
Boston   Sydney   Tokyo   Toronto

ACADEMIC PRESS LIMITED
24–28 Oval Road
London NW1 7DX

U.S. Edition Published by
ACADEMIC PRESS INC.
San Diego, CA 92101

This book is printed on acid-free paper

Copyright © 1996
ACADEMIC PRESS LIMITED
Second printing 1997

A catalogue record for this book is available from the British Library

ISBN 0–12–283485–2

Typeset by LaserScript, Mitcham, Surrey
Printed and bound in Great Britain by Hartnolls Ltd, Bodmin, Cornwall

Preface

As with the previous Editions, this book is intended to be an introduction to recent research and theory concerning thought processes in normal human adults. The major topics dealt with are (i) thinking directed at solving problems, (ii) less directed forms of thinking such as are found in daydreaming and (iii) creative thinking. While these topics are largely considered from the perspective of the information processing approach, which is currently dominant in cognitive psychology, some historical background is also provided (particularly in the first chapter). In the final chapter, an attempt is made to assess the progress achieved within the information processing approach to thinking and to indicate promising directions for future research. To help the interested reader go more deeply and widely into the various topics raised in the book, I have made suggestions for further readings at the end of each chapter.

A major change in this Third Edition is the provision of a chapter on propositional reasoning. In addition, there has been a general up-dating of material throughout to reflect some of the many developments over the eight years or so since the Second Edition appeared. To make space for new material there has also been some pruning. Among the topics and approaches given more extended discussion in this Edition are: Cognitive science; connectionism; analogical reasoning; insight; search and working memory in chess; medical expertise; practice and expertise; decision making; propositional reasoning; social contract and optimality approaches to rule testing; and models of creative processes.

The level of treatment is pitched at students who already have some background in psychology. As well as students and teachers concerned with courses on the psychology of thinking, I hope that the book will also be of interest to researchers, teachers and practitioners in other areas of psychology and in related disciplines, such as education, cognitive science and artificial intelligence.

While preparing this Edition I benefitted greatly from discussions of issues in the study of thinking with many fellow psychologists and cognitive scientists. Among those who helped me in this way, I would particularly like to thank Robert Logie, Pertti Saariluoma and Norman Wetherick for their contributions to my thinking about working memory, expertise and reasoning respectively. Of course, it should not be assumed that they agree with my final treatment of the topics concerned.

Production of this book was greatly facilitated by excellent assistance from Caroline Green and Val Wynn, both of whom I am pleased to acknowledge here.

January, 1996   K J Gilhooly

Contents

1

Introduction

Thinking is an activity that has long intrigued and puzzled psychologists and philosophers – and continues to do so. Since all valuable innovations in the arts and sciences originate from fruitful thinking, it is a process of evident importance. At a more prosaic level, thought is frequently required to deal effectively with the various frustrations that arise in everyday activities. Even when not dealing with any pressing problems, thinking is always occurring, during periods of wakefulness, albeit often in a free-floating daydreaming fashion. It is desirable to obtain a good theoretical understanding of thinking, not only for the sake of pure knowledge, but also with a view to helping people to think more effectively. This book, then, aims to review recent attempts, involving new approaches, techniques and experiments, to increase our understanding of thinking. The focus will be on thinking in normal adult humans, particularly problem-directed thinking, undirected daydreaming and creative thinking.

I. PRELIMINARIES

A. Characterizing thinking

The term 'thinking' will be taken as referring to a set of processes whereby people assemble, use and revise internal symbolic models. These models may be intended to represent reality (as in science) or conceivable reality (as in fiction), or may even be quite abstract with no particular external interpretation intended (as in music or pure mathematics). This text will be mainly concerned with the first case, which is typical in problem solving. Thinking directed toward problem solving may be regarded as exploring a symbolic model of the task to determine a course of action that should be the best (or at least be satisfactory). A symbolic model often enables the thinker to go far beyond the perceptually available information (Bruner, 1957), and to anticipate the outcomes of alternative actions without costly overt trial and error. The first psychologist to describe thinking explicitly in terms of running symbolic models appears to have been Kenneth Craik (1943; see also Zangwill,

1980). To illustrate his analysis, Craik used the example of a bridge builder determining a viable design by exploring symbolic models of possible bridges, rather than by overt and costly trial and error with real bridges.

The general view of thinking adopted here is 'reflexive' in that it encompasses the activity of psychologists as well as the activities of psychologists' subjects. Psychologists seek to assemble symbolic models of how humans (including themselves) assemble and utilize symbolic models. As Wetherick (1979, p. 105) has put it, "cognitive psychology seeks to model man's model-making capacities". To aid in the development of models of thinking, psychologists present experimental tasks to their subjects and record the resulting behaviour in varying degrees of detail. The psychologist's interpretation of the behavioural data should, using the approach presented here, take account of the way in which the subjects model (or interpret) the experimental task. As will emerge in later chapters, it is frequently the case that behaviour which seems unintelligible or irrational becomes clear and sensible when an understanding is achieved of how the task has been interpreted by the subjects.

As well as varying in degree of directedness (problem solving v. daydreaming), thought is also often considered to vary in modality. Subjectively, thinking often seems to involve inner speech or visual, auditory, or other forms of imagery. For example, reporting the sixth letter in the alphabet after 'E' would generally involve the experience of inner speech. On the other hand, deciding whether an irregular shape was the same as another irregular shape at a different orientation (Shepard and Metzler, 1971) would generally involve an experience of visual imagery. Subjective experience, then, suggests the existence of different internal 'languages', or distinct sets of symbols (verbal, visual, etc.), with their own rules of combination. Some translation rules must also exist to enable one to go from a word to an image and vice versa. Although the experience of imagery is not denied by current theorists, the functional role of imagery has been questioned. Imagery might be merely ephiphenomenal, i.e. like factory noise, a non-functional byproduct of the important processes. For instance, it has been strongly argued (Pylyshyn, 1973) that the meaning of both verbal and non-verbal representations is conveyed by an underlying abstract conceptual code. Taking this view, a visual image is generated on the basis of a symbolic description of the object being imaged, but it is the symbolic or propositional description that is important, rather than the image itself. To use one of Pylyshyn's examples, two images of a chessboard might be pictorially identical, but one image might be based on an abstract encoding that includes the relationship 'Black Queen attacks White Bishop' while the other might not. In Pylyshyn's view, the important thing about an image is the propositions that it is derived from, rather than any 'pictorial' properties. The opposing point of view is that images can convey 'appearance' information better than propositions. The obtained patterns of reaction times to tasks that would appear to involve image comparing, rotating and scanning have been taken as supporting this latter view (Kosslyn and Pomerantz, 1977). But interpretations in propositional terms always seem possible and it is not yet clear which position is correct (Kosslyn, 1981; Pylyshyn, 1981) or even whether the question is empirically decidable (Anderson, 1978). However, it does appear that spontaneous or instructed use of strategies involving imagery in problem solving makes different information available and can facilitate solution (e.g. Antonietti, 1991).

B. Characterizing problems

Given the strong emphasis on problem solving in this text and in the general literature on thinking, the question arises 'what is a problem?' The definition offered by the Gestalt psychologist Karl Duncker (1945, p. 1) is still serviceable. He wrote that "a problem arises when a living organism has a goal but does not know how this goal is to be reached".

This is a useful initial formulation that signals a number of points. First, that a 'task' set by an experimenter is not necessarily a problem for a given individual. Whether it is a problem or not depends on the subject's knowledge and on his or her ability to locate relevant knowledge, should he or she have it. Second, a problem may vanish or be dissolved if the person changes their goals. A third point is that a problem does not exist effectively until the person detects some discrepancy between their goals and the situation they find themself in.

Most psychological studies of problem solving (especially, as we shall see, those within the information-processing framework) have dealt with well-defined problems. If we accept Reitman's (1965) useful proposal that problems in general can be viewed as having three components (a starting state, a goal state and a set of processes that may be used to reach the goal from the starting state), then a problem is well defined if all three components are completely specified. Problems in mathematics, in logic and in various board games tend to be well defined. Although well defined, such problems can be very difficult and the psychologist is faced with the task of explaining how we humans, with our various limitations, manage to solve geometry, chess and problems of a similar scale in reasonable times. Of course, it will be still more difficult to explain how we tackle those ill-defined problems that are more typical of real life than the well-defined variety.

Ill-defined problems leave one or more components of the problem statement vague and unspecified. Problems can vary in degree of definedness (Reitman, 1965, Ch. 5); for example, from 'make a silk purse out of a sow's ear' (which leaves possible methods unspecified), to 'make something useful from a sow's ear', (which has a vague goal and unspecified methods), to 'make something useful from some part of a pig' (which leaves vague the goal, the starting state and the methods available).

It seems a reasonable strategy for psychologists to start by studying people's ways of handling apparently well-defined problems and then to move on to consider ill-defined tasks. Perhaps people tackle ill-defined tasks by seeking a well-defined version of the problem, which they then work within until the problem is solved or a new definition is tried. If this is so, then studies with well-defined problems will be relevant to part of the process of solving ill-defined problems. Indeed, processes of defining, or interpreting, the problem are also important in well-defined tasks and some attention has recently been given to task interpretation processes that must play a role in both well- and ill-defined tasks (Kochen and Badre, 1974; Simon and

Hayes, 1976). Some studies relating to task interpretation processes will be discussed in later sections.

Another useful distinction is that between *adversary* and *non-adversary* problems. In an adversary problem the person is competing with a thinking opponent, while in non-adversary problems the struggle is with inert problem materials (real or symbolic) that are not reacting to what the person does with a view to defeating him or her (despite what the problem solver may feel). Both these sorts of problem will be dealt with in future chapters.

A third distinction that has become increasingly important in problem-solving research is that between *semantically rich* and *semantically impoverished* problems (Chi *et al.*, 1982). To a large extent, this distinction refers to the solver's view of the problem. A problem is semantically rich for solvers who bring considerable relevant knowledge to the problem. For example, if someone has just been told the basic rules of a game that they have never encountered before, then a problem in that game would be semantically impoverished for that person, but the same problem would be semantically rich for an expert player of the game. Many artificial puzzles used in studies of problem solving are semantically impoverished for most subjects. Until relatively recently, most studies of problem solving focused on semantically impoverished puzzles, particularly in the case of non-adversary problem solving. More recently there has been considerable interest in the study of semantically rich non-adversary tasks such as computer programming and physics problem solving. Such studies frequently involve contrasts between the behaviour of subjects for whom the problems concerned are semantically rich (experts in the area) with that of subjects for whom the problems are semantically impoverished (novices in the area). See Chapters 3 and 4 for further discussion of semantically rich problems.

II. APPROACHES TO THINKING

Historically, a number of theoretical approaches have been taken to the topic of thinking. The principal early approaches were those of classical introspectionism, behaviourism, Gestalt theory and neobehaviourism. More recent work has been dominated by the information-processing approach. Although this text is written largely from the point of view of the currently dominant information-processing approach, a brief historical overview will now be given to help set recent developments in perspective.

A. Early approaches

1 Introspectionism

In the late nineteenth and early twentieth century the classical introspectionists, such as Wundt and Titchener, took conscious experience to be their subject matter and attempted to analyse consciousness into elementary sensations. A good analogy for the introspectionist endeavour is with chemistry. As chemists analyse complex compounds into chemical elements, so the introspectionists sought to analyse complex experiences into elementary sensations. Such analyses were to be made by means of the classical introspective report. To produce a classical introspective report the subject was required to adopt a special attitude or 'set' such that the 'meaning' of the experience was to be ignored in favour of the component sensations. So, instead of a report, for instance, that one saw 'a large red book', a report of 'an experience of a red-coloured slightly trapezoidal shape' was expected. At this point, it is worth distinguishing between 'classical introspectionism', with its emphasis on reporting in the language of sensations, and 'ordinary' introspective reporting in everyday terms. The latter form of introspection is used quite widely in the current study of thought (Ericsson and Simon, 1984, 1993), as will be seen in future chapters. Classical introspectionism, by contrast, has fallen into disuse. One reason for the decline of the method of classical introspection was that it led to conflicting reports which could not be easily reconciled. In particular, the question of thinking without images aroused considerable controversy between the introspectionists of Wurzburg (who reported imageless thought under certain circumstances) and those of Leipzig and Cornell who adamantly insisted that thought was always accompanied by imagery even although it might be very feint.

As well as the difficulty of resolving conflicts on such basic matters as imageless thought, the introspectionist approach was, in any case, limited in its scope to the consciousness of specially trained, sane, adult human subjects. To tackle unconscious thought processes or those of children, the insane, untrained subjects and animals would require very different approaches (Miller, 1960). The early behaviourists offered a radical alternative to classical introspectionism and this alternative was eagerly adopted by many psychologists.

2 Behaviourism

The early behaviourists (e.g. Watson, 1913) changed the focus of psychology from conscious experience to observable behaviour. Their dominant theoretical notion was the 'stimulus–response link'. As a topic of study, 'thought' was displaced from its centre-stage position by 'learning'. Thorndike, an important precursor of Watson, had paved the way for this development through his studies of trial-and-error behaviour during problem solving in cats (Thorndike, 1898). Cats placed in puzzle boxes displayed considerable trial-and-error behaviour before escaping and, on being returned to the boxes after each trial, they were only a little faster at escaping on each successive trial. There was no sign of 'insight' leading to sudden solutions that could then be repeated without error when the cats returned to the puzzle boxes. Ruger (1910) found similar patterns of results in studies of humans working with manipulation puzzles. Thorndike and Ruger suggested that thought in problem solving could be described as *covert* trial and error, similar to the *overt* trial and error observable in their subjects' behaviour. Notions of 'insight' or 'understanding' were felt to be unnecessary.

3 Gestalt

A contrasting view was put forward by the Gestalt psychologists, who objected to the different forms of 'elementarism' represented by the classical introspectionists and the early behaviourists. Gestalt theory focused especially on perception, rather than on thinking or learning, and the importance of perceptual organization was particularly stressed. Thus, in dealing with thinking and problem solving, the Gestalt theorists emphasized the way in which the problem was perceived as a determining factor in task difficulty. The solving process was described as one of perceptual restructuring in which the problem comes to be seen in such a way that the solution is obvious. Examples of purely perceptual restructuring would include suddenly seeing the alternative interpretation of an ambiguous drawing or coming to see a face hidden in a puzzle painting. In the problem-solving area, 'restructuring' may be illustrated by the following anecdotal example (discussed by Wertheimer, 1945, Ch. 4). When the famous mathematician Gauss was a 6-year-old schoolboy he amazed his teacher by being able to give immediate answers to problems requiring the sum of successive whole numbers from 1 to N. Gauss was able to do this, not by rapid addition, but by restructuring the task. In the case of adding the following series of numbers (1, 2, 3, 4, 5, 6, 7, 8, 9, 10), Gauss noticed that each number from the left increases by one and each number from the right decreases by one. Thus the numbers can be regrouped into pairs that all have the same sum [(1, 10), (2, 9), (3, 8), (4, 7), (5, 6)]. There are five pairs in this example, each of which sums to 11, and so the answer to the original question is 55. In general, the number of pairs will be $N/2$ and the sum of each pair will be $N + 1$; hence the formula that the sum of such a series ending in an even number is given by $(N/2) \times (N + 1)$.

For the Gestalt theorists, then, problem solving involved 'insight', which was an appreciation of how the solution was necessitated by the nature of the problem; this insight would come through a restructuring of the subject's perception of the problem. Some important early Gestalt research on problem solving was carried out with animal subjects. Presumably, if insight could be convincingly demonstrated with animals, then its occurrence in humans could scarcely be denied. So, Kohler (1925), on the basis of his famous series of studies with apes, claimed that his animal subjects suddenly solved manipulation problems, after periods of overt inactivity (interpreted as periods of thought).

Behaviourist critics argued that trial and error was evident in Kohler's behavioural records and that the results could be explained simply by trial and error. They also pointed out that prior experience with the tools (sticks) used in the tasks was necessary for solution (Birch, 1945). To Gestalt replies that, even if trial and error had occurred, it was not blind or random, the behaviourist retort was that random trial and error had never been postulated, but rather trial and error biased by prior learning. The issue of trial and error v. insight was also taken up within the more constrained area of discrimination learning. Krechevsky (1935) reported data apparently showing sudden solutions by rats of discrimination learning tasks together with response patterns that could be interpreted as evidence of hypothesis-testing. The response patterns in question showed consistent responding to some irrelevant cue, such as position or size of the stimulus, when brightness was the relevant cue. However, Spence (1936) showed that these response patterns could be produced by gradual accretions and reductions of response strength to the cues in the task and so could be explained in simpler, less mentalistic terms than those proposed by Krechevsky.

Studies of human problem solving were not neglected by the Gestalt school. Karl Duncker (1945) examined in detail solution attempts to a range of problems involving mathematical or practical contents. The task known as the 'X-ray' or 'radiation' problem was studied particularly closely by Duncker.

The radiation problem was posed as follows (Duncker, 1945, p. 1): "Given a human being with an inoperable stomach tumour, and rays which destroy organic tissue at sufficient intensity, by what procedure can one free him of the tumour by these rays and at the same time avoid destroying the healthy tissue which surrounds it?". The subject was usually also given a sketch (see Fig. 1.1) and told that someone had visualized the situation in that way, but that this simple approach of sending a beam of rays straight through to destroy the tumour would not do, since the rays would destroy healthy tissue on the way to the tumour.

Subjects were asked to think aloud as they worked on the problem and the resulting records or protocols indicated a tendency to work backwards from the overall goal to subgoals which, if achieved, would lead to solution. So, for instance, the major goal of 'treating the tumour by rays without destroying healthy tissue' could be achieved if the subgoal of 'avoiding contact between rays and healthy tissue' could be attained. In the most thoroughly discussed protocol, this particular subgoal governed much of the subject's efforts. However, solution was not obtained until an alternative subgoal was set up of 'lowering the intensity of the rays on their way through healthy tissue'. This subgoal led to the solution of using a lens to focus the rays on the tumour so that lethal intensity is reached only at the focal point.

While Duncker investigated the development of insight, the opposite phenomenon of problem 'blindness' or ('misleading sets') was studied by Luchins (1942) in a series of experiments using water jar problems. In these tasks the subject was

Fig. 1.1 *Sketch given to subjects working on X-ray problem (Duncker, 1945). The oval represents a cross-section through the body with the tumour in the centre. The radiation apparatus is on the left, sending a beam through the tumour.*

asked to say how one could get exactly a specified amount of water using jars of fixed capacity and an unlimited source of water, e.g. given three jars (A, B and C) of capacity 18, 43 and 10 units respectively, how could you obtain exactly 5 units of water? The solution may be expressed as $B - A - 2C$. After a series of problems with that same general solution, subjects had great difficulty with the following problem: given three jars (A, B and C) of capacity 28, 76 and 3 units respectively, how could you obtain exactly 25 units of water? In fact, the solution to this problem is very simple (i.e. $A - C$), but when it comes after a series of problems involving the long solution ($B - A - 2C$) many subjects fail to solve or are greatly slowed down compared with control subjects.

A related block to effective problem solving, known as 'functional fixity', was also identified by work in the Gestalt tradition. Functional fixity tends to arise when an object has to be used in a new way in order to solve some problem. The classical study of functional fixity was carried out by Duncker (1945) using the 'box' (or 'candle' problem). In this task subjects were presented with tacks, matches, three small boxes and three candles. The problem was to put the candles side by side on a door, in such a way that they could burn in a stable fashion. For one group of subjects the boxes were empty but for the other group (experimental group) the boxes were used as containers and held the matches, tacks and candles. The solution is to use the boxes as platforms and fix them to the door using the tacks. It was found that the solving rate was much higher in the control than in the experimental group. Duncker explained this result in terms of a failure to perceive the possible platform function of the boxes when they were presented as containers. Functional fixity has been independently demonstrated and further investigated in a number of later studies (e.g. Birch and Rabinowitz, 1951; Adamson and Taylor, 1954; Glucksberg and Weisberg, 1968; Glucksberg and Danks, 1968). Glucksberg has proposed an alternative interpretation of the effect, in terms of failure to notice the boxes as separate units when they are presented as containers. Whatever the detailed explanation, the phenomenon appears to be a robust one and is doubtless one source of difficulty in real-life problem solving.

4 Neobehaviourism

The Gestalt investigators helped keep the study of thought processes alive in the 1920s and 1930s while behaviourists focused on associative learning in humans and the white rat. In the face of studies such as Duncker's on the X-ray problem, the simple S–R approach to extended chains of thought appears quite inadequate. Even in the case of maze problem solving by rats, it was becoming evident that richer internal processes would have to be postulated within behaviourist theory. Thus the notion of a 'mediating response' (r_m) was introduced into neobehaviourist analysis. 'Mediating responses' are seen as implicit covert responses that generate 'mediating stimuli' (s_m), which can elicit further mediating responses or overt behaviour. Chains of mediating stimuli and responses are taken to represent thought sequences. In many problems, various alternative sequences of actions might lead to the desired goal and such alternatives could be explored via mediational chains without overt trial and error. To take Berlyne's (1965) example, a resident of Boston may have many possible ways of travelling to New York involving different routes and different forms of transport. In thinking of how to make this journey the Bostonian subject would, on the neobehaviourist analysis, 'embark' (covertly) on one mediational chain out of those available. The alternative chains may be assumed to vary in strength of association to the problem stimulus, i.e. they form a hierarchy, ordered from strongly associated to weakly associated chains. If the person is told that their dominant chain (air route, say) is blocked (e.g. airport closed), the next most dominant chain would tend to be evoked. Such a hierarchy of mediational response sequences is an example of a *habit-family hierarchy* (Hull, 1934).

Maltzman (1955) proposed an extension of the habit-family hierarchy notion which would permit hierarchies of habit-family hierarchies. Thus a problem stimulus could be associated in varying degrees of strength with a number of different habit-family hierarchies. Furthermore, the 'nesting' of hierarchies within hierarchies could continue to many levels. These elaborate structures of mediating stimuli and responses are known as *compound* habit-family hierarchies. As Berlyne (1965) pointed out, when stimulus–response associations are organized in this way, the actual course of action followed will result from selection of a hierarchy at the highest level, then from selection of a subhierarchy within the first hierarchy, and so on. At each stage, 'selection' would be made automatically on the basis of habit strength. This kind of scheme could, albeit in a cumbersome way, represent results, such as those of Duncker on the X-ray problem, that show subjects following one general direction (corresponding to selection at a high level of the compound hierarchy) down to a fair degree of detail (corresponding to selection at lower levels). Duncker's subjects abandoned directions and selected different ones when success was not obtained. In neobehaviourist terms, continued failure within a given hierarchy of responses would reduce the relevant habit strengths and thus increase the probability of alternative hierarchies being evoked. Berlyne (1965) developed such ideas in an ambitious book (*Structure and direction in thinking*) that attempted to demonstrate how neobehaviourist theory could account for directed thought. However, by the time Berlyne's work appeared, the information-processing 'revolution' that still dominates cognitive psychology had begun (see, for example, Miller *et al.* (1960) for an important early manifesto of the new approach), and Berlyne's neobehaviourist notions had little impact.

Although precursors of the modern information-processing approach can be identified in researchers active before the Second World War, such as Selz (see De Groot, 1965; Frijda and De Groot, 1981), developments in cybernetics and computer technology appear to have been necessary before psychologists in general felt secure in ascribing 'goal directedness' and complex internal processes to people. Such concepts were felt to be open to charges of 'mentalism', until implemented on machines such as guided missiles and computers. The information-processing approach, now dominant in cognitive psychology, will be discussed in the next section.

B. The information-processing approach

1 Basic ideas

The main stimulus for the development of the information-processing approach to thinking was the arrival of the computer. The basic idea of the information-processing approach is that, in cognitive aspects, the human can be regarded as a computer-like system that codes, stores, retrieves and transforms information. Computers work by following programs, which are essentially lists of step-by-step instructions. The instructions can be conditional, that is, can involve simple decisions so that the computer can be instructed to jump from one part of the program to another, depending on the outcome of intermediate operations, thus making the system very flexible. Furthermore, complete groups of instructions (subroutines) can be given labels and activated by those names. This facility for creating and using subroutines greatly increases the ease and flexibility of programming. Since both computers and humans flexibly manipulate symbols, it is tempting to seek computer analogies and metaphors for human processes. Such analogies span a continuum of detail from vague verbal similarities between human and machine at one end to working computer programs that are intended to simulate (i.e. mimic) human processes at the other end. At an intermediate level of detail are flow charts or outlines of the organization and sequencing of major processing steps and decisions. Many information-processing analyses are at this level.

Broad verbal analogies between human and computer provide an orientation for thinking about human processes. Within the loose constraints of this orientation, models of greater specificity can be constructed. If a model is at the flowchart level, then at least a definite sequence of broad steps has been specified and it may be possible to derive predictions from the flowchart itself. Furthermore, the flowchart may be used to guide construction of a model at the most detailed and completely specified level, viz. that of a running program. Thus, the flowchart is a useful summary of the main features of the program. Indeed, it can be argued that the flowchart level is the most fruitful one (not too vague and not too detailed) for making comparisons between human and computer processes. However, having a running program corresponding to a given flowchart is a reassuring guarantee that the flowchart describes something that works.

2 Simulation

The virtues and problems of simulation level models will now be considered in more detail. First, it may be noted that computer simulation is a general method that can be applied in all fields that involve the study of complex processes. For instance, the economy could be theoretically represented by a large number of variables (wages, prices, employment levels, balance of payments, exchange rates, etc.) which are all related to one another. An economist might speculate that a particular pattern of relationships holds among the main economic variables, and this hunch could be tested by programming a computer to behave in accord with the economist's model. Many predictions could then be generated and checked against subsequent events (or degree of fit to past events could be assessed) and the simulation model could be revised to improve its predictions and ultimately provide a better understanding of the process being modelled.

In a similar way simulation can be used to explore and test ideas about human information processing. If we thought that humans solved, say, logic problems by going through a certain sequence of decisions and operations, we could program a computer to go through the same sequence on a number of such problems and compare the computer's performance with that of a sample of human subjects. If the computer tended to take more steps on the problems that humans found more difficult or to make the same patterns of mistaken conclusions as humans, then the theory would gain support from such results. Furthermore, the computer could be made to print out every operation and decision that it made and the resulting record could then be compared with the records produced by humans 'thinking aloud' as they worked on the problems. Comparison of human 'thinking-aloud' records and the computer's report of the steps taken by the program could be used in attempts to assess the degree of detailed match between computer and human processes. However, in practice, there are many difficulties in assessing the degree of match between two such multidimensional records.

3 Capacity limitations

Whatever process is to be simulated, a clear and unambiguous model is required, since a computer program cannot work unless it is completely specified. So, one benefit of simulation is that it forces the theorist to be clear and unambiguous – properties that have sometimes been felt lacking in psychological theories and models! Of course, a simulation model should not invoke processes that exceed human capabilities. Knowledge of human limitations is derived from studies of basic information-processing tasks (e.g. recognizing familiar symbols, comparing symbols, reproducing previously presented symbols, and so on). The following broad picture seems to emerge from such studies. Humans have a vast *long-term memory* capacity which is so organized as to permit generally rapid recognition of familiar symbols and retrieval of information associated with recognized symbols. Familiar symbols representing both presented information and associated retrieved information can be held temporarily in a small-capacity *working memory system*. Memory span studies initially suggested a capacity of about 5–9 symbols for this system (Miller, 1956).

Detailed research and theorizing on human memory has led to more elaborate models in which both long-term memory and working systems are seen as involving a number of interrelated components. So, long-term memory has been analysed into semantic and episodic memory, (Tulving, 1983), with semantic memory being decomposed further into lexical and encyclopaedic memory (Lachman, 1973). Working memory, in turn, has been analysed into three main subsystems comprising a central executive, an articulatory loop and a visuospatial scratchpad (Baddeley,

1986, 1992). However, from the point of view of research on thinking, the fine structure of memory has not normally been taken into account; a general distinction between unlimited long-term and limited short-term storage systems has usually been taken to be adequate. More recently, studies have begun to be made of the relative roles of central executive, articulatory loop and visuospatial scratchpad in reasoning (Gilhooly *et al.* 1993) and in mental arithmetic (Logie *et al.* 1994).

It may be noted that many studies in the memory literature have focused on the transfer of information from temporary storage in working memory to permanent storage in a long-term memory. From the point of view of problem-solving studies, the reverse traffic is more relevant. Problem solving may often be viewed as involving the application of rules which take inputs from working memory, locate appropriate symbols in long-term memory and place those symbols in working memory, displacing old symbols if working memory capacity is exceeded.

In addition to storage capacity limitations, an important processing limitation is also generally acknowledged on the number of operations that can be carried out simultaneously. At the level of problem solving, the human information-processing system is assumed by most workers in the field to be serial, i.e. only one operation is carried out at a time. This is a convenient assumption for computer simulation, since virtually all current computers are serial devices. Also, there is little solid empirical evidence that humans can explore more than one line of problem development at a time. However, the notion of unconscious work progressing in parallel with the single conscious mainstream of thought has been invoked (e.g. Neisser, 1963b), especially in connection with creativity, and the possibility cannot be ruled out *a priori*. Further discussion of this issue will be found in Chapter 10 on creative processes and in the final overview in Chapter 11.

The assumptions of (a) separate long-term and short-term working memories, and (b) serial symbol processing, jointly serve to define a model of thinking that has been widely accepted within the information-processing approach. Hence, following Simon and Kaplan (1989), I will refer to this as the *standard model* of thinking. Although the standard model may well ultimately prove insufficient to cover all aspects of the topic, performance in a number of task areas has been successfully analysed within its confines and many examples will be found in the following chapters of research based on its assumptions.

Recently, an approach known as *connectionism* (see Quinlan, 1991, for an overview), which espouses considerable parallel processing among simple units and little or no symbolic processing, has been explored extensively, with some success, especially in the areas of learning and memory. Possible applications of connectionism to thinking and comparisons with the standard model are discussed in Chapter 11.

4 Artificial intelligence

Before going on to discuss applications of the information-processing approach, it should be pointed out that simulation programs are by no means the only ones that tackle problems hitherto the preserve of humans. Within the area of computer science there is a thriving subdiscipline known as *artificial intelligence* (AI) that attempts to construct programs capable of such achievements as playing master-level chess, interpreting pictures and understanding natural language, among other undoubtedly intelligent activities. However, unlike simulation programs, AI programs are not restricted to processes that humans might conceivably use. Many chess programs, for example, are greatly superior to the ability of humans to look ahead exhaustively for a number of moves, and cannot be considered to be simulations.

However, AI research has been a useful source of ideas about possible human processes and of terminology for describing problems and methods. For example, in the field of memory, Quillian's (1968) program for natural language comprehension led to some very fruitful notions about human semantic memory (Collins and Quillian, 1969; Collins and Loftus, 1975), while the General Problem Solver program (Newell and Simon, 1972) has been a valuable source of ideas about human methods in problem solving (e.g. Egan and Greeno, 1974), and the 'production system' approach to programming in AI has been very influential in computer models of cognition, such as Anderson's (1983) ACT* and Newell's (1990) SOAR models, discussed in Chapter 4.

5 Cognitive science

As has been noted in previous sections, both psychological analyses of human problem solving and AI syntheses of computer problem solving view problem solving as a form of information processing. Thus, both humans and suitably programmed computers are seen as flexibly manipulating symbols in order to solve problems. Viewing natural and artificial information processing as essentially similar is the perspective of the emerging discipline known as cognitive science (Gardner, 1985). Cognitive science takes as its topic *knowledge acquisition and use*, in general, whether by artificial or natural systems.

In the case of problem solving, the focus of cognitive science is on real life, complex, knowledge-rich problem areas, in which extended effort is required for solution. A typical cognitive science study will examine in detail the performance of a small number of subjects on a complex task and will often lead to a computer program model of the processes underlying performance. Thus, a combination of psychological and computational skills is brought to bear on understanding the task performance. (Also, since the task is usually complex, task expertise is an additional requirement among the experimenters.) Thus cognitive science is typically an interdisciplinary enterprise and is generally regarded as representing a promising fusion of inter-related subject areas (principally, psychology, computing, linguistics and philosophy). It has, however, been criticized on general methodological grounds by Skinner (1985) and on philosophical grounds by Searle (1984, 1990). These criticisms will be considered in more detail in Chapter 11, in the context of the examples of cognitive science work discussed in the intervening chapters.

III. SUMMARY AND CONCLUDING COMMENTS

In this chapter thinking has been characterized as an internal symbolic activity. This activity may be tightly directed to specific goals, as in problem solving, or it may be free-floating, as in daydreaming. Thinking directed towards problem solving involves exploring a symbolic model of the task to determine a useful course of action without overt, and possibly costly, trial and error. Following Duncker (1945), problems were defined as arising when an organism has a goal that it does not know how to reach.

Problems can vary in the degree to which they are well or ill defined. Most research has focused on well-defined problems (drawn from puzzles, games, logic, maths) but it is hoped that results from these studies will be relevant to ill-defined problem solving to the extent that people tackle such problems by first converting them into well-defined variants.

A second useful distinction is between adversary and non-adversary problems. In non-adversary problems the solver has to manipulate inert materials (concrete or symbolic) to reach a goal, whereas in adversary problems there is an additional layer of complexity caused by having to counter a rational opponent whose goals are contrary to those of the solver. A third distinction was drawn between semantically rich problems, in which the solver brings a large mass of relevant knowledge to bear, and semantically impoverished problems, in which little or no prior knowledge is available to aid in solving. After a long period of neglect, the solving of semantically rich problems has become an area of intense study over the past few years.

A variety of approaches have been taken to the topic of thinking in the history of psychology. The principal approaches have been those of classical introspectionism, early behaviourism, Gestalt analysis, neobehaviourism and information-processing. Although the field has been dominated by the information-processing approach since the early 1960s, the earlier approaches were reviewed above to give some historical perspective. To summarize, the introspectionists focused on the analysis of consciousness into elementary sensations, while the early behaviourists stressed observable behaviour and the importance of learning. The Gestalt school emphasized organization in thought and perception, and argued strongly for the role of insight and restructuring in problem solving. The neobehaviourists attempted to explain the internal processes of thought in terms of covert chains of mediating responses and (response-produced) mediating stimuli. The resulting analyses could be stretched to deal with extended problem solving, as in Duncker's X-ray problem, but only in a rather cumbersome fashion.

The currently dominant information-processing approach takes the computer as its key metaphor for the mind. In cognitive aspects, this approach sees people as computer-like systems that code, store, retrieve and transform information. Within this approach, models for thinking in particular tasks have been proposed in greatly varying degrees of detail. An intermediate level of analysis in terms of broad steps and decisions (flow chart level) has probably been the most prevalent and useful.

Most information-processing models for various tasks accept certain limitations on cognitive capacities. More specifically, it is generally accepted that processing is serial at the problem-solving level and that, while long-term memory is vast, working memory is very limited. These memory and processing limitations are key elements of what may be referred to as the 'standard model' for thinking. According to this standard model, thinking involves serial symbol manipulations between long-term and working memory, in accord with rules or programs stored in the long-term memory. Throughout this text, and particularly in the final chapter, the standard model assumptions will be considered against the data resulting from recent psychological research on thinking.

IV. FURTHER READING

Dominowski, R.L. and Bourne, L.E. (1994). History of research on thinking and problem solving. In R.J. Sternberg (Ed.), *Thinking and problem solving*, pp. 1–35. Orlando, FL: Academic Press.

Simon, H.A. (1990). Invariants of human behavior. *Annual Review of Psychology* **41**, 1–19. A broad but succinct overview of the standard information processing approach to higher mental processes.

2

Solving puzzles

What mental processes are involved in solving, or attempting to solve, problems? Since there is an indefinite number of problems, varying greatly in content and form, this question is too broad and needs to be divided into more specific questions to be manageable. This 'splitting up' has been reflected in research practice, and efforts have been directed at the mental processes involved in tackling particular problems, or classes of problems. It is, of course, hoped that similar processing limits will emerge over a variety of task areas. In Chapter 1 distinctions were drawn between well- and ill-defined problems, between adversary and non-adversary problems, and between semantically rich and semantically impoverished problems. These distinctions will help organize the discussion of research in this and following chapters.

Within the field of problem solving, certain methodological tendencies are quite marked and deserve some consideration at this point, before going on to deal with studies of particular topics. For instance, much research has focused on well-defined problems in which the goal, starting state and permissible actions are all clearly specified. A major reason for using such problems is to increase the chances that all subjects will interpret the tasks concerned in the same way. Such unanimity would be useful in that the theoretical task of explaining problem-solving behaviour would be simplified if all subjects could be assumed to start with a similar model of the task to be worked on. Even if there is some variation in interpretation, the degree of variation is likely to be less for well-defined than for ill-defined tasks. A further tendency, until relatively recently, was for studies of non-adversary tasks to be limited to unfamiliar and rather artificial puzzles. The main reason for using artificial material was to equate degree of familiarity with the task over subjects. The effects of familiarity (or expertise) in the task area were initially studied in connection with adversary problems, such as chess, in which people vary widely in skill level. An additional tendency has been to use small-scale tasks that are usually solvable within one hour or less. This tendency probably grew up for the very practical reason that subjects often cannot spare a longer time to take part in experiments. Thus, studies of non-adversary problem solving have often focused on puzzles that are well defined, small scale, artificial and unfamiliar. As indicated already, there are some advantages in using such materials, but there are also drawbacks, particularly in that generalization to problems not fitting the typical description (well defined, small scale, etc.) must be somewhat uncertain. However, even within the typical methodological constraints, problem content and structure vary widely. So, it is not obvious, in advance, whether similar processes and limitations will show up across the various different, but typical, laboratory tasks. The current chapter includes consideration of this issue and focuses on well-defined non-adversary puzzles.

The contents of the remainder of this chapter will now be indicated. First, I will introduce some terminology and approaches (largely from outwith psychology) that have proved useful in describing well-defined problems and solving processes. In broad terms, using one approach (state–action representation), the possible manipulations of the problem material are seen as generating an often vast network of possible paths leading to numerous intermediate states, and the solver is regarded as searching the resulting mental 'maze' or 'tree' of possibilities for a path to the goal. A second approach (problem reduction) involves attempting to divide problems up into more manageable sub-problems. Again, this leads to a 'tree' of possible divisions of the problem. How these notions have been used in the analysis of human problem solving will be discussed with reference to a range of laboratory tasks, from well-defined examples (e.g. missionaries-and-cannibals puzzles) to less well-defined cases (e.g. cryptarithmetic). The issues of task interpretation processes, analogy and insight will then be addressed. Finally, the chapter closes with a brief summary and some concluding comments.

I. STATE–ACTION REPRESENTATIONS

A. Graphs and trees

Many well-defined problems can be represented as involving a search for a suitable series of operations that will transform the starting state of the problem into a state that meets the goal requirements. In general, the possible sequences of actions and intermediate states can often be represented by diagrams composed of points (or 'nodes'), which represent the actions that transform one state into another. Such structures of 'nodes and arcs' are known in mathematics as 'graphs' and can be used to represent many phenomena. A special form of graph which is frequently useful is the *tree*. In a tree graph the connections are directional and there are no loops or returns to earlier nodes. The appearance of such graphs is reminiscent of an upside-down tree, with the starting node at the top of the page and its descendants branching out down the page. The possible sequences of actions and intermediate states in well-defined problems can often be represented by this special form of graph and the resulting diagrams are known as *state–action trees* (Wickelgren, 1974). Take, for example, the 8-puzzle (Nilsson, 1971) as shown in Fig. 2.1. The numbers are on tiles in a 3 × 3 frame. One cell of the frame is always empty, so that an adjacent tile can be moved into the empty cell, thus moving the empty cell also.

The possible sequences of moves in this 8-puzzle can be represented by a state–action tree (Fig. 2.2) in which states of the puzzle generated by making the possible moves are depicted.

The first three levels of the tree are shown in Fig. 2.3 (assuming that no move is immediately 'undone'). There are over 100,000 states that can be reached from the start. One of these is the goal. You may find it instructive to seek the solution path for the puzzle shown in Fig. 2.3

A major characteristic of state–action trees is the rapid way in which they grow. If there are m alternative actions per state, then there will be m^n possible sequences of n actions; in other words, with n actions one could reach any one of m^n states. So, for example, with four alternative actions (moves) available from each state, one could reach any of 1024 ($= 4^5$) different states in just five steps. The difficulty is in finding a short path to a goal state with little search of the state–action tree.

Fig. 2.1 *An example 8-puzzle. The tiles are to be moved so that the goal state is reached from the given starting configuration.*

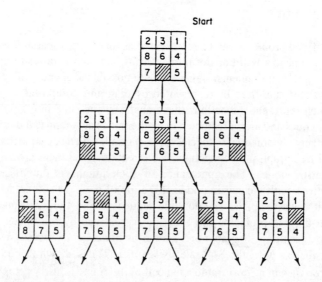

Fig. 2.2 *First three levels of the state–action tree for the example 8-puzzle.*

In the fields of AI and operations research, ideas have been developed about searching state–action trees that are useful for discussing problem solving by both people and machines, and a sample of these notions is outlined in the following sections.

B. Basic search methods

In principle, paths from starting states to goal states can often be found by systematic searches. The two main search schemes are known as '*depth first*' and '*breadth first*' searching. Depth-first searching follows up just one state from each state examined until either the goal or a dead end is reached. (A 'dead end' would be a state that could not be developed further.) On encountering a dead end, a depth-first search would 'back up' to the preceding state and follow up another hitherto unexplored branch. In terms of the 8-puzzle example a depth-first search could develop as indicated in Fig. 2.3.

There are no dead ends in the 8-puzzle search tree and so a depth-first search would never back up, but would continue indefinitely or until the goal was reached. The order of examination of the states is indicated by the circled numbers in Fig. 2.3.

As depth-first search proceeds, the memory load grows relatively slowly, just by one intermediate state per level of depth. Breadth-first search is much more stressful in terms of memory load.

In breadth-first searching, all states at a given level are examined before using the moves from each state to check all the next level states. The resulting pattern of search is illustrated for the 8-puzzle example in Fig. 2.4. The circled numbers in the figure indicate the order in which states would be examined in a breadth-first search.

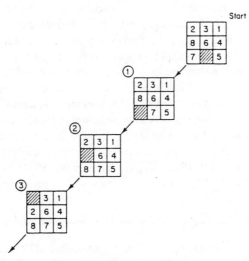

Fig. 2.3 *A depth-first search of the 8-puzzle state–action tree. The circled numbers indicate the order in which states are examined.*

Fig. 2.4 *A breadth-first search of the 8-puzzle state–action tree. The circled numbers indicate the order in which states are examined.*

Breadth-first searches involve ever-increasing memory loads as search progresses downwards through ever-expanding trees of possibilities. In return for high memory load, breadth-first search is *algorithmic*, that is, it will always find a goal state and, furthermore, it will be a goal state that is a minimum number of moves from the start. (An algorithm is a procedure, possibly inefficient, that is guaranteed to solve all members of a given class of problems.) By contrast, depth-first searches will not necessarily find the goal. They can be diverted down infinitely long byways and so fail to solve. Also, any solutions reached by depth-first search are not necessarily the best ones in terms of number of moves from the start to the goal.

A compromise form of search that mixes depth- and breadth-first methods is known as '*progressive deepening*'. This method consists of searching depth first up to some limit, then backing up and continuing search down all branches up to the depth limit, until the entire tree has been searched to the depth limit or the goal has been located. If the goal has not been found within the first depth limit, the limit is increased by some fixed amount and search continues in the same way until the new depth limits are encountered or a goal state is located. This method is of additional interest because rather similar strategies have emerged from studies of human search processes in chess (De Groot, 1965; Wagner and Scurrah, 1971; Newell and Simon, 1972; Charness, 1981b; Holding, 1985; see Chapter 3 for further details).

C. Selective search

Search of a state–action tree can often be made more efficient by selecting promising states for further development on the basis of an evaluation of how close the states are to the goal.

In the classical 'hill climbing' method, the exact value of the goal state is not known and the solver tries to find the best state in the state–action tree. The task is rather like that of a real climber in thick fog, who wishes to reach the highest spot in the area. He or she can certainly find a peak by first testing out one pace in the four main directions and taking a pace in the direction that moves to the highest spot of the four tested, and then repeating this process until a spot is reached from which no move yields an improvement. This method is sure to find a peak, but there is no guarantee that it will be the highest peak, if there are foothills around. If the climber has an altimeter and knows the height of the highest peak then he or she could backtrack from any mistakenly climbed foothills and keep trying until the desired peak is reached.

Hill climbing can be useful but it does have hazards. Apart from the 'foothill' problem just alluded to, there is also the 'plateau problem' and the 'ridge problem'. If a plateau is reached then no steps (actions) lead to any marked improvement and much wandering results. On a ridge, it might be that none of the four principal directions leads to improvement, although some other intermediate direction might (Winston, 1984, Ch. 4).

A better procedure than hill climbing is known as '*best first*'. In this method, forward motion is from the best state encountered so far, no matter where in the search tree. For such a procedure to work the solver must remember the evaluations that have been made of previously encountered states.

For any selective search method to work, a useful '*evaluation function*' must be developed which expresses the 'promise' of an intermediate state as a function of its characteristics, e.g. in attempting the 8-puzzle a simple evaluation function would be to calculate the average distance of the pieces from their target positions. This should be better than nothing, although it is certainly suboptimal and poorer than those functions that Doran and Michie (1966) developed for their Graph Traverser program that successfully tackles 8- and 15-puzzle tasks.

II. PROBLEM REDUCTION APPROACH

State–action approaches to problem solving involve direct attempts to manipulate the problem materials (mentally or in reality) in worthwhile directions. A more roundabout, but often more useful, approach is known as '*problem reduction*'. The basic idea is to convert a single complex problem into a number of (easily) solved sub-problems. 'Factoring' or dividing a problem into sub-problems, each of which can be solved separately, is generally a very useful procedure when it can be applied. Newell and colleagues (1962) give the example of safecracking. If ten dials each with two possible positions have all to be set correctly before a safe will open, then one try in 2^{10} (i.e. 1024) will be correct and on average around 500 trials would be needed to find the correct combination (assuming sampling without replacement from the possibilities). If, however, each dial clicked when it was in its own correct position, one would need on average only 1.5 trials per dial, i.e. around 15 trials for the whole set. So when this problem is reduced from a single task to ten small ones, the savings in terms of expected search effort are dramatic (a 97 per cent reduction in the number of trials required).

Of course, problems do not always yield to such a simple 'factoring' approach. In the 8-puzzle, for example, one would not get far by trying to set the eight pieces separately because getting one piece correct may disrupt those that have been set previously. Also, a more complex problem–sub-problem structure may be required in which the sub-problems themselves need further reduction.

A rather general method for developing sub-problem structures is *'means–end'* analysis. In this, the solver compares the goal with the starting state and selects one of the ways in which they differ as a goal for the first sub-problem. The solver then selects from memory an action or 'operator' relevant to reducing this difference. If the first selected operator cannot be applied, because its preconditions are not met, then a new sub-problem is generated, viz. to reduce the difference between the current state and the operator's preconditions. This new subgoal causes a relevant operator to be selected and so on. The 'means–end' process develops a tree of sub-problems and, as in state–action trees, some backing up will often be necessary.

Making travel plans provides a real-life example of means–end analysis. If the problem is to travel from London to New York, the difference between the starting state and the goal is a large distance. Large distances can be reduced by using aeroplanes (the first operator). But to use a plane one needs to have a ticket and to be at the airport, that is, the preconditions of the first operator have to be met. These preconditions define two sub-problems. The 'ticket' problem may be solved by using a travel agent, but to use a travel agent the would-be traveller must be in communication with one and so a new 'communication' sub-problem arises . . . and so on, until the solving of the subsidiary problems resolves the overall problem. Means–end analysis is especially useful when the number of alternative actions is very large, because it offers rules for selecting actions for further exploration. Only actions relevant to approaching closer to the goal are selected with this method.

The usefulness of the means–end approach was demonstrated by the success of Newell and Simon's *General Problem Solver* (GPS) program. This program incorporated means–end analysis and achieved a fair measure of success with a range of problems including integral calculus, symbolic logic, missionary-and-cannibal puzzles and the Tower of Hanoi (Ernst and Newell, 1969). Comparison of the steps taken by the GPS program and the thinking-aloud record of a human subject, when both tackled a symbolic logic task, indicated a promising degree of match between the problem-solving processes of humans and GPS. Other evidence for means–end analysis in human problem solving may be found in Duncker's (1945) thinking-aloud records from subjects attempting the X-ray problem (discussed in Chapter 1).

III. EXPERIMENTAL STUDIES

In this section I will review experimental studies of human puzzle solving in which there is no element of competition or conflict with another rational being. We will first consider tasks, such as 'missionaries-and-cannibals' and water jug problems, to which the state–action approach can be applied quite directly, then a task that lends itself to a problem reduction approach (the Tower of Hanoi), next an example of a task in which the 'space' that the solver works in is less obvious (i.e. cryptarithmetic) and, finally, studies of how task representations are constructed from problem descriptions and the roles of analogy and insight in problem solving.

While considering the experimental studies discussed in this chapter, it might be useful to keep the following questions in mind.

(1) Under what conditions do humans adopt state–action as against problem reduction approaches? What factors of problem structure or prior experience are relevant?

(2) Both state–action and problem reduction methods require search. What factors shape human search patterns? What affects the depth and breadth of search? Can limits of working memory be related to the search strategies adopted in various tasks? What factors of problem structure or prior experience are relevant?

A. Move problems

The two main examples of problems that can be easily described in state–action terms and that have been studied extensively are the 'missionaries-and-cannibals' and 'water jars' tasks. These are also referred to as 'move' problems, in which movements of units or materials are required to transform the starting state into the goal state.

1 Missionaries-and-cannibals tasks

The first study of the 'missionaries-and-cannibals' problem that used a state–action approach seems to have been carried out by Thomas (1974). He used a variant of the task in which 'hobbits' replaced the missionaries and 'orcs' replaced the cannibals. The 'hobbits-and-orcs' problem requires that the solver produce a sequence of moves to transport three hobbits and three orcs across a river. The only way to cross the river is by use of a boat, and the boat can carry one or at most two creatures. At least one creature must be in the boat for it to cross. The major constraint in the problem is to avoid having the hobbits ever outnumbered by orcs on the same side of the river, since, as is well known (Tolkien, 1966), the orcs will gang up and devour the hobbits at the slightest opportunity.

This problem can be readily represented as a 'state–action' graph in which states of the problem are specified by (a) the numbers of hobbits and orcs on the starting (left) side and (b) the position of the boat (on right or left bank). Actions consist of moving one or two creatures from where the boat is to the opposite bank. At each state a number of actions are conceivable; some are 'illegal', i.e. result in consumption of hobbits, some take the subject backwards to a state already visited, and one, or at most two, advance toward the solution state. The 'legal' search space is represented in Fig. 2.5 and the solution can be read from the diagram. Each state is specified by a three-digit code: (1) the number of hobbits on the starting side; (2) the number of orcs on the starting side; (3) the location of the boat – '1' if on the starting side, '0' if on the other side.

The transitions are labelled to represent corresponding actions, e.g. 1H1O means that one hobbit and one orc were transported on the move.

In Thomas's study subjects tackled the problem on a computer display which showed the current state of the problem. The computer changed the display in accord with the subject's decisions about moves if the moves were legal; otherwise the computer informed the subject of the error and invited another try.

The relative difficulties of decisions are indicated by the graphs of times to choose and error rates per state (Fig. 2.6 and 2.7). The greatest difficulties were experienced in states 321 and 110.

Thomas notes that these states may be difficult for different reasons. It may be pointed out that state 321 does have three legal moves, of which one is helpful. There are also two illegal moves possible in this state. Furthermore, at state 321 there is the possibility of 'cycling' from 321 to 310 to 331 to 220 to 321. So there are more alternative responses at 321 than at other states. The difficulty at 110, however, may be due to the apparent progress that is required at that point. This conflicts with the general 'hill climbing' approach of moving to ever closer approximations to the goal. In going from 110 to 221 the solver actually appears to be getting further from the goal rather than closer. Wickelgren (1974, pp. 85–88) puts this problem into a general class of 'detour' problems that pose difficulties for 'hill climbing' methods.

As well as a (control) group of subjects who worked through the problem from the normal starting state, a part-whole group first solved the problem from the halfway state, 110 to 000. Then the part-whole group was given the whole problem from the normal starting state (331).

Table 2.1 *Average moves in each half of the hobbits–orcs problem (Thomas, 1974)*

	First half of task	Second half of task
Control group ($n = 71$)	13.0	15.5
Part-whole group ($n = 44$)	10.8	14.3
	(First attempt = 12.0)	

The part-whole group had prior experience of the second half and then tackled the whole problem. The control group worked through the whole problem in the normal way, without prior training.

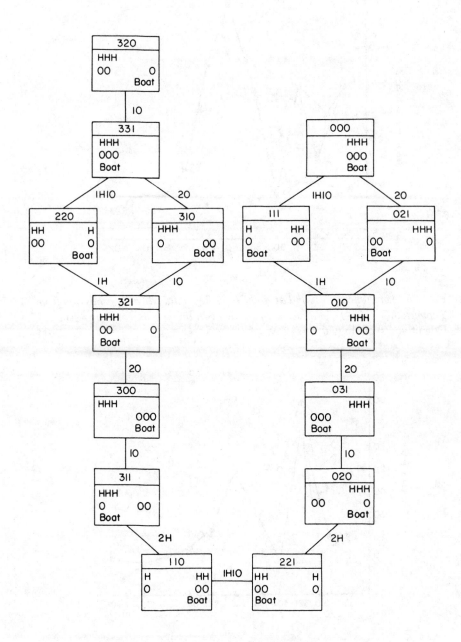

Fig. 2.5 *State–action graph of hobbits–orcs problem. See text for further explanation. Reproduced with permission from Thomas, J.C. (1974). An analysis of behavior in the hobbit–orcs problem.* Cognitive Psychology **6**, *257–269.*

Fig. 2.6 *Mean time to respond at each state. Reproduced with permission from Thomas, J.C. (1974). An analysis of behavior in the hobbits–orcs problem.* Cognitive Psychology **6**, *257–269.*

Fig. 2.7 *Proportion of errors at each state. Reproduced with permission from Thomas, J.C. (1974). An analysis of behavior in the hobbits–orcs problem.* Cognitive Psychology **6**, *257–269.*

The results (Table 2.1) indicate that the part group learned something from doing the second half that helped in tackling the first half. Interestingly, the control group did not appear to have benefited from the first half when they tackled the second half. Furthermore, when the part group repeated the second half while attempting the whole problem, they did *worse* than on the first time through. Apparently, a strong context effect occurred when subjects reached state 110 while solving the whole problem. This seems to support the idea, based on Wickelgren's analysis, that people tackling the whole problem are reluctant to reverse the apparent flow of moves in the direction of solution, but the 'detour' is less apparent without the background of progress through the earlier states.

Finally, from an analysis of the distributions of total times to solve, using a statistical technique devised by Restle and Davis (1962), Thomas inferred that some three or four major cognitive steps were involved in solving.

These steps would be decisions about whole blocks of moves, blocks that were then run off with increasing speed. At the end of each preplanned block of moves a longer pause would be evident while the next major decision was taken. The plot of latencies over states was consistent with about three such major decision points (Fig. 2.6). However, subsequent studies, some of which will be described next, suggest that subjects tackle this problem by making only very 'local' move-by-move decisions, rather than higher-order strategic decisions.

Simon and Reed (1976) examined a more complex version of the hobbits–orcs or missionaries–cannibals task than that studied by Thomas. In the Simon and Reed study, subjects were required to solve a problem involving five missionaries and five cannibals (the 5MC task). In this problem the boat can hold up to three people. The state–action graph for this problem is shown in Fig. 2.8. There are 27 legal states and, although there are only a few possible moves per state, subjects find the task quite difficult. For example, although it can be solved in 11 moves, one of Simon and Reed's naive groups averaged 30.6 legal moves to solution.

Simon and Reed put forward a model involving *strategy shift* during solving. According to their model, people start out with a 'balancing' strategy that leads them to try to have equal numbers of missionaries and cannibals on each side, but they switch at some point to a 'means–end' strategy in which legal moves that maximize the number of people on the target side are preferred (as long as missionaries are not outnumbered). Additionally, the model assumed that subjects performed a local 'anti-looping' test to avoid reversing the move made on the immediately previous trial. This was suggested because at each step it is possible to go back to the preceding state. Some randomness was built into the model by an assumption that people would sometimes make random moves and would not always check for loops.

The model was tested against data from two experiments. In experiment 1 a control group tackled the problem without any special hints while an experimental 'sub-goal' group was told that, on the way to solution, a state would be reached in which three cannibals were on the target side, on their own, and without the boat (state L in Fig. 2.8). In experiment 2, subjects solved the same problem twice, thus producing data on training effects.

Fig. 2.8 *State–action space for the five missionary–five cannibal (5MC) problem. The four-digit code for each state represents the number of missionaries and cannibals on the left and right banks. The position of the boat at each state is marked with a small star.*

In each condition, estimates were made of the model's five parameters. These parameters were the probabilities of (1) shifting strategy, (2) checking for loops, (3) making a random move, (4) the rate of increase in the probability of loop checking and (5) the rate of decrease in the probability of moving at random. It was found that providing a sub-goal (experiment 1) facilitated performance of the experimental subjects and this was reflected in an increase in the probability of shifting strategy from 'balance' to 'means–end' in the experimental group as compared with the control group.

Similarly a second attempt at the task (experiment 2) led to an improved performance, which was reflected in a larger estimated strategy shift parameter on the second attempt than on the first. Furthermore, the model predicted quite closely the average number of times, within each condition, that subjects made each possible move. Thus, the data can be interpreted reasonably well within the framework of this model – a model that involves only local decisions with no extensive forward planning or look ahead beyond the immediate alternatives. It may be that this is the case for the 5MC problem, while the 3MC problem, which Thomas (1974) studied, may permit more strategic planning; or it may be that Simon and Reed's analysis was not sensitive enough to uncover features of performance not consistent with their model. Thomas used latency and error data in his analysis, whereas Simon and Reed ignored error trials (which were approximately 20 per cent of all trials), and did not use latencies.

2 Water jugs tasks

A somewhat similar style of model exploration is found in Polson and co-workers' studies of water jug and missionaries-and-cannibals tasks, to which we now turn.

Atwood and Polson (1976) have developed a model for solving the following sort of water jug problems. Given three jugs (A, B, C,) where A can hold 8 units, B 5 units and C 3 units, A is initially full, and B and C are empty. The subject's task is to find a sequence of pourings that would divide the contents of the largest jug evenly between the largest and the middle-sized jug. In pouring, water is transferred until the jug the subject is pouring from is empty or the jug being poured into is full. Water cannot be added or discarded during the course of solving the problem. Such problems can be succinctly represented by state–action graphs, as in Fig. 2.9.

As can be seen from the state–action graph there is ample scope for 'looping'. Of course, the subject sees only the current state at any one time and has to envisage the successor states and evaluate them mentally. Under such conditions these problems are generally found to be difficult, e.g. the (8, 5, 3) problem can be solved in seven moves yet it took a naive group 26 moves on average.

The Atwood and Polson model combines assumptions about state evaluation, look ahead and memory processes. It assumes that subjects look ahead only to a depth of one step and that they evaluate the immediate successors of the current state by means of an evaluation function that sums the discrepancies between the target (goal) quantities in jugs A and B and the quantities in each successor state considered.

Fig. 2.9 State–action space for water jugs problems. Each state has a three-digit code showing the amount of water in each of the three jugs.

The actual evaluation function is:

$$e_i = c_i(A) - G(A) + c_i(B) - G(B)$$

where $c_i(A)$ is the number of units in jug A in state i and $G(A)$ is the number of units in jug A in the goal state. The smaller e_i is, the more the evaluated state is like the goal state. It is assumed that working memory can hold information up to some small number, r, of possible moves. At the beginning of the problem all moves are new and the one with the best evaluation will be selected. Information about that move is stored in long-term memory with some *probability s*. In future decisions, 'old' moves tend to be avoided, unless there are no 'new' moves.

Experiment 1 involved two conditions. In condition 1, subjects solved a practice problem (6, 4, 1) then the (8, 5, 3), the (24, 21, 3) and the (8, 5, 3) task. The (24, 21, 3) problem could be solved by applying the 'means–end' evaluation heuristic already outlined, whereas (8, 5, 3) required a 'detour' (i.e. a move to an 'unacceptable' state with a much poorer evaluation than the current state). It was predicted that tackling the (24, 21, 3) problem first would strengthen reliance on the means–end strategy, and so make the (8, 5, 3) problem more difficult, and that the (8, 5, 3) would be harder than (24, 21, 3) problem. In experiment 2, all subjects did the practice problem (6, 4, 1) followed by one of (8, 5, 3), (4, 9, 5), (12, 7, 4) or (16, 10, 3) problems.

As the model predicted, (8, 5, 3) was considerably more difficult than (24, 21, 3), but there was no order effect, in that doing (24, 21, 3) first did not hinder performance of (8, 5, 3). Analysis of both experiments indicated that the number of acceptable looping moves was the main determinant of problem difficulty.

The number of visits per problem state was quite well predicted by the model when the parameters were set such that information about three possible moves could be held in working memory, and information about a visited state entered long-term memory with probability of 0.90.

3 A general model?

Jeffries *et al.* (1977) described and tested an extension of Atwood and Polson's water jug model that can handle missionaries-and-cannibals problems. The extended model assumes that moves are selected on the basis of state evaluation processes and memory processes. Possible moves are evaluated in terms of how close they come to the goal state. The following general evaluation function is proposed.

$$e_i = aM_i + bC_i + cP_i$$

where M is the number of missionaries, C is the number of cannibals and P is the number of MC pairs, on the target side in all cases.

By varying the parameters (a, b and c), pure means–end, balancing, cannibals- or missionaries-first strategies can be represented, as can mixed strategies. The proposed memory processes are the same as in the water jug model. Information about a small number of moves (r) being currently considered is stored in working memory. Information about states actually visited is stored in long-term memory with some probability (*s*).

It is assumed that move selection may involve up to three stages. First, all 'acceptable' moves are considered. These are moves that do not lead to a 'worse' state than that already occupied.

Moves to new 'acceptable' states are more likely to be taken than moves to 'old' states (i.e. states recognized as having been entered already). If a move is not selected at this stage, the subject then seeks any move leading to a new state ('acceptable' or not). If all immediate successor states are 'old', the next stage begins and the subject simply selects the best of the *r* states under consideration. Finally, once a move is selected it may or may not be screened for *illegality*. If illegality is detected, the selected move is dropped and the process returns to the point where the illegal move was selected and continues from that point. So, this model permits illegal moves as well as legal ones.

Some 25–35 subjects tackled four variants of the missionaries-and-cannibals problem. These variants had the same structure but were couched in terms of (1) hobbits and orcs, (2) elves and men I (elves disappear if outnumbered by men), (3) elves and men II (custom requires elves and men to be paired or for three elves to be together) and (4) silver and gold (a monk must convey six talismans through a forest; gold talismans must never outnumber silver talismans on either side of forest).

Quite good fits to the state-to-state transition frequencies were obtained using the following parameter values over all problems.

$$\alpha = 0.70, \beta = 0.15, s = 0.85, r = 2$$

where α is the probability of picking a new move at stage 1, β is the probability of picking an old move at stage 2, s is the probability of storing information about a visited state in long-term memory, and r is the number of successor states about which information is held in working memory.

The evaluation function was

$$e_i = 3M_i + C_i + 2P_i$$

(*Note*: A wide variety of functions would lead to similar results.)

The illegal move detection parameters varied across problems. However, the general pattern of results was very similar over task variants.

The model was supported by reasonable fits between its predictions and the data, including illegal move data over all conditions. It is an attractive model in that it relates missionaries-and-cannibals tasks to water jug tasks and so reduces the fragmentation so prevalent in the problem-solving area. More critically, the model has a rather large number of free parameters (9) and has been fitted only to the three missionaries-and-cannibals task. It would be interesting to see an extension to the five missionaries-and-cannibals task, in which it could be compared directly with Simon and Reed's 'strategy shift' model. Also, the model deals only with the move data and not at with latencies (cf. Thomas, 1974). Again, it would be interesting to see extensions in that direction. Finally, the model does not seem to offer a ready explanation for the effects of hints and prior experience – effects that are dealt with by Simon and Reed's model.

A subsequent study (Atwood *et al.* 1980) focused on the question of the degree of planning used by subjects in the water jug task. The Jeffries *et al.* model proposes that people look only one move ahead. Subjects were given a number of water jug problems under different memory-aiding conditions. For some subjects the immediately available successor states were presented on each trial, for others the successor states were shown and were also marked to indicate whether they had been visited before. This manipulation should help reduce looping moves. Control subjects worked under the normal conditions of problem presentation. Analysis indicated that very good fits to move data could be obtained without assuming any look ahead beyond one level. These data then support the Jeffries *et al.* model. However, we must note that a large number of free parameters are involved and that the subjects were naive with respect to the task.

4 Puzzle solving with partial understanding

Polson and Jeffries (1982) reported a further extension of their general model to more complex tasks in which subjects are likely to detect major sub-goals and organize their problem solving accordingly. In particular, Polson and Jeffries considered the 'hobbits, orcs and gold' task. As the name suggests, this is a hobbits-and-orcs task combined with the concurrent task of moving some bags of gold across the river, one at a time. Two main versions of this problem were explored, viz. a non-interaction and an interaction version. In the interaction version, if all three orcs and all the bags of gold are left alone on the same side of the river, the orcs will steal the gold. Three strategies were distinguished. First, there was a gold-first strategy in which some combination of travellers was used to move the gold across the river, before then moving the travellers. Second, there was a travellers-first strategy, in which the travellers sub-problem was solved first and then the gold sub-problem. Finally, there was a combined strategy in which subjects attempted to solve both sub-problems simultaneously. The combined strategy is the most efficient. The travellers-first approach was used extremely rarely and the combined strategy was a little more prevalent than the gold-first approach (which led to a need for detouring in the interaction versions of the problems). Data obtained from variations of the problems, with differing numbers of gold bags, were well fitted by assuming that (a) subjects did recognize two sub-goals and pursued these independently and (b) there was a probability that subjects would realize (in the interaction problems) that a single bag of gold had to be left on the starting side until near the end of the task. Generally, deciding on the gold move is not a problem, and the model combines such decisions with decisions on the travellers' movements which are made in the same way as in the model already outlined for the simple 'hobbit-and-orc' problems. Polson and Jeffries thus indicate how the solving of complex puzzles with a clear and easily appreciated goal structure may be modelled by modest extensions of models developed for simpler tasks.

5 Tower of Hanoi problem

In the classical Tower of Hanoi (or Tower of Brahma) problem the subject is presented with three vertical pegs on one of which are n discs piled up in order of size, with the largest on the bottom. The task is to transfer the entire stack of discs from the starting peg to a target peg, moving only one disc at a time and never placing a larger disc on top of a smaller one. The spare peg may be used as a temporary holding place. If there are n discs, then the minimum number of moves required is $2^n - 1$. Thus the four-disc version in Fig. 2.10 would require a minimum of 15 moves.

According to legend (Raphael, 1976), some monks near Hanoi are working on a 64-disc puzzle, and when they complete it the world will end. However, even if they make no mistakes or wasted moves it will take them nearly a trillion years to finish, at one move per second!

Research with small versions of this puzzle suggests that subjects come to impose a goal–sub-goal (or problem–sub-problem) structure on the task (Egan and Greeno, 1974; Luger, 1976). For example, the four-disc task may be structured as follows:

(1) Solve the three-disc puzzle of moving the top three discs from peg 1 to peg 2, so that disc 4 can be moved to the target peg 3. (8 moves)
(2) Now solve the two-disc puzzle of moving the top two discs from peg 2 to peg 1, so that disc 3 can be moved to the target peg 3. (4 moves)
(3) Now solve the one-disc puzzle of moving the top disc on peg 1 to peg 2, so that disc 2 can be moved to peg 3. (2 moves)
(4) Finally, move disc 1 from peg 1 to peg 3. (1 move)

Following the above structure the problem is solved in the minimum of 15 moves, and the solution was guided by splitting up (reducing) the task into sub-problems. A possible 'problem reduction' tree for the four-disc task is shown in Fig. 2.11.

Egan and Greeno (1974) reported a study in which some subjects had prior experience with three-disc problems before tackling five- or six-disc puzzles. Other subjects attempted the difficult tasks without prior experience. The error profiles for all groups indicated that they performed better as important goals were near

Starting peg   Target peg

Fig. 2.10 *A Tower of Hanoi problem. The stack of discs is to be moved from the starting peg to the target peg, moving only one disc at a time and never placing a larger disc on a smaller one.*

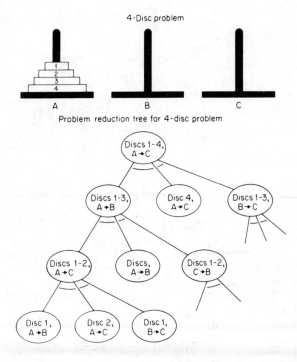

Fig. 2.11 *Part of problem reduction tree for the four-disc Tower of Hanoi problem. The overall task is successively reduced into sub-problems until sub-problems solvable in one move are reached.*

accomplishment. Also, they tended to perform worse (i.e. make more moves off the best solution path) when they were at points in the task that were remote from satisfying important goals.

Further evidence that a goal–sub-goal structure is commonly induced by this problem comes from studies by Luger (1976). The state–action graph for Tower of Hanoi problems clearly shows sub-spaces corresponding to the sub-problems (see Fig. 2.12).

By tracing subjects' paths through such state–action graphs, Luger has found that subjects generally (1) follow goal-directed paths, in that each successive step tends to approach a goal or sub-goal, and (2) whenever a sub-goal state is reached the preferred path exists from the space of the just-completed sub-problem to enter a new sub-problem space. However, Luger's analysis is not conclusive regarding strategies, since, as Simon (1975) has shown, a number of rather different strategies could produce minimum solution paths.

Simon (1975) considered three main alternative strategies. The first, 'goal recursion', is essentially the one already outlined. As he points out, this strategy requires a list of goals and sub-goals to be kept in working memory and the list grows

Fig. 2.12 *Part of the state–action graph for a three-disc Tower of Hanoi problem. The upper nine states correspond to two-disc problems (the left-hand side to one such sub-problem and the right-hand side to another). On leaving the upper nine states, further two-disc sub-problem spaces are entered. Reproduced with permission from Cognitive psychology: learning and problem solving (Part 3), Unit 28, D303. Milton Keynes: Open University Press.*

with the number of discs, so that by the time ten discs are tackled, the list would be completely unwieldy. For large numbers of discs at least, a different strategy is needed. The second strategy, the 'perceptual' strategy, is much less demanding on memory. The main steps are: (a) identifying the largest disc (label it k) not yet on the target peg; (b) to identify the largest disc obstructing movement of k to the target peg; (c) if there is no obstructor, make the move; (d) if there is an obstructor, establish the goal of moving the obstructor to the other peg (neither the source nor the target of k), then recurse, for the obstructor, through steps (b) and (c). This strategy involves perceptual tests but a much more limited load on memory – only one goal need be in working memory at any one time, no matter how large the stack. Finally, Simon describes a 'move pattern' strategy, which also involves very little memory load, that could be used with large versions of the Tower of Hanoi problem, but whose rationale is obscure. This strategy can be described as follows:

(1) On odd-numbered moves, move the smallest disc.
(2) On even-numbered moves, move the next smallest disc that is exposed.
(3) If peg S is the initial source peg, T the target peg and O the other peg, then, if the total number of pegs is odd, the smallest disc is always moved from S to T to O to S, and so on, while, if the total number of pegs is even, the smallest disc is always moved in the opposite cycle: from S to O to T to S, and so on.

While people can follow such a strategy, if they are told about it, it seems unlikely that it would be easily discovered spontaneously. The strategy makes very small demands upon either pattern recognition or working memory, and can be applied to any number of discs.

Simon's analysis alerts us to the existence of alternative strategies (even within this well-structured task) that can produce identical patterns of moves but involve very different demands on memory and perceptual processes. Clearly, further data on reactions to task variants (increasing number of discs, for instance), further response measures (e.g. latencies) and verbal protocols would be useful in determining which strategies actually tend to be followed under which conditions. Karat (1982) used move latencies as well as move patterns and task variants to test a model for naive performance in the Tower of Hanoi. The model derives from Polson and Jeffries' analyses of puzzle solving discussed in the previous section of this chapter. Karat assumed that subjects searched the problem space guided by two strategies. These are, first, to have as a sub-goal moving the largest disc to the goal peg and, second, to avoid returning to just-visited problem states. A model incorporating these assumptions about decision latencies yielded good fits to move and latency results from three- four- and five-disc problems.

An important factor in performance is the degree of experience that the solver has with the task. Anzai and Simon (1979) allowed a single subject four attempts at a five-disc version of the Tower of Hanoi problem. The instructions urged the subject to seek a good solution procedure. Over the four attempts, distinct strategies evolved. The earliest was a form of forward search from the starting state, with a check against repetitions of previously obtained positions. Thus, a form of state–action representation seems to have been used initially. Subsequently, a strategy similar to Simon's (1975) 'perceptual' strategy was evolved and this in turn gave way to a 'pyramid' strategy in which the subject saw the task as one of moving sets and subsets of discs. This final strategy is essentially the same as Simon's (1975) 'goal recursion' strategy. These results are suggestive of an order of acquisition of alternative strategies with task experience. Anzai and Simon (1979) have proposed some plausible mechanisms for strategy improvement. For example, if a short sequence of moves leads to a desired sub-goal, then remember that sub-goal–sequence association and use it next time the same sub-goal is sought. However, since this experiment involved but a single subject, the results are only suggestive and do not allow confident generalization. The study does serve as a reminder that strategy change within subjects exists, and indicates how it might be examined further.

B. Cryptarithmetic

The missionaries-and-cannibals, water jugs and Tower of Hanoi tasks have clear, simple structures. In such tasks subjects were successfully represented as working with state–action or problem reduction representations that followed, quite directly, from the problem statements. In the case of *cryptarithmetic* tasks, the permissible actions and the problem states are relatively more open to differing definitions (and so such problems represent a step toward less well-defined types of problem).

Newell and Simon (1972) attempted a detailed analysis of behaviour on the following cryptarithmetic task. (The solution is on page 40. You may find it instructive to attempt the task at this point.)

DONALD + GERALD = ROBERT

Given D = 5 and that each letter stands for a different digit from 0 to 9, find the assignment of digits to letters that makes the sum correct.

This problem could, in principle, be tackled by trying out all possible mappings of nine digits to nine letters in a pure trial-and-error manner. However, there are 9! (= 362,880) such mappings and so a serial processor testing five mappings per minute would require about 1 month to solve.

Since human subjects can solve in 15–20 min, we can rule out pure trial and error on their part.

Whatever human subjects do, Newell and Simon claim that they work within some definite *problem space* and that attempts to solve can be seen as searches through the problem space. By a 'problem space' is meant the set of possible states of knowledge that a solver can be in with respect to the problem. The problem space is essentially defined by the distinctions and relationships that the solver uses while working on the task. Clues about the problem space used by a particular subject can be gained by examining thinking-aloud records or 'protocols' obtained while the problem is worked through.

The beginning of a thinking-aloud protocol from this task is shown in Fig. 2.13. The subject concerned here (S3) makes use of information she has inferred about in equalities, parity (i.e. oddness or evenness of numbers) and whether there are carries or not from column to column. She also makes assignments by calculation and, later on, by hypothesis. Hypothesized assignments are rejected if they lead to contradictions. Newell and Simon conclude that S3 is working within what they call the 'augmented problem space' for cryptarithmetic. This may be contrasted with a 'basic space' that deals only in assignments and contradictions, and does not use information about parities and carries.

Newell and Simon propose that a person's movement through the problem space can be represented by a *Problem Behaviour Graph* (PBG). The subject is envisaged as moving through a series of 'states of knowledge' (some of the knowledge may be of provisional assignments or hypotheses). Movement from state to state is mediated by operations that modify current knowledge states into a different knowledge state. It is possible to return to previously visited knowledge states (though the subject may not realize that this has happened). Four broad operations were distinguished in S3's protocol.

(1) *Process column* (PC): extract whatever information can be inferred from a given column in view of other information available in the current knowledge state.
(2) *Assign value* (AV): assign a digit to a letter.
(3) *Generate* (GN): generate possible values for a given letter, in view of available information in the current knowledge state.
(4) *Test digit* (TD): check whether a particular digit could be assigned to a given letter, in view of information available in the current knowledge state.

There are ten different letters and each of them has one numerical value.
 Therefore, I can, looking at the 2D's – each D is 5; therefore, T is zero. So I think I'll start by writing that problem here. I'll write 5, 5 is zero.
 Now, do I have any other T's? No, but I have another D. That means I have a 5 over the other side.
 Now I have 2 A's and 2 L's that are each – somewhere – and this R – 3 R's. Two L's equal an R. Of course, I'm carrying a 1 which will mean that R has to be an odd number because the 2 L's – any two numbers added together has to be an even number and 1 will be an odd number. So R can be 1, 3, not 5, 7 or 9.
 (The experimenter asks at this point, 'What are you thinking now?')
 Now G – since R is going to be an odd number and D is 5, G has to be an even number.
 I'm looking at the left side of this problem here where it says D + G. Oh, plus possibly another number, if I have to carry 1 from the E + O. I think I'll forget about that for a minute.

Fig. 2.13 *Beginning of thinking-aloud record (protocol) from subject working on the DONALD + GERALD problem. Reproduced with permission from Newell, A. and Simon, H.A. (1972).* Human problem solving, *pp. 230–231. Englewood Cliffs, NJ: Prentice-Hall.*

Part of the PBG for S3 is shown in Fig. 2.14. The PBG for the complete protocol involved 238 states. Note that there is no automatic procedure for producing a PBG for a given protocol, despite some preliminary proposals (Bhaskhar and Simon, 1977). Deriving PBGs from such protocols is largely a matter of judgement. The major pitfalls in PBG construction are that the graph will be (a) too superficial (will miss important details), (b) too disaggregated (over-detailed), or (c) be epi-phenomenal (will be in terms of the wrong problem space).

At the various states in the PBG, alternative operations would often be possible and the question arises of the strategy by which operations are chosen. The order in which letters are solved provides a clue to strategy. Newell and Simon report that those subjects who solve tend to substitute numbers for letters in approximately the same sequence, i.e. first, T = 0 then E = 9, R = 7, then A = 4 and L = 8, then G = 1, then N = 6, B = 3 and finally O = 2.

The structure of the task allows subjects to concentrate on the column whose entries are most constrained by virtue of previous information or by the nature of the column, e.g. O + E = 0 is constrained and very informative. Processing the most constrained columns first in this way greatly cuts down the amount of trial and error and leads to the observed order of solving.

Newell and Simon proposed a fine grain analysis that is intended to account for the state-to-state transitions in the PBG and to be a specific implementation of the general strategy of 'focusing on the most constrained columns'. Their analysis is in terms of 'production rules'. A production rule is of the form: 'If condition C applies, take action A'. A collection of such rules forms a production system. Computer programs can be written in the form of such systems, and a number of researchers (e.g. Baylor and Gascon, 1974; Young, 1974; Anderson, 1983) have found pro-duction systems to offer a useful way of building models. Production rules are reminiscent of stimulus–response links, but are more flexible. The conditions may

Key: PC(1) = Process column 1
      GNC   = Get next column
      GC(R) = Get column containing R
      GN(R) = Generate possible values for R

Fig. 2.14 *Part of the Problem Behaviour Graph (PBG) for S3. The boxes represent states of knowledge and the arrows represent operations that move the subject from state to state. Reproduced with permission from Newell, A. and Simon, H.A. (1972).* Human problem solving, *p. 174. Englewood Cliffs, NJ: Prentice-Hall.*

refer to memory contents, goals or observed states of the world; the actions may be overt or internal. Each action leads to a new state of affairs which in turn triggers a new rule, and so on.

Newell and Simon were able to account for around 90 per cent of state-to-state transitions in the PBG with just 14 production rules. It should be noted, however, that the rules were not sufficient to form a complete running production system, and the analysis appears to have been carried out by hand rather than by computer.

Finally, Newell and Simon extended their analysis to other related problems and to new subjects. Broadly similar results were obtained, but some novel problem spaces were tried out by at least one of the subjects (S8). For instance, there was a 'typographical space' in which similarities in appearance between letters and digits were sought as a guide to the answer. There was also a 'cryptogram space' in which rules were sought to associate digits to letters on the basis of letter position in the alphabet. Solution is unlikely within these spaces. Evidently, the initial phase of developing an understanding of the task (i.e. a problem space) is crucial to late action. So, we now turn to some studies directed at task comprehension or problem space construction.

C. Understanding task instructions

In a typical laboratory study of puzzle solving the subject is presented with written or spoken instructions from which he or she must develop a representation of the task. Despite the evident importance of the task interpretation stage, relatively little work has been carried out on it.

Simon and Hayes have reported some studies which indicate how the topic can be tackled within the information-processing framework. They propose that understanding instructions involves two sub-processes (Hayes and Simon, 1974), which they label the *language process* and the *construction process*. The language process deals with the basic interpretation of the sentences in the instructions and draws on the subject's knowledge of syntax and semantics. After every sentence or two, the construction process tries to build up an internal model of the task and the operators available to deal with the task. It is assumed that the internal model can be represented by list-processing notions, i.e. the internal representation involves symbols, lists of symbols and operations that change symbols on lists or transfer symbols from list to list.

A computer model (called UNDERSTAND) incorporating these ideas was developed and compared (albeit loosely) with human protocol data obtained using the Tea Ceremony problem (Hayes and Simon, 1974). The Tea Ceremony (TC) problem is an isomorph of the Tower of Hanoi (TOH), i.e. it has the same abstract structure but differs in form. In the TC problem there are five tasks of varying 'nobility' and three participants. Initially, all tasks are the responsibility of one participant (host) and the goal is to transfer all the tasks to a specified other participant (the most senior guest). The major constraints are that only the least noble task that a person is performing can be transferred and it can be transferred only to someone who does not already have a less noble task. A TC task can be translated into a TOH task and vice versa by using the correspondences below.

Tea Ceremony	Tower of Hanoi
3 participants	3 pegs
5 tasks	5 discs
Nobility of tasks	Size of discs

The UNDERSTAND program incorporated sufficient methods to produce from the problem text a list-processing representation of the task that could, in theory, serve as input to a GPS-like program for solving the problem. However, some differences emerged between the program and human protocol data. For instance, the program alternated between language and construction processes but never returned to earlier parts of the text to reanalyse them for possible misunderstanding. The human subjects, in contrast, went back, re-read and reinterpreted certain portions when they realized that their first interpretation of the task was leading to difficulties. Also, when the problem was attempted, subjects often went back to the instructions and modified earlier mistaken attempts at understanding. The program thus requires extra flexibility to make it a closer simulation.

Hayes and Simon's (1974) analysis suggests that list-processing operations are used in the task representation that is finally constructed as a result of the understanding process. An interesting check on this idea was reported on in a study involving further isomorphs of the Tower of Hanoi (Simon and Hayes, 1976). Subjects were presented with 'monster' problems, e.g. in which three monsters of different sizes each hold a differently sized globe and have to transfer globes so that they end up holding globes proportionate to their size. Variants of the problem required that the globes be shrunk or expanded to attain the desired consistency of monster-to-globe assignments. Despite differences in the surface descriptions, all problems could be represented by a common abstract structure. Simon and Hayes (1976) argued, however, that the UNDERSTAND program and human subjects would reach different representations for problems of *transferring* items as compared to problems of *changing* items. In list-processing terms, if each monster is represented by a list of globe names (i.e. the globes it is holding), then a 'transfer' task requires symbols to be shifted from list to list while a 'change' problem involves replacing symbols on lists. In both cases the moves must be in accord with the task constraints. It happens that the change representation requires a more complex testing procedure to ensure that proposed moves are legal than does the transfer representation, and so it was predicted that change problems would take longer. Consistent with this analysis, Hayes and Simon (1977) found that the change tasks took almost twice as long (28.1 min) as the transfer tasks (16.9 min).

Human subjects' comments showed a tendency to modify the names or labels that they used with certain of the problems as they continued to work on them. This was the case where the monsters were referred to by variable names (e.g. the monster with the small name) that would not be directly appropriate later on (e.g. in a task that involved name swapping). Subjects would replace variable names by shorter permanent ones (e.g. 'the first monster', 'the left-most monster'). These changes presumably helped to reduce demands on working memory.

To sum up, it appears that people are more flexible in constructing and revising problem representations than the UNDERSTAND program, but that, like the program, they interpret the instructions in terms of list structures and general-purpose operators, presumably drawn from long-term memory.

D. Analogy in problem solving

A possible route to solving a problem is to try to solve it by analogy with some other problem for which a solution is known. The problem for which the solution is known, is technically referred to as the *base* or *source* problem and the problem for which a solution is sought is known as the *target* problem. A matching is sought between features of the target and base problems in the hope that a matching solution will be useful for the target task. This process is generally called *analogical mapping* (Gentner, 1980; 1983; Holyoak, 1984). A helpful analogous problem may be sought within the same domain as the current problem or in a quite different domain. Extremely difficult problems of theory development in science have sometimes been solved by means of such inter-domain analogies. Examples from the history of science include the model of the heart as a pump, the planetary model of the atom and the billiard ball model of gases. In these examples there were valid mappings at a structural or conceptual level that led to useful solutions. Thus, nucleus and electrons could be usefully matched to sun and planets, leading to the useful conclusion that the electrons revolve around the nucleus because of attraction and weight differences in a way similar to the behaviour of planets in the solar system. At a more modest level, Polya (1957) recommended seeking out analogous known problems when tackling new geometry problems, and Clement (1982) found that expert physicists spontaneously developed simpler analogue problems when searching for solutions to novel physics problems.

1 Studies of remote analogies

A series of studies by Gick and Holyoak (1980, 1983) has revealed some of the conditions under which analogies are detected and used in the case of solving ill-defined puzzles which draw on real-world non-technical knowledge. The main problem that Gick and Holyoak used in their experiments is Duncker's (1945) radiation problem (which was introduced in Chapter 1). In this task, the subject has to find a way in which a doctor could destroy a tumour deep inside an imaginary patient's body, without surgically operating or damaging surrounding tissue. A source of radiation is provided. The solution involves a convergence of weak rays on the tumour. Gick and Holyoak (1980) examined the effects of making analogous problems and their solutions known to subjects faced with the radiation problem. In the first experiment, each subject read one of three military stories and then had the story available for reference while tackling the radiation problem. In one story a general captures a fortress by attacking it with groups of soldiers from a number of directions simultaneously (mines on all the approach roads prevent a direct concentrated attack). In the second story, one road to the fort is left unmined and a concentrated onslaught succeeds. In the third story, a tunnel is constructed to get inside the fort. Experimental subjects were told to try to use their story problem as a hint in solving the radiation problem. Control subjects did not receive the story problems or, of course, the hint. Subjects' solutions were classified as to whether they invoked convergence of rays, use of an already existing passage (e.g. the oesophagus) or use of an operation. The three story-problems led to production of corresponding solutions for the radiation problem (that is, the first story was associated with convergence solutions, the second with 'open passage' and the third with 'operation' solutions). Thus, subjects could and did use analogous problems to solve the radiation task (at least when instructed to do so). Subsequent experiments, with hints to use the story analogues, also showed that the closer the analogy the better the 'transfer'; that memorized stories could also be used, with a hint, as well as currently present stories; and that timing of the story (before beginning the radiation task or after a period of work in the task) had no effect. Overall, spontaneous use of the analogies was low; however, the 'no hint' groups did somewhat better (roughly 30 per cent solving) than controls (roughly 10 per cent solving), who had had no analogous stories. Gick and Holyoak (1980) surmised that the level of encoding of the stories for memory may have been too specific to be very helpful in the problem-solving context, where more general similarities would be useful in mediating transfer.

This consideration led to the studies reported by Gick and Holyoak (1983) which concerned the development of problem schemata from analogous problems. A problem *schema* (plural: schemata) is a general solution concept which applies to a class of problems. Gick and Holyoak proposed a schema for 'convergence' problems, which can be summarized by the principle: 'If you need a large force to accomplish some purpose but are prevented from applying such a force directly, many smaller forces applied simultaneously from different directions may work just as well'. Gick and Holyoak reported three individual experiments in which they attempted to bring about the induction of schemata by (a) presenting single analogous problems and having subjects summarize them or (b) presenting an analogous problem plus a statement of the underlying principle of the solution, or (c) using single analogue problems with or without diagrams. None of these manipulations using single analogue problems was effective in improving performance in subsequent target problems. A further three experiments involving two story analogues proved more successful. Performance in the target radiation task was particularly good, even without a hint, when the story analogues were dissimilar to each other and subjects either extracted a principle from the stories or were told one. It seems then that extraction and use of a relevant ('convergence') problem schema was most facilitated by prior exposure to dissimilar analogues, for which the key principle was made explicit. Under such conditions roughly 60 per cent of subjects solved without any hint being given; this compares with a 10 per cent solution rate for control subjects receiving no story analogues.

Subsequent studies (Holyoak and Koh, 1987; Keane, 1988) indicated that single analogues can be useful, especially when they are closely analogous to the target problem. In one study Keane used either a very close analogy involving a surgeon treating a brain tumour by radiation or the more remote analogy of the general taking a fort by a simultaneous attack on it with small groups of soldiers. Despite a week's delay between memorizing the analogue story problem and tackling the radiation problem, subjects retrieved the literal analogue quite readily but only rarely the remote analogue. A similar result was obtained by Keane in a further study where analogous stories involving military applications of rays and lasers were retrieved readily on tests with the radiation problem, while the standard 'general' analogue was rarely retrieved. Holyoak and Koh (1987) have examined the relative roles of structural and surface similarity between analogue and target problems. They used as their analogue task two versions of the 'lightbulb' problem. In one lightbulb problem, a broken filament has to be fused together without damaging the glass; converging low-intensity laser beams provide a solution. In the second version, the filament has fused and needs to be jarred apart, without breaking the glass bulb: converging ultrasound waves are the solution. Each problem was also presented either as stated above or with the 'glass breaking' constraint removed and a statement that the instruments available were individually of insufficient power. In all four versions of the problem story a convergence solution was given. Relative to the target radiation problem, the degree of *structural* similarity was highest when the container-damage constraint applied, and the degree of surface similarity was highest when the instrument was the laser (which is more like an X-ray that is ultrasound). Prior study of the lightbulb problem produced greatest transfer (without hint) to the radiation problem when both structural and surface similarity were high. Both structural and surface similarity had comparable effects before a hint to use the story analogue. After a hint, structural similarity was more influential in reaching solution. Holyoak and Koh suggested that both structural and surface similarity play a role in automatic retrieval of problem analogues, but that structural similarity is crucial if the analogue is to be applied successfully. Overall, these studies suggest that successful spontaneous use of remote inter-domain analogies is hard to demonstrate even in favourable laboratory conditions. Indeed, as Perkins argues (1981, pp. 89–91), the use of novel remote analogies is probably also very rare outside the laboratory.

Work by Gick and McGarry (1992) has indicated that initial failure to solve a source problem can facilitate solution of later analogous problems. This has been demonstrated in the context of the mutilated chequerboard (MC) problem, given in Fig. 2.15.

To solve the problem subjects have to conceptualize the colours of the 64 squares as paired up, since a domino must cover both a black and a white square; removing two squares of the same colour makes it impossible to cover the remaining 62 squares with 31 dominoes. An analogous problem is the dance problem. If there are 32 men and 32 women initially and two women leave, can the remaining 62 people form heterosexual dancing pairs? Subjects readily realize that dancers cannot now

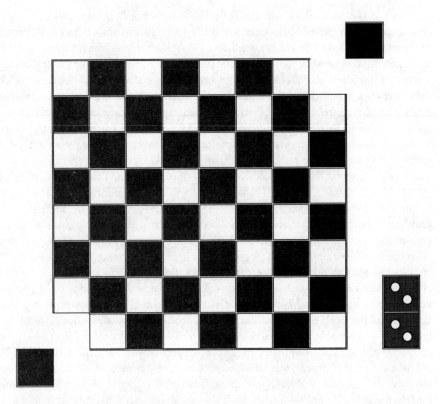

Fig. 2.15 *The mutilated chequerboard (MC) problem. You are given a chequerboard and 32 dominoes. Each domino covers exactly two adjacent squares on the board. Thus, the 32 dominoes can cover all 64 squares of the chequerboard. Now, suppose two squares are cut off at diagonally opposite corners of the board. If possible, show how you would place 31 dominoes on the board so that all the remaining 62 squares are covered. If you think it is impossible, give a proof of why.*

form all male–female pairs. Gick found poor transfer from the dance problem to the MC problem. However, if subjects were given first the dinner party problem shown in Fig. 2.16, which they typically failed to solve, and then the dinner party solution, good transfer occurred to the MC problem. Gick and McGarry were able to conclude that similarities between target and source solution *processes*, not just similarities in content or structure, could underlie successful analogies.

2 Studies of close analogies (examples)

Under some conditions even close analogies that should be available to subjects are

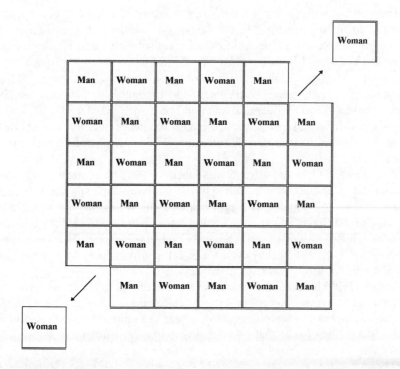

Fig. 2.16 *The dinner party problem. Thirty-six people, 18 men and 18 women, are at a dinner party, as illustrated schematically above. The 36 people are seated at 18 tables. Each table seats only two people, a man and a woman, who are sitting immediately next to each other, in either a horizontal or a vertical direction. If two people leave, as illustrated by the arrows, can 17 tables be arranged to seat the other 34 people? The people are not allowed to move. Explain your reasoning. After Gick and McGarry (1992).*

not retrieved or applied appropriately. This is a cause for concern in that teaching by use of *examples*, which are a form of close analogy, is a commom strategy in textbooks and lecture courses. Reed and co-workers (1985) found very little transfer from study of a worked example in word algebra problems to test problems having identical solutions.

(Two completely analogous word algebra problems are:

(1) A car travelling at a speed of 30 mph left a certain place at 10.00 am. At 11.30 am another car departed from the same place at 40 mph and travelled the same route. In how many hours will the second car overtake the first?

(2) A car travels south at the rate of 30 mph. Two hours later a second car leaves to overtake the first car, using the same route and going at 45 mph. In how many hours will the second car overtake the first?)

Transfer was even poorer when the test problems had related but not identical solutions to the example problems. Having the solutions of the examples continuously available aided transfer in the identical solution cases. However, transfer appears to have been largely based on 'blind' substitution of test item quantities into the example solutions, with frequent substitution errors indicating lack of understanding. More elaborate explanation of the example solutions was helpful in promoting transfer to the identical solution test items. Transfer to related but not identical problems was poor over the manipulations of solution availability and degree of explanation. It appears that an example will not be helpful unless it is itself clearly understood.

Ross (1984, 1989) and Ross and Kennedy (1990) have stressed the role of reminding of previous examples during problem solving. Ross and Kennedy demonstrated that being reminded of a previous example which had the same solution structure (but different contents) as a current test item not only aided performance on the that test item but also on subsequent problems having different contents but the same solution, that is, subjects learn something from applying a prior example which carries forward to subsequent items.

Bassok (1990) has also shown transfer from examples to test items dissimilar in content, such as from compound interest calculations in a banking example to population growth problems in ecology, where the same mathematical principles apply. She further found that transfer was markedly better when the quantities involved in the example and transfer test problems were of the same type (e.g. both rates or both simple amounts), suggesting that type of variable was a feature used by subjects in encoding problems.

Finally, with regard to the use of examples, it is noteworthy that studies of effective learners compared with less effective learners in complex domains (mechanics and statistical computing) have found that extensive use of examples is a characteristic of better learners (Chi *et al.* 1989; Green and Gilhooly, 1990).

3 Theoretical approaches to analogy

The process of using analogies in problem solving can be divided into two main stages. First, a candidate base analogy is retrieved from long-term memory. Second, a mapping is established between the candidate base analogy and the target. Theorists have tended to address these two phases separately, with most attention being given to the mapping process. Accounting for mapping is a more tractable matter since the subject is dealing with just two specific items, the base and the target, whereas, in retrieval an indefinitely large pool of candidates has to be considered. Further, subjects can usually make some mapping between base and target but cannot always retrieve candidate bases from long-term memory, particularly if base and target are superficially dissimilar (Gick and Holyoak, 1980, 1983; Holyoak and Koh, 1987; Keane, 1988).

Gentner and Gentner (1983) proposed a 'structure-mapping' theory of analogical thinking. This approach presupposes that subjects represent the target and base as well-defined structures of *objects* and *predicates*. Objects are the mental entities that comprise the base and target in the subject's representation. Gentner and Gentner pointed out that these 'objects' need not be concrete tangible objects, rather they may be coherent separable parts of a complex object or even fictional objects. Different subjects may well represent the same material in quite different ways; but, once the objects are set in a particular representation, they will then be used in subsequent mapping operations. Predicates can be *attributes* of objects, *relationships* between objects or *higher-order relationships* between relationships. Take a possible representation of a solar system, for example. This is represented as a structure of objects (sun and planets); the objects have attributes (mass, heat, colour etc.); there are relationships between objects (sun is more massive than planet, planet attracts sun, sun attracts planet, planet revolves around sun); and higher-order relationships (e.g. if an object x is more massive than object y, then y will revolve around x). The higher-order relationship links together the relative mass and revolving around relationships in a *systematic* way. The two lower-level relationships are thus not accidental but are implied by a higher-level rule in the representation.

Having formed the structured representation of the base example, it can now be mapped on to the target. It is assumed that the subject has an initially impoverished representation of the target consisting of objects and attributes but without the crucial relationships. Mapping the objects from the base on to the target objects (e.g. sun to nucleus, planets to electrons) permits application of the base relationships to the target objects. For example, that there is a force attracting peripheral and central objects; that the central object is more massive than the peripheral ones. It is assumed then that relationships are carried over but that attributes are not. Further, it is suggested that relationships that are linked by higher-order relationships or rules are more likely to be carried over than more isolated relationships. So, in the solar system–atomic structure example, relationships of mass and revolving around would be carried over because they are linked together, while the relationship *hotter than* which is isolated would not be imported from base to target. The structure-mapping theory has been embodied in an artificial intelligence program known as the Structure Mapping Engine (SME) (Falkenhainer *et al.*, 1986), which attests to its internal coherence.

Gentner and Gentner (1983) explored the empirical implications of structure-mapping theory in two experiments on analogies for electricity. These studies concerned two alternative analogies for electrical flow through circuits with batteries and resistors in parallel or in series. The analogies were electricity as like flow of fluid through pipes and as like the movement of crowds through passageways. In the 'fluid' analogy, voltage is mapped to pressure, current is mapped to flow rate, resistance is mapped to pipe width and batteries are mapped to reservoirs. In the 'crowd' analogy, voltage is mapped to the amount of pushing in the crowd, current is mapped to the number of people per unit time and resistance is mapped to gates in the passageway, but no clear mapping exists between batteries and any aspect of the crowd model. Subjects given electrical circuit problems could be divided into those spontaneously using fluid or crowd analogies. Those using the fluid analogy performed better on battery problems than resistor problems. Those using the crowd analogy did better on resistor problems than on analogies. A second study briefly trained subjects in one or the other analogy before they tackled circuit problems. Similar, if weaker, results were obtained in this second study. It appears that the brief training was not sufficient to establish the fluids base analogy sufficiently to permit adequate mapping. This result underlines the importance of having a good understanding of the base domain before it can function effectively in analogical problem solving.

An alternative 'constraint–satisfaction' approach has been put forward by Holyoak and Thagard (1989, 1990). This connectionist approach proposes that, in seeking a good mapping, a network of nodes is set up where each node represents a possible mapping between base and target elements (e.g. in the X-ray task with the general story as base, one node might represent the doctor–general mapping and another node the rays–army mapping). Clearly there are many possible mappings. Some mappings support one another while others do not. For example, the doctor–general mapping supports the army–ray mapping since army and ray relate to general and doctor in the same way and army and ray are both means available to the agents in the story. Other conceivable mappings such as fort–rays are not consistent with the (correct) mappings of doctor and general. Links between mutually consistent mappings are positive and those between mutually inconsistent mappings are negative. If such a network is set up with plausible link weights between the nodes repre- senting possible mappings, then the network settles into a stable state where the most active units represent the best analogical mapping the system can find (Holyoak and Thagard, 1990). (The program to carry out the parallel constraint satisfaction is known as ACME, standing for Analogical Constraint Mapping Engine.) A result for the lightbulb and radiation problem reported by Holyoak and Thagard is essentially the standard correct mapping. Hence the system is adequate to the mapping task. Holyoak and Thagard have also gone a step further and developed a model to simulate the retrieval of candidate base analogues given a target. This model is known as ARCS (Analogical Retrieval by Constraint Satisfaction). Competing possible base or source analogues are activated by degree of surface similarity, and an initial structure mapping begins simultaneously between all candidate sources and the target until one mapping passes a threshold of fit and is then selected for further mapping attempts. The model can be interpreted as suggesting that consider- able unconscious activity takes place before a candidate source analogue reaches consciousness for 'verification' or rejection. Among other tests the system has been explored on a database containing synopses of 25 plays by Shakespeare. When given 'Hamlet' as a target, the system yielded a psychologically plausible result by activating other tragedies, such as 'King Lear', but not comedies.

Keane and colleagues have pointed out that both the ACME and SME models previously discussed do not take into account the limitations of working memory, and have proposed an alternative model, the Incremental Analogy Machine (IAM), which does explicitly respect human processing limitations (Keane and Brayshaw, 1988; Keane et al., 1994). IAM works in a serial fashion, building up a single mapping bit by bit; if the first mapping is unsatisfactory, a fresh one is attempted.

Empirical support for the IAM approach was obtained in a study of the following type of analogy task (Holyoak and Thagard, 1989.)

A	B
Bill is tall	Fido is hungry
Bill is smart	Blackie is friendly
Tom is tall	Blackie is frisky
Tom is timid	Rover is hungry
Steve is smart	Rover is friendly

The task is to decide which items in list A match which items in list B (ignoring the meanings of the words). The solution is that Steve matches Fido, Bill matches Rover, Tom matches Blackie, smart matches hungry, tall matches friendly, and timid matches frisky. The key to solving is to attend to the 'singletons' in each list; these must match and the rest follows. The IAM model correctly predicted that problems with the singletons early in the lists would be solved faster than problems with the singletons late in the lists. ACME and SME were not sensitive to this order effect (Keane *et al.*, 1994).

A good analogy often elicits a feeling of insight. The next section considers some recent research which focuses on the notion of insight in problem solving.

E. Insight revisited

1 Issues

The Gestalt approach to problem solving, which was outlined in Chapter 1, stressed the notion of 'insight' as against blind trial and error. One definition of insight is that it is an understanding of how the solution is necessitated, given the nature of the problem. This 'accomplishment' definition is probably widely acceptable. A less widely acceptable view is of insight as a *special* distinct process that leads to good sudden solutions usually after a period of no progress and which is not reducible to the ordinary processes of recognition, retrieval, goal-setting, and so on. The notion of insight as a special irreducible process is often associated with the Gestalt approach. However, the corpus of Gestalt writings is sufficiently large and vague that this assertion can be both supported and denied by suitably selective quotation (for example, see Dominowski, 1981; Weisberg and Alba, 1981b; Ellen, 1982). Setting aside the historical controversy, there has been a recent renewal of interest in the concept of insight. As Sternberg (1987) has put it, one can distinguish the 'special process' approach from the alternative 'nothing special' approach to insight. Currently, the 'nothing special' approach is associated particularly with Weisberg (1986, 1988), Perkins (1981) and Sternberg (1987). A particular test-bed for these opposing views has been the set of problems often referred to as 'insight' problems. Such problems have the characteristic that a misleading representation is usually formed initially, within which solution is impossible, and so a less obvious representation must be found, or developed, in which the solution is generally quickly found (and understood).

Metcalfe (1986a, 1986b) and Metcalfe and Weibe (1987) have investigated subjects' metacognitions about insight and non-insight tasks, and found differences that support the insight–non-insight distinction. In her 1986a study, Metcalfe asked subjects to indicate their feeling of knowing answers to general knowledge questions which they were unable to answer at first sight and to insight problems. There was a strong correlation between feeling of knowing ratings and recognition test perform-ance on the general knowledge items, but there was no correlation between feeling of knowing ratings before tackling the insight problems and success at solving them. This suggests that insight problems do indeed involve a sudden illumination or understanding that cannot be predicted in advance. Further, Metcalfe (1986b) ex-amined feelings of 'warmth' or closeness to solution while subjects tackled insight problems, and found a striking pattern in warmth ratings leading up to solution, viz. that the ratings stayed essentially flat until solution was reached, whereupon they were maximal. This pattern is consistent with an all-or-none development of insight. Interestingly, she also noted that ratings just before wrong answers were higher than ratings just before correct answers. This may reflect the fact that most 'obvious' answers to insight problems are incorrect. Metcalfe and Weibe (1987) found that non-insight problems showed a steady increase in warmth rating to solution while insight problems showed an all-or-none pattern, which further supports the view that insight problems are evoking some special process. In terms of evaluation functions discussed earlier, it seems that subjects can apply such functions to guide search in non-insight, incremental, problems (such as the Tower of Hanoi) but that the nature of insight problems precludes the use of evaluation functions until a good repre-sentation is found (Kaplan and Simon, 1990).

2 Fixation and the 9-dot task

Subjects are often described as 'fixated' on the initial inappropriate representation, and such fixation may be classed as a major obstacle to 'insight' (e.g. Scheerer, 1963). Weisberg and Alba (1981a) sought to examine the role of one possible source of fixation in the 9-dot task, which is often classed as an 'insight' problem. In the 9-dot problem, the subject is faced with a 3 × 3 array of dots, arranged as follows:

●　●　●

●　●　●

●　●　●

The subject's task is to draw four straight lines through all the dots without lifting his or her pen from the paper. If you are not familiar with this problem, you may find it instructive to try to solve it, before reading further. Naive subjects usually find the problem to be very difficult. Why? Until recently the generally accepted view was that subjects assumed that lines drawn had to remain in the square shape formed by the dots. Since the problem cannot be solved on that assumption, most subjects failed to solve. If you have been trying to solve and have not succeeded, try again, in the light of this hint. (The solution is given at the end of this chapter.) However, Weisberg and Alba (1981a) found that while none of their subjects solved without the hint, only 20 per cent solved when given the hint. Therefore, they concluded that a fixation on staying within the square array of dots was not the whole explanation for the difficulty of the 9-dot task. A similar result has also been reported by Burnham and Davis (1969). Weisberg and Alba carried out further studies using the 9-dot task and a simpler but analogous 4-dot problem. They found that only quite specific hints, such as the experimenters drawing in two lines of the solution, going outside the square, were helpful. Overall, Weisberg and Alba concluded that the concepts of 'insight' and 'fixation' were not helpful in discussing problem solving in the 9-dot task; instead, they emphasized the role of highly problem-specific knowledge.

Dominowski (1981) raised the point that, although fixation may not be a useful explanatory concept, there was still a need to explain persistence and change in problem representations and directions of attack on problems. Ellen (1982) also commenting on Weisberg and Alba's findings, stressed the restructuring of problem representations as a source of insight (in the sense of a sudden understanding of how the goal is to be reached). Weisberg and Alba (1982) replied that such 'perceptual' accounts of problem solving had not been helpful despite a long history. In an empirical study, Lung and Dominowski (1985) found that practice with other dot-connecting problems which required extension of lines beyond the dot pattern facilitated subsequent performance in the 9-dot problem. They also found facilitations from strategy instructions that stressed the need to extend solution lines beyond the dots. These results counter Weisberg and Alba's (1981a,b, 1982) view that only very detailed specific solution information will facilitate in the 9-dot task. A more general solution schema can apparently be formed for a class of dot-connecting problems.

3 Processes underlying 'insight'

Sternberg   The reader may well feel that the issue of 'insight' has become lost in the minutiae of the 9-dot and related tasks. Indeed, it appears that the 9-dot task is not an ideal test-bed for the study of insight. Sternberg (1987) reports findings from a broader range of tasks which, he argues, reflect different *forms of insight*. In particular, Sternberg distinguishes three types of insight. First, he proposes insights of *selective encoding*. These involve selecting relevant from irrelevant information. Typically, real-life problems present a mass of information, only a fraction of which may be relevant to the solution. It may be that once the key pieces of information are selected, the solution is obvious. However, it might be the case that the problem requires a new way of combining or interrelating the key pieces of information. If so, Sternberg argues, an insight of *selective combination* is required. A third form of insight proposed by Sternberg is insight of *selective comparison*. This involves relating newly acquired information to information in long-term memory, for example by analogy.

Sternberg and Davidson (1982) examined performance on insight problems, such as the following:

(1) If you have black socks and brown socks in your drawers mixed in the ratio of 4 to 5, how many socks will you have to take out to make sure of having a pair of socks of the same colour?
(2) Suppose you and I have the same amount of money. How much must I give you so that you have 10 dollars more than I?
(3) Water lilies double in area every 24 hours. At the beginning of the summer there is one water lily on a lake. It takes 60 days for the lake to become covered with water lilies. On what day is the lake half-covered?

The first problem is presumed to mainly require selective encoding, the second to require selective combination and the third both selective encoding and combination. (The answers are given at the end of this chapter.) On the basis of subjects' written protocols while they tackled 12 such problems, selective combination was the most common strategy. However, selective encoding was more successful and use of both selective encoding and combination was most successful. A further study of selective comparison indicated that subjects would use related prior examples, especially if the fact of relevance was pointed out. This is very similar to the findings of Gick and Holyoak (1980) on use of analogy in problem solving discussed above.

Overall, Sternberg's analyses and results support the view that there are multiple routes to 'insight', in the sense of understanding a problem solution. However, the postulated processes of selection, combination and comparison are not in themselves 'special'. Rather, with certain types of problem these processes in various combinations can lead to a 'special' state of problem understanding or 'insight'.

Kaplan and Simon Kaplan and Simon (1990) interpreted insight in terms of changing problem representations, and explored in detail how subjects attained a good representation of the Mutilated Chequerboard (MC) problem, which was discussed in an earlier section on analogy in problem solving. A key feature of a good representation of the MC problem is the explicit inclusion of 'parity'. This is the notion that the squares of the chequerboard form pairs of black and white squares; a domino must cover a black and a white square and this cannot happen if the board is mutilated by having two corner squares of the same colour removed. Kaplan and Simon found that when subjects noticed parity as a feature of the board then solution was quickly reached thereafter. Of course, most subjects do not notice parity initially. Kaplan and Simon showed that the noticeability of parity could be manipulated by the way the board was presented. In order of difficulty, a board of uncoloured squares was most difficult, then a board of black and pink squares, then one with the words 'black' and 'pink' on the squares, and finally a board with squares marked 'bread' and 'butter' was easiest. From problem-solving protocols it was clear that subjects would search for new representations after unsuccessful attempts within an early representation. An important heuristic for developing new representations was that of *noticing invariants*, i.e. facts about the problem that always seemed to hold over repeated attempts. An example invariant in this task is that the two squares that cannot be covered are always of the same colour, opposite to the colour of the two squares that were removed. Not all invariants in the task are relevant to solution, but within the limited set of invariants is the parity feature that is the key to solution. Kaplan and Simon then explain insight as resulting from a search process at the level of problem representation (or problem space). As with search processes within representations (spaces), questions about how search is controlled arise and lead again to the idea of heuristics. This approach goes some way to taking the mystery out of insight and would seem well worth extending to other insight tasks.

Ohlsson Ohlsson (1984, 1992) follows an information-processing approach similar to that of Kaplan and Simon, and seeks to explain insight as the breaking of an *impasse* in problem solving. Typical insight problems tend to produce an initial representation that is misleading. Ohlsson proposes that subjects generate possible actions or *operators* by retrieval from long-term memory, guided by the cues in their current problem representation. By a process of spreading activation, possible operators are activated and retrieved; if applied they lead to new problem states, and so on, until solution or an impasse is reached. An impasse is a state in which no new operator is retrieved; subjectively the person experiences a 'blank'. Undoubtedly this is a common experience in tackling problems of any difficulty. Impasses can be overcome by changing problem representation so that new operators can be cued. Ohlsson outlines three ways in which a problem representation may be changed, viz. *elaboration, re-encoding* and *constraint relaxation*.

Elaboration involves adding information to the representation by observing pre-viously unnoticed features. For example, in the MC problem elaboration might involve noticing that the squares form pairs. Kaplan and Simon found this elabor-ation to be the key to solving.

Re-encoding involves completely changing the encoding rather than simply adding more information. Ohlsson (1990) reported clear examples in the case of geometry problems where complex figures can be construed and reconstrued as different combinations of squares, rectangles, parallelograms and triangles.

Constraint relaxation involves changing the goal representation to a less demanding form. For example, as we have seen already in this chapter, one source of difficulty in the 9-dot problem is the tendency to overconstrain the goal so that the four lines are kept within the square array of dots; relaxing this constraint to allow lines outside the square shape makes the problem easier.

Ohlsson (1992) pointed out that changing representation does not guarantee solution immediately or in the long run. He suggested distinguishing partial insights which lead eventually to solution and complete insights which lead immediately to solution. How is immediate solution following impasse-breaking possible? The proposal is that some changes in representation elicit operations or actions that lead to solution in one step, which is within the scope of mental look-ahead. Such restructurings give the experience of complete and sudden insight. Partial insight restructurings lead to solution after more extended search, which exceeds the limited scope of mental look-ahead.

Overall, Ohlsson's approach is a very promising marriage of Gestalt concerns and information-processing approaches to problem solving. Contrary to Sternberg (1987), Perkins (1981) and Weisberg (1988), Ohlsson suggests that insight *is* 'special' in that it critically involves restructuring followed by rapid solution, while non-insight problem solving involves working within a single representation maintained throughout the solving process. However, he is *emphatically not* arguing that insight is a special 'magical' process that cannot be analysed.

IV. SUMMARY AND CONCLUDING COMMENTS

The following picture seems to emerge from the studies reviewed above of processes involved in solving small-scale well-defined non-adversary problems (puzzles). The person faced with a novel laboratory puzzle spends some time building up a symbolic model of the task materials, the available operations and the desired goal (Simon and Hayes, 1976). The person's model of the task determines the problem space within which he or she will work to explore consequences of possible actions. Two kinds of problem representation that could be used in modelling a problem were distinguished, viz. state–action and problem reduction. With a state–action representation, the solver explores the consequences of alternative actions forwards from the starting state, whereas the problem reduction representation involves breaking the overall problem into more manageable sub- and sub-sub-problems. Models of the solving process that postulated state–action representations and heuristic searches of the resulting state–action space gave reasonable fits to data from missionaries-and-cannibals and water jug problems (Polson and Jeffries, 1982). These models proposed only a small degree of mental look-ahead, involving two or three immediate successor states, thus reflecting working memory limitations as proposed by the 'standard' model of thinking. Problem reduction approaches were implicated in cryptarithmetic (Newell and Simon, 1972) and Tower of Hanoi problems (Luger, 1976). In the case of the latter task, preliminary evidence (Anzai and Simon, 1979) suggests that degree of acquaintance with the problem may be influential in determining the adoption of one approach or another. On initial exposure to a Tower of Hanoi task, Anzai and Simon's subject adopted a state–action representation but switched to a problem reduction representation when more experience of the task had been gained.

On the question of when and why, in general, people adopt state–action or problem reduction approaches, it does not seem possible to give definite answers at present, because few, if any, studies have been carried out with this question in mind. Intuitively, a problem reduction approach seems more likely in tasks that permit a large number of possible actions. After all, problem reduction offers a useful way of cutting down on the number of actions to be considered at each step. Within a given task area, it may well be that a problem reduction approach is more likely with subjects experienced in that area than with naive subjects. Some experience with the task area is probably required to enable subjects to learn which differences between starting states and goal states are relevant and in what order these differences are best dealt with. The results of Anzai and Simon are consistent with this view. Further studies are still needed, especially of problem formulation and interpretation as a function of task structures and subject experience, to help answer this question. This general topic of strategy and representational changes with increasing experience in a problem area will be taken up again in Chapter 4.

Analogies and examples can play a role in suggesting useful formulations (Gick and Holyoak, 1980, 1983; Keane, 1988; Bassok, 1990). However, remote unprompted analogies appear to be rarely used (Perkins, 1981). Modelling of analogical problem solving has been developed to a sophisticated degree, especially of the matching process, but with less progress on modelling the retrieval process (Gentner and Gentner, 1983; Holyoak and Thagard, 1990; Keane *et al.*, 1994). Suitable formulations and reformulations may lead to sudden understanding of how the solution is to be accomplished (i.e. *insight*). It is somewhat controversial as to whether such states of insight should be regarded as 'special'. However, they appear to be achieved by means of intelligible processes, such as selection, combination and comparison (Sternberg, 1987) or problem restructuring by means of these or other heuristics (Ohlsson, 1984, 1992; Kaplan and Simon, 1990). Insight would seem to be dependent on restructuring and to that extent could be classed as 'special', but not in the sense of being a magical uninterpretable process.

The tasks considered in this chapter have been unfamiliar puzzles and so solution processes could not draw greatly on expertise stored in long-term memory (except perhaps in the case of analogical problem solving). The unfamiliarity of puzzles is useful from the point of view of controlling for level of prior experience among the subjects, but it must also be seen as a limitation on the problem-solving conditions being studied. It is quite possible that, when working in more familiar domains, people can usefully structure a task more rapidly and look ahead further than they can with unfamiliar types of task. The next chapter concerns an area in which this possibility can be checked: the area of board games, in which fresh problems can readily be generated within frameworks that vary greatly in familiarity between novice and expert players. Chapter 4 goes on to consider expertise in non-adversary problem solving.

V. FURTHER READING

Kahney, H (1993). *Problem solving: current issues*. Milton Keynes: Open University Press. This book offers very readable discussions of approaches to problem solving, especially analogical problem solving

VI. APPENDIX: PROBLEM SOLVING

A. *9-Dot problem*:

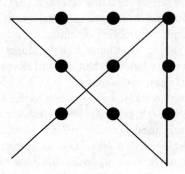

B. *'Insight' problems*:

(1) Three
(2) 5 dollars
(3) 59th day

3

Expertise 1: Adversary problems

In tackling adversary problems solvers must consider not only their own possible sequences of actions but also those of an opponent. The games of chess, GO, bridge and poker provide good examples of adversary problems and have been studied from psychological, artificial intelligence (AI) and normative points of view. (The normative approach is concerned with how best to play the games concerned.) Psychologists have found it helpful to use some of the terminology and concepts that have been developed in the normative Theory of Games (e.g. Von Neumann and Morgenstern, 1944) and in studies of machine game playing. Accordingly, I will first outline the basic notions of 'game tree' and 'minimax' and then briefly describe AI developments in chess before going on to studies of human game playing.

I. GAME TREES AND THE MINIMAX PRINCIPLE

In board games the possible sequences of moves and counter-moves from a given position can be represented by state–action trees known as 'game trees'. If it is possible to look ahead from the start to all the possible endings of the game then the best starting move can be chosen by application of the 'minimax' principle. This principle was illustrated by Newell and Simon (1972) for the artificially simple two-move game shown in Fig. 3.1. The first player determines his or her best move by looking ahead to the possible endings and then works backwards, applying the minimax strategy to assess the work of intermediate states. This strategy assumes that the opponent will do their worst to you and that you will always choose the best alternative available. Working backwards, minimaxing would label W3 as (–), W2 as (–) and W1 as (0), and recommend W1 as the best starting move, since it is found to lead to a draw whereas the other moves must lead to losses.

The problem with a simple application of this approach to many games, including chess, is that in order to determine the value of a move the player must consider the opponent's possible replies and then his or her own replies to each of the opponent's replies to those, and so on. In theory, a 'brute force' program could generate such information and select the best move on each trial. Unfortunately, the tree of

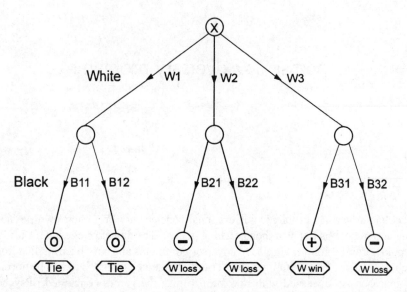

Fig. 3.1 *Minimaxing in a game tree (see text for further explanation). Reproduced with permission from Newell, A. and Simon, H.A. (1972)* Human problem solving, *p. 669. Englewood Cliffs, NJ: Prentice-Hall.*

possibilities is just too big – approximately 10^{120} possible sequences of moves in chess and only 10^{16} microseconds per century to explore them all.

The cognitive effort required to explore all the possible chess games is just too much for any present or likely future machine, or for any human. Computers and humans can investigate and keep track of the consequences of relatively few moves, and then only to a limited extent. So, for humans or computers to play reasonable chess, some strategies or heuristics must be available to restrict search to plausible moves and to evaluate lines of development in the absence of complete information about their remote consequences.

II. ARTIFICIAL INTELLIGENCE AND CHESS

Some of the early chess programs are worth a brief consideration. In 1956 and 1958 a computer called MANIAC at Los Alamos was programmed to play chess using the following methods. At each turn the machine looked ahead to a depth of four turns and considered *all* legal moves on each turn. In other words, given a starting position of the board, all of the average 30 moves were generated, then all the opponent's replies, then all machine replies and finally all the opponent's replies to those replies. On average, $30^4 \sim 800,000$ continuations were generated. Each of the near 1 million possible states of the board after four moves was then evaluated by adding a measure of material advantage and piece mobility. A minimaxing procedure was then followed to work back up the tree of possibilities to find the best first move. This program is near the brute force end of a sophistication continuum and could not be regarded as a simulation. According to Newell and Simon (1972), the program played rather weak chess and was susceptible to serious blunders, even though close to a million possibilities were considered. Presumably, many of the possible moves were not really worth looking at and the evaluation of possibilities may have been too crude to select good moves.

Additional sophistication was introduced into a program devised by an IBM programmer named Bernstein in 1958. Instead of considering all legal moves at each step, Bernstein's program considered only seven, which cut the size of the tree at depth four, from near 1 million branches to around 2500.

The program incorporated about eight so-called 'plausible move generators', each of which was related to some feature of the game, such as king safety, development, defence, attack, etc. When the program had to select a move it generated seven alternatives by applying the generators in a priority order. For each of those seven alternative moves, seven opponent moves were generated, and so on to a depth of four moves. So, this program searched the tree of possibilities very selectively. The end positions, four moves ahead, were evaluated by numerical measures of material strength, defence area controlled and mobility of pieces. The program then minimaxed back up the tree to select its 'best' move. The program's play is reported to have been rather uneven: sometimes it played well for a series of moves, and then displayed glaring blind spots. Although not a great deal of evidence is available about the program's performance, it appears to have been an improvement over the less selective MANIAC program in method and in end results. Further details on early chess programs can be found in Newell and Simon (1972) and in Bell (1978).

The 1977 world champion computer chess program (CHESS 4.6) exploited the speed and storage space of modern machines and examined an average of 400,000 successor positions per move. It looked ahead about four or five moves and could beat 99.5 per cent of rated human players, although it was relatively weak in the end-game. CHESS 4.6 is clearly not human-like in its methods (Levy, 1978).

Still further progress in machine chess has been achieved in the program known as DEEP THOUGHT (Hsu *et al.*, 1990). Using special-purpose hardware and improved search heuristics, this program searches on average some 15 moves ahead and in fluid situations can continue search up to 60 moves ahead. Millions of possible board states are examined per second and, although it is an advance on previous programs, it is not yet invincible to the top human players. As with the previous chess programs outlined above, DEEP THOUGHT's methods depart drastically from those feasible for human players.

Although a number of advances have been made in computer chess playing since the late 1950s, almost all the programs seem to possess the same kind of structure. They all search ahead through a tree of possibilities with some heuristic restrictions on the search, evaluate positions at the end of the search, and minimax. (This general structure was anticipated by Shannon, one of the founders of information theory, in 1950.) Essentially all the programs choose moves in given chess positions, rather than play a chess game with an overall plan, although the end product may look quite planned.

The effort to develop chess-playing programs helps reveal the difficulties faced by any system that deals effectively with complex adversary problems. How do humans tackle such difficulties? This question is addressed in the following sections.

III. EXPERIMENTAL STUDIES OF HUMAN ADVERSARY PROBLEM SOLVING

A. Human chess play

1 Search in chess: early studies

Perhaps the most direct way to try to find out about thought processes during chess play is to present subjects with a chess problem and ask them to think aloud as they decide which move should be made next by one of the players (usually white). This method was followed by De Groot (1965), Wagner and Scurrah (1971), Newell and Simon (1972, Ch. 12) and Charness (1981b).

De Groot was particularly interested in possible differences between players of differing degrees of expertise. Five Grand Masters and five expert players were given the same position and thought aloud while choosing a move. The search trees they developed could be abstracted from their protocols, and De Groot reported the summary statistics shown in Table 3.1.

A number of points emerge from these data. First, there was little or no difference in the quantitative aspects of the search patterns of the Grand Masters and the experts. The only major difference was in the quality of the move finally chosen. (Move quality was rated by independent experts.) Both groups looked ahead to

Table 3.1 *Average protocol statistics for De Groot's position A*

Variable	Grand masters ($n = 5$)	Experts ($n = 5$)
Time to choose move	9.6 min	12.9 min
No. of different first moves considered	4.2	3.4
Maximum depth of search (moves)	6.8	6.6
Total no. of moves considered	35.0	30.8
Rated value of move selected (max. = 9)	8.2	5.2

From De Groot (1965) *Thought and choice in chess*, Table 12, p. 319. Reprinted by permission of Mouton Publishers, The Hague.

similar maximum depths (about 6–7 moves), considered a similar number of possible first moves (about 4) and a similar total number of first moves and subsequent replies and counter-replies (30–55). Although, as Hearst (1977) suggested, the Grand Masters might be able to search deeper and broader if they were sufficiently motivated (e.g. in competition), it is still noteworthy that they consistently reached a better conclusion without any more search than the weaker players. Also, of course, the amount of sheer search is very small compared with that of the best computer chess programs. (According to Levy (1978), the program CHESS 4.6 sometimes examined around 3 million possible positions that could be reached from the current position before choosing a move, while De Groot's players were averaging around 35 possible positions.)

As well as being more selective in search than most chess programs, the way in which human chess searches develop is also different from the way program searches usually develop. De Groot's players and those of Wagner and Scurrah followed a progressive deepening method in which the same small number of alternative first moves were returned to repeatedly and generally followed up in greater depth on each occasion that they were re-examined. Re-examinations to greater depth were quite often immediate, but delayed re-examinations were also fairly frequent. Progressive deepening offers a way of gradually building up in long-term memory a representation of a long sequence of moves that would overload working memory. Also, the method permits repeated checks of apparently promising lines, in case some danger has been overlooked.

Finally, we note that human players do not search to a fixed depth but to a 'quiet' position where no immediate exchanges are possible. Such positions appear then to be evaluated on the basis of some salient feature or 'general impression' (e.g. 'awkward for black') rather than in terms of some explicit combinatorial weighting of many features (which is how the programs tend to make evaluations).

How is it that expert human chess players can be so selective to such good effect when they search for a next move? According to a much investigated hypothesis the answer may lie in the extensive repertoire of chess patterns and schemas built up by experts over many years study of the game. These patterns help the expert players structure their perceptions of the board appropriately and could be attached to recommendations for possible actions, in a production system organization. Evidence suggesting this possible explanation was obtained from a task that De Groot and colleagues found was much easier for master players than for amateurs. This is the chess memory task described in the next section.

2 Chess memory and perception

De Groot (1965) put chess positions, taken from actual games, in front of subjects for 2–15 seconds; then he removed the positions and asked subjects to reconstruct them. Chess masters could reconstruct the positions without error (91 per cent correct), while poorer players made many errors (41 per cent correct). (There were 20 of 24 pieces on the board in the positions concerned.)

A clue to the chess masters' performance was given by another finding from De Groot's laboratory. In an unpublished study in 1964, Lemmens and Jongman found that, when good and poor players were shown boards with the 20 or so pieces *arranged at random*, both groups did equally poorly. [See Vincente and De Groot (1990) for detailed background to the random positions study, and Vincente and Brewer (1993) for an illuminating study of systematic errors in the reporting of the chess memory studies in the literature, including *mea culpa* Gilhooly (1988). Typically, the random position control condition has wrongly been ascribed to De Groot (1965) rather than Lemmens and Jongman.] The finding of expert superiority in memory only for meaningful boards corroborated some early Russian studies (Djakow *et al.*, 1927) which found chess masters not to have superior visual memory in general. Chase and Simon (1973a,b) verified the basic findings of Lemmens and Jongman with larger-scale studies and argued that the chess memory data are consistent with the view that perceivers of the chessboard store about seven familiar units or 'chunks' (Miller, 1956) in short-term memory during the inspection period irrespective of their skill level. However, the chess masters' seven chunks of information are much richer than those of the novices, i.e. they are larger units. Similarly, if you have learned to read in a given language you could reproduce about seven words after brief exposure to a set of random words, whereas a non-reader of the language might manage to reproduce only about seven letters (especially if the words were difficult for the non-reader of the language to pronounce).

Chase and Simon (1973a,b) sought to demonstrate quite directly the proposed superiority of master players' chunks compared with those of weaker players. In their study, three players varying in skill were given chess perception and memory tasks. The perception task required the subjects to reconstruct on one board a chess position that remained in view on another board. The main variables of interest were the numbers of pieces placed following each glance at the stimulus board, the times between piece placements, and the nature of the relationships between the pieces placed between one glance and the next. For all players the average number of pieces placed after a glance was similar (between two or three). However, the masters' glances were significantly shorter, indicating more rapid encoding. The chess recall tasks were similar to those of De Groot and involved 5 seconds' presentation followed by board reconstruction. Times between placements of pieces were recorded and intervals of 2 seconds or more were taken to correspond to boundaries between chunks in recall. On this basis, the number of pieces per chunk varied systematically (if not dramatically) with skill level, from 2.5 to 1.9 pieces per chunk from strongest to weakest player. Pieces within a single chunk tended to have relations of defence and attack, to be close together and to be of common colour and type. Thus, Chase and Simon's studies indicated that, compared with weaker players, the stronger player encodes chess information more rapidly when perceiving the board and encodes a given position in larger chunks when recall is required.

Research on chess perception and memory is relevant to chess playing in that players seek to structure board positions in terms of familiar patterns before trying to choose a move. De Groot and others have found that, when a chess position is given and the player must select a move, the first 15–30 seconds are occupied with gathering information about the situation in order to build up an internal representation of the position. Players do not begin to explore possible moves until an initial perceptual preparatory phase is complete. Indeed, it is sometimes suggested that the initial perception or structuring of a problem is the most important stage in problem solving in general. The early chess simulation programs did not take account of this perceptual phase (nor do most current AI programs). However, Simon and Barenfeld (1969) have reported a program labelled PERCEIVER which can simulate eye movements in the first 5 seconds of examining a chess board for the next move.

PERCEIVER begins with a central fixation point and follows lines of 'attack' or 'defence' as they are noticed and stores relationships of attack–defence between pairs of pieces. In this way it builds up a representation of the board position. Very few data on eye movements in chess are available, but PERCEIVER's successive fixations on a particular board have been compared with Russian eye movement data for a single expert subject (Tikhomirov and Poznyanskaya, 1966). Both program and subject tended to focus on the same squares, and the overall patterns were similar. Similar scanning data emerged from studies of blind players' manual explorations of boards before moving (Tikhomirov and Terekhov, 1967). Recent eye movement studies by Charness and Reingold (1992), using more sensitive recording equipment, bear out the patterns obtained by the earlier researchers. Further data would be useful to refine the program, but Simon and Barenfeld were mainly concerned to demonstrate the possibility of simulating the initial perceptual phase; they succeeded in that aim.

Further evidence on expertise and chess perception has been gathered by Saariluoma in a range of tasks: selective enumeration, total enumeration and threat detection. In the selective enumeration task subjects are asked to count the number of specific types of pieces, such as bishops or knights, in real or random positions. Saariluoma (1984, 1985) found that experts were faster and that both experts and novices were slowed down to the same extent by random boards compared with real-board positions. However, in total enumeration tasks (Saariluoma, 1990a), in which subjects had to count simply the total number of pieces on the board irrespective of type, there were no effects of expertise or of position meaningfulness. Taken together, these results indicate that the expert's advantage begins with more rapid feature discrimination, leading to faster identification of the different pieces on the board. Studies of threat detection (Saariluoma, 1984) also showed an expert advantage in speed of detecting checks and one-move mate threats, which indicates that experts are tuned to detect critical patterns on the board.

To sum up on the evidence so far, the expert chess player apparently detects and stores about as many 'chunks' as a poor player but the better player's 'chunks' or units are larger. Thus a good player 'structures' a given situation differently from a poor player and, in a sense, 'sees' the same problem quite differently from a poor player (and importantly is more likely to register critical threat patterns). The advanced coding scheme of the expert is, of course, bought with many years of study.

The extended study required is consistent with Simon's suggestion that a slow serial system with limited short-term memory, equipped with a discrimination learning program, could come to recognize many thousands of chess patterns over a lifetime's play.

3 The Memory-Aided Pattern Perceiver (MAPP) model

Simon and Gilmartin (1973) converted the general notions sketched by Simon and Barenfeld (1969) into a working computer model for the chess memory task. This model, known as the Memory-Aided Pattern Perceiver (MAPP), assumed that a position is encoded as a set of chunks (pattern labels) that occupy a limited-capacity short-term memory. The pattern labels are then decoded during the position reconstruction phase. The chunks or pattern labels are produced by a pattern recognizer that seeks to match board configurations to known patterns stored permanently in a long-term memory. The pattern-recognizing component consists of a discrimination net that is organized around salient pieces. It is assumed that the skilled player has a large discrimination net that incorporates a great many different patterns, while the weaker player has fewer patterns available with which to describe any given position. The program can thus simulate different levels of expertise by varying the number of patterns in its long-term store.

Two versions of MAPP were explored. One had 894 patterns available and the other 1144 patterns. Given the same board positions, the more 'knowledgeable' version was able to encode the positions more efficiently into its short-term memory and thus scored better on position reconstruction than the less knowledgeable version. The 'knowledgeable' version's performance seems to be intermediate between that of a master player and a Class A (good amateur) player according to comparisons between the program and human data on positions used by Chase and Simon (1973a) (see Table 3.2).

Simon and Gilmartin estimate that a MAPP-like system could replicate master level performance on the chess memory task with between 10,000 and 100,000 patterns in long-term memory. Assuming the model has some validity, similar estimates would apply to the store of patterns available to the human master.

Table 3.2 *Percentage of pieces placed correctly by MAPP (with 1144 patterns in long-term memory) and Chase and Simon's (1973a,b) Ss after 10 seconds exposure.*

Position	Master (%)	MAPP (%)	Good amateur (%)
Set 1	62	43	34
Set 2	81	54	49

From Simon and Gilmartin (1973) *Cognitive Psychology* 5, 29–46. Reprinted by permission.

Acquisition of this order of patterns is certainly possible over many years of study, since a well-educated person's vocabulary, for instance, has been estimated at around 75,000 words (Oldfield, 1966). Furthermore, the estimated number of patterns required may be reduced if, as Holding (1985, p. 109) has pointed out, it is assumed that the patterns are not simply arrangements of particular pieces on particular squares. If the chunks remain recognizable when shifted a few squares or if they are changed from black to white, then the estimated number of patterns needed for master level performance can be reduced to the more manageable levels of 500–5000 patterns.

Some of MAPP's assumptions have been tested independently by Frey and Adesman (1976) and by Charness (1976). Frey and Adesman confirmed the importance of chunking by showing that recall of a position, the development of which had been shown from the start in a sequence of 2-second 'snapshots', was better than recall of the same position shown without its development. Presumably the chess patterns were more evident when their build-ups were known. The effect was present for three levels of player and tended to be stronger for the more expert players. Also, memory performance was better for positions that had been built up in a meaningful order than for those built up in a random order. Again, skill level was an important factor in performance in both order conditions. However, when Frey and Adesman examined the assumption that the chess chunks are stored in a limited capacity short-term memory, the results were contrary to expectations based on MAPP. Subjects were presented with chess positions for 8 seconds and then required to count backwards from a three-digit number for either 3 seconds or 30 seconds before attempting to reconstruct the position. The counting backwards procedure is usually assumed to 'clear' short-term memory by preventing rehearsal and/or displacing the contents of short-term memory (Brown, 1958; Peterson and Peterson, 1959). This manipulation had only a very slight effect. Correct recall after 3 seconds of interpolated activity was 13.1 pieces and after 30 seconds was 11.6 pieces. These data cast doubts on the assumption that chunks are held in short-term memory.

Further strong evidence against the 'short-term memory assumption' was reported by Charness (1976). He carried out a number of studies using 5-second presentation and Brown–Peterson interference paradigms. The 30-second interpolated tasks varied in complexity and modality (shadowing digits, summing digits, copying symbols, rotating and then copying symbols, studying other chess problems, naming pieces on a chessboard). Recall of chess positions was reduced by only about 6–8 per cent by the most effective of these manipulations. (Control conditions indicated that recall of trigrams was affected by some of the interpolated tasks.) As usual, skilled players performed better across all the memory task conditions than weak players. One interesting effect was a marked increase in time to place the first piece as a function of interpolated processing. It appears that the interpolated tasks did have some effect on ease of retrieval but not such as to reduce *accuracy* of retrieval. The degree to which memory for briefly presented chess positions resists interference strongly suggests that the information is stored in long-term rather than short-term memory. Charness, and Frey and Adesman, suggest a 'depth of processing' interpretation whereby the skilled player can encode to a deeper level, more rapidly, than the less skilled player. However, even the least skilled players used in the experiments discussed here appear to have encoded sufficiently deeply to be little affected by interpolated processing tasks of the type found to be very effective by Brown and the Petersons in the recall of verbal materials.

4 Age and skill in chess

The studies of chess perception, memory and play discussed so far have focused on individual differences in skill and have proposed that strong and weak players differ in the efficiency of their chess-encoding schemes. Charness (1981a,b) investigated possible player-age effects additional to skill effects. Ageing is generally thought to affect memory operations, particularly those of retrieval, and so Charness hypothesized that players of equivalent skill, but widely differing ages, might differ in the underlying processes that yielded similar molar results (i.e. similar skill ratings).

Charness (1981a) assembled a sample of 34 chess players who varied independently in age (16–64 years) and skill level (skill ratings ranged from 1283 to 2004). The players were presented with four positions in which they had to choose a move while thinking aloud. Next, they were asked to evaluate end-game positions rapidly as being wins, draws or losses for white. After this task, the players were asked unexpectedly to recall the four initial positions by reconstructing them. Finally, a recognition task was administered in which the subjects attempted to identify the first four problem conditions among a set of 26. Only skill level was predictive of performance in the move-choosing task and in the end-game evaluation task. Skill level was positively, while age was negatively, related to chess recall scores. Measures of chunk size in recall were obtained using a procedure similar to that of Chase and Simon (1973a,b) described above. This indicated that chunk size was positively related to skill and negatively related to age, i.e. the older subjects made use of more but smaller chunks in recall than did younger subjects of similar skill level. These results then suggest that differences in encoding efficiency may not be sufficient to explain differences in skill levels. It should be noted, however, that Charness's (1981a) memory task involved delayed testing while the usual chess memory study has involved immediate memory. A follow-up study (Charness, 1981c), however, confirmed the result by showing age effects on immediate recall of chess positions, independent of skill level.

Charness (1981b) followed up the question of possible differences in the processes underlying move selection between older and younger players by analysing thinking-aloud records produced in his 1981a study. Analysis of these records indicated that the more skilled players searched more extensively and deeply than the less skilled. This result departs from De Groot's (1965) finding, based on fewer subjects (see Table 3.1), that skill level was independent of search depth or breadth. The discrepancy is probably due to the wider range of skills sampled by Charness. The average maximum depth reported by Charness (5.7) is similar to that reported by De Groot (6.7). Also, Charness found that the older players searched less extensively, though as deeply, as younger players and did not differ in quality of move finally chosen.

So, given similar skill levels the older player searches less extensively than the younger player, yet reaches conclusions of similar value. Perhaps older players can evaluate possible positions more accurately and dispense with the prolonged checking and verifying more typical of younger players. More sensitive 'evaluation functions' could compensate for the apparently poorer encoding of chess positions by older players, indicated both by Charness's delayed memory study (1981a) and by his further results showing age effects on immediate recall of chess positions (Charness, 1981c).

5 Counter-evidence to the pattern recognition theory of chess skill

The results of Charness described in the previous section may have raised some doubts in the reader's mind about the analysis of chess skill in terms of pattern storage and recognition. In its strongest form, the pattern recognition theory proposed by Chase and Simon states that chess skill is explained by superior memory storage and recognition of familiar patterns. Holding (1985, 1989) pointed out that the reverse is in many ways more plausible, i.e. that superior storage and recognition of chess patterns is explained by greater skill. Charness's results show that the same skill level can be achieved even when chess memory performance varies. At the least, this implies that chess memory cannot be the sole determinant of chess skill.

Holding and Reynolds (1982) tested the further possibility that skill differences could be shown even when no memory differences were present. They did this by having high- and low-rated players attempt (a) to recall random positions after 8 seconds exposure and (b) to decide on the best move when they were shown the correctly reconstructed random positions. As usual, there was no skill effect on memory for the random positions. However, there was a marked linear increase in the quality of the moves chosen by the players as their skill ratings increased. Such a trend cannot be explained by the pattern recognition theory of chess skill.

These results have thus led to a re-evaluation of the pattern recognition theory and have made other difficulties with the theory appear more salient. For instance, the sizes of the chunks reported by Chase and Simon (1973a,b) are rather small (2–4 pieces) to represent important chess patterns and the exact mechanisms for linking pattern recognition to choice of moves is unclear. Indeed, Holding (1985) lists some 40 objections to the pattern recognition theory of chess skill. Rather than chess skill being determined by chess memory it seems that chess memory is an incidental side-effect of chess skill. Consistent with this view, Pfau and Murphy (1988) found that ratings of chess skill in 60 players were better predicted by a tactical skill test, a positional judgement test and a 75-item chess knowledge test ($r = 0.70$ with the criterion) than by memory scores following 5-second exposures of chess positions ($r = 0.44$ with criterion). General chess *knowledge*, rather than chess memory for specific patterns, appears to be critical to chess skill.

6 Re-examination of human search in chess

The results of De Groot (1965), which showed few differences between highly skilled and less skilled players in their search patterns, helped to motivate the concentration of research on the pattern recognition hypothesis. In view of the difficulties with that hypothesis, research attention has begun to switch back to human search in chess; this is particularly evident in the work of Holding (1985, 1989), Charness (1981b, 1989) and Saariluoma (1990a,b).

From analyses of thinking-aloud records obtained from 34 players in a move-choosing task, Charness found steady increases in the depth, breadth and speed of search as skill increased from ratings of 1283 to 2004; similar findings were also reported by Holding and Reynolds (1982). Thus, it appears that De Groot's early results may have been somewhat misleading and reflected the small sample sizes and the relatively small range of skill levels used in his study. Some complications arise from more recent studies. Charness (1989) retested one of his 1981 subjects (D.H.) after a 9-year gap, during which D.H. had progressed from an intermediate 1600-point skill rating to 2400 points (International Master level). Although D.H. showed major gains in chess recall, evaluation and chunking over the 9-year period, his search patterns had not changed. Saariluoma (1990a,b) found an intermediate effect in that top-level players (Grand Master, International Master) searched less than intermediates, who searched more than novices. Quality of move chosen did increase with expertise, but amount of searching did not. It appears then that, at the top levels of chess skill, players can achieve better results with less search than intermediate-level players.

One important aspect of search, which may vary with skill and allow more efficient search, is evaluation. If poor evaluations are made at the limits of search, then the choices made at the top level of the search tree are likely to be in error. Indeed, it has been shown in computer studies that, when evaluation procedures are poor, deeper look-aheads can lead to worse decisions than shallower look-aheads (Pearl, 1983).

Holding (1979) investigated the relationship between overall skill level and quality of evaluation. He asked 50 players to assess the relative advantages of whichever side the players thought was winning. The assessments were made on a 10-point scale over ten board positions. The results indicated clearly that judgements of which side was winning were much better in the more skilled players and that the different classes of player differed in the degree of discrimination they showed among the game positions. Thus, more skilled players used a wider range of the scale than the weaker players. Holding also compared the subjects' judgements with evaluations of the positions delivered by Slate and Atkin's (1977) highly rated program, CHESS 4.5. This program assigns overall scores to positions on the basis of features such as king defence, pawn structure, rook connection, file control, and queen mobility and attack. The program's evaluations correlated very highly with those of the top half of Holding's players ($r = 0.91$). The correlation with the lower half of Holding's sample was lower, but still striking ($r = 0.80$). These results suggest a reasonable measure of analogy between the factors entering into human chess evaluation and those incorporated into the evaluation function used in the CHESS 4.5 program.

7 Working memory and long-term memory in chess skill

Some recent studies have returned to the role of working memory in chess skill, using the model of working memory developed by Baddeley and Hitch (1974; Baddeley, 1986, 1992). In this model, as outlined in Chapter 1, working memory is divided into three main components known as the phonological loop, the visuo-spatial scratchpad and the central executive. The first two components store and rehearse phonological and visuospatial material while the central executive handles strategic decisions, reasoning and problem solving with the aid of the storage systems. Baddeley and colleagues have developed a range of tasks that selectively load one or other of the systems. Thus, the phonological loop may be occupied by *articulatory suppression* in which the subject repeats a short word over and over (e.g. 'the, the, the, the . . . '); the visuospatial scratchpad may be occupied by a *visuo-spatial suppression task* such as moving a hand repeatedly in a prescribed pattern; and the central executive may be occupied by a *central executive suppression task* such as random generation of digits. If a task of interest is impaired when subjects concurrently carry out a suppression task, then the relevant working memory system is implicated in the main task. Thus, for example, visuospatial suppression affects use of visual mnemonics, and articulatory suppression affects rote verbal learning (Logie, 1986), but not vice versa. What can these techniques reveal about chess?

Saariluoma (1991a, 1992) found that visuospatial suppression has a marked effect on move generation, mate detection and the encoding stage of chess memory tasks. No effect was found for articulatory suppression. These results suggest a major role for the visuospatial scratchpad in chess play but no strong role for the phonological loop. Rather similar results were also found by Baddeley and colleagues (Bradley *et al.*, 1987; Baddeley, 1992), together with a marked effect of central executive suppression on chess recall and move generation.

Thus, it appears that exploration of possible move sequences involves the readily disruptible visuospatial part of working memory and the central executive. In the expert, working memory systems are backed up by long-term memory in which new information from chess positions is readily stored and retrieved. In addition to the evidence from interference studies such as those of Charness (1976) and Frey and Adesman (1976) for the role of long-term memory in recall of briefly seen positions, rather dramatic evidence of long-term memory capabilities comes from studies of blindfold chess. Playing a single game of chess while blindfolded may seem difficult enough but expert players can successfully play a large number of simultaneous games while blindfold. They are given their opponents moves verbally and must store the current state of the simultaneous games (up to 50 is not unheard of) in memory. (See Holding (1985, pp. 48–49) for a history of blindfold play.) Saariluoma (1991b) examined blindfold chess experimentally, using a number of successive games rather than simultaneous games. He found large expertise effects as well as strong interfering effects of concurrent visuospatial suppression tasks, but little effect of articulatory suppression. Again, it appears that the visuospatial component of working memory plays a key role in a chess skill; in the case of blindfold chess, the visuospatial scratchpad is assumed to be used in updating the board image and in generating moves.

B. Memory, perception and play in GO

A number of the basic findings reported by De Groot, Chase and Simon and others for chess have now been replicated for a range of games. In the case of GO, Reitman (1976) showed superior board reconstruction, after brief exposure, by a master level player compared with a beginner. A typical GO board position is shown in Fig. 3.2. As with chess, the Master's recall superiority held only for positions that were meaningful and not for random positions. Reitman was also able to show that the way in which the Master structured meaningful positions was rather complex, and involved perception in terms of overlapping clusters of pieces rather than simply as independent chunks or as hierarchically nested chunks and subchunks.

Further aspects of internal representation and perceptual scanning in board games have been examined in the contexts of both GO and GO-moku. Both these games use the same board and the same black and white 'stones' or counters; but GO is the more complex game.

First, Eisenstadt and Kareev (1977) were able to show that subjects represented the same board configurations differently, depending on whether the configurations were presented as coming from a GO or a GO-moku game. Subjects were shown

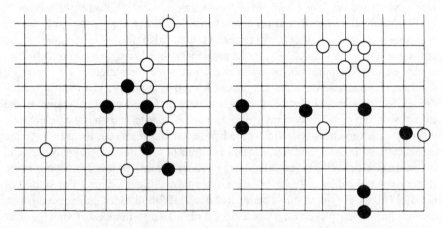

Fig. 3.2 *An example of meaningful (left panel) and random (right panel) GO board patterns. Reproduced with permission from Reitman, J.S. (1976). Skill perception in GO: deducing memory structures from inter-response times.* Cognitive Psychology **8**, *336–356.*

positions and told either that the positions were from a GO game or a GO-moku and asked to decide what the best move would be for one of the players. After they had done this and an intervening task, they were unexpectedly asked to reconstruct the position that they had originally worked with. Different pieces were of critical importance for the GO and GO-moku interpretations, and the accuracy of the reconstructions of the positions of the critical pieces varied in line with the interpretations. So, it can be concluded that people encode the board position in a manner relevant to the game they are playing.

This result suggests that people look for patterns typical of (or important to) the game in which they are engaged. Scanning the board may then be guided by expectations about types of patterns to be found. Indeed, Simon and Barenfeld's (1969) simulation of scanning in chess successfully assumed that scanning followed lines of attack and defence. Eisenstadt and Kareev (1977) suggested that Gestalt principles of similarity, proximity and continuity might also play a role, especially in GO-moku since its basic game-specific patterns are straight lines.

In particular they examined the extent to which players detected an important type of configuration known as an 'open-three'. This pattern has two forms, continuous and non-continuous, as shown below.

X/X/X   /X/X/ /X/

continuous   non-continuous

If a player does not notice that their opponent has constructed an open-three and so fails to block it, they will lose the game. The winner is the first to establish a row of five pieces in his or her colour, and an unblocked open-three is bound to lead to a winning line.

Additionally, open-threes can be either non diagonal (high proximity) or diagonal (low proximity).

Subjects played against a computer program and the proportion of trials on which they failed to respond to open-threes was recorded. As would be predicted from the Gestalt principles, probability of responding was greater for open-threes on non-diagonals v. diagonals, and for continuous v. non-continuous patterns. These results indicate that Gestalt principles had a strong effect on scanning with this material.

C. Bridge

Expertise in a third game, bridge, has also been studied. Successful bridge play involves memory demands in that a bridge player benefits if he or she can remember the cards that have been played in the preceding rounds and what the bid was at the initial auction stage. So, in addition to a working memory load involved in planning which sequence of plays to attempt at a given point, a player also has to remember which cards have already been played and what happened during bidding. Thus, accurate memory is essential for good play. As with chess and GO, we might expect skilled players to demonstrate superior memory for bridge information, indicating a large repertoire of familiar patterns in long-term storage. Evidence reported by Engle and Bukstel (1978) and by Charness (1979) bears out this expectation.

Engle and Bukstel (1978) gave four subjects (an expert, a life master, an average player and a novice) three tasks. First, the subjects played ten hands of bridge and were then given an unexpected memory test for the cards in the ten hands. An intentional memory task required subjects to reconstruct four bridge hands from one deal, where the cards within each hand were arranged either systematically or at random. Finally, a perception task required subjects to reconstruct stimuli similar to those used in the memory task after brief glances at the stimulus. The higher the level of bridge expertise of the subject, the better his or her performance on the structured tasks, but no effect of expertise on the unstructured tasks was found.

Charness (1979) confirmed these results in a study that had a firmer empirical basis, since it used 20 subjects of varying degrees of bridge ability. The subjects were given the following tasks: planning the play of a contract, rapid bidding, incidental learning and recall memory for structured or unstructured bridge hands. Performance on all tasks, except memory for randomly arranged hands, was strongly positively related to bridge expertise level.

A further result from this study was that memory performance declined with age of the player, independently of level of expertise (although it may be noted that age had no effect on recall of randomly arranged hands). This suggests that, as in chess, skill differences in bridge cannot be explained simply in terms of differences in pattern encoding.

Frensch and Sternberg (1989) examined the degree to which novice and expert bridge players represented bridge information in terms of deep or surface features. It was expected that novices would organize their knowledge mainly on the basis of perceptual features, but that more experienced players would use more abstract strategy-based features [cf. the work of Chi et al., (1981) and Larkin (1983) on physics expertise, discussed in Chapter 4]. Subjects played 12 bridge games against a computer such that half the games were under normal conditions. In the experimental conditions, three manipulations were introduced. In the first manipulation, the suits and face cards were given new nonsense names. In the second, the order of face cards and suits was changed, and in the third a rule change was introduced so that the player who won the last trick did not get to lead the next trick but rather the honour went to the player of the lowest card. As expected, the experts were more affected by the third, structural, change than by the perceptual level changes, while the reverse held for the novices. Thus, the experts' bridge knowledge and processing was at a deeper level than that of the novices.

D. Poker

Chess and GO are games of complete information in which the opponent's material strengths and weaknesses are available to inspection. In many real-life cases of adversary problem solving such complete information is not available and partial information must be relied on, thus introducing probabilistic considerations. Bridge clearly involves some uncertainty about where particular cards lie, and poker even more so. Thus poker playing has been studied as a microcosm of problem solving in uncertain conditions.

Lopes (1976) reported experiments on how poker players' internal models of the game and of their opponents' styles of play influence decision making in a modified version of five-card stud poker. In stud poker, players initially receive one card face down and one card face up. Normally a round of betting follows in which some players might drop out. A further card is dealt face up to the remaining players and another round of betting ensues. This procedure continues until five cards have been dealt (or until only one player remains active). Final rounds of betting are then held between those players left in the game. Lopes used a simplified task in which subjects saw two hands (four cards face up, one face down) together with the amounts bet on those hands, and had to make various judgements and side bets. They rated the likelihood that a pair of sevens could beat both opposing hands and then bet on the pair on sevens. The results supported the view that the subjective probability of beating both hands was a multiplicative function of the probabilities of beating each of the individual hands. The subjective probability estimates were generally accurate reflections of the objective probabilities. The more likely the players judged that they would win, the larger the bet they would make. Interestingly, when in further conditions, subjects were told that some hands and bets were from 'conservative' (low bluffing) players and others from 'average' players, they varied their bets to take into account the different bluffing tendencies of their imaginary opponents. As Lopes concluded, this series of studies showed that performance was affected by the players' model of the probabilities of having the winning hand and by the model of the opponents' bluffing tendencies.

Findler (1978) explored computer models of processes underlying play in the related game of five-card draw poker. In draw poker all cards are hidden from the players, except their own. Five cards are dealt initially and a first betting round is followed by the discarding of up to four cards and the drawing of replacements. All that a given player knows is his or her own cards, the number of cards drawn by other players and the bets made. Thus, draw poker involves even more uncertainty than stud poker. Findler has developed a number of programs to play draw poker that incorporate both fixed static strategies and adaptive learning routines. The 'simplest' strategy is that of the *mathematically fair player* who decides when and what to bet in accord with the objective odds of winning, but takes no regard of other players' styles of betting. This strategy serves well against unsophisticated opposition but is vulnerable to bluffers who bet enough to make the perceived risk of losing unacceptable to the mathematically fair player. A more useful static strategy uses the objective odds and incorporates an index of the desirability of staying in the game at a particular juncture. This index takes into account the number of other players left in the game, how long they have remained in, and how much extra must be bet to stay in the game. Programs embodying this strategy do well in competition with the mathematically fair player. A number of learning programs have also been devised that attempt to take account of opponents' playing styles as relevant evidence accumulates during a game session. Such programs that update models of opponents were the most successful investigated, and it seems likely that good human players also use similar processes. Indeed, Findler reports that human players usually cannot tell whether they are competing with other humans or with an adaptive program when the game is played over computer terminals.

IV. SUMMARY AND CONCLUDING COMMENTS

In this chapter recent studies of processes involved in adversary problem solving have been reviewed. From the game theory literature on how best to tackle such problems, came the useful notions of game trees and minimaxing. These ideas have been taken up both in analysing human play of board games and in developing AI programs capable of high-level performance in chess and other games. Board games provide a useful focus for studying thought because they permit the generation of an indefinite number of fresh problems within tight frameworks.

This is very useful from the AI point of view since the basic rules of such games can be readily programmed. From the point of view of studying human processes, an extra benefit of games as research tools is that people's experience of particular games varies widely, and so studies of the effects of varying familiarity with the task area can readily be carried out. In comparison with traditional studies of non-adversary problems then, a strong emphasis on the effects of experience is found in the study of human game playing. De Groot (1965) reported little difference between good and excellent chess players in depth of look-ahead or breadth of search, or in other easily quantified aspects of mental search, and yet the excellent (master-level) players almost always choose a better move. It may be noted in passing that the depth of look-ahead (5–6) reported by De Groot, and by Charness (1981b), is markedly larger than that assumed by the successful models for water jug and missionary-and-cannibal problems discussed in Chapter 2. This difference may be due to the complete unfamiliarity of those non-adversary problems compared with the relative familiarity of the chess task to the subjects concerned. One would expect to obtain quantifiable differences in search patterns between novices and good chess players [and the results of Charness (1981b) and Holding and Reynolds (1982) support this expectation]. However, since De Groot's results appeared to rule out a search-based explanation for the superior move choices made by master-level players compared with good amateurs, other explanations were sought. A possible explanation for skill differences in chess was suggested by data on memory for chess positions after brief exposures. Master-level players could reconstruct complete board positions much better than weaker players. This difference held up only if the board position made 'chess sense'. The level of playing skill made no difference to recall of positions constructed by arranging pieces at random on the board. Similar results have been reported for GO (Reitman, 1976) and bridge (Engle and Bukstel, 1978; Charness, 1979).

Simon and Gilmartin (1973) put forward an explanation for the chess memory results in terms of 'chunking' (Miller, 1956) in working (or short-term) memory. The master-level player was assumed to have a larger store of patterns in long-term memory with which to label board configurations and thus could find pattern labels that encoded the position more economically than the weaker player. Support for this view came from the successful simulation program, MAPP. The notion that the 'chunks' are held in short-term memory until recall is no longer plausible following Charness's (1976) and Frey and Adesman's (1976) reports of little or no effects from interpolated tasks on chess memory. These results suggest, rather, rapid encoding in long-term memory. They do not, however, directly damage the major assumption of the pattern recognition model for chess skill, viz. that master-level players have a more advanced coding scheme than weaker players.

More direct evidence against the pattern recognition model for chess skill comes from studies by Charness (1981a,b,c) and Holding and Reynolds (1982). Charness found that when older and younger players were equated for skill level, the older players had poorer immediate and delayed memory for chess positions, i.e. a difference in memory not reflected in a skill difference. Conversely, Holding and Reynolds found that when players chose moves in random positions, clear skill differences emerged but there were no memory differences for the positions, i.e. a difference in skill not reflected in a memory difference. These results jointly and separately make the simple pattern recognition model of chess skill untenable.

In chess, working memory and, in particular, the visuospatial scratchpad and the central executive components have been shown to play a role in generating moves and in encoding new positions for later recall (Saariluoma, 1991a, 1992a; Baddeley, 1992). The special task of blindfold chess play clearly implicates long-term memory and shows the expert's ability rapidly to encode and retrieve chess information (Saariluoma, 1991b).

Both the artificial intelligence (Findler, 1978) and the human experimental (Lopes, 1976) studies of poker playing underline the need to consider players' internal models of adversaries as well as of the task materials.

Overall, then, the implications of the studies of adversary problem solving are quite consistent with those of investigations of non-adversary problem solving. Both lines of research indicate the role of internal models in problem solving and are consistent with the view that the human subject searches trees of possibilities in a serial fashion, making use of a limited working memory backed up in the case of domain experts by a high-capacity long-term memory.

There is no sign of parallel searches of different branches of the game tree in chess, for instance. A small-capacity working memory appears to be implicated in view of the limitations on look-ahead depth within a single exploratory sequence, although these limits seem to be overcome by building up long-term memory representations of longer sequences by use of progressive deepening strategies. More general use of long-term memory is indicated by the role of general chess knowledge, indicated by the results of Pfau and Murphy (1988), for example, which show chess skill ratings to be closely related to scores on chess knowledge tests.

V. FURTHER READING

Saariluoma, P. (1995). *Chess players' thinking*. London: Routledge. This provides a thorough review of research on all aspects of chess skill, as well as setting out the author's own approach.

4

Expertise 2: Non-adversary problems

This chapter deals with solving semantically rich non-adversary problems. First, I consider research in the domains of physics, mathematics, computer programming, political science and medicine. The findings in these studies mainly bear on the quantitative and qualitative differences in performance between experts and novices. I then go on in the second major section to discuss recent findings and models regarding the acquisition of expertise.

I. EXPERT–NOVICE COMPARISONS

A. Physics

At the textbook level, at least, physics is a formal domain that includes a set of principles logically sufficient to solve physics problems. The problems posed to physics students are essentially well defined. The major difficulty in solving physics problems lies in selecting which principles to apply, rather than in applying the principles to generate equations. How, then, do skilled physicists select useful principles to apply to problems? Perhaps expert subjects have developed a repertoire of familiar problem categories and have associated each category with relevant principles? (This is a similar hypothesis to the pattern recognition model of chess skill discussed in Chapter 3.)

One technique that has been used to investigate this hypothesis involves asking subjects to sort or categorize problems according to their similarity. Chi and co-workers (1982) asked advanced PhD and undergraduate students to sort physics problems on the basis of similarities in how they would solve them, but without actually solving them. The results showed no evidence of *quantitative* differences between the two skill groups, such as number of categories used or time to categorize. However, *qualitative* differences were apparent in the categories into which novices and experts sorted the problems. Novices grouped together problems which were similar in '*surface structure*', that is, they were similar in terms of the objects and key words referred to in the problem.

In contrast, experts did not sort on the basis of similar surface structures. Instead, their categories reflected sortings on the basis of '*deep structure*', that is, in terms of major principles involved in solution, such as 'conservation of energy'. This result suggests that, in the case of the expert, knowledge useful for tackling a particular problem is accessed when the problem is first perceived.

Part of the skill of expert physicists then lies in their ability to categorize a problem appropriately. An appropriate categorization may then help the subject to access large-scale units for solving problems (i.e. 'groups' or 'chunks' of related principles). Larkin (1978) set out to examine this by having two experts and one novice think aloud while solving textbook physics problems. If principles useful for solving particular types of problems are stored as groups or chunks, this might be reflected in the solver's generation of 'bursts' of related equations. If no such chunks exist, then equations should be generated at random intervals over time. Also, if chunking develops with experience, novices should show less pronounced evidence for chunking than experts. Hypothesized chunks were constructed by Larkin and physicist colleagues such that each chunk contained one fundamental principle together with those subsidiary principles commonly applied with the fundamental principle. Consistent with the hypothesis, Larkin found that the pairs of equations generated by experts with intervening times of 10 seconds or less were typically 'same chunk' pairs. Those with intervening times of 15 seconds or more tended to be 'different chunk' pairs. In contrast, the novices' temporal data fitted well a random distribution curve, suggesting that, for novices, principles were accessed individually rather than as part of a large-scale method.

However, these findings were not replicated by Chi *et al.* (1982), who used the same method of analysis. If anything, their results contradicted the hypothesis, as their novices seemed to generate a greater number of related principles in close succession. Unless the discrepancy can be resolved, it cannot be concluded that storage of equations in long-term memory differs for experts and novices. It may be that Chi *et al.*'s novices generated clusters of equations as a result of a problem-solving strategy rather than because of structure in long-term memory. (A problem-solving strategy that might produce such results is to generate all principles known, in the hope that some are recognized as useful.)

The sorting experiments of Chi *et al.* indicated marked differences in problem representation between experts and novices. Are there differences in the way experts and novices build up representations of specific problems before attempting solutions?

Larkin (1978) addressed this question through the analysis of think-aloud proto-cols produced by expert physicists as they solved a problem. She found that experts engaged in an extensive qualitative analysis of the problem before generating equations. By 'qualitative analysis' is meant a phase in which the subject makes inferences essential to solve the problem. It seems that this phase lays the foundation for the successful selection of principles appropriate to solution. Chi *et al.* (1982) found that novices also carry out a qualitative analysis of a problem. However, the difference between experts and novices lies in the quality of inferences made, as novices often fail to draw necessary inferences and so work with less useful representations of the problems. It is also noteworthy that experts typically produce and make better use of diagrams in tackling physics problems (Larkin and Simon, 1987; Anzai, 1991; Hegarty, 1991).

Differences between experts and novices in their long-term knowledge bases have now been discussed, but we have not yet examined differences in strategies employed by solvers differing in level of expertise. Larkin *et al.* (1980) found that novices used a 'working backwards' strategy, whereas experts used a 'working forwards' strategy when solving physics problems. In more detail, novices solved a problem using a 'naive' representation, which provided little guidance in selecting principles for application. Thus, novices fell back on a means–end analysis which involves working backwards from the unknown to the given, gradually eliminating differences be- tween the written equations and an equation that would provide the desired answer. Experts, however, worked forwards from the given to the goal, suggesting that they have the solution procedure available as one 'large functional unit', as Larkin (1979) described it. Thus, it seems that problem-solving is primarily *search driven* for the novice and *schema driven* for the expert.

B. Mathematical problem solving

The research in physics discussed above suggests that the ability to categorize a problem correctly in terms of relevant principles facilitates the problem-solving process. The correct perception of a problem seems to cue a 'problem schema' which suggests a straightforward stereotypical solution method. At the other extreme an incorrect perception can send the solver up a blind alley. Problem perception, then, is clearly an important component of problem-solving performance. What changes occur in problem perception with skill acquisition? If researchers could identify the critical changes, then training might capitalize on this and enhance problem-solving performance. This issue was addressed in an experiment by Schoenfeld and Hermann (1982) in the domain of mathematical problem solving.

Schoenfeld and Hermann's study replicated previous findings that novices sort problems on the basis of surface structure while experts sort on the basis of deep structure. Their results also showed that after a 1-month long course in mathematical problem solving, an experimental group of subjects subsequently sorted problems significantly more often on the basis of deep structure than did a control group who had received training in computer programming. As would be expected, the course, which focused on general mathematical problem-solving heuristics, enhanced performance of the experimental group in solving mathematical problems.

Schoenfeld (1983) has pointed to the importance of what may be called *self-management, executive* or *metacognitive* skills in expert mathematical problem solving. Such skills concern the deployment of effort and involve frequent monitoring of progress with decisions to change broad direction of activity if necessary. Schoenfeld gave the example of having 20 minutes to work on a problem. In such a case, the decision to spend 10 minutes calculating an area is strategic and may determine overall success or failure. In his study, Schoenfeld set both experts and novices unusual problems which evoked search in both groups. The experts' search was better monitored and protocols showed frequent assessment of progress, of possible actions and of difficulty of goals and sub-goals. Novices tended to follow a single line of search with little monitoring. It is plausible that similar metacognitive skills are important in a range of domains, and indeed similar reports can be found in Larkin's 1983 study of physics problem solving, in Jeffries *et al.*'s (1981) study of programmers and in Green and Gilhooly's (1990) work on statistical computing.

C. Computer programming

A number of studies have examined problem-solving skill in the context of computer programming. Adelson (1981) addressed the question of how novice and expert programmers represent and use programming concepts. In each trial of Adelson's study, novice and expert programmers were shown 16 randomly ordered lines of Polymorphic Programming Language (PPL) code drawn from three short programs. Subjects were then asked to free-recall as many items as possible at the end of each of nine trials. Experts recalled more lines of code than novices. In addition, average chunk size for experts (i.e. lines of code recalled with inter-response times of 10 seconds or less) was larger than that of the novices. Novices clustered terms from the same syntactic category (e.g. all 'FOR' statements together) whereas experts clustered items belonging to the same program function (e.g. a sorting routine). These results suggest that both experts and novices have categories for elements of a programming language, the novices' being syntactically and the experts' being semantically based. The results do not, however, indicate whether the programmers' memory performance was due to encoding or retrieval.

A similar study was carried out by McKeithen *et al.* (1981). Subjects of three skill levels were shown a 31-line Algol W program in either normal or scrambled version for five 2-minute study trials. Skill level was found to predict recall performance for the normal version but not the scrambled version, replicating the Chase and Simon (1973a,b) results for random chess patterns. Differences in the way subjects organized recall were also examined and connections were found between high expertise and a particular organization of concepts in Algol W. While the data do not prove that this organization produces expertise, they do show that experts know more or less the same things, and know them in the same way, as indicated by the fact that several chunks were common to the experts.

The studies just outlined by Adelson (1981) and McKeithen *et al.* (1981) appear somewhat contradictory. Adelson reported an expert–novice difference on memory for scrambled programs, while McKeithen *et al.* reported no such difference in their scrambled program condition. Also, Adelson's finding seems to contradict the well-established result in a number of fields, that experts and novices do not differ in recall of randomized unstructured material. On this latter point, Adelson argued that the scrambled programs were potentially meaningful when reorganized by experts, while a scrambled chess pattern could not be reconstructed into a meaningful form.

The former point is a little harder to deal with. Why should two apparently similar studies produce discrepant results? However, examination of the details of the experimental procedures in the two studies gives some clues. Adelson used a line-by-line presentation, allowed 20 seconds per line, the material consisted of three small programs, extended free recall was allowed (8 minutes per trial) and, finally, the recall score was simply the number of lines correct irrespective of order. McKeithen *et al.* (1981) differed in every one of these experimental parameters. They presented the whole of a 31-line program to be learned at once, allowed 2 minutes of study (i.e. just under 4 seconds per line) per trial; the recall period was only 3 minutes, and recall was scored in terms of lines in correct order. Overall, it would seem that McKeithen *et al.*'s version of the scrambled program memory task was considerably more difficult than Adelson's. (Adelson's experts averaged scores of about 75 per cent correct whereas McKeithen *et al.*'s appear to have averaged about 20 per cent correct in the scrambled conditions). This difficulty factor may have suppressed any possible expert advantage in imposing structure on the randomized program. There would appear to be a need for further parametric research to clarify the conditions under which expertise advantages will or will not show in memory for scrambled programs.

A study by Ehrlich and Soloway (1984) examined the use of 'tacit' plan knowledge by expert programmers. Ehrlich and Soloway argue that expert programmers use higher-level knowledge to code programs for ease of recall, and that this higher-level knowledge is in the form of script-like plans that represent certain stereotypical actions in a program. Since experts may be unaware of using a structure such as the 'running total loop plan', the focus of the study is on 'procedural' as opposed to 'declarative' knowledge. The technique involved was a 'fill-in-blank' task, and used the programming language PASCAL. Problems concerned the initialization of variables and context effects. Results were consistent with the hypothesis that experts use tacit knowledge, enabling them to react appropriately to constraints operating on the initialization and updating of variables, and to contextual constraints implicit in a program. Skilled programmers seem to engage in a process of selecting from memory an appropriate plan and adapting this to meet the needs of the current situation.

A subsequent study by Soloway *et al.* (1988) found that experts' *comprehension* of programs was aided by knowledge of 'rules of programming discourse' as well as knowledge of the programming plans mentioned above. Rules of programming discourse specify the conventions of programming, e.g. that the name of a variable should match its function. Expert and novice programmers were given functionally identical pairs of programs such that one member of each pair conformed to the rules of programming discourse and one did not. The subjects' task was to fill in a blank line in each program. It was found that experts scored significantly better than novices when the programs followed the programming discourse rules but the difference between the groups disappeared when the programs did not follow the rules. Thus, part of the skill of programming is to know and use rules that make programs more readily intelligible as well as meeting their objectives.

D. Problem solving in political science

Political science problems differ from physics, mathematics and programming problems in that they are typically ill defined, i.e. the goal is often vaguely stated, candidate operators may not be defined and often there is not a generally agreed-upon solution. Given these additional considerations, how do individuals solve such ill-defined problems and to what extent does the political science expert resemble the expert in better defined domains?

These questions were tackled in a study carried out by Voss and co-workers (1983), who employed think-aloud protocols obtained from expert and novice solvers. The problem for the subjects was to suggest how to increase crop production in the Soviet Union. One interesting feature of this study was that the researchers also collected protocols from two kinds of non-expert 'experts': individuals expert in political science but not in the domain-area of the Soviet Union, and subjects expert in a totally different domain (chemistry). This design helps to 'unconfound' some expert–novice differences by attempting to distinguish general world knowledge and general problem-solving strategies from domain-related strategies.

The results showed that experts tended to review the problem initially and then build a representation of the task. This seems to correspond to the qualitative analysis carried out by physics experts. Their approach was to find one general solution to the problem, such as 'greater capital investment in agriculture', which would also solve a number of subordinate problems. The proposal of a general solution was followed by extensive exploration of the ramifications of the solution and by supportive argumentation. Social scientists unfamiliar with the field of the Soviet Union tended to fall back on general knowledge of the political science area, but did utilize domain-related strategies. The chemists, however, lacked both the knowledge base and domain-related strategies and thus performed at the same level as novices. Thus, experience within the domain provides for the acquisition of knowledge and strategies, which may be content-independent, such as problem conversion, or content-dependent, such as historical analysis.

Voss *et al.* (1983) concluded, first, that learning within the domain involves the development of networks providing information about relations among concepts and facts. Second, the individual acquires knowledge of the interdependencies that exist within a domain, and this knowledge facilitates the development of arguments in support of solutions. Third, the knowledge base becomes hierarchically organized so that some problems, such as 'lack of fertilizer', become subordinate to a more abstract problem, such as 'lack of capital investment'. In general terms, Voss *et al.* concluded that the political science expert is like the chess master, in whom experience brings about the development of a large repertoire of recognizable 'patterns'. Unlike physics, where 'exposing learners to selected, special cases' (Larkin, 1979, p. 112) may be crucial, it is suggested that exposure to a wide *variety* of problem types is important in developing skill in political science problem solving.

Later studies by Voss *et al.* (1991) of problem solving in international relations also indicated that experts engaged in much richer analysis of problem scenarios than did novices. Voss *et al.* (1991) used a task involving the then hypothetical situation of moves by West and East Germany towards reunification. The subjects' task was to indicate the likely response of the Soviet Union to such moves. Experts began by developing a representation of Soviet Union's historical and current goals and perceptions. From their representations experts identified one likely course of action. Novices, in contrast, engaged in little representation of the task but developed many alternative responses that the Soviets might have made. Voss *et al.* showed that the impression of expert problem solving in political science that emerges from these laboratory studies (extensive historically based analysis constraining predic- tions and recommendations) matches quite well the documented behaviour of expert advisers to the US Presidents in response to the real crises of Korea in 1950 and of Cuba in 1962.

E. Medicine: diagnostic problem solving

This section focuses on the roles of deep and surface knowledge in the acquisition and exercise of human medical expertise, with special reference to the task of diagnosis. By 'deep knowledge' we are referring to knowledge of underlying physiology and anatomy (i.e. 'basic science') as opposed to the 'surface knowledge' of symptom–diagnosis associations or previously experienced cases ('clinical knowledge'). In the traditional medical curriculum deep knowledge is acquired first through formal study and is then supplemented with clinical knowledge of cases and useful 'surface' rules, largely obtained through experience and (guided) practice. Some curricula now endeavour to interweave basic science and clinical strands in a problem-based approach. Which pedagogic style is more effective in the long run is currently a controversial issue (Norman, 1988).

1 Task analysis

The basic task in medical diagnosis is to place the patient into an appropriate disease class so that suitable treatment can be given. In general terms, this task is fraught with difficulty and may be characterized as a type of *ill-defined problem* (Reitman, 1965; Pople, 1982), that is, the starting state of the problem, the means available and the goal state are not well specified, unlike, say, chess where the starting state, goal and means available (the legal moves) are all completely specified. The problem may begin with a patient entering the general practitioner's surgery and complaining of a pain. The site of the pain, its intensity, frequency, character and determinants are not given but have to be sought. The means available to determine the patient's state are not neatly defined, but encompass all the questions that could be asked and all the laboratory tests that might be requested. The set of possible diseases is vast and still may be incomplete. A conservative estimate puts it at 1000 known diseases or disorders (Evans, 1989). The ICD (International Classification of Diseases) (Israel *et al.*, 1980) suggests the figure is nearer 3–5000.

Perhaps the patient has some new and as yet unrecognized disorder. Whether a correct diagnosis has been made is not always easy to determine without performing an autopsy. If the usual treatment for the diagnosed disorder works, then the diagnosis was probably correct; but at the time the diagnosis is made, it is generally the best-fitting hypothesis out of a number of possible candidates rather than the only possible answer.

2 Process studies of diagnosis

An important early study (Elstein *et al.*, 1978) used thinking-aloud methods in realistically simulated settings to produce overviews of the whole process of diagnosis and to seek possible differences in approach between more and less skilled diagnosticians. The approach used was to identify, by peer judgement, a 'criterial' group of doctors (*n*=17), reputed to be particularly good diagnosticians, and a 'non-criterial' group of doctors (*n*=7) not so reputed. All the doctors were experienced in internal medicine. 'High-fidelity' simulations of diagnostic tasks were arranged by having actors play the parts of patients and by using a normal consulting room as the setting. If a physical examination was deemed desirable by the doctor, appropriate results would be provided. Three problems were used, drawn from real cases and representing disorders from the sub-areas of haematology, gastroenterology and neurology.

The doctors were encouraged to think aloud during the diagnostic session, to report what they had been thinking at natural breaks in the diagnosis and, finally, during a stimulated recall period in which they watched a videotape of the diagnostic interview, to report what they had been thinking.

The results were analysed in terms of hypothesis generation, hypothesis testing, and efficiency of information gathering and utilization. Surprisingly, perhaps, no quantitative differences emerged in hypothesis processing or information use patterns between the criterial and non-criterial groups. A similar finding emerged from Gale and Marsden's 1983 study of diagnostic processes in final-year medical students, house officers and registrars in a London hospital. These results are reminiscent of De Groot's (1965) reported lack of differences in search processes between more and less skilled chess players. The lack of differences in the Elstein *et al.* study might be due to a lack of spread of true expertise between the groups, or to small sample sizes limiting the power of the study, or to the small number of problems. There was a lack of intra-individual consistency over problems concerning accuracy and other process measures, suggesting that specific knowledge differences may have been critical. Similar findings of high intra-individual variability have been reported in many studies of diagnostic performance in medicine (see McGuire, 1985, for a review; also, Swanson, 1987).

Despite the lack of skill-related differences, a number of interesting findings emerged which give an overall picture of diagnostic thinking in experienced doctors. The main features of this picture were as follows. Hypotheses were generated very early in the process, usually within the first few minutes. Considerations of disease incidence seemed relatively important in hypothesis generation while *considerations of underlying pathophysiological processes were infrequent.* The number of hypotheses actively considered at any one time was quite small, of the order of two or three. This limited number is consistent with working memory constraints.

The general approach may be characterized as one of *hypothetico-deductive reasoning.* The initial hypotheses are elicited from long-term memory by the presented symptoms and signs (reasoning forwards). These hypotheses are then tested, by deducing what further symptoms should be present for each hypothesized disorder and then checking for their presence or absence (reasoning backwards). Thus, one of the maxims of expertise research, that experts work forwards, was contradicted by this study of medical diagnosis. The reason would appear to lie in the structure of the task. Not all the necessary information is presented initially, unless the diagnostic problem is particularly easy, and so, normally, a representation adequate to support pure working forwards cannot be developed without seeking further information. The search for further information is most efficiently guided by working back from possible hypotheses to associated symptoms.

As Swanson and Stillman (1990) have noted, Elstein *et al.*'s (1978) work showed that the differences between more and less successful solvers were in the details of the structure and organization of knowledge that supported the diagnostic process. The implication is that expertise is highly domain specific and tied to knowledge rather than process. This conclusion is also supported by Grant (1989) and Balla, *et al.* (1990).

3 Medium-fidelity studies of diagnosis

The studies by Elstein *et al.* (1978) and by Gale and Marsden (1983) attempted to mimic the real diagnostic situation closely. As Elstein *et al.* put it, such studies may be called 'high-fidelity' simulations. Less 'ecologically valid' but more convenient arrangements have also been explored. For example, Johnson and colleagues (1981) had three groups of four subjects (students, trainees and experts) think aloud while they worked on four cases which were presented in data files. The information was available only in the same fixed order for all subjects, thus removing the need for information search. Since information search is a key part of normal diagnosis, this procedure is lacking in ecological validity. However, some plausible differences emerged. The experts quickly developed a candidate set of hypotheses, consisting of closely related diseases, and could use the available data to distinguish correctly among the hypotheses. The less skilled subjects tended to work with more distinct 'textbook' cases of diseases as hypotheses, and were not so successful at using the data to distinguish among hypotheses. Further analysis of the same study by Feltovich *et al.* (1984) indicated that the experts always used the 'Logical Competitor Set' (LCS), which is the set of all competing physiologically similar diseases. Further, the experts were better able to decide among the similar possibilities. As with Elstein *et al.* and Gale and Marsden, the conclusion was that *the experts' advantage lay in superior knowledge of interrelated diseases rather than in diagnostic approach.*

Patel and Groen (1986a) examined protocols from seven expert cardiologists in a task involving diagnosis of acute bacterial endocarditis and explanation of under-lying pathophysiology. The task departed from the realistic in that all the necessary information was made available on a single display for a period of 2.5 minutes, and diagnosis and explanation had to be done from memory. The main result was that forward working from data to diagnosis characterized the four successful diagnoses, whereas those making incorrect diagnoses displayed a mixture of forward and backward reasoning. The correct forward reasoning of the successful diagnoses was interpreted as reflecting the activation of causal rules derived from the physicians' underlying knowledge base. The task information was such that pure forward rea-soning could be successful; this was not so in Elstein *et al.*'s tasks in which information search was required for solution.

Norman *et al.* (1989) examined diagnostic expertise in dermatology, in a study requiring subjects to provide a diagnosis as quickly as possible to 100 slides representing both typical and atypical instances of some 20 common skin disorders. It was found that typical slides produced a constant proportion of errors at all higher skill levels and that experts still made a significant number of errors, even on these relatively easy slides. The findings were interpreted as consistent with the notion that specific prior experience in the form of previous examples has an important role in this diagnostic task and that retrieval of similar previous patient information guides diagnosis of current cases.

4 Probe studies

Although the process studies outlined above gave a general overview of the shape of the diagnostic process, they were less revealing about differences in knowledge structures between more and less expert subjects. As in the chess domain, it seemed likely that differences in *memory* for new relevant information would be indicative of different schemata being brought to bear. Although a number of early studies on memory for case information failed to find any expert superiority (e.g. Claessen and Boshuizen, 1985), when recalls were scored in terms of *propositions* correctly recalled rather than in more superficial ways, the normal expert superiority effect was obtained (Patel *et al.*, 1986b). However, this intuitively reasonable result proved somewhat misleading: subsequent studies using the 'clinical case representation paradigm' and a wide range of expertise levels reported more complex but still interpretable patterns of findings.

5 Clinical case representation studies

The clinical case representation paradigm is an extension of the simple memory paradigm. Subjects varying in expertise are presented with a short text detailing a patient's history, complaints and any relevant additional laboratory findings. After a short while (2–3 minutes), the text is removed and the subject is asked (a) to recall the text, (b) to state the most likely diagnosis in their view and (c) in some studies, to give a pathophysiological explanation.

A number of studies of this type have found that subjects of intermediate levels of expertise recall the information better than either more or less expert subjects (Claessen and Boshuizen, 1985; Patel and Medley-Mark, 1985; Patel and Groen, 1986b). Accuracy of diagnosis, however, increased monotonically with expertise level. A promising interpretation by Schmidt and Norman (1988) suggests that the *different forms of knowledge* brought to bear on the task by the novice, intermediate and expert groups can explain the apparently paradoxical 'intermediate effect'. It is argued that novices have only lay knowledge plus some limited knowledge of basic biology but little knowledge of disease types and processes. Intermediates have acquired extensive 'book-learning' of the pathophysiology, linking signs and symptoms to diseases, but do not have extensive experience of real patients. Their approach to a newly presented case is likely to be one of slow elaborate reasoning from first principles. The experts have compiled their pathophysiological knowledge so that the diagnostic process becomes relatively automatic and effortless. In support of this view, studies by Boshuizen *et al.* (1987) and Patel *et al.* (1989a) indicated relatively *little reference to pathophysiology during expert diagnosis*. Further, it is suggested that, through extensive experience with real patients, experts have developed knowledge in the form of 'illness scripts' containing prototypical information about diseases. Such scripts, when activated by cues in the case description, could lead quickly to a diagnosis with little 'deep' processing. The proposed explanation may be summed up in depth of processing language by saying that the novices process shallowly because they cannot do otherwise, the experts process shallowly because that is all they need do to solve the problem, while the intermediates process deeply because they can and that is their best hope of reaching a solution.

Schmidt *et al.* (1988) examined the interpretation outlined above in an extensive study involving five groups of 24 subjects varying in expertise from first-year health science students to internists with 2 years' experience. Each group was further subdivided into three groups of eight who studied a case under different time constraints. In addition to recalling the case and giving a diagnosis, subjects were asked to produce a pathophysiological explanation. The 270-word text describing the case was presented for 3 minutes 30 seconds, 1 minute 15 seconds or 30 seconds. The results (see Figs 4.1 and 4.2) indicated a monotonic increase in diagnostic accuracy with expertise level for all exposure times.

At the longest exposure time, memory for the text showed a clear intermediate superiority effect, which was replaced by an expert superiority effect at the shortest exposure. With the medium exposure, recall showed only a slight intermediate superiority effect. It seems, then, that when time was limited the intermediate-level subjects could not engage in deeper pathophysiological processing and so lost their advantage in terms of text recall. The hypothesis also suggested that intermediates and experts used different knowledge when processing the case. This was borne out by the results on the relationships between expertise, exposure time and extensiveness of pathophysiological information reported. At all exposure times there was a significant intermediate superiority effect on the extensiveness of the pathophysiological explanation. This supports the view that *experts make little use of*

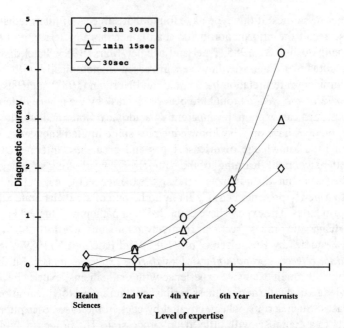

Fig. 4.1 *Average accuracy of diagnosis as a function of expertise and processing time. From Schmidt and Boshuizen (1993), reprinted by permission of Psychonomic Society, Inc.*

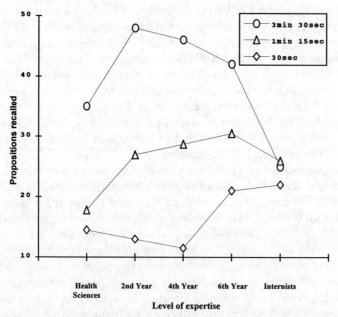

Fig. 4.2 *Number of propositions recalled from the acute bacterial endocarditis case as a function of expertise and processing time. From Schmidt and Boshuizen (1993) reprinted by permission of Psychonomic Society Inc.*

pathophysiological reasoning when the case can be solved in other less effortful ways.

A second study by Schmidt and Boshuizen (1993) explicitly primed subjects with relevant pathophysiological information by having the subjects recall as much pathophysiological knowledge as they could regarding endocarditis for 30 seconds or for 3 minutes 30 seconds before seeing an endocarditis case text. The more expert subjects produced more pathophysiological information at both priming intervals, but on recall following 30 seconds' study of the case, there was still an intermediate superiority effect and intermediates were most affected by the degree of priming. These results are consistent with the previous interpretation that intermediates use more pathophysiological knowledge during case study than do novice or expert subjects.

6 Illness scripts in long-term memory

The study by Schmidt and Boshuizen (1993) discussed above provided some indirect evidence that 'illness scripts' may be a useful idea in describing expert knowledge. The notion of an illness script, as developed by Feltovich and Barrows (1984), is of a stereotyped sequential schema (or frame) with three main elements: *enabling conditions, faults* and *consequences.* Enabling conditions are the causal conditions under which the disease emerges and include backgound and contextual factors (e.g. age, sex, occupation, social class). Faults are the major malfunctions (bacterial infection, metabolic disorder, trauma, etc.). Consequences are the signs and symptoms associated with a particular malfunction.

Evidence of the possible use of illness scripts in expert diagnosis comes from a study by Hobus *et al.* (1987). Expert and novice subjects were presented briefly with 'enabling condition' information only, on a number of cases. With this background type of information experts were considerably more accurate in proposing a diagnosis than novices. Further, recall of the 'enabling conditions' information was better for the experts than the novices. Most interestingly, recall of this information was significantly correlated with diagnostic accuracy among the expert group but showed a near zero correlation in the novice group. This last result suggests that the 'enabling conditions' information was indeed used by the experts in making their judgements.

A related study by Hobus *et al.* (1989) addressed rather more directly the question of mental representation of prototypical patients. If expert knowledge is organized around illness scripts, then information characteristic of such scripts should be salient in prototypical descriptions. Accordingly, Hobus *et al.* (1989) asked novices and experts to produce descriptions of prototypical patients in response to 18 complaint–diagnosis pairs. The resulting experts' prototypes contained considerably more contextual features relating to 'enabling condition' information than did the novices' prototypes, which contained more features relating to signs and symptoms than did those of the experts.

7 Effects of priming with deep knowledge and of related expertise on diagnosis

Patel and colleagues have carried out a number of studies using a priming approach to investigate how subjects of varying levels of expertise use relevant deep knowledge which has been made highly available (Patel and Medley-Mark, 1985; Patel *et al.*, 1987, 1988, 1989b). They have also examined transfer between domains of medical expertise and the differences in approach between researchers and practitioners (Patel *et al.*, 1986a, 1990). Many of these studies have been summarized by Patel *et al.* (1989a).

The priming studies involved presenting relevant short physiological texts before or after presentation of a clinical text which was to be summarized and interpreted diagnostically. Briefly, the results indicated that unprimed student subjects produce relatively little basic science reasoning in interpreting clinical texts, although junior students tended to produce more than senior students. The more senior students tended to produce more clinical reasoning. Priming with basic science information before or after case presentation was of little help in reaching more accurate diagnoses, suggesting that subjects found it difficult to integrate this information with the clinical case information.

In studies of experts operating within and outwith their fields (in the latter case they are dubbed 'sub-experts'), both practitioners and researchers have been used as subjects. Patel *et al.* (1986a), found that researchers given tasks within and outwith their domain tended to work backwards and to use more basic science knowledge in both cases, whereas the practitioners worked forwards and used little basic science knowledge when in their domain and worked backwards but still with little basic science when outwith their domain. Essentially similar results were also found using different subjects and domains by Patel and colleagues (1990). Thus it seems that medical researchers generally draw on basic science knowledge while practitioners draw on more 'surface' clinical knowledge. These tendencies seem explicable given the different professional goals of the two groups of subjects. For the researchers the main goal is for detailed understanding, without strong time pressures, whereas for the practitioners it is for rapid remedial action with no need for deep-level explanation.

8 Conclusions on expertise in medical diagnosis

Compared with other areas of expertise that have been subject to cognitive–psychological investigation, medical diagnosis is a relatively complex domain in which many different types of knowledge are involved and in which the problems are not very well defined. However, thinking-aloud and knowledge-probing techniques have proved useful in the study of medical expertise as in other areas of expertise, and a number of interpretable results have been found regarding the use of deep knowledge in diagnosis.

From studies of tasks requiring memory for medical information, experts draw on compiled 'script'-like knowledge (when sufficient cues are present at least) and this usually delivers a reasonable diagnosis with very little processing of the textual information. Subjects at an intermediate level of skill apply pathophysiological reasoning, a slow and effortful activity, in order to understand the text, and this deep processing results in good memory performance. Novices cannot proceed beyond a superficial processing of the text and so have poor memory performance. To sum up, studies of memory for medical cases support the view that experience in medical diagnosis in clinical settings leads to the development of knowledge in terms of 'illness scripts' which facilitate rapid diagnosis *without the direct activation of pathophysiological knowledge*. Thus, it seems that psychological research has borne out a common intuition among practitioners that diagnostic skill depends on clinical experience, for which book-learning is a poor substitute.

It seems that deep knowledge is mainly invoked when explanation rather than remedial action is the dominant goal, as evidenced by the prevalence of patho-physiological reasoning among researchers as compared with practitioners given the same cases for diagnosis (Patel *et al.*, 1986a 1990). It may be that the lack of evidence for deep reasoning found in the studies of diagnosis outlined here arises from methodological limitations in that the cases used may have been too simple to require such reasoning from experts. For the future, it would be desirable for researchers to use more realistic and difficult tasks to assess when and how deep model use occurs in practice.

F. Interim summary and conclusions

In the areas reviewed (physics, mathematics, computer programming, political science and medical diagnosis) expert–novice comparisons indicate that experts form better representations of problems in their field and generally reason forwards from the givens to a solution. However, this 'working forward' pattern tends to break down with problems that are unfamiliar for the expert. Particularly in the case of medical diagnosis, a mixed pattern of working forwards and backwards appears in the hypothetico-deductive approach of both experts and novices. As in other domains, the expert's initial formulation of the diagnostic problem is better; the alternative hypotheses considered by experts in diagnosis are more similar to one another than those considered by novices, and experts have better-tuned knowledge of what evidence is or is not consistent with alternative diagnoses.

Thus far, our focus has been on cross-sectional contrasts of the knowledge possessed by experts but not by novices. But how does the transition from expert to novice take place? Studies and theories bearing on this question will be discussed below.

II. DEVELOPMENT OF EXPERTISE

Both empirical studies and theoretical developments will be considered under this heading.

A. Empirical studies

Real expertise takes a long time to develop. The figure of 10 years' study and practice is generally accepted as a rough minimum for high-level performance in a wide range of areas [see Holding (1985, p.33) for relevant results on the time between starting play and first major successes in chess play]. Because of the long time periods involved, it is difficult to obtain longitudinal data on the course of development of expertise. The full process is clearly beyond the methods of laboratory-based cognitive research. One approach is to concentrate on relatively small-scale or narrow skills, and to try to obtain information on factors relating to particular well-established changes on the route from novice to expert. This approach was adopted by Sweller *et al.* (1983) in their studies of the shift from working backwards to working forwards. Another line of attack is to carry out more fine-grained cross-sectional analysis. This is exemplified by the work of Lesgold (1984) on the development of skill in the interpretation of X-ray plates. Lesgold and colleagues did not simply compare 'experts' at one end of the scale with 'novices' at the other, but examined performance at a number of points along the skill continuum. A third approach is to examine retrospective accounts of practice given by subjects with varying levels of skill, as exemplified by Ericsson *et al.*'s (1993) work on musical skill. These three lines of empirical research on expertise development will be discussed in the following sections.

1 Strategy changes

Sweller *et al.* (1983) reported a series of experiments concerning the shift in strategy from working backwards to working forwards that characterizes the change from novice to expert in many fields. To make the research problem tractable, they focused on a narrow cognitive skill, consisting of the ability to solve certain problems in kinematics. The domain of kinematics problems was restricted to those soluble using one or two of a set of three equations ($V = at$; $s = vt$ and $v = 0.5V$). In the first experiment, subjects tackled 25 different problems of which the middle 13 were repeated five times. Thus, subjects experienced a total of 77 problems. The subjects' problem-solving steps could be readily classed as either showing a working backwards or a working forwards approach, and Sweller *et al.* found a significant tendency for working forwards to occur more often with increased practice. This result is of interest because it demonstrates differences within individuals over time as against the more usual demonstration of cross-sectional differences in strategy use.

Previous research (Mawer and Sweller, 1982; Sweller and Levine, 1982) had indicated that use of a means–ends or working backwards strategy might hinder the acquisition of knowledge about a problem area. However, the previous studies had concerned maze-learning and some simple symbolic rule-learning tasks, and so might not generalize to the more complex area of cognitive skills. Sweller *et al.* (1983) examined the effects of reducing the use of means–ends strategies on expertise development. They did this using kinematics problems, as in the study of practice effects. One group of subjects worked through 12 problems, each with a specific goal set (e.g. 'given v and t, find the distance travelled'); a second group worked through problems that had a non-specific goal (e.g. 'given v and t, calculate the value of as many variables as you can'). Both groups received four specific goal problems at the start and a different set of four specific goal problems at the end.

The subjects who had worked with specific goal problems showed little use of forwards working on either the initial or final four problems (around 12 per cent in both sets). However, the subjects who had worked with the non-specific goals showed a marked increase (from 12 per cent to 75 per cent) in use of working forwards between the initial and final problems. Thus, use of non-specific-goals in training promotes use of a working forwards strategy in subsequent specific goal tasks. A subsequent study showed that (a) use of non-specific goals in training also positively affected moves to solution and (b) similar results held in geometry tasks as well as in kinematics. An interesting effect of the greater expertise acquired through the non-specific goal procedure is that the more effective, working-forward subjects were more susceptible to 'set' effects than the less effective, working-backward comparison subjects. As in the water jugs studies of Luchins (1942), discussed in Chapter 1, subjects displayed 'set' by adopting a longer solution path when a shorter one was available (e.g. in the kinematics problems, by ignoring possible use of $V = at$ and instead using $s = vt$ followed by $v = 0.5V$). This is taken as evidence of the development of problem schemata in the non-specific goal conditions.

Overall then, Sweller *et al.*'s results suggest that expertise is acquired more rapidly if the training problems have non-specific goals. The proposed explanation is that specific goals induce in the novice a means–ends approach in which attention is focused on reducing the differences between the current state and the overall goal. This reduces the likelihood of learning connections between problem givens and actions. Reduced goal specificity shifts control of moves from the goal to the problem-givens. (In the case of the kinematics problems, knowledge of the givens was in fact sufficient to categorize the three main types of problems, since the same givens always had the same goal.) The results obtained by Sweller *et al.* are undoubtedly intriguing and suggestive of links with 'exploration learning'. However, a question mark must hang over the generality of these results, given that they have been established in narrow skill areas compared with the full-blown forms of expertise addressed in the more typical cross-sectional study.

2 Performance changes in radiology

While practice may indeed make perfect, it may not do so in a smooth and regular way, especially when complex skills with many components have to be acquired. The work of Lesgold and colleagues [see Lesgold (1984) for an accessible account] addresses the development of skill in the domain of radiological diagnosis and has produced some striking results.

First, the domain should be explained. In radiology the physician has to know the relationships between variations in anatomical structure and the black and white patterns seen on X-ray plates. Given a plate, the task is to infer the underlying pathology (if any). Lesgold (1984) reported frequently finding a non-linear, U-shaped curve of performance over beginning, intermediate and expert radiologists; that is, beginners and experts were better at X-ray plate interpretation than subjects of intermediate levels of experience.

Apparently, beginners rely on a few clear surface features of the plates that will sometimes lead to a correct diagnosis, but, because the complete context must be taken into account, cannot permit high-level performance. The expert can take the context into account and so performs well. However, the intermediate-level subject is attempting to take context into account, but often failing to do so correctly. This leads to a higher error rate. However, these short-term losses in efficiency are a necessary step on the way to expert performance.

Lesgold *et al.* (1988) pointed out that acquisition of expertise may be similar to long-term developmental processes, in which U-shaped growth curves are not un-common. For example, initially, young children usually handle irregular plurals and past tenses correctly, learning each as a separate item; but then, as they learn the regular rules, performance on the irregular words deteriorates because the rules are applied to the irregular words as well as to the regular ones. Later, the regular and irregular words come to be disassociated and performance improves once more (Brown, 1973).

3 The role of deliberate practice

Simon and Chase (1973, p. 402) noted that nobody had achieved grand master level performance in chess with less than 10 years of 'intense preparation'. A '10-year rule' also seems to operate in many other domains of expertise, such as music (Sosniak, 1985) and mathematics (Gustin, 1985) [see Ericsson *et al.*, (1993), for further examples]. Ericsson *et al.* point out that sheer exposure to the task domain does not necessarily result in better performance. For example, in Chase and Ericsson's (1982) study of practice in the digit memory span task, a subject who simply kept rehearsing digits showed no improvement in span over trials while those who practised relating digit strings to prior knowledge showed massive improvements. What is required for the development of expertise is deliberate practice aimed at improvement. In many spheres (e.g. most sports and musical skills) tutors have devised practice activities for beginners and intermediates to aid the transition to expertise, and further practice activities to maintain expert levels. Such schemes generally incorporate a programme of distibuted practice with ample rest periods between practice sessions. Beyond a certain point the gain of continuing a practice session diminishes and may even become detrimental to motivation and interest. However, as subjects become older and more experienced, in most domains they can tolerate longer practice sessions.

Ericsson *et al.* (1993) investigated the practice habits of a samples of music students, professional musicians and amateurs. In the case of violin players, the students were divided by their teachers into 'best' and 'good', and students of music education ('teachers') and middle-aged professional violinists were also included. Diaries kept by the student subjects indicated markedly higher levels of weekly practice for the two most skilled groups (average 24.3 hours per week) than for the least-skilled, music teachers group (average 9.3 hours per week). Curiously, the student diary study also revealed that more-skilled subjects tended to take short naps in the afternoons (average napping 2.8 hours per week) while less-skilled subjects did not (average napping 0.9 hours per week). This difference may well reflect a strategy for recovering from more intense and extensive morning practice in the higher skill groups. Student and professional subjects were asked to estimate the average amount of deliberate practice they had carried out each week for each year from age 4 to 20 years. The resulting estimates were multiplied by 52 to give estimates of accumulated hours of practice. The results in Fig. 4.3 clearly show how the student groups separate out on this measure as the years pass. The best students' plot matches well that given by middle-aged professionals. A similar plot is given in Fig. 4.4 for estimates by expert and amateur pianists matched in age, and again shows a clear divergence in accumulated hours of practice with expertise.

These results attest to the role of deliberate practice in the development of expertise.

B. Theories of the acquisition of expertise

Despite the paucity of hard data on the acquisition of cognitive skills, a number of theories of varying scope have been put forward. In the following sections, four theories of broad applicability are discussed: Ericsson's Skilled Memory theory (Ericsson and Pennington, 1993; Ericsson and Kintsch, 1995), Anderson's (1983) ACT* theory, Holland et al.'s (1986) Framework for Induction theory, and Newell's (1990, 1992) SOAR theory.

1 Ericsson's Skilled Memory Theory

Ericsson and Pennington's (1993) exposition of Skilled Memory theory represents a welcome attempt to form bridges between the study of memory and that of problem solving. Too often these areas of study are pursued largely in isolation from one another. It is clear that in real 'everyday' problem solving, memory processes must be implicated, and equally that memory tasks in everyday life often have marked problem-solving components.

A salient generalization in expertise research is that experts remember new information in their fields better than do novices. This result was initially established in the area of chess by De Groot (1965) and has subsequently been replicated in a broad range of areas. As Ericsson and Pennington point out, such memory advantages are highly specific to the particular domains concerned and do not reflect any general superiority in basic memory capacities for experts. The specificity of such memory advantages goes against the view of expertise as a result of superior basic

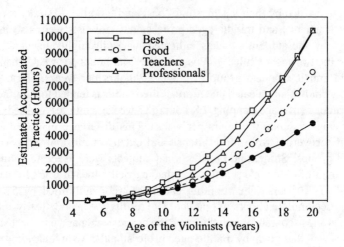

Fig. 4.3 *Accumulated amount of practice alone (based on estimates of weekly practice) as a function of age for the middle-aged violinists (△), the best violinists (□), the good violinists (○) and the music teachers (●). Reproduced with permission from Ericsson, K.A., Krampe, R.T. and Tesch-Rohmer, C. (1993). The role of deliberate practice in the acquisition of expert performance.* Psychological Review. **102**, *211–245.*

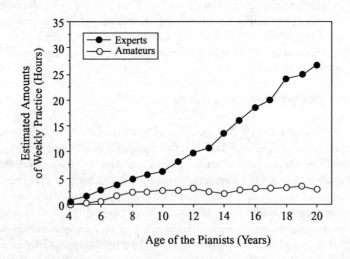

Fig. 4.4 *Estimated amount of time for practice alone at the piano as a function of age for expert and amateur pianists. Reproduced with permission from Ericsson, K.A., Krampe, R.T. and Tesch-Rohmer, C. (1993). The role of deliberate practice in the acquisition of expert performance.* Psychological Review **102**, *211–245.*

capacities (the 'talent' view; Ericsson and Smith, 1991). Rather, the memory results have been taken as support for the 'knowledge' view that expertise results from the accumulation of a large repertoire of domain-specific schemata which enable ready categorization of problems into familiar types and support memory for fresh information in the domain. However, as Ericsson and Pennington point out, sheer knowledge accumulation is unlikely to be whole story and the development of skills in anticipation (e.g. in typing) and in memory are also likely to be involved.

Consideration of memory skills, as in Ericsson and Polson's (1988a,b) studies of waiters and Chase and Ericsson's (1981, 1982) studies of practice effects in digit span tasks, has led to the Skilled Memory theory (Ericsson, 1985), which is also applicable to expert memory performance (Ericsson and Kintsch, 1995). According to this theory, skilled memory involves rapid storage of presented information in long-term memory via associations with existing information and retrieval via appropriate cues. Thus, in the digit-span task, subjects who had extensive prior knowledge of running times associated chunks of digits with typical times for various distances and recalled via those distance–time links. Use of such mnemonic methods enabled Chase and Ericsson's (1982) subjects to recall lists of over 80 rapidly presented digits (far in excess of the typical 7–9 digits).

What of areas of skill in which the main activity is not one of memorizing? As we have seen, expert memory is generally better for domain materials than novice memory, even although the skill does not focus on memory performance. It is proposed that experts have *incidentally* developed skilled memory for their domains, rather than having done so *intentionally*, as Chase and Ericsson's subjects did. Experts have extensive background knowledge of their domain in long-term memory, to which new information can readily be linked; retrieval is then by appropriate cues determined at the time of encoding.

Ericsson and Pennington's analysis is consistent with the traditional 'standard' model of human memory as consisting of a limited-capacity short-term or working memory backed up by an essentially unlimited-capacity long-term memory. What they have proposed is that experts circumvent the limitations of short-term working memory by rapid storage in and retrieval from long-term memory.

As a final comment, the extended working memory concept may be applicable to the processing of difficult problems at the edge of expertise. Such problems can tax scientists and artists for months or even years, and any solutions are often regarded as creative. Helmholtz in 1896 (Woodworth and Schlosberg, 1954, p. 838) noted that for successful solution of difficult problems: 'It was always necessary, first of all, that I should have turned my problem over on all sides to such an extent that I had all its angles and complexities 'in my head' and could run through them freely without writing.' In other words, the complex problem representation had to be in extended working memory to overcome the limitations of focal short-term working memory, before solution was possible. Thus, the notion of extended working memory looks promising in the analysis of extremely difficult problem solving, as well as in cases of more routine expert problem solving.

2 Anderson's ACT* theory

Anderson's Adaptive Control of Thought (ACT) approach has evolved through a number of versions into its current form, ACT* (Anderson, 1983). ACT* is intended as a general framework for understanding cognition, but it particularly addresses the acquisition of cognitive skills. Anderson stresses the time-honoured distinction between 'knowing that' and 'knowing how'. The latter knowledge is said to be 'procedural' and the former 'declarative' in his system. Declarative knowledge takes the form of propositions and is converted only slowly into action by means of general interpretive procedures (e.g. following a recipe). Procedural knowledge takes the form of production rules, discussed in Chapter 2, which permit rapid and appropriate action. Skill acquisition involves, first, the conversion of declarative into procedural knowledge and, second, refinements of procedural knowledge. The initial conversion is labelled *knowledge compilation*. In computing, a 'compiled' program is one that has already been translated from a high-level language into machine code and in this form is ready to be run. Initially in skill acquisition then, declarative knowledge is used, possibly from textbooks or from instructors' verbal guidance. Declarative knowledge is converted only slowly into procedural form. Anderson argues plausibly that rapid knowledge compilation would be maladaptive. Since compiled knowledge controls behaviour quite directly, it is important that such knowledge be 'tried and tested'.

Knowledge compilation is seen as involving two sets of processes: *proceduralization* and *composition*. Proceduralization creates highly specific rules that eliminate any need to search long-term memory during skilled activity. For example, through repeatedly using a new acquaintance's telephone number, the need to consult directories or to search long-term memory for the number reduces as a new production is formed, the conditional part of which is the goal of dialling the acquaintance's number and the action of which is simply to dial the appropriate sequence. The other process, composition, smooths performance by collapsing a repeated sequence of actions into a single sequence (a 'macro-operation').

The refinement or tuning stage of skill acquisition involves sub-processes of generalization, discrimination and strengthening. Generalization creates general rules from more specific ones, where the action parts of the rules are the same.

Anderson (1983, p. 242) gives an example from the game of bridge. Suppose the following two rules are known:

Rule 1: IF I am playing no trump and my dummy has a long suit,
THEN
try to establish that suit and then run that suit.
Rule 2: IF I am playing spades and my dummy has a long suit,
THEN
try to establish that suit and then run that suit.

ACT* would form a generalized rule from these two rules:

Rule 3: IF my dummy has a long suit,
THEN
try to establish that suit and then run that suit.

Discrimination works in the reverse direction, by adding necessary extra conditions to rules when they prove to be too general. All rules in the system have their own current strength level, and the strength of a rule is adjusted up whenever it is applied and adjusted down if punishment results. The conditions of rules with a greater strength index are matched more rapidly and thus come to dominate rules of lesser strength.

Overall, Anderson's system copes well with many of the standard observations regarding skill acquisition. For example, repeated composition would collapse sequences of operations into a macro-operation that could be applied as soon as a familiar problem was detected; this would produce a working-forward pattern of activity, typical of expert performance. Again, proceduralization and strengthening produce the typical speed-ups, automatization and susceptibility to set that result from repeated exposure to familiar types of problems. Some difficulties are that composition has been shown formally to be inadequate to explain the development of expert skill in solving algebraic equations (Lewis, 1981); also, the theory makes no provision for the development of new rules, as against the refinement and modification of old ones. This last point is taken up by Holland *et al.*'s theory, to which we now turn.

3 Holland et al.'s Processes of Induction

The framework proposed by Holland *et al.* (1986) takes production rules as the basic building blocks of knowledge. They distinguish three types of rule: (1) empirical rules; (2) inferential rules which modify existing empirical rules; and (3) system-operating rules which serve performance functions, such as resolving conflict among competing rules or automatically adjusting strengths assigned to rules.

Unlike earlier production system models which have generally envisaged serial processing, Holland *et al.* allow a degree of parallel processing, in that a number of rules can 'fire' at once. One result of a rule firing is that a 'message' is posted on a 'message list'; the messages on the message list can then trigger other rules, which place new messages on the message list . . . and so on. At any one time all the rules in the system are eligible for firing, but only those rules whose conditions are matched completely get a chance to post messages. All the rules with completely matched conditions enter a strength competition and only those above a threshold strength actually fire and post messages.

How does this framework apply to acquisition of cognitive skills? The speed-up of performance typical of the expert may be accounted for by rule strengthening. Holland *et al.* note that rule strengthening following success raises the question of 'apportion of credit'. If only the last rule in a long sequence is strengthened, then earlier rules that set the scene for later success, will not be strengthened. The solution offered takes the form of the picturesquely named 'bucket brigade' algorithm. In this scheme, strength increments are passed back along the sequence of linked rules that led to success. Rules that may have fired in parallel but did not form part of the successful sequence are not strengthened. The strength increments are larger at the end of the sequence than at the beginning. This feature accounts for the usual result that behavioural chains are best established in reverse order (Millenson, 1967).

New rules are produced by modifications of old ones. Two main types of rule modification are *specialization* and *generalization*. Specialization is invoked when an over-general rule leads to error. In such a case, any unusual condition that held when the rule fired is added to the rule's old conditions to produce a new, more specialized, rule. If a number of different rules are formed such that they all lead to the same action but have different conditions, then generalization seeks to produce a single rule to cover all the conditions of the separate rules. Novel rules (rather than modified or strengthened rules) are formed by a genetics-like process, whereby rules are broken up into component conditions and actions and are recombined to form new ones.

An interesting point stressed by Holland *et al.* (1986) is that new rules do not replace old rules, but rather co-exist with earlier learning. Thus, physics graduates, for example, will have the rules of both newtonian and pre-newtonian mechanics (acquired before formal physics instruction, in their 'naive physics' stage of life). This explains why a person who can readily solve textbook physics problems will exhibit more developmentally primitive rules when faced with a real-life physics problem. For example, most college students in a study by McCloskey (1983) believed that, if they walked along carrying a ball and then dropped it, the ball would land directly under the point where it was released. Similarly, in the First World War, hand-held bombs dropped from aeroplanes very frequently overshot their targets (McCloskey and Kaiser, 1984). 'Dissociations' of textbook knowledge from every-day beliefs are consistent with Holland *et al.*'s framework.

4 Newell's SOAR theory

Newell and colleagues (1990, 1992) have developed an ambitious approach, known as SOAR (State, Operator And Result). SOAR is intended to be a unified theory of cognition, comprising a single set of mechanisms to explain all cognition. As with Anderson's ACT* and Holland *et al.*'s Process of Induction (PI) theories, SOAR's building blocks are production rules. The SOAR theory proposes a far higher degree of parallelism than ACT* or PI and allows all matched rules in long-term memory to fire and place their outputs in working memory. This implies a very capacious working memory – far from the assumptions of limited working memory prevalent in cognitive psychology. Seriality enters when selection is made of which fired rule should cause action to occur. Selection is made by decision rules, taking goals into account. If a decision cannot be made an *impasse* is said to exist and a new goal is set up to resolve the impasse. Further rules are then evoked, producing a possibly extensive search with further impasses and further sub-goals until the initial impasse is resolved. The sequence of actions that resolved the impasse is then *chunked* into a single rule, which can then be applied should that particular situation recur. Newell's chunking is similar to the compilation process of ACT* and can reproduce the typical pattern of speed-up observed in skill acquisition, known as the power law of practice (Newell and Rosenbloom, 1981). Although SOAR appears computationally adequate to tackle a wide range of tasks, its psychological plausibility has been questioned (e.g., Card, 1992; Carlson and Detweiler, 1992; Chipman, 1992; Lewandowsky, 1992; Remington et al., 1992).

III. SUMMARY AND CONCLUDING COMMENTS

This chapter has reviewed research concerned with characterizing differences in knowledge and strategy between more and less skilled solvers of problems in a range of semantically rich domains. Most of this research has been cross-sectional, with relatively few studies yielding data on the transition from novice to expert. Nevertheless, some quite detailed theories of cognitive skill acquisition have been proposed and three approaches based on production system notions discussed (Anderson, 1983; Holland et al., 1986; Newell, 1990, 1992).

From the studies of expert–novice differences in physics, mathematics, computer programming, political science and medical diagnosis, it seems that experts spend relatively more time in representing problems and then usually work forward from the givens to the solution. Novices spend less time on initial representation and usually attempt to work backwards. However, when problems are difficult even for experts (e.g. medical diagnosis), then a mixed working forwards and backwards pattern has been observed. With very difficult problems, it is surmised that experts too will show a fairly pure means–ends analysis, working-backward approach (Gick, 1986). While it is generally agreed that experts have acquired extensive problem schemata that support richer representations of problems and facilitate working forward, the processes of schemata acquisition are difficult to observe, in that expertise in most areas requires several years of practice (10 years is an often-cited number). In many ways, explaining the acquisition of expertise is a problem on a developmental scale, and is not easily tackled in the typical laboratory study. Sweller et al. (1983) have focused on very narrow skills, e.g. using three equations in kinematics. While this research is suggestive, it is not clear how well it relates to full-scale acquisition of expertise in broader domains, such as physics. Sweller et al.'s experimentally based recommendations of using non-specific goals during training are plausible and should be testable in real-life studies of physics teaching.

The work of Lesgold et al. (1988) is valuable, notably in its use of a number of levels of experience in the subjects. The use of just two levels (expert and novice) could easily hide important trends, such as the U-shaped curve of performance against experience in radiology.

Ericsson and co-workers' (1993) studies of musical expertise have shown the utility of diary studies and retrospective estimates of practice habits in detailing the critical role of deliberate practice in developing and maintaining high-level skill.

The theoretical approaches of Anderson, Holland *et al.* and of Newell are somewhat similar in that they are all based on production systems. Anderson's is the best developed and most closely tied to experimental data. However, Holland *et al.*'s framework seems promising and incorporates useful notions of parallel processing and of evolution of new productions, lacking in Anderson's ACT*. Although Newell's SOAR is undoubtedly widely applicable, it has drawbacks in terms of psychological plausibility, particularly with reference to working memory assumptions (Broadbent, 1993).

Future research may profitably focus on (a) performance and learning of experts when dealing with problems at the limits of their expertise and (b) longitudinal studies of expertise acquisition.

IV. FURTHER READING

Ericsson, K.A. and Smith, J. (Eds) (1991). *Towards a general theory of expertise*. Cambridge: Cambridge University Press.
Sternberg, R.J. and Frensch, P.A. (Eds) (1991). *Complex problem-solving*. Hillsdale, NJ: Lawrence Erlbaum Associates.

Both the above contain a wide range of useful papers reviewing developments in expertise research.

5

Deductive reasoning 1: Categorical syllogisms

This chapter and the next two deal with reasoning and continue the theme of considering how people 'go beyond the information given' in a task to reach a solution. The preceding three chapters concerned studies of how people tackle problems that involve extensive mental searches and, in the case of experts, an extensive long-term memory of relevant problem schemata. By contrast, the reasoning tasks to be considered here would not appear to require extensive mental searches or extensive prior knowledge structures. Nevertheless, the tasks to be dealt with are frequently found to be difficult despite their apparent simplicity.

The reasoning problems discussed in this chapter and the next two may be broadly classed as 'deductive' and 'inductive' respectively. In *deductive* tasks, people are required to determine what conclusion, if any, necessarily follows when certain given statements are assumed to be true. For example, taking as true that "All the guard dogs in Scotland weigh over 70 pounds", and that "Fido is a guard dog in Scotland", it can be concluded necessarily that "Fido weighs over 70 pounds". In the case of *inductive* reasoning, two categories of task can be distinguished and these may be labelled *hypothesis testing* and *hypothesis generation*. In hypothesis testing, people are required to determine the implications, if any, of some particular observation(s) for the truth of possible generalizations (hypotheses). For example, observations of guard dogs, their weights and geographical locations would bear on the generalization given above on guard dogs in Scotland. In hypothesis generation, the person has or can obtain observations (e.g. weight, colour, barking volume, colouration, geographical location) on the objects of interest (e.g. guard dogs) and seeks to make a plausible generalization.

The topics of deductive and inductive reasoning are closely related and both have been studied extensively in recent years. In the case of deductive reasoning, at least, clear normative theories exist (some of great antiquity) and human performance can be compared with ideal benchmarks. Departures from the normative benchmarks raise questions about the extent of human rationality, which will be discussed as we proceed. To keep the text to a manageable length, I will largely deal with selected 'prototypical' instances of the two types of inference.

I. CATEGORICAL SYLLOGISTIC REASONING

A fairly common type of deductive problem in everyday thinking is to determine what conclusion, if any, must follow from certain assumptions about category membership. The main features and principles of categorical reasoning were first identified and systematically developed by Aristotle (384–322 BC); see Nidditch (1962) for a clear account of the development of formal logic from Aristotle to the twentieth century. Because the classical argument form of the categorical *syllogism* provides small-scale instances of such deductive problems, it has been widely used in laboratory studies of reasoning. Technically, a syllogism is any argument consisting of two premises and a conclusion, and so includes linear syllogisms (e.g. "Tom is taller than Fred, Fred is taller than Bill, therefore?") as well as categorical syllogisms. However, it is common in the literature to use the term 'syllogism' to refer to categorical syllogisms unless otherwise specified, and this usage will be followed here. The main features of syllogistic arguments may be conveyed by a few examples. Consider the following:

All mammals have backbones.
All dogs are mammals.
Therefore, all dogs have backbones.

Since the third statement (the conclusion) follows necessarily from the first two (the premises) this is a *valid* syllogistic argument and may be compared with:

All cats are mammals.
All dogs are mammals.
Therefore, all dogs are cats.

In this case the conclusion plainly does not follow from the premises and the argument is invalid. It should be noted that the validity of an argument is independent of the truth of the premises. So, for example, the following is a deductively valid argument:

All cats have nine lives.
All dogs are cats.
Therefore, all dogs have nine lives.

A *valid argument* is simply one in which, if the premises are true, then the conclusion is also, necessarily, true.

In addition to validity, syllogisms can be varied in many other ways for experimental purposes. For example, they may be varied by changing the quantifiers ('some', 'all') used in the argument; the terms may be abstract or concrete; the premises and conclusion may be negative or affirmative; the propositions in the argument may be empirically true or false . . . and so on. Clearly, many features of the task can be readily manipulated. A number of variations are also possible in the response requirements. Subjects can be asked to produce valid inferences from given premises; to judge a possible conclusion as valid or not; or to select a valid conclusion from a set of possibilities. Early studies (e.g. Wilkins, 1928) established some of the main factors associated with the difficulty of syllogisms, such as concreteness. Intuitively, the invalidity of an argument seems less clear when the terms are abstract, for example:

All P's are M's.
All S's are M's.
Therefore, all S's are P's.

This abstract argument may well be accepted, even though it exhibits the same invalid pattern as a previous concrete example that led from true premises to the conclusion that 'all dogs are cats'. The role of concreteness in facilitating syllogistic reasoning was established experimentally by Wilkins. She found that syllogisms that employed concrete terms resulted in more correct deductions than syllogisms in abstract form. Some 81 subjects were given a series of problems like the following:

All good ballet dancers have many years of training.
Some of the dancers in this musical comedy have had many years of training.
Therefore:

(1)   Some of the dancers in this musical comedy are good ballet dancers.
(2)   All good ballet dancers are in this musical comedy.
(3)   Some of the dancers in this musical comedy are not good ballet dancers.

Or, the same thing in symbols:

All A's are B's.
Some C's are B's.
Therefore:

(1)   Some C's are A's.
(2)   All A's are C's.
(3)   Some C's are not A's.

The instructions were 'to put a plus sign before every conclusion which you are sure follows necessarily from the given statements . . . a minus sign before every conclusion that does not necessarily follow from the given statements . . .'. The average score was 76 per cent correct for the letter terms and 84 per cent for the syllogisms expressed in familiar words. Why, even in the case of concrete syllogisms, did the subjects accept so many invalid conclusions? Misunderstanding of the use of the term 'some' could have caused errors. In logic, 'some' means 'at least one and possibly all' whereas in normal usage it means 'not all but at least one'. Thus, in logic, it is not valid to infer from 'some X are Y' that 'some X are not Y'. An additional proposal has been that there is an 'atmosphere effect' which leads subjects to accept invalid conclusions. This proposal has generated a long-lasting controversy which will now be surveyed.

A. The 'atmosphere effect' controversy

1 Basic results

All C's are M's.
All D's are M's.
Therefore, all D's are C's.

The above argument is invalid. (In logic it is known as the 'fallacy of the undistributed middle.' For a syllogistic argument to be valid, at least one of the premises must make a statement that applies to every member of the class denoted by the middle term [see Wetherick (1989) for details]. When a statement asserts something about all instances of a term, then that term is said to be *distributed*. Taking statements about S's and M's there are three types of statement in which M is distributed, viz. "All M's are S's", "No M's are S's" or "Some S's are not M's". In these statements the middle term is distributed; something is asserted of all cases of the middle term. The first two examples are probably clear, but the third, "Some S's are not M's", is less obvious. The M term is distributed here because *some* of the S's are excluded from *all* of the M's.) To account for the common fallacy of the undistributed middle, Woodworth and Sells (1935) hypothesized an 'atmosphere' effect which predicted that the form of the premises would influence people's expectations about the form of the conclusion. They proposed that if both premises involve the universal ('all'), people are disposed to accept an 'all' conclusion. Similarly, if both premises are particular ('some'), people will be disposed to a 'particular' conclusion. Similar predictions apply if both premises are negatively particular or universal; in such cases, the preferred conclusion is predicted to be negatively particular or universal, respectively. With mixed premises it is proposed that: (1) a negative premise creates a negative atmosphere even when the other premise is affirmative; and (2) a particular premise creates a particular atmosphere, even when the other premise is universal. To test the atmosphere hypothesis, Sells (1936) presented 65 subjects with 180 syllogisms, using abstract material; for example:

> If all Z's are Y's
> and all X's are Y's
> are all X's then Z's?
> True, probably true, false or indeterminate? (Correct answer – indeterminate)

The meaning of 'some' in logic was explained in advance. Of the 180 syllogisms 52 were valid and 128 invalid. With the invalid syllogisms, the conclusions that accorded to the atmosphere of the premises were predominantly accepted as true/ valid conclusions, in accord with the hypothesis.

Sells and Koob (1937) reported a similar result in a study that required subjects to draw their own conclusions from premises rather than merely to judge already set out conclusions. This study required subjects to 'work quickly', which would probably favour an atmosphere effect.

How might atmosphere operate? The suggestion is that one becomes quickly 'set' or adjusted to the total impression of the presented situation and responds accordingly. This would lead to fast responses, some of which would be correct. Accurate reasoning, on the other hand, surely requires analysis of the situation, and noting of relations – presumably a slower, more deliberate, process than is suggested by the atmosphere hypothesis.

As a model, the atmosphere hypothesis proposes very superficial processing with minimal understanding, and it may be correct, when abstract problems are given to untrained subjects working under time pressure.

2 Conversion errors and probabilistic inference

More than 20 years after Woodworth and Sells proposed the atmosphere hypothesis, an alternative was put forward by Chapman and Chapman (1959). First, they collected some fresh data by giving subjects 42 syllogisms that had no valid conclusions, for example:

Some L's are K's.
Some K's are M's.
Therefore:
(1) No M's are L's.
(2) Some M's are L's.
(3) Some M's are not L's.
(4) None of these.
(5) All M's are L's.

The correct conclusion is (4). Subjects tended to be wrong on these items and the kind of error made depended on the form of syllogism. The study involved 14 main types of syllogism and the atmosphere effect predicted the preferred errors on many of these. But it failed on syllogisms that involved premises of the following type:

	Some X are Y			Some X are not Y
A		and	(B)	
	No Y are Z			No Y are Z

The predicted response for both (on atmosphere) is 'Some Z are not X', but in fact subjects tended to choose 'No Z are X', especially on (A) but split fairly evenly between the universal and the particular conclusions on (B). Chapman and Chapman (1959) proposed that their results could be better explained by the operation of two reasoning errors that they called 'conversion' and 'probabilistic inference'. There are two conversion errors. These are to assume (1) from 'all X are Y' that 'all Y are X' and (2) that 'some A's are not B's' implies 'some B's are not A's'. That these are errors is shown clearly by concrete material. 'All women are human' does not imply that 'all humans are women'. Again, 'some humans are not politicians' does not imply that 'some politicians are not human'. However, the Chapmans argued that conversions often happen to be correct with real material (e.g. 'all three-sided figures are triangles') and they suggest that subjects tend to make conversions unless they have information to the contrary (which they do not have with abstract material). Probabilistic inference involved 'plausible reasoning' that is not strictly valid, deductively speaking, e.g. 'Some cloudy days are wet', 'Some wet days are unpleasant', therefore 'Some cloudy days are unpleasant'. The Chapmans report that the joint operation of illicit conversion and probabilistic inference accounts better for their obtained error patterns than does the atmosphere hypothesis. This is largely on the strength of improved predictions for the types of syllogism mentioned above. With other syllogisms the alternative hypotheses make the same predictions. It is notable that the Chapmans' results differ from those of Sells on the 'crucial' syllogisms. (Sells' results favoured the atmosphere prediction.) To sum up, the Chapmans have presented a plausible alternative to the atmosphere hypothesis, an alternative that is congenial to a cognitive approach; however, their data do not represent a complete demolition of the atmosphere hypothesis.

In 1969 Begg and Denny re-examined the atmosphere *v.* illicit conversion etc. controversy and provided a brief reformulation of the atmosphere hypothesis, which covers most of the obtained effects. They proposed two principles:

(1) Whenever at least one premise is negative, the conclusion is negative and otherwise it is positive.
(2) Whenever at least one premise is particular (some), the conclusion will be particular, otherwise it is universal.

These two principles can be combined for any pair of premises to predict the preferred conclusion.

For most syllogisms these assumptions predict the same results as the conversion and probabilistic inference hypothesis. Begg and Denny (1969) analysed error patterns on 45 syllogisms, representing the main types and, again, found that atmosphere predicted the majority choices very well. They also reanalysed the data of Sells (1936) and Chapman and Chapman (1959). There was great consistency among the three sets of data and, on the average of the three studies, the atmosphere predictions were more often upheld than the conversion and probabilistic inference predictions.

Begg and Denny emphasized that their study was not informative about the processes that lead subjects to error; but their results do support the use of the atmosphere 'formula' as a convenient predictor of error patterns, even if the underlying processes may not be as described by the atmosphere hypothesis.

Wason and Johnson-Laird (1972) brought up some other points which suggest that, at the least, the atmosphere hypothesis is inadequate as a complete explanation; for example, from Sells' own data, when subjects are given:

All B are A.
All C are B.

they accept the correct conclusion 'All C are A' twice as often as the incorrect conclusion 'All A are C'. Both are equally predicted by the atmosphere hypothesis. Again, Wilkins' (1928) data show that the atmosphere effect is weaker with familiar as opposed to abstract or unfamiliar material and the atmosphere hypothesis does not explain this difference.

Wason and Johnson-Laird (1972) ran a further informative study. This differed from most of the previous experiments in that the subjects were simply given the premises and asked to draw a conclusion. They were not asked to evaluate given conclusions or to select one from a multiple choice list. Also, the premises they were given permitted valid inferences to be drawn [cf. Sells (1936) and Chapman and Chapman (1959)]. Wason and Johnson-Laird found that there were reliably more errors *incompatible* with atmosphere (average of 3.9 per problem) than compatible with atmosphere (1.8 per problem). Further, the tendency to conform to atmosphere varied from one sort of problem to another. They concluded that the atmosphere explanation left something to be desired and, in view of the 'anti-atmosphere' evidence, went so far as to suggest that "Perhaps there is no atmosphere effect in syllogistic reasoning at all, but merely an amassed set of data which, when casually viewed, give rise to the illusion of such a phenomenon" (1972, p. 139). Another attack on the atmosphere hypothesis that has led to some interesting work was developed by Henle (1962) and this will be discussed next.

3 Henle's defence of 'rationality'

The atmosphere notion portrays people as non-logical and as under the influence of non-rational sets; on the other hand, Chapman and Chapman's (1959) hypothesis suggests that people are somewhat rational – but may misinterpret premises (leading to illicit conversion) and may draw plausible but not strictly warranted conclusions from premises (probabilistic inference). This second kind of approach is more consistent with the views put forward by Henle (1962) in an influential paper that argued for the essential logicality of everyday thinking.

Henle argued that many apparent instances of illogical thinking may involve the implicit introduction of additional premises, the ignoring of some of the given premises and the misinterpretation of still other premises, but she claimed the *inferences* are generally rational, given the subject's real premises. Henle here supports an old view that the laws of logic and the laws of thinking are the same, as opposed to the more recent view that thinking is not intrinsically logical and conforms to logical paths only under special circumstances. She illustrated her points with typical responses given by a sample of graduate students to syllogisms that one might come across in everyday life, for example:

> It's important to talk about things that are in our minds.
> We spend so much of our time in the kitchen that household problems are in our minds.
> Therefore, it's important to talk about household problems.

Subjects were asked to assess the validity of the argument and to give their reasons. Some subjects failed to accept the task at all, and did not distinguish logical validity from factual truth, e.g. "No it's not important to talk about things in our minds unless they worry us". In a number of cases, subjects tacitly restated premises or the conclusion, so that the intended meaning was changed. [Since Henle's syllogisms omitted quantifiers they were open to changes of this sort. Indeed, to digress slightly, omission of quantifiers is a prime source of crooked and confused

thinking according to Thouless (1953, p. 24).] Other examples showed that subjects sometimes omitted entire premises or introduced premises that had not been given.
Henle concluded

> that when subjects arrive at apparently invalid conclusions, or when they fail to spot a fallacy, they often do so because they have worked with materials different from those intended or because they have undertaken a task different from the one intended. In such cases, if we consider the materials and task as they were actually understood by individual subjects, we fail to find evidence of faulty reasoning. It must be concluded that the presence of error does not constitute evidence that the laws of logic are irrelevant to actual thinking. The data tend, rather, to support the older conception that these laws are widely discernible in the thinking process.

Although Henle's final conclusion from her informal study of a small, highly educated, sample may be regarded as debatable, she made a sound point in stressing the need to consider subjects' interpretations of the task materials and goals. It is easy to assume that subjects interpret a task exactly as the experimenter intends and then go on to make extraordinary blunders, which the experimenter is perplexed to explain. Consideration of possible interpretations may well make subjects' behaviour more intelligible. The notion that people may follow a *mental logic*, which shares at least some basic rules with formal logic, has been pursued by researchers such as Braine (1990), Rips (1983, 1994), O'Brien (1993) and Macnamara (1986), and some of that work is discussed in a later section on propositional reasoning.

4 Misinterpretation of premises: further evidence

The question of premise interpretation was again taken up by Ceraso and Provitera (1971), who examined the ambiguity of the traditional statements used in syllogistic tasks. There are four basic statements, obtained by combining universal or particular quantifiers, positively or negatively. These statements are:

(A) All A are B.
(I) Some A are B.
(E) All A are not B.
(O) Some A are not B.

and are traditionally labelled A, I, E and O. These labels come from the initial vowels of the Latin words 'affirmo' and 'nego', meaning 'I assert' and 'I deny' respectively. An A statement can refer to two different situations, an I statement to four situations and an O statement to three, while an E statement is unambiguous and refers to only one state of affairs. These points should become clearer by reference to Euler circles (see Fig. 5.1). If, as seems likely (Begg and Harris, 1982; Newstead and Griggs, 1983), many subjects misinterpret the traditional ambiguous premises, then apparently mistaken conclusions (e.g. those attributed to atmosphere effects) may be valid inferences based on misconstrued premises.

Ceraso and Provitera (1971) gave subjects syllogisms in which the premises were given a definite interpretation. For example, instead of "Some A's are B's", subjects were told "Some of the A's (but not all) are B's, but all of the B's are A's". Another

Fig. 5.1 *Venn diagrams showing possible interpretations of the traditional premises of syllogistic logic.*

group of subjects were given the traditional syllogism statements. The subjects with the clarified premises performed much better (averaging 2.5 errors per 13 syllogisms) compared with the traditional group (who averaged 5.5 errors per 13 syllogisms). Also, the responses of the subjects receiving traditional syllogism could largely be explained by proposing that they tended to interpret their premises in a more restricted way than was intended by logic.

Even with the modified premises, some difficulties still arose, which seemed to be related to the multiple possibilities that could follow from certain premise combinations. Subjects do not seem to analyse completely all the possible consequences of such premise combinations. Rather they develop one possible consequence and adopt it as the conclusion. This leads to an over-restricted conclusion which is *consistent* with the premises but not necessarily true. For example, from:

All B are A.
All B are C.

subjects tended to conclude 'All A are C' rather than the more general and correct deduction 'Some A are C'. Ceraso and Provitera (1971) dubbed this an example of 'could be' reasoning. Wason and Johnson-Laird (1972) reported other evidence supporting the notion of premise misinterpretation and incomplete analysis of consequences. They also suggested that when subjects have drawn a plausible consistent conclusion they are reluctant to try to *falsify* it by, for example, checking whether the negative of the initial conclusion is also consistent with the premises.

B. Approaches based on set-theory

1 Erickson's model

Erickson (1974, 1978) has also considered the problems of premise interpretation and inadequate analysis of proposed conclusions. He found consistent patterns of interpretations that held over large student samples drawn from four different universities. When subjects were asked to draw Euler diagrams corresponding to the statement 'All A are B', approximately 40 per cent of responses were in terms of a set identity interpretation while 60 per cent were in terms of a set inclusion interpretation (see Fig. 5.2). It may be noted that studies in which subjects choose among pesented Euler diagrams have generally found a markedly lower rate of identity choices (e.g. Griggs and Warner, 1982, Newstead, 1989. However, the drawing test as used by Erickson may be more relevant to the syllogism task in which subjects must make their own interpretations rather than choose between pre-packaged interpretations. The identity and inclusion interpretations would logically lead to different conclusions if they were used in syllogistic reasoning.

Erickson (1978) focused his research on 'AA' syllogisms, in which both premises are 'A' statements, i.e. are affirmative universals. Since subjects were quite self-consistent and tended to interpret all universal statements in the same way, he could then consider only identity–identity and inclusion–inclusion interpretations of the premises in AA syllogisms.

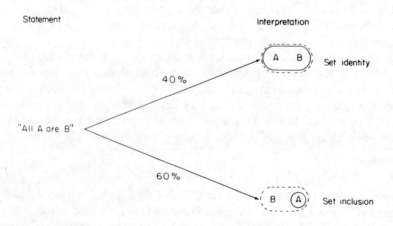

Fig. 5.2 *Distribution of interpretations given to the universal affirmative premise by Erickson's (1974) subjects.*

At this point we must consider an aspect of the structure of syllogisms that it has been possible to ignore up to now. This aspect relates to the terms and their arrangement within the syllogism. A syllogism involves three terms (category or individual names). The premises state the relationships of one term (the middle term, M) to a predicate term (P) and to a subject term (S). A valid conclusion states the relationship that must hold between the S and P terms. So, a typical example reads, 'All M are P. All S are M. Therefore, 'all S are P', in accord with the tradition that the first statement relates M and P and the second relates S and M. Clearly, the order of the terms within each premise can be varied in two ways. Putting together the combinatorial possibilities for two premises yields four syllogistic patterns known as the four *figures* (see Table 5.1).

Erickson (1978) pointed out that the possible conclusions consistent with the premise interpretations of AA syllogisms differed over the four figures. Fig. 5.3 illustrates the conclusions consistent with the figures. Note that only one conclusion follows from the identity–identity interpretation over all figures. When subjects were given Euler circles representing the different AA premise interpretations, their drawn Euler circle conclusions were generally consistent with the premises and showed reliable (and different) distributions over the possible conclusions for the four argument figures.

On the basis of (a) the estimated proportions of subjects making identity–identity and inclusion–inclusion interpretations, and (b) the estimated proportion that would produce each alternative conclusion from each premise–premise interpretation, Erickson was able accurately to predict the proportion of subjects that would draw each of the possible conclusions (A, E, I, O) to AA syllogisms in the four figures. The data from five independent studies were fitted very well by predictions based on the above analyses. Thus, there is a good measure of support for Erickson's model, which proposes a three-stage process of: (1) premise interpretation, (2) combination of interpreted premises to yield a conclusion, and (3) response formation depending on the conclusion and on the task demands (e.g. draw a diagram, give a verbal statement, select one from a list of alternatives, etc.). This analysis is quite consistent with Ceraso and Provitera's (1971) results, which showed that disambiguated premises improved performance. Erickson's three-stage model would explain Ceraso and Provitera's results by assuming that correct interpretations at stage 1 were made more likely by the clarified premises.

Table 5.1 *Possible syllogistic figures*

Figure I	Figure II	Figure III	Figure IV
M–P	P–M	M–P	P–M
S–M	S–M	M–S	M–S
S–P	S–P	S–P	S–P

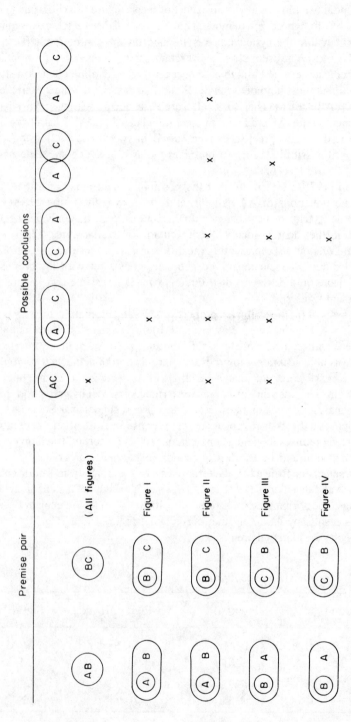

Fig. 5.3 *Conclusions consistent with set identity and set inclusion interpretations of two universal affirmative premises. The consistent conclusions are marked 'X' for each syllogistic figure. Reproduced with permission from Erickson, J.R. (1978). Models of formal reasoning in R. Revlin and R. Mayer (Eds), Human reasoning p. 43. Washington, DC: V.H. Winston.*

2 The transitive-chain model

Guyote and Sternberg (1981) have proposed a rather complex model, which, like Erickson's (1978), assumes that subjects represent premises in set-theoretic terms. They draw a distinction between a 'competence model' and a 'performance model' of syllogistic reasoning. This is akin to the competence–performance distinction in psycholinguistic theory. In psycholinguistics, 'competence' is the ability possessed by an idealized speaker of a language, which, for example, permits that speaker to class sentences as grammatically acceptable or not; a performance model details why actual performance falls short of ideal performance, e.g. why spoken language is not always grammatically correct. Usually, constraints on processing, such as limited working memory, are invoked to explain departures from ideal competence. Similarly, Guyote and Sternberg (1981) first presented an idealized competence model which would allow perfect performance on syllogistic tasks, and then detailed constraints on performance.

According to the competence model, subjects carry out two main steps when presented with premises and with a list of alternative conclusions from which one must be selected. The two main steps are: (a) encoding the premises, and (b) combining information in the premises.

In the encoding stage the category relationships between the terms in each premise are represented symbolically. Each possible interpretation of the two premises is made and given corresponding symbolic representations. Thus, unlike Erickson (1978) or Ceraso and Provitera (1971), it is assumed that *all* possible interpretations are made. *All* combinations of the possible interpretations of the two premises are then considered, to determine what conclusions may follow. Note that since two premises of form 'I' each have four possible interpretations, 16 combinations would have to be considered in such a case. The combination rules attempt to form 'transitive chains' linking the 'end' terms (subject and predicate) via the middle term of the syllogism.

The performance model involves stages of (a) encoding the premises, (b) combining information from the premises, (c) selecting a label to describe the combined representations (where the label is one of the four traditional statements, A, I, E, O or 'no valid conclusion'), and (d) making a response on the basis of a match between the label and the conclusions offered for evaluation. The performance model assumes that the encoding stage is carried out completely and without error. In the combination stage it is assumed that errors can creep in because subjects are limited in the number of pairs of representations that they encode. It is assumed that the subject always combines at least one pair of representations but never more than four pairs (due to working memory limitations). The subject's choice of pairs to combine is based on simplicity. Simpler pairs are dealt with in preference to those involving more complex representation. In choosing a label for the combined representations, which represent possible inferences, subjects are assumed to be biased to 'strong' labels and to labels that match the 'atmosphere' of the premises [as defined by Begg and Denny (1969)]. The 'stronger' the label, the less ambiguous is its interpretation in set-inclusion terms. Thus, the labels in order of strength are E, A, O, and I.

To test their complex performance model, Guyote and Sternberg (1981) first expressed the model in mathematical terms and then assessed its fit to data from five studies. These studies involved a wide range of syllogistic problems, varying in both form and content. The mathematical model required five parameters to be estimated from the data, but once these were obtained it yielded a good fit to percentage correct scores and latencies over the problems used in the five studies. Indeed, their model gave better fits to the data than did mathematical versions of Erickson's model (1974, 1978), although these had more parameters than that of Guyote and Sternberg (1981).

Despite good overall fits to data, the model suffers from the inherent implausibility of its assumptions regarding complete encoding [which are countered empirically by Ceraso and Provitera (1971)]. Furthermore, as Johnson-Laird (1983) has pointed out, the model makes it impossible for subjects to reason, with understanding, when more than four premise combinations need to be considered before a correct conclusion can be drawn. Also, as is explained in the next section, there are certain effects ('figural effects') that this and other set-theory based models cannot explain.

Finally, it is worth noting an incidental observation of Guyote and Sternberg (1981) that subjects' scores on a test of spatial ability correlated considerably better with syllogistic reasoning performance than did scores on verbal ability. This suggests that some form of spatial representation is used in syllogistic reasoning (but, as the next section indicates, it may not be in the form of 'mental Euler circles').

C. Mental model approaches

1 Figural bias, figural difficulty and origins of the mental model approach

A series of studies by Johnson-Laird and colleagues (Johnson-Laird, 1975; Johnson-Laird and Steedman, 1978) has revealed an interesting effect due to the figure of the syllogism, and this effect can be accounted for by models of syllogistic inference developed by Johnson-Laird. In the experiments in question, subjects had to draw conclusions from syllogistic premises dealing with concrete but uncontroversial matters, e.g. 'Some of the parents are scientists; all of the scientists are drivers; therefore . . .?' This particular form of syllogism, in which the subject term has not been specified and conclusions are to be drawn rather than chosen from a list, tended to elicit the conclusion 'Some of the parents are drivers' rather than the equally valid 'Some of the drivers are parents'. On the other hand, the premises 'Some of the scientists are parents; all of the drivers are scientists' would tend to elicit the conclusion 'Some of the drivers are parents' rather than the also valid 'Some of the parents are drivers'. Indeed, throughout their experiments premises of the form 'A–B; B–C' (i.e. conventionally figure IV in Fig. 5.3, with C assumed to be the subject-term) produced a bias towards conclusions of the form 'A–C' (even if 'C–A' conclusions were also valid).

This strong effect, dubbed the *figural bias* effect, had not been noticed hitherto, perhaps because of the widespread use of forced choice-testing formats that would not include the unorthodox (from the classical point of view) conclusion 'A–C' to the 'A–B; B–C' syllogism. This conclusion is unorthodox because it has taken the first premise as relating subject to middle term, while, traditionally, the first premise has related predicate to middle term. Johnson-Laird pointed out that traditionally 64 'moods' of syllogism were recognized since the two premises and the conclusion have to be chosen from the four sentence moods (A, E, I, O) giving $4^3 = 64$ possibilities. Combining the 64 moods with the four figures (explained in a previous section) yields $64 \times 4 = 256$ different syllogistic structures. While this number had been taken for granted by psychologists, Johnson-Laird observed that one could in fact generate twice as many. Logicians had decided to arrange their syllogisms so that the subject of the conclusion always appeared in the second premise, but the logic of the argument is not really affected if the subject term (S) happens to appear in the first premise, as in

S–M
M–P
___
S–P
cf. traditional figure I,
M–P
S–M
___
S–P

It seems that failure to consider all 512 possible syllogisms led to the figural bias effect remaining undiscovered until recently. However, it may be noted that Dickstein (1978), in a careful study which took into account of confounding factors such as premise moods and validity, found that conventional figure IV syllogisms were markedly harder than conventional figure I syllogisms using a standard multiple choice response procedure. Thus there is a *figural difficulty* effect with multiple choice responses which Dickstein interpreted in terms of the relative ease of forward working from S to P in figure I as against the need to work backwards from P to S and convert in the case of figure IV.

Strikingly, the figural bias effect is not predicted by previous approaches. The atmosphere hypothesis, the conversion and probabilistic inference hypothesis, Erickson's or Guyote and Sternberg's set-theoretic approaches are alike in failing to predict any effect of figure on preferred conclusion direction when no topic has been specified in advance. In view of this and other problems with the earlier approaches, Johnson-Laird and Steedman (1978) put forward a theory for syllogistic reasoning, initially known as the *analogical* theory and later as *mental models* theory. [A preliminary version was reported by Johnson-Laird (1975).]

2 The analogical model

The broad stages proposed by the theory are mostly similar to those suggested by other analyses (e.g. Erickson, 1978). They are: (1) interpretation of premises; (2) an initial *heuristic* combination of the representations of the two premises; (3) the formulation of a conclusion corresponding to the combination of premises; and (4) a *logical test* (or series of tests) of the initial heuristic combination which may lead to the conclusion being modified or abandoned. In terms of broad stages, the main novelty is the provision of a final testing stage that can lead back to a changed combination of information in the premises, which in turn may be tested again. In terms of detail, an explicit information-processing model was developed that incorporated a number of distinctive ideas.

First, the premise representations are assumed to take the form of list structures. A clue to the possible use of list-structure representations in this task came from one of the subject's retrospections on how he had tackled the syllogisms. In connection with the premise "All the artists are beekeepers", he reported, "I thought of all the little artists in the room and imagined that they all had beekeepers' hats on" (Johnson-Laird and Steedman, 1978, p. 77). This remark suggested the hypothesis that a class is represented by thinking of an arbitrary number of examples. So, to represent the above premise, the reasoner imagines an arbitrary number of artists and tags each of them as a beekeeper. Since the sets are not identical one should add an arbitrary number of beekeepers not linked to artists to the representation. The elements in the representation may be images, or verbal or abstract items; the important feature is the relationship between the elements, rather than their exact nature. The structure of the representation of the current example may be taken to have the form:

artist   artist   artist

↓   ↓   ↓

beekeeper   beekeeper   beekeeper   (beekeeper)

(The arrows represent the relationships 'is a'.) It is asserted that this representation is structurally analogous to what reasoners think when they understand the sentence "All artists are beekeepers". The proposed representation is a list-structure and this has the advantage of being readily encodable in computer programming. In list-structure terms, each entry on the artist list has stored with it the address of a corresponding beekeeper on the beekeeper list and there are entries on the beekeeper list that are not connected to entries on the artist list. It is notable that such list-structure notions were also found useful by Simon and Hayes (1976) in their analysis of problem comprehension, discussed in Chapter 3.

Having fixed on a representation of the individual premises, the next step is to combine them in some way. Johnson-Laird proposed that there is a heuristic bias towards forming connections that link up all the classes if possible. So, given:

All A are B   a   a

                ↓   ↓

                b   b   (b)

and
Some B and C   b   (b)

                     ↓

                     c   (c)

these would be combined to yield the structure:

a   a

↓   ↓

b   b   (b)

↓

c   (c)

This structure readily suggests the invalid conclusion 'Some a's are c's', (this conclusion is often erroneously made). To draw a conclusion the paths between end-terms must be considered. Taking the structure resulting from the initial combination of 'All A are B' and 'Some B are C' the paths would be labelled:

+   ?

a   a

↓   ↓

b   b   (b)

↓

c   (c)

One path is positive and one indeterminate. (Negative paths can arise if the negative operators 'no' and 'not' occur in the premises. For the sake of simplicity negatives will not be considered here.) The path labelling of the above structure would lead to the (erroneous) conclusion 'some a are c', in accordance with the principle that "where there is at least one positive path the conclusion is of the form 'some X are Y', unless there are only positive paths in which case it is of the form 'all X are Y; in any other case no valid conclusion can be drawn". To avoid invalid conclusions, it is proposed that logical tests are applied to the combined representation in an attempt to remove links between end-items without damaging the correctness of the individual premise interpretations. In the example, "All the artists are beekeepers. Some of the beekeepers are chemists", the initial combined representation has an artist tagged as a beekeeper, who in turn is tagged as a chemist. This particular beekeeper–chemist linkage can be broken without losing the initial meaning. The modified representation would not include any artist positively linked to any chemist. No conclusion could be drawn and the final overt answer would correctly so indicate.

The analogical theory, then, proposes a heuristic combination of premises to yield a tentative conclusion, followed by a logical testing process. Differences in persistence of testing preliminary conclusions could well lead to differences in the conclusions finally drawn by different individuals to the same premises.

The theory was expressed in the form of a computer program and its performance compared with that of human subjects on a set of 64 problems. With some syllogisms the process of testing does not lead to any modifications (hence thoroughness of testing does not matter). Such syllogisms were predicted to be easier than those to which the model would produce a modified conclusion after testing. This prediction was upheld (80.4 per cent correct on predicted 'easy' problems v. 46.5 per cent correct on others). Also, the model predicts the figural bias effect because the directionality of the linkages in the figures in question leads naturally to the particular ordering of terms most often observed in subjects' conclusions. Further support for the theory comes from responses to those premises that do not permit a valid conclusion to be drawn. Invalid syllogisms in figures I and IV, in which it is easy to form paths in the initial representation, are predicted to be more difficult than invalid syllogisms in the other figures. The predicted difference was upheld by 18 of 20 subjects.

Although the original analogical model was more successful than previous analyses in coping with a wide range of results in syllogistic reasoning, later data, reported in the next section, caused the analogical model to be revised considerably.

3 Figural bias: a process explanation?

Johnson-Laird and Steedman's (1978) analogical model explained figural bias as arising from biases in scanning the structures representing the combined premises. Another possibility, which was mentioned in passing in the 1978 paper, is that the figural effect arises from the process of *combining* the premise representations in working memory. That is, with the A–B, B–C premises subjects can encode the first premise and then add on to it a representation of the second premise (A–B, B–C) with a resulting bias toward a conclusion of the form A–C. In the case of B–A, C–B premises, since the middle terms are not adjacent, it would be necessary to store the second premise in working memory first, then encode the first premise to make the combination (C–B, B–A), giving a bias toward C–A conclusions.

Johnson-Laird and Bara (1984) obtained relevant data from an experiment concerning conclusions given to syllogisms that were presented for brief exposures (10 seconds). Even with this short exposure there were clear figural effects; more significantly, however, there were unpredicted effects, due to figure, on the frequency of responses indicating 'no valid conclusion'. The A–B, B–C figure yielded the fewest such responses and the B–A, B–C figure produced the most. This result cannot be explained by Johnson-Laird and Steedman's (1978) analogical model, and so Johnson-Laird and Bara (1984) proposed that the figural effect reflects the process of integrating premises within working memory. With short presentations subjects experience difficulty in effecting combinations of premises in certain figures (such as B–A, B–C, in which re-ordering of premise models is needed to effect premise integration) and thus have a high rate of (incorrect) conclusions that 'no conclusion can be drawn'.

It has also been pointed out (Johnson-Laird, 1983; Johnson-Laird and Bara, 1984) that for certain syllogisms two or three combined models of the premises are possible and that all the possible models must be considered before a correct conclusion can be drawn. Johnson-Laird (1983, p. 104) reported data from studies which find that the rate of drawing correct conclusions declined sharply as the number of possible combined models increased from one to three. Johnson-Laird (1983) proposed that these results are due to the load on working memory occasioned when more than one model must be constructed and evaluated. Using dual task methods, Gilhooly *et al.* (1993) found support for the general notion that syllogisms load working memory, particularly the central executive and phonological loop components of the Baddeley–Hitch working memory model (Baddeley, 1992; see also Chapter 1 for an outline of working memory theory). However Gilhooly *et al.* (1993) did not directly address the issue of whether multiple-model syllogisms impose a greater load on working memory than single-model syllogisms.

4 A note on notation

The notation used to express the mental models theory has changed at least three times (Johnson-Laird and Steedman, 1978; Johnson-Laird and Bara, 1984; Johnson-Laird and Byrne, 1991, 1993). The changes are illustrated in Table 5.2, which shows three mental models representations for the four syllogistic statements. The changes from Johnson-Laird and Steedman (1978) to Johnson-Laird and Bara (1984) made spatial aspects of the representation more salient and gave spatial representations to both 'is a' and 'is not'. This second notation also made it easier to represent the differences in premise integration processes dependent on figure, in terms of spatial reorganization. The changes between Johnson-Laird and Bara and Johnson-Laird and Byrne made the representation of '*exhaustiveness*' explicit, where before it had been implicit. The implicit existence of other possible individuals not explicitly represented is also indicated in the third notation. The Johnson-Laird and Byrne notation facilitates extension of the approach to tasks other than the syllogism. The initial simplicity of a subject's introspection about imagining little artists with beekeepers' hats on has been left far behind!

5 Mental models and syllogisms: criticisms

Mental models theory is continually evolving in both notation and substance, and has been extended to a wide range of reasoning tasks (Johnson-Laird and Byrne, 1991, 1993). The frequent changes in the theory make it difficult to pin down and evaluate. Although it is surely an impressive exercise in model building, some possible problems have been pointed out by a range of critics. For example,

Table 5.2 *Mental models representations of four syllogistic statements*

Syllogistic statement	Johnson-Laird and Steedman (1978)		Johnson-Laird and Bara (1984)		Johnson-Laird and Byrne (1991)	
(A) All A are B	a	a	a = b		[a]	b
	↓	↓				
	b	b (b)	a = b		[a]	b
			Ob		...	
(I) Some A are B	a (a)		a = b		a	b
	↓		Oa	Ob	a	b
	b (b)				...	
(O) Some A are not B	a	a	a		a	
	⊥	↓	a		a	
			———————		a	
	b	(b)	Oa	y	[b]	
				y	[b]	
					...	
(E) No A are B	a	a	a			
	⊥	↓	a		[a]	
			———————		[a]	
	b	b		y		
				y	[b]	
					[b]	
					...	

Notes:	Each column is a possible individual.	Each row is a possible individual.	Each row is a possible individual.
	(b) means b may or may not exist.	Ob means b may or may not exist.	'...' means there may be other types of individual not represented.
	↓ means 'is a'	= means 'is a'	
	⊥ means 'is not'	A line is a barrier representing a negative 'is not' relationship.	[a] indicates that a is exhaustively represented in the model, so that all a's have the same relation to b as do the explicitly represented individuals.

Wetherick and Gilhooly (1990, 1995) and Ford (1995) have indicated other possible explanations of figural bias and of the number-of-models effect on difficulty.

Figural bias may simply be due to subjects picking as the topic of the argument the first end-term which is the topic of its premise. If the topic of the argument is not specified (which it would be in a real argument), the subject has an ambiguous situation and would seem justified in resolving it in accord with the normal rhetorical practice that the topic is mentioned first and then commented on.

The apparent effect of multiple models may be due to application of a simple heuristic known as 'matching' whereby subjects take as conclusion the quantifier that makes the smallest positive commitment of those in the premises. This predicts a preference order of E over O, O over I, and I over A. By examining detailed response patterns in a multiple choice presentation, Wetherick and Gilhooly (1990) found that a majority of subjects followed this matching strategy (with a smaller group making more logically sanctioned choices) Similar patterns were found by Gilhooly *et al.* (1993) and were also noted by Rips (1994, p. 246) in a re-analysis of the results of Johnson-Laird and Bara (1984). It turns out that single-model syllogisms can be solved correctly by matching but that multiple-model syllogisms cannot. Thus, the apparent effect of multiple models on difficulty may be due to use of a matching heuristic rather than to mental model strategies being followed.

The mental models approach to syllogisms assumes that all subjects approach the task in the same way and no explicit mechanisms of change or improvement are provided. However, in any large sample of subjects, some will get most syllogisms correct, a few will be at guessing level and the remainder will be shown the typical variations in item difficulty discussed here and addressed by the mental models approach. Galotti *et al.* (1986) found that subjects classed on a pre-test as 'good reasoners' (but who had no training in formal logic) either used or quickly developed short-cut rules that would preclude laborious exploration of multiple model possibilities. For example, better subjects used the rules that two particular premises could only yield no valid conclusion and similarly that two negative premises must give no valid conclusion. Ford (1995), in a detailed study using concurrent verbal and written protocols, found that her sample of 20 subjects divided clearly into a group that used primarily verbal rules and representations and a group that used spatial representations akin to Euler circles supplemented by a verbal representation. Both groups solved at about the same level as each other and displayed similar patterns of difficulty over syllogisms, as reported by Johnson-Laird and Bara (1984), but showed little or no sign of using representations similar to those postulated by mental models theory.

II. SUMMARY AND CONCLUDING COMMENTS

From the evidence reviewed in this chapter, what answer can be given to the often raised question, "Do people think logically?"? If the criterion of logical thinking is reaching conclusions consistent with those of formal logic, then one must answer that people are not always logical reasoners. They do make errors. Indeed, according to one authority (Erickson, 1978, p. 41), 'in fact, for most syllogisms the modal response is incorrect". However, the errors do not appear to be random and various suggestions have been made regarding the processes underlying both errors and correct responses.

A proposal of completely non-logical processing is embodied in the atmosphere hypothesis. This hypothesis is consistent with many typical responses to syllogistic tasks; however, it is 'over-inclusive' and is thus consistent with many possibilities that tend not to happen. Furthermore, it does not cope well with fine-grain effects, such as the figural bias effect or the often correct choice of 'no conclusion' by subjects. The atmosphere hypothesis always predicts that some conclusion can be drawn, but, at least some of the time, people can appreciate that certain syllogisms are inconclusive. An alternative proposal is that various 'illogical' processes which have some plausibility may jointly produce many errors. In particular, illicit conversion of premises and probabilistic inference have been proposed by Chapman and Chapman (1959). However, the empirical evidence distinguishing this suggestion from the atmosphere hypothesis is not strong (Begg and Denny, 1969). Again, the figural bias effect and many fine-grain features of reasoning data are not dealt with by this hypothesis.

Henle (1962) put forward the influential view that people do reason logically, but frequently misinterpret the premises or the task demands, thus producing overt errors. Indeed, Henle (1978, p. xviii) has gone so far as to say, "I have never found errors which could unambiguously be attributed to faulty reasoning". Unfortunately, this may reflect the difficulty, in principle, of obtaining falsifying evidence for the Henle position. No matter what response is given, a suitable interpretation of the premises (or task) can be inferred to make the response seem 'logical'. Clearly, some independent check on premise and task interpretation is required when considering individual examples. However, most research has involved the more indirect methods of group analysis. For example, Ceraso and Provitera (1971) showed that clarified, unambiguous premises led to many fewer errors than traditional ambiguous premises. This is consistent with the Henle position. Erickson (1974, 1978) proposed a specific form of 'Henle' model in which premise interpretation was assumed to take the form of mental Euler circles. Using the proportions of people in one group who interpreted universal affirmative (A) statements as set identity and as set inclusion, he was able to predict the obtained proportions of alternative conclusions to AA syllogisms, in the four different figures, for independent groups of subjects. Again, this result is consistent with the Henle approach. A stronger test would have been to compare the inferences of subjects classed as 'set-identity interpreters' with those of subjects classed as 'set-inclusion interpreters' of AA premises.

Guyote and Sternberg (1981) presented a more wide-ranging theory than Erickson's but which was also based on the notion of mental Euler diagrams. Complete and error-free premise interpretation was assumed. However, subjects were assumed to be constrained by working memory limits when combining premise interpretations; these limits were taken to underlie the relative difficulty of syllogisms. Although Guyote and Sternberg's 'transitive chain theory' predicted performance well over a wide range of syllogisms, its assumptions of complete and perfect premise interpretation are implausible; furthermore, the theory cannot explain figural bias effects.

An alternative proposal is contained in Johnson-Laird's (1975, 1983; Johnson-Laird and Steedman, 1978; Johnson-Laird and Bara, 1984; Johnson-Laird and Byrne, 1991, 1993) analysis reasoning in terms of mental models. In the 1984 model most of the individual variability in reasoning behaviour is not attributed to differences in the premise interpretation stage but to different degrees of thoroughness in constructing possible models of premise combinations. Differences in syllogism difficulty are explained in terms of the number of models required to represent the premise combinations. Figural bias effects are explained in terms of preferred ways of combining premise representations. Although Johnson-Laird's mental model theory is the most comprehensive current approach to syllogistic reasoning, it has been subject to numerous criticisms including lack of specificity in determining number of models per syllogism (Garnham, 1993), over-complexity and lack of concordance with verbal reports of problem-solving processes (Ford, 1995; Wetherick, 1993) and lack of allowance for individual differences in strategies (Galotti et al., 1986; Ford, 1995).

How might syllogistic reasoning relate to the processes of problem solving discussed in earlier chapters? On the surface, syllogistic tasks are well defined and appear to require but one 'move' from a given starting state (the premises) to a goal state (a valid conclusion). However, from the review in this chapter, a variety of processes seems to be involved. First, as in all problems, the starting state has to be defined by the subject. In dealing with syllogisms, this is the process of premise interpretation. Since premises are frequently ambiguous, alternative interpretations are often possible, although it would appear that only one interpretation is considered at a time, i.e. a serial search among interpretation possibilities is undertaken. Indeed, it often seems that only one interpretation is derived (Erickson, 1974). Once an interpretation of the premises has been made, by using general procedures, presumably stored in long-term memory, more than one conclusion might often be drawn (e.g. 'strong' or 'weak' conclusions). According to Johnson-Laird's (1983) analysis, it seems that rather lax 'evaluation functions' are often used to determine whether a possible conclusion is valid or not. There seems to be a tendency to accept conclusions that are consistent with the premises, but which are not required by them. To the extent that there is a search among alternative conclusions, it seems to be a serial search. Frequently, however, it seems that, if the first conclusion drawn is acceptable to the subject, then alternatives are not generated.

There is nothing in the syllogistic reasoning data to counter the view that, when problem solving, we work as limited-capacity, slow, serial processors of information. Indeed, recent analyses (Johnson-Laird, 1993; Rips, 1994) have particularly stressed the role of working memory limitations in syllogistic reasoning, and such limitations have been demonstrated empirically by means of dual-task studies (Gilhooly et al., 1993).

III. FURTHER READING

Henle, M. (1962). On the relation between logic and thinking. *Psychological Review*, **69**, 366–378. This very readable paper contains Mary Henle's classic statement in defence of human rationality. Much later research can be seen as amplifying or reacting against her position.

Johnson-Laird, P.N. and Byrne, R. (1993). Precis of "Deduction". *Behavioral and Brain Sciences*, **16**, 323–380 (and ensuing commentaries and rejoinder). This is a good summary of recent developments in the mental models approach coupled with a lively debate between critics of the approach and Johnson-Laird and Byrne.

Rips, L.J. (1994). *The psychology of proof: deductive reasoning in human thinking*. MIT Press: Cambridge, MA. Rips provides a thorough exposition of his influential mental logic approach to reasoning.

6

Deductive reasoning 2: Propositional reasoning

I. PROPOSITIONAL LOGIC

Propositional logic concerns arguments consisting of sequences of simple statements linked by connectives such as *and*, *or*, *not* and *if . . . then* to form compound statements; for example, "Either the Minister did not hear the question or she is reluctant to take a stand. She did hear the question. Therefore she must be reluctant to take a stand." Analysis of such arguments seems to have begun among stoic and megarian philosophers at about the same time (*c.* 350 BC) as Aristotle was developing the logic of categorical reasoning (Nidditch, 1962). For generality, simple statements may be represented by letters, **p**, **q**, **r**, etc., and so typical propositional arguments would be as follows:

(1) If **p** then **q**; **p**; therefore, **q**.
(2) If **p** then **q**; not-**q**; therefore, not-**p**.
(3) Not (**p** and **q**); **p**; therefore, not-**q**.
(4) (**p** or **q**) and (not (**p** and **q**)); **p**; therefore, not-**q**.

Propositional logic has become highly formalized into alternative propositional calculi. These calculi divide into two broad groups: *proof-theoretic* and *model-theoretic*. Within each group of calculi, alternative formalizations have been developed. Proof-theoretic approaches divide into *axiomatic* and *natural deduction systems*. The axiomatic approach is mainly of mathematical–logical interest and seeks the minimum number of axioms (unproven assumptions) and operators from which all else can be derived. For example, with just one operator, '|', which takes two terms (say, **p** and **q**) and can be defined as 'not both **p** and **q**', the whole propositional calculus can be derived [see Garnham and Oakhill (1994), for further details].

The '|' or stroke operator is not particularly intuitive; in contrast, natural deduction systems make use of inference rules, many of which are intuitively appealing. Given the inference rules, proofs of theorems can be derived from given assumptions by repeated applications of the rules. A few typical inference rules are as follows:

Modus Ponens: if **p** then **q**; **p**; therefore **q**.
Modus Tollens: if **p** then **q**; not-**q**; therefore, not-**p**.
Double negation: not (not-**p**); therefore, **p**.

Proofs are often facilitated by the method of *Reductio ad Absurdum*. In this method, if **p** is to be proved, assume not-**p** is true; if that assumption leads to a contradiction (e.g. **q** and not-**q**), then not-**p** must be false and hence **p** is true. Natural deduction systems suggest plausible models for human reasoning and have been inspirational for mental logic theorists (Braine *et al.*, 1984 Braine, 1990; O'Brien, 1993; Rips, 1994), who propose that humans have an intuitive grasp of at least some inference rules and an ability to apply rules sequentially to prove or disprove claimed consequences from premises.

Finally, *model-theoretic* or *truth-table* approaches to proof define the basic operators in terms of truth tables which show how the truth value (T, true, or F, false) of an operator varies with the truth values of the component statements. Example truth tables are as follows:

p	and	q
T	T	T
T	F	F
F	F	T
F	F	F

p	implies	q
T	T	T
T	F	F
F	T	T
F	T	F

p	or	q
T	T	T
T	T	F
F	T	T
F	F	F

To assess a composite argument, the truth table for the premises and conclusion is drawn up. If the conclusion is always true when the premises are true, then the argument is valid. For example, consider the following argument (Copi, 1954): "If I work then I earn money, and if I don't work then I enjoy myself. Therefore, if I don't earn money then I enjoy myself." Is this a valid argument or not? To apply the truth table method it will help to symbolize the components of the argument as 'W' = 'I work', 'M' = 'I earn money' and 'E' = 'I enjoy myself', '→'= 'implies'.

W	M	E	(W → M)	(not-W → E)	(not-M → E)
T	T	T	T	T	T
T	T	F	T	T	T
T	F	T	F	T	T

T	F	F	F	T	F
F	T	T	T	T	T
F	T	F	T	F	T
F	F	T	T	T	T
F	F	F	T	F	F

From the truth table above, whenever the premises are both true (rows 1, 2, 5 and 7), the conclusion is also true and so the argument is valid.

This truth-table approach provides a normative analogy for the mental model-based explanation of human reasoning [e.g. Johnson-Laird (1983), discussed in Chapter 5 on syllogisms), which proposes that subjects consider alternative models of the world in which the premises are true (corresponding to key rows of the truth table) and determine whether the conclusion is also true in all such worlds (Evans *et al.*, 1993, p. 22).

II. PSYCHOLOGICAL STUDIES

A. Conditionals

The conditional 'if . . . then' has attracted a considerable volume of research in the psychological study of reasoning. While the conditional can be clearly defined in the context of formal logic by means of truth tables, the meaning of 'if . . . then' in everyday usage is quite variable, and this variety of meanings may underlie some of the departures between subjects' performance in conditional reasoning tasks and predictions from logic. Varying interpretations of the conditional in reasoning tasks may produce non-normative performance.

1 Conditional rules in propositional logic

Conditional rules are of the abstract form, 'if **p**, then **q**', and are also known as 'implication' rules. In propositional logic there are two main valid inference patterns involving such rules (viz. Modus Ponens and Modus Tollens) and two main fallacies (viz. Affirming the Consequent and Denying the Antecedent). These are shown in Table 6.1. (Note that a tilde (˜) means 'not', so that ˜**q** is to be read as 'not-**q**'.)

Another way of thinking about the implication rule is to consider how its truth or falsity varies as a function of the truth of the component terms. The two terms in the rule can be independently true or false, yielding four combinations. The status of the rule given these combinations is represented in Table 6.2, which shows the 'truth table' for implication.

A different form of implication is the 'if and only if' rule of equivalence (also known as a '*biconditional*'). In the case of equivalence, from '**q** if and only if **p**', one can validly assert '**p**' given '**q**' (Affirming the Consequent) and 'not-**q**' given 'not-**p**' (Denying the Antecedent). Misinterpretations of material implication as equivalence

Table 6.1 *Valid and fallacious inference based on implication*

Valid inferences			Fallacious inferences		
1. (Modus Ponens)	If **p** then **q**		1. (Denying the Antecedent)	If **p** then **q**	
	p			~**p**	
	∴ **q**			∴ ~**q**	
2. (Modus Tollens)	If **p** then **q**		2. (Affirming the Consequent)	If **p** then **q**	
	~**q**			**q**	
	∴ ~**p**			∴ **p**	

and vice versa are possible sources of error in conditional reasoning.

2 Everyday usages of the conditional

The truth-table definition of implication states that if the antecedent is false the implication is always true. Thus, 'if it is day then it is night' is true at night but is false in the day, and 'if three is an even number then the moon is square' is always true. Rules with always-false antecedents are of little use in real life and are generally be seen as 'irrelevant' rather than true (Johnson-Laird and Tagart, 1969). Normal usage then departs from the strict two-valued logic of true *v.* false and allows the third option of 'irrelevant'. A further divergence of ordinary usage from the artificially simple truth-functional definitions of implication and equivalence is that natural 'if . . . then' statements usually have definitional, causal, temporal, contractual or deontic (i.e. regarding permissions and obligations) meanings that permit or invite additional inferences. We rarely deal with arbitrary pairings of statements (e.g. 'if it is snowing then it is 4 pm') outside of logic exercises. We are more likely to deal with causal statements such as 'if acid is spilled on the table it will stain', temporal statements such as 'if it is 4 pm, the train will leave', definitional statements such as

Table 6.2 *Truth table for implication*

p	→	**q**
T	T	T
T	F	F
F	T	T
F	T	T

T = true; F = false; → = 'implies' of 'if . . . then'.

'if a figure has three sides it is a triangle', contractual statements such as 'if you cut the grass, I will give you a cold beer' or permission statements such as 'If you are 18 years old, you may legally purchase alcohol in the UK'. If, as is plausible, subjects interpret conditionals in reasoning tasks as having one or other of the extra overtones present in normal conditional usage, departures from the truth-functional pattern may be expected.

3 Basic results

Conditional inferences   A number of studies have examined performance with abstract or concrete but arbitrary conditionals (e.g. 'if there is an A then there is a 7' or 'if it is Wednesday then Mr Jones eats fish'). Subjects have been asked to say whether each of the four possible arguments – Modus Tollens (MT), Modus Ponens (MP), Affirming the Consequent (AC) and Denying the Antecedent (DA) – are valid for such arguments. Summarizing over a range of studies (e.g. Taplin, 1971; Evans, 1977; Marcus and Rips, 1979; Rumain *et al.*, 1983; Markovits, 1988), subjects typically perform with near 100 per cent accuracy in the case of MP, about 60 per cent correct on MT and about 50 per cent correct on the two fallacies (in terms of material implication), AC and DA.

Suppression effects   It has been suggested that apparent fallacies in conditional reasoning may arise from misinterpretation of the premises (Rumain *et al.*, 1983). For example, from the premise, 'If there is a dog in the box, then there is an orange in the box', subjects may assume this also means, 'If there is not a dog in the box then there is not an orange in the box'. From this extended interpretation, conclusions that are fallacies on the official narrower interpretation follow validly; so, 'there is not a dog' implies there is not an orange and 'there is an orange' implies there is a dog, on the extended interpretation.

Rumain and co-workers found that additional alternative antecedents, such as 'If there is a tiger in the box then there is an orange in the box', block such misinterpretations and so suppress the fallacies of AC and DA. The rates of valid conclusions, MP, and MT were not affected.

Interestingly, additional antecedents have also been found to block valid inferences of MP and MT (Byrne, 1989). Byrne used pairs of conditional statements in which the second statement was an additional condition; for example:

If she meets her friend then she will go to a play.
If she has enough money then she will go to a play.

When subjects were given as true that 'She meets her friend', the rate of correct MP conclusions was far lower than with the single conditional premise. Similarly, when given as true that 'she did not go to the play', the rate of valid MT conclusions also dropped sharply. The rates of the fallacies DA and AC were not affected. It appears that the additional premises are interpreted as forming a conjunctive condition ('If she meets her friend and she has enough money then she will go to the play'). Thus, as with the case of alternative conditions (Rumain *et al.*, 1983) the interpretational aspect is crucial (Fillenbaum, 1993).

B. Extended arguments

1 Early results

Thus far we have focused on simple conditional arguments with few premises from which a conclusion could be reached by application of a single rule. In extended arguments a long sequence of rules may be required to establish whether a given conclusion follows or not. For example, does it follow from 'If there is not both an M and a P on the blackboard then there is an R' that 'If there is no M, then there is an R' (Rips, 1983)?.

Early studies of such tasks were carried out by Moore and Anderson (1954a,b). However, Moore and Anderson presented the tasks as ones of '*recoding*' in which certain symbol strings were to be recoded into others using given rules to transform or rewrite strings. Subjects had a sheet of paper with 12 rules for manipulating symbolic expressions containing letters connected by dots (.), wedges (v), horse-shoes ($\supset$) and tildes (˜). These symbols stand for 'and', 'or', 'implies' and 'not' respectively in symbolic logic, but subjects were not told of the correspondence. The recoding or rewriting rules corresponded to rules of symbolic logic, e.g. 'A implies B → ˜B implies ˜A', meaning that 'A implies B' can be rewritten or recoded as 'not-B implies not-A'. Equipped with the rewriting rules, subjects were given recoding tasks (equivalent to proof tasks), such as moving by a sequence of recodings from (R implies ˜P).(˜R implies Q) to ˜(˜Q.P).

Newell and Simon (1972) applied their GPS model (see Chapter 2 for intro-duction to GPS) to extended arguments, using Moore and Anderson's results as data to compare with the model. GPS solves by selective goal-driven search, guided by means–ends analysis. Along the way, sub-goals of reducing differences between the current state and the goal state are set up. Where possible, problems are reduced into manageable sub-problems. Overall, the GPS model matched the general shape of human performance in the Moore–Anderson task, indicating that subjects carried out a selective problem reduction-oriented search for paths from the starting state (the premises) to the goal state (the conclusion). Newell *et al.* (1958) had earlier developed the Logic Theorist (LT) program specifically for logical proof problems, and GPS was a generalization of LT. Newell *et al.*'s task analysis of proof problems showed clearly that selective search was essential in this domain as the number of possible rules that could be applied at any stage was usually large, resulting in an exponentially growing tree of possible problem states. Thus a simple exhaustive forward search would not be a feasible way to solve proof problems of any length. GPS (and LT) adopt heuristic approaches, which often solve with little search but are not guaranteed to solve. In mathematical logic various practical algorithmic methods have been devised which will prove a conclusion, if it follows, from given premises.

However, these methods are not intuitive and do not suggest plausible models for human reasoning (e.g. resolution theorem proving; Robinson, 1965).

It may be that the Moore–Anderson data are misleading in that the logical nature of the task was not made clear to the subjects. More recent studies have used data from subjects attempting to prove or disprove extended arguments where the logical nature of the task has not been obscured but is overtly stated.

2 Natural deduction approaches

Braine et al. Braine *et al.* (1984) proposed that people generally have available a set of elementary inference schemas that permit direct inferences when the schema conditions are met. For example, one schema (Disjunctive Syllogism) may be represented as:

p or **q**; not-**p**
Therefore, **q**

Thus, given any two statements represented by **p** and **q**, if it is true that either **p** or **q** or both are true and that not-**p** is also true, it follows that **q** must be true. The schemas proposed by Braine *et al.* (1984) are based on those of Braine (1978), which are related to those proposed by Osherson (1975) and Johnson-Laird (1975). Braine *et al.* (1984) proposed some 16 inference schemas on which subjects make few errors and rate as unproblematic when given problems that should directly evoke individual schemas.

To be a complete theory of reasoning, from presentation of problems to output of answers, some further machinery is needed to explain (a) comprehension of the linguistic statements making up the problem, (b) the programme used to decide which schema to apply at any given time (because often a number of schemas may be applicable) and (c) any fallback procedures for making plausible responses when the schema-based approach has failed.

Braine *et al.* (1984) suggested three sources of error in reasoning: *comprehension, heuristic inadequacy* and *processing* errors. Comprehension errors occur when the subject interprets the premises in a way unintended by the experimenter. In their experiments, Braine and co-workers sought to minimize such errors by devising problems in which the best known misinterpretations would not affect the conclusions reached, and also by piloting their problems to ensure good agreement between subjects and experimenters on the meaning of the premises. Heuristic inadequacy errors arise when the subjects' reasoning programme cannot find a correct line of reasoning. This was addressed by having a mixture of problems, some of which yielded to *direct* reasoning, in which forward working from the premises would yield solutions in a few steps, and some of which involved *indirect* reasoning, in which suppositions and/or *reductio ad absurdum* methods would be needed. The reasoning programme proposed by Braine *et al.* includes rules to control the application of schemas (essentially conflict resolution rules as discussed in Chapter 4), which prevent redundant inferences being made. Generally the programme will find a minimum length proof of the direct problems used (which were quite short). Direct methods may fail because of processing errors, such as attentional failures or memory overloads. If direct methods are not adequate, the indirect methods may be attempted but these may not be available to all subjects and are presumed to be more demanding than direct methods.

Three experiments were run to explore Braine *et al.*'s theory. All experiments involved direct reasoning tasks requiring one step only to solve or one-step plus a contradiction, or multistep problems in which a short chain of schemas was required. In addition there were control problems in which the conclusion was identical to the premise or negated the premise, and a small number of indirect problems. Subjects were presented with premises one line at a time at their own pace and finally with a tentative conclusion line which they had to judge as true or false. An example multistep problem is as follows:

> There is an L or a W.
> If there is an L then there's not an E.
> If there is a W then there's not an E.
> There is an E or an O.
> There is an O?

In the first experiment, solution latency was the main measure. In experiments 2 and 3, rated task difficulty was obtained on a 1–9 scale and proved to be a useful response measure. (Rated difficulties showed good consensus between subjects, were normally distributed and discriminated well between problems). In all cases, successive premise sentences remained on display as they accumulated, so that memory load was minimized.

Braine *et al.* argued that subjective problem difficulty would depend partly on the length of the problem statement in words and, more interestingly, on the difficulty of the schemas used in solving the problem. The rated difficulty data in experiment 3 were used to estimate the parameters of a linear model incorporating problem length (in words) and weighted difficulties of the 13 reasoning schemas thought to be applicable in direct reasoning problems. The resulting equation correlated 0.92 with obtained difficulty ratings over 60 problems. Assuming that all schemas were equally difficult (by weighting them all as '1') significantly reduced the correlation to 0.79. Thus, simply taking account of the number of reasoning steps without considering their difficulty led to a poorer fit to the data.

The model equations derived from study 3 data also fitted well the data from study 2, both for a set of problems shared between the two experiments and for a set of problems unique to experiment 1. Problem length and schema difficulty seemed to contribute independently to rated problem difficulty, since length and total schema difficulty per problem were uncorrelated.

The latency data from experiment 1 presented some difficulties of interpretation since the final conclusion latency, taken to be a measure of reasoning time, would be inflated by the length of the conclusion to be read and would be reduced by any anticipatory reasoning carried out as the premises accumulated on the screen. Ways were found to adjust the raw conclusion latencies to take these factors into account and the adjusted latencies correlated moderately ($r ~0.40$) with both problem length and summed schema difficulty.

Errors did not correlate with problem length but did correlate with the sum of reasoning step difficulty weights ($r = 0.73$).

Overall, Braine *et al.*'s theory met with a good measure of support from their experiments and its success lends support to the more general mental logic approach.

Rips' Natural Deduction approach   Rips (1983, 1994) shares the assumption of Braine *et al.* (1984) that human deductive reasoning involves the application of mental inference rules. Within this shared mental logic approach he has proposed a detailed model with some important differences to that of Braine *et al.* The model was first put forward under the name ANDS, standing for A Natural Deduction System (Rips, 1983). Recently it has been modified and extended into new areas (e.g. categorical syllogisms); the newer version is labelled PSYCOP, standing for Psychology of Proof (Rips, 1994). The original ANDS model will be our main target of discussion, followed by a brief consideration of PSYCOP.

Rips (1983) assumed that subjects have available 11 inference routines or rules corresponding to standard logical rules, such as Modus Ponens and Disjunctive Syllogism, which we have introduced earlier. Another example rule included in Rips' system is DeMorgan's law which is as follows:

Not (**p** and **q**)
Therefore, not-**p** or not-**q**

The inference rules of ANDS are divided into forward-working rules, which lead to new assertions from the premises and already derived assertions, and backward-working rules, which are triggered by goals and sub-goals and lead to new sub-goals being generated and perhaps to new assertions also. Working backwards from the overall goal (conclusion) to sub-goals and sub-sub-goals was a feature of GPS (Newell and Simon, 1972) and is common in problem-solving programs and in analyses of human problem solving (see Chapter 2). In this respect ANDS differs from Braine *et al.*'s system which works forwards only.

The operation of the system may be introduced with the aid of an example problem. Consider the following:

If there is not both an M and a P on the blackboard, then there is an R.
Therefore, if there is no M, then there is an R.

The subject's task is to decide whether the conclusion follows from the premise. The ANDS line of proof would be as follows:

(a) If there is not both an M and a P on the blackboard, then there is an R. (Premise)
(b) If there is no M or no P on the blackboard, then there is an R. (Consequence of a)
(c) Suppose there is no M on the blackboard. (Supposition)
(d) Then there will be an R. (Consequence of b and c)
(e) Therefore, if there is no M there will be an R. (Consequence of c and d)

While reaching the proof, ANDS maintains in working memory both a tree of assertions and a tree of sub-goals (e.g. sub-goals of proving R and of proving not-M arise in course of the proof). Thus, working memory plays an explicit role in the ANDS model. As Rips (1983, p. 42) writes, "Reasoning in ANDS means constructing a proof in working memory." The ANDS working memory structure at the conclusion of the above proof is represented in the Fig. 6.1.

Suppositions (together with their consequences) and sub-goals are placed in subsidiary nodes of the assertion and sub-goal trees respectively. The accumulation of information in working memory is dependent on the order in which rules are applied, and this order depends in turn on the processing component of the model. The inference rules or routines are represented as production rules in a production system (see Chapter 2). The rules are ordered in priority with the simplest working-forward rules considered first, then the more complex working-backward rules. The first rule to match the current working memory state fires and changes the working memory state accordingly. Checks are built in to the conditions of the rules to prevent redundant looping and the generation of clearly irrelevant inferences. The backward rules, in particular, help to keep search focused on relevant goals. A potential source of within- and between-individual variability in the model is the provision that the rules are not necessarily perfectly available at all times. Rather, each rule for a given subject can have a different probability that it will be available. The rule availability probabilities are the major parameters of the model.

The ANDS model has been subject to three main forms of empirical assessment: comparison with protocols, examination of predictions regarding memory for proofs, and fit of model to acceptability judgements of a range of arguments. These will now be considered in turn.

Fig. 6.1 *ANDS working memory structure at the conclusion of the proof of the argument:* If not both M and P then R; therefore, if not M then R. *After Rips (1983). Copyright © 1983 by the American Psychological Associaiton. Adapted with persmission.*

The model was partly derived from examination of protocols of subjects assessing the acceptability of arguments and so reasonable fit to those protocols is not remarkable. However, the model's fit was also assessed with further protocols and compared with Osherson's (1975) model. Some 32 protocols were rated by two independent judges on a 0–5 scale for the degree to which the protocols reflected the proofs generated by ANDS and by Osherson's model. The mean similarity rating for ANDS was 3.64, which was significantly higher than that for the Osherson model (3.21). These results then offer some support for the psychological plausibility of ANDS.

Since the ANDS model makes specific memory assumptions, predictions about memory for lines of proofs can be made. Previous experiments on text memory (e.g. Meyer, 1975) found that high-level facts closely related to the main theme of the text are better recalled than low-level details (the levels effect). ANDS memory tree structure suggests that high-level assertions should be recalled better than subordinate suppositions. Marcus (1982) tested this prediction in a study in which subjects listened to simple proofs, which they then tried to recall. As predicted, recall of supposition lines was markedly poorer than that of control lines of text. These results lend some support to the memory assumptions of ANDS.

The main empirical test of ANDS comes from a study of the acceptability of arguments. Thirty-six subjects were given arguments such as the following, and asked to say whether the argument was valid or not:

If Judy is in Albany or Barbara is in Detroit, then Janice is in Los Angeles.
Therefore, If Judy is in Albany or Janice is in Los Angeles, then Janice is in Los Angeles.

Using the ANDS model, subjects would carry out the task by trying to develop a proof, which could be done using three rules (R4, R9 and R11). If each rule is available with probabilities $p4$, $p9$ and $p11$, the probability of reaching the proof would be $p4*p9*p11$. However, if one or more steps are unavailable, then subjects might still hazard a guess with probability pg and that guess will be correct with a probability of 0.5. If subjects do not guess (with probability $1-pg$) following failure to prove the conclusion, then they are assumed to respond 'unacceptable'. Thus, on the assumptions so far, the overall probability that subjects say 'acceptable' to the above argument should be $p4*p9*p11 + 0.5*pg(1 - p4*p9*p11)$. In fact, there is an alternative route to solution which must be taken into account in the finally correct formula for the example problem, but the general procedure indicated leads to formulae for any valid argument. In the experiment, 32 arguments were devised representing triples of rules. These arguments were given together with 40 filler items (simple valid arguments) and 32 invalid arguments to 36 subjects.

The valid arguments were accepted as valid on 50.6 per cent of trials with a range of 16.7–91.7 per cent over problems. Invalid arguments were accepted as valid on 22.9 per cent of trials. Overall, then, subjects did discriminate between valid and invalid arguments but the error rate was quite high compared with the findings of Braine *et al.* However, Rips' problems all involved a theoretical minimum of three steps, whereas those of Braine *et al.* often involved fewer steps. The model's parameters were estimated from the proportion of correct judgements over the 32 valid problems. The best-fitting set of availability parameters gave a correlation of 0.93 between predicted and observed proportions correct. The availability estimates proved reliable and were generally plausible. For example, the intuitively clear Disjunctive Modus Ponens rule, which states:

If **p** or **q** then **r**
p
Therefore, **r**

was available with $p = 1.0$. Interestingly, the Or introduction rule, which states:

p
Therefore, **p** or **q**

had a very low availability ($p = 0.197$). Braine *et al.* (1984) also noted that this rule caused difficulty in their study and seemed non-intuitive to many subjects. Quite likely this rule is relatively unavailable for pragmatic reasons (Grice, 1975) in that the extra information in the conclusion seems irrelevant and by conversational convention should have been mentioned in the premise if it was known.

The ANDS model thus received a good measure of support from the studies of protocols, memory for proofs and correctness of validity judgements. The model has been modified recently by Rips (1994) to form the more general PSYCOP model which contains a larger repertoire of inference rules and altered control processes, although the core principles remain as before. The PSYCOP model was applied to the task of proof comprehension in which subjects read proofs one line at a time at their own pace, trying to understand the proof as they proceeded. When PSYCOP could anticipate a line by means of a forward rule, subjects' times to understand that line were relatively fast. When PSYCOP needed a backward rule to prove that a line followed, then times on such lines were relatively long. Further, the new model could explain quite well the patterns of results obtained in simple conditional inference tasks (Marcus and Rips, 1979), in which examples of all possible forms of conditional syllogisms with antecedents and consequents affirmed or denied are judged for validity. Yet more evidence for PSYCOP's generality was obtained by equipping it with suitable inference rules for categorical syllogistic reasoning. When availability parameters were estimated from mean correct validity judgements from 20 subjects over 256 categorical syllogisms, the PSYCOP model predictions correlated 0.88 with the obtained data (Rips, 1994). Thus, there is evidence that PSYCOP could be a useful general model for deductive reasoning, both categorical and propositional.

3 Mental models

The mental models approach, originally developed for the case of categorical syllogisms, has now been extended to cover propositional reasoning (Johnson-Laird and Byrne, 1991; Johnson-Laird *et al.*, 1992). The basic notion is that the meaning of connectives (and, or, if, etc.) can be represented by mental models of states of affairs in which the connectives are true. Deductive propositional reasoning then begins with the construction of a set of mental models that represent the first premise. As premises are added, the set of models is modified and a conclusion is drawn from the final set of models. The approach is derived from the formal truth-table or model-theoretic approach discussed above. Full truth-table representations quickly become bulky and could not reasonably be implemented in unaided working memory. Mental models, it is argued, offer more economical forms of representation that appear psychologically plausible, although this has been challenged (Bonatti, 1994; O'Brien *et al.*, 1994). In more detail, mental model representations can be *initial* and involve *implicit* models or be *explicit* and involve *fleshed out* models. Both implicit and explicit models may involve *exhaustiveness* tags, or not. It is proposed that most inferences in daily life are made using initial models which represent only those contingencies corresponding to the simple propositions in the premises. So, for example, on the mental models approach, the initial representation of 'if p then q' would be:

[p] q
. . .

The first line of this representation is to be interpreted as meaning that there is a 'p' and a 'q' and that every 'p' is also associated with a 'q', i.e. 'p' is exhausted relative to 'q'. This first line is a model; the second line '. . .' is an ellipsis, indicating that further models are implicit and may be made explicit or 'fleshed out' if need be. (Note that each *line* of these representations of connectives is a model. The representational scheme differs from that used with categorical syllogisms where each line represented a different individual and a set of lines constituted a model of a premise or conclusion. In the propositional case, each premise is represented by a set of models with one model per line.)

A fleshed out, explicit, representation for the conditional 'if p then q' would be as follows:

p q
~p q
~p ~q

Initial and explicit representations of the main connectives are shown in Table 6.3. (For consistency with previous usage in this book '~' has been used as a negation tag where Johnson-Laird uses '¬'.)

Johnson-Laird *et al.* (1992) applied the mental models theory to 61 of the problems used by Braine *et al.* (1984) and compared the theoretical number of models required to solve these problems with the difficulty ratings reported by Braine *et al.* For example, given the following problem:

If e or k, then o
e and v
therefore, not-o

Table 6.3 *Initial and explicit models for the main propositional connectives in recent mental models theory.*

	Model			
Connective	**Initial**		**Explicit**	
p and q	p q		p q	
p or q		Inclusive		Exclusive
	p	p q		p ~q
	q	p ~q		
		~p q		
If p, then q		Conditional		Biconditional
	[p] q	p q		p q
	. . .	~p q		~p ~q
		~p ~q		
p only if q	[p] q	p q		p q
	~p [~q]	~p q		~p ~q
		~p ~q		

Each row represents an alternative model. ~ is a symbol for negation. After Johnson Laird *et al.* (1992). Copyright © 1992 American Psychological Association. Reprinted with permission.

The first premise would yield the following models:

```
e                    o
        k            o
   . . .                    (two explicit models)
```

The second premise gives the following models:

```
e          v            (one explicit model)
```

The reult of combining the premises is:

```
e                    o          v
e          k          o          v     (two explicit models)
```

Thus, five explicit models are needed on the way to the conclusion that the proposed conclusion does not follow.

Over 61 problems, the total number of explicit models per problem correlated 0.73 with rated problem difficulty reported by Braine *et al.* (1984). Thus, the results are consistent with the notion that the more explicit models in a deduction the harder the task should be.

Other tests of the theory have concerned the basic phenomena of 'if . . . then' reasoning and the relative difficulty of various connectives. The theory is consistent with the usual finding that Modus Ponens is easier than Modus Tollens for conditionals because Modus Ponens requires only one (initial) model whereas Modus Tollens requires three explicit models. The theory is also consistent with the approximate equality of difficulty of Modus Ponens and Modus Tollens with 'only if' as a connective. In the case of 'only if', negatives are explicitly represented. For example, 'p only if q', is represented as:

[p]   q
~p   [~q]
          . . .

These initial models allow Modus Ponens and Modus Tollens without any fleshing out and with equal difficulty, but both deductions should be more difficult than Modus Ponens with ordinary conditionals, as is observed (Evans, 1982).

Further data reported by Johnson-Laird *et al.* (1992) showed that, as predicted on the basis of the number of models involved, exclusive disjunctions were harder than conditionals and that Modus Tollens was easier in biconditionals than in conditionals. Also, it was found that with very difficult double disjunctions, erroneous conclusions corresponded to possible models of the premises with a significant frequency.

Criticisms of mental models approach to propositional reasoning.   Johnson-Laird *et al.* (1992) stated that the mental models theory "is in principle simple to refute: an easy deduction that depends on many models violates its principal prediction" (p. 436). O'Brien and colleagues (1994) accepted the challenge and have presented data from tasks that would appear to require many models but which subjects handle well. For example, consider the following problem:

If O or K or R or C, then X
If E or F or G or H, then Y
K
F
What follows?

In O'Brien *et al.*'s study 100 per cent of subjects answered correctly, 'X and Y', despite the problem requiring a total of some 58 models of which up to 15 must be considered simultaneously. Similar results were obtained with other problems which should have been difficult in terms of number of models but were solved readily. In general, as the number of conjuncts or disjuncts increases in a conditional the number of mental models required expands very rapidly and quickly reaches untractable levels at which working memory would be heavily overloaded. (For example, with ten conjuncts, a conditional would require some 2047 models). A similar point regarding tractability was also made by Bonatti (1994). In response, Johnson-Laird *et al.* (1994) argued that subjects would not blindly generate models unnecessarily and would realize that only a small part of the premises needs to be represented, which could be done with a manageable number of models.

Another issue raised by O'Brien *et al.* (1994) is the apparent failure of the mental models theory to rule out certain invalid conclusions. For example, consider the problem:

If A and M then S
A
M
Therefore what?

S is the correct inference and would be predicted by the mental models theory. However, the theory would also predict S as the conclusion when the premises (and models) are:

If A and M then S   [A M] [S]
                              [S]
                              . . .
A   A
Therefore what?

S is predicted here because the way in which premise models are combined would yield a conclusion representation consisting of two models:

[A M] [S]
A   [S]

From which S follows, because it is present in both lines/models. Over a number of such problems, subjects consistently responded 'nothing follows' rather than the conclusions expected on mental models theory (O'Brien *et al.*, 1994). Johnson-Laird *et al.* (1994) replied that, although O'Brien *et al.*'s analysis was correct for mental models theory using only initial models without exhaustivity tags, the incorrect deductions are blocked when the intermediate version of the theory is used in which initial models with exhaustivity are applied. (The AI version in which all models are fully explicit also blocks the unwarranted conclusions.) However, O'Brien *et al.*'s analysis is based on a fleshed-out representation *with exhaustivity*, which appears to make Johnson-Laird *et al.*'s defence misplaced.

However, Johnson-Laird *et al.*'s argument is based on subjects representing the conditional with an initial model with exhaustivity rather than a fleshed-out model with exhaustivity. If the conditional in the example argument is represented as:

[A M] S
. . . .

Then adding A as a premise gives:

A M S
A

which blocks the inference S.

The defence case then seems to hinge on subjects adopting an initial representation with exhaustivity; an initial representation without exhaustivity or a fleshed-out representation with exhaustivity would not block the unwarranted inferences discussed here. There would appear to be a need to establish independently which representations are being used to determine whether the representations do predict behaviour. If initial representations with exhaustivity are typical of intermediate-level reasoners, and initial models without exhaustivity are typical of unskilled reasoners, and fleshed-out models with exhaustivity are typical of more skilled reasoners, Johnson-Laird *et al.*'s defence would seem to suggest that, as skill increases, performance on the invalid arguments discussed here would improve at first and then decline. If such a counter-intuitive prediction could be upheld, the mental models theory would be strengthened considerably.

III. SUMMARY AND CONCLUDING COMMENTS

Propositional reasoning concerns arguments involving connectives such as 'and', 'or', 'not', 'if . . . then'. Logicians have developed formalized systems based on very restricted interpretations of the connectives which permit necessarily true conclusions to be drawn from given premises. Everyday uses of connectives such as 'if . . . then' are highly varied (e.g. causal, temporal, definitional, deontic) and importation of these interpretations into tasks intended to be of a simple logical nature probably underlie the many departures from logic reported in the literature.

Extended arguments, where a chain of inferences is required from starting statement to conclusions, have been investigated, particularly in the mental logic approach (Rips, 1983, 1994; Braine *et al.* 1984). Heuristic search, subject to working memory constraints, seems to account well for behaviour in extended logical proof tasks (Newell *et al.* 1958, 1972; Rips, 1983, 1994; Braine *et al.* 1984). This finding supports the general view that logical reasoning is a special case of problem solving.

The mental models approach has been applied to simple and extended propositional reasoning tasks (Johnson-Laird *et al.* 1992). The extended theory introduces new concepts and symbolism which make the implications of the theory more difficult to assess. For example, subjects might use one of four different representations (initial or extended, with or without exhaustivity). The diverging implications of these representations have generated considerable controversy (Bonatti, 1994; Johnson-Laird *et al.* 1994; O'Brien *et al.* 1994), particularly over whether mental models theory would predict unrealistic working memory loads when implications have highly disjunctive antecedents.

The theme of how people understand and use conditional statements (implications) is also a major issue in the next chapter, which focuses on inductive reasoning.

IV. FURTHER READING

Rips, L.J. (1994). *The psychology of proof: deductive reasoning in human thinking*. MIT Press: Cambridge, MA. Rips provides a thorough exposition of his influential mental logic approach to reasoning.

O'Brien, D.P., Braine, M.D.S. and Yang, Y. (1994). Propositional reasoning by mental models? Simple to refute in principle and practice. *Psychological Review* **101**, 711–724.

Johnson-Laird, P.N., Byrne, R.M.J. and Schaeken, W. (1994). Why models rather than rules give a better account of propositional reasoning: a reply to Bonatti and to O'Brien, Braine and Yang. *Psychological Review* **101**, 734–739.

The above papers set out clearly the major conflicts between mental logic and mental models accounts of propositional reasoning.

7

Inductive reasoning:
Testing and generating hypotheses

In the last two chapters we considered studies of deductive inference from statements (premises) that were to be taken as true. Somewhat different but related tasks arise when one has to test statements (hypotheses) for truth against external data. Detectives and scientists, for instance, constantly face the inductive problem of deciding whether certain hypotheses are true or false. A possible general approach is to follow the 'hypothetico-deductive' method. In this technique, implications are *deduced* from the hypothesis and are then checked empirically for truth or falsity. If the implications of the hypothesis turn out to be true, then the hypothesis is supported, otherwise it can be rejected – on the grounds that if validly drawn inferences from the hypothesis lead to empirically false conclusions then the hypothesis *must* be false. Whether the apparently simple prescription embodied in the hypothetico-deductive method is descriptive of behaviour in the face of inductive problems has been the topic of numerous studies, a selection of which will be considered in this chapter.

Our review will start with tasks in which people are given both a particular hypothesis to test and sources of potentially relevant data. Next, we will discuss a range of more complicated tasks in which people are required both to generate and to test their own hypotheses. The hypothesis-generating and testing behaviour of scientists in real life will be considered in the final substantive section.

I. THE FOUR-CARD SELECTION PROBLEM

Wason (1966, 1968) devised the following deceptively simple paradigm in which to explore hypothetico-deductive reasoning. Suppose you are given four cards showing:

| E | K | 4 | 7 |

Each card has a letter on one side and a number on the other. Your task is to name the cards that need to be turned over to test the following statement: "If a card has a vowel on one side, then it has an even number on the other side". You may find it instructive to pause here and decide on your answer before reading on.

On the 'official' intended interpretation of the rule as one of material implication (see discussion of conditional reasoning in Chapter 6), the most common answers are wrong. Why they are wrong, and what the correct answer is, should become clearer with the aid of a more concrete example. Take the statement 'Paper ignites at 481°F'. If we had a furnace set at 481°F, we could test this proposed rule by inserting samples of paper and noting whether they ignite or not. A difficulty arises, in that no matter how many different samples of paper conform to the rule there could always be as yet untried papers that would not. Thus, no matter how many 'positives' are recorded, the rule can never be absolutely verified; it would be falsified if just one sample failed to ignite at 481°F. This is a general characteristic of such universal hypotheses and the example should alert us to the need to consider potentially falsifying data as well as potentially supporting data in testing proposed rules. Suppose now that a study was conducted on what sorts of things ignite at 481°F and that four cards are available representing four individual experiments. On one side of each card is listed the type of material put into the furnace, and on the other side whether it burned or not. Which of the four cards below would have to be turned over to test the hypothesis, 'If it is paper, it will ignite at 481°F'?

| Paper | Plastic | Burned | Did not burn |

Clearly we must look at the 'Paper' card to see whether it burned or not. The 'Plastic' card can be ignored as irrelevant. Surprisingly, perhaps, the 'Burned' card need not be turned over. Once we know that the material burned, whether the material was paper or not does not affect the status of the hypothesis. No information regarding the hypothesis could be gained by turning over the 'Burned' card, so it should be left untouched. The 'Did not burn' card should definitely be turned over, since it would be falsifying if 'Paper' were on the other side.

Similarly, in the abstract version, i.e. 'If vowel on one side, then even number on the other side', the cards showing 'E' and '7' should be examined because they are potentially falsifying. The '4' and the 'K' cards may be left unturned since the truth of the hypothesis would not be affected no matter what is on their other sides.

The kind of rule involved in the four-card task has been extensively used in studies of hypothesis testing. Before reviewing the empirical research, we will briefly set out the logic of such rules in a little more detail, for the benefit of readers who have not read the previous chapter or who have but would like a reminder. The rules are of the abstract form, 'If p, then q', and are known as 'conditionals' or 'implication' rules. In propositional logic there are two main valid inference patterns involving such rules and two main fallacies. These are shown in Table 7.1. Note that '~' before a letter means 'not', so that ~q is to be read as 'not-q'.

Another way of thinking about the implication rule is to consider how its truth or falsity varies as a function of the truth of the component terms. The two terms in the rule can be independently true or false, yielding four combinations. The status of the

Table 7.1 *Valid and fallacious inferences based on implication*

Valid inferences		Fallacious inferences	
1. (Modus Ponens)	If **p** then **q** **p** ∴ **q**	1. (Denying the Antecedent)	If **p** then **q** **˜p** ∴ **˜q**
2. (Modus Tollens)	If **p** then **q** **˜q** ∴ **˜p**	2. (Affirming the Consequent)	If **p** then **q** **q** ∴ **p**

rule given these combinations is represented in Table 7.2, which shows the 'truth table' for implication.

A. Basic results

In testing a rule of the form 'if p then q', there are four possible cases that might arise: pq, p˜q, ˜pq and ˜p˜q. (Remember ˜q is to be read as 'not-q'.) In logic, only the second case (p˜q) is inconsistent with the rule while the remainder are consistent (see Table 7.2).

When subjects are given a conditional rule to test and the opportunity to observe what is paired with cases of p, q, ˜p, ˜q in the four-card task, they almost always select the cards showing p and q, rather than the logically correct p and ˜q cards. The results of four typical studies by Watson and co-workers are given in Table 7.3.

One way to describe these results is to say that subjects are 'set' for verification and so choose the potentially verifying cards (p, q) and ignore the potentially falsifying case (˜q). (Note: p is potentially falsifying as well as verifying.)

Subjects generally recognize that the ˜q card falsifies the rule if the ˜q card is turned over to reveal p, but rarely examine it spontaneously.

Table 7.2 *Truth table for implication*

p	**→**	**q**
T	T	T
T	F	F
F	T	T
F	T	F

T = true; F = false; → = 'implies' or 'if . . . then'.

Table 7.3 *Results from four experiments on the four-card selection task*[a]

Selection	Frequency
pq	59
p	42
pp~q	9
p~q	5
Others	13
	$N = 128$

a   From Johnson-Laird, and Wason (1970), with permission.

B. Procedural variations

Wason and others examined a number of procedural variables in an attempt to locate the sources of difficulty in this task. For example, in one study (Wason, 1969) the task materials were made strictly binary (with only two possible letters and numbers) but this had no effect. Thus the source of the difficulty was not confusion induced by the sheer number of possibilities in the 'Vowel–even number' cards.

It was suggested that subjects might have been confused by the expression 'the other side of the card' and might have misinterpreted this to mean 'the side face downward'. Wason and Johnson-Laird (1970) therefore presented subjects with cards that had all the information on one side and used masks to hide the appropriate part of the card. Again, no facilitation occurred. Goodwin and Wason (1972) made a duplicate set of fully revealed cards available to subjects while they performed the task with equivalent partially masked cards. The fully revealed cards could serve as aids to memory or imagery in solving the problem. This had a slight but non-significant beneficial effect on choice of the ~q card. But most subjects still chose the q card.

Perhaps the apparent 'set' for verification could be broken by instructions that emphasize falsification? However, Wason (1968) found that instructions to pick cards that 'could break the rule' did not enhance performance.

Perhaps more familiarity is required with the rule? Wason and Shapiro (1971) trained subjects to construct or evaluate instances of the four types of cards (pq, p~q, ~pq, ~p~q) for 24 trials in relation to a given rule. They were then given the selection task with four more partially concealed cards in relation to the same rule. The 'construction' group did a little better than normal, while the 'evaluation' group showed averagely poor performance. However, the difference between the groups was not significant.

A more successful method of rule familiarization was devised by Legrenzi (1971). He first gave subjects instances of four types of cards. The cards had a triangle or a circle on their left and right half. The cards were clearly marked as '+' or '–' and the subjects had to express a rule in their own words to describe the assignment of cards to the '+' and '–' categories. They were given partially covered cards and asked which ones should be uncovered to test the rule. The 'rule discovery' subjects were compared with 'yoked' subjects presented with the discovered rules and the selection task. The 'rule discovery' subjects performed significantly better than the controls.

Interestingly, the rules 'induced' by the experimental subjects were rarely in the form of conditional sentences, but were more usually in terms of 'either . . . or' e.g. 'circle on right or two triangles together' instead of 'if circle on left, then circle on right'. In a second study subjects were required to find a rule of the form 'if . . . then' that fitted the figures. Again, rule discovery subjects did very much better on a selection task than control subjects simply given the rule.

Performance on reasoning tasks is often improved by concrete material. The task of testing conditional rules does not seem to be an exception. Wason and Shapiro (1971) found considerable improvement when the task was presented in terms of four journeys. The four cards were said to represent journeys, with names of towns (destinations) on one side and modes of transport on the other. Subjects were given cards marked, face up, as follows:

and were told that the cards represented journeys made by the experimenter. The proposed rule to be tested was 'Every time I go to Manchester, I go by train'. (*Answer*: turn over 'Manchester' and 'Car' cards.)

Subsequent analyses of this thematic effect by Gilhooly and Falconer (1974), and by Bracewell and Hidi (1974) indicated that the concreteness of the terms and the presence or absence of a concrete relationship contributed separately to improving performance on the task. [Despite this early accumulation of data in favour of the thematic effect, it should be noted that Manktelow and Evans (1979) failed to replicate many of the relevant results and thus cast some doubt on the strength of the effect.]

Further facilitation of performance was reported when the task was made very lifelike and concrete by Johnson-Laird and co-workers (1972). Subjects were asked to imagine that they worked in the Post Office, sorting letters. Their task was to discover whether the following rule had been violated: 'If a letter is sealed, then it has a 5d. stamp on it'. Envelopes were provided either sealed or not and bearing either a 4d. or a 5d. stamp on the side that was showing. A parallel abstract condition had the following rule: 'If an envelope has a D on one side, then it has a 5 on the other side'. Again, suitable envelopes were provided to test the rule. Some 24 subjects were given both tasks in a balanced order. Of these, 22 were correct in the concrete condition; only two were correct in the abstract condition. Surprisingly, perhaps, there was no transfer from the concrete to the abstract form of the task.

In the context of rules using realistic material, Van Duyne (1974) found a high success rate when the rule was known to be false (e.g. 'If a student studies philosophy, then she is at Cambridge'). Further, in a later study (Van Duyne, 1976), more logical reasoning was obtained with rules that the subjects believed to be 'sometimes true' as against 'always true', (an example of the latter case is, 'If it is glucose then it is sweet'). Pollard and Evans (1981) extended this to include rules thought to be 'usually false' and 'always false', and found that perceived falsity had a significant effect on response frequencies in the direction of better (i.e. falsifying) performance.

In sum, it appeared from these early studies that the main facilitating effects on selection task performance were those of (a) using realistic material, (b) allowing rule familiarization through discovery learning and (c) using rules of dubious truth value.

C. 'Insight' model

Wason tried to induce 'insight' into the task by means of post-task discussions or 'confrontations'. When subjects made a wrong selection they were asked to consider the ~q card. Could it be relevant? Could it falsify? It was pointed out that it might have p on the other side. What then? Subjects were shown the reverse of the ~q card (p) and asked whether the rule still held.

On the basis of such 'dialogues', Johnson-Laird and Wason (1970) proposed a model for insight into the task. They proposed three levels of insight. First, there is the level of no insight, in which the person is fixated on verification and chooses p or p and q (depending on whether he or she thinks the rule is reversible or not). The second level, partial insight, is obtained when it is realized that potentially falsifying cards should be examined as well as potentially verifying cards. This leads to a choice of p, q, ~q. The third level, complete insight, consists in realizing that only cards that could falsify should be selected, i.e. p and ~q.

Some evidence in support of the 'insight' model was obtained from studies in which subjects wrote down their reasons for selecting or not selecting each card (Goodwin and Wason, 1972). These results were claimed to provide independent support for the model in that the choices were justified by reasons consistent with the insight model.

The 'insight' model explains errors partly in terms of misinterpretation of the rule as reversible, but mainly in terms of failure to appreciate the importance of potentially falsifying information in rule testing. Two main types of alternative explanations have subsequently been put forward. The first type focuses on the ambiguities of the task and essentially follows a similar line to that taken by Henle (1962, 1978) in connection with syllogistic reasoning. The second type proposes an 'atmosphere-like' explanation known as the 'matching bias' hypothesis. This sup- poses that people have a tendency simply to select cards that match the terms mentioned in the rule. These alternatives will be discussed in the following sections.

D. Interpretation factors

A number of investigators have pointed to ambiguities in the standard four-card task. Typical patterns of performance on the task might be explained in terms of people making interpretations different from that intended, but reasoning correctly on their interpretations.

Smalley (1974) distinguished three sources of ambiguity.

(1) Is the rule 'reversible' or not? i.e. does p → q also mean q → p, or not?
(2) Does the rule refer to both sides of the card or just to the showing side?
(3) Is the task one of verification, falsification, or both? Putting together these ambiguities leads to $(2 \times 2 \times 3) = 12$ possible interpretations of the task. These 12 interpretations logically require certain patterns of card selection. Smalley showed that such interpretations occurred and that his subjects' choices were consistent with their interpretations.

Bracewell (1974) gave some subjects a 'clarified' statement of the task (cf. Ceraso and Provitera's (1971) syllogism experiment discussed in Chapter 4). The rule was given as follows:

> If either the showing face or the underside face of the card has a J on it then 2 is on the remaining face. This hypothesis should not be interpreted to mean that 2 only occurs with J.
>   Please indicate the card or cards it is necessary to examine in order to see if the above hypothesis is false.

The success rate with clarified instructions (seven of 12) was much higher than that obtained with standard instructions (one of 12).

The beneficial effects of realistic material would be attributed, on the 'interpretation' view, to reductions in ambiguity with such material. A rule, such as "If I go to London, I go by car', is unlikely to be interpreted as reversible (i.e. as implying 'If I go by car, I go to London') because the reversed version is implausible. No such plausibility checks would prevent reversal of an abstract rule. In the 'Post Office' variant, the nature of task – to seek potentially falsifying information – fits the thematic structure and so makes the task less ambiguous.

The interpretation approach was strongly criticized by Evans and colleagues, and they put forward a radical alternative to previous approaches. This work is discussed below.

E. 'Matching bias'

Evans (1984; Evans and Lynch, 1973; Wason and Evans, 1975) put forward the view that, in the abstract version of the selection task, most people simply select the cards showing the symbols mentioned in the rule, i.e. the responses match the input and no 'deeper' processing is involved. One main source of evidence for this view is the finding that with a negative form of the rule ('If B on one side, there will not be 3 on the other') the success rate is high. Most subjects choose the 'B' card and the '3' card. Wason and Johnson-Laird's 'insight' model would predict selection of 'B' and the 'not 3' card by naive subjects working under a verification set.

Interestingly, when subjects are given both the negative and the affirmative form of rule in succession, they tend to be correct on the negative and wrong on the affirmative. Furthermore, they give 'verification' reasons in the negative case. Evans argues that the reasons given are often *post hoc* rationalizations and that behaviour in this task is actually determined by an unconscious matching bias. The 'matching bias' proposal is clearly reminiscent of the 'atmosphere' hypothesis in syllogistic reasoning in that superficial processing is proposed with little understanding of the logic of the task assumed.

Evans (1980; Evans and Wason, 1976) argued that the data on card selection and justification of selections may be explained in terms of two modes of thought labelled 'Type I' and 'Type II'. Type I processes are conceived to be non-verbal and non-introspectible (and it seems to be suggested, non-logical) while Type II processes are verbal and apparently 'rational'.

If responses are made on the basis of a Type I process, and the subjects are asked 'Why did you do that?', it is proposed that they will generate rationalizations, using Type II processes to do so. As Evans (1980a, p. 235) pointed out, "The 'rationalization' itself a form of reasoning: the subject asks, in effect, 'Given the structure of the problem and the instructions, what reason could I have had for the response I made?'" Consistent with this approach, Evans and Wason (1976) found that when subjects were asked to justify various answers presented to them as being 'correct solutions' to the selection task, they confidently gave reasons for accepting all the answers, including wrong answers. Thus, it is possible in the normal selection task that responses are made on a basis unknown to the subjects, but that they can construct reasons (rationalizations) for their responses if asked. This demonstration by Evans and Wason seriously undermines Goodwin and Wason's (1972) arguments, in favour of the 'insight' model, which were based on subjects' justifications of their choices. The Goodwin and Wason analysis assumed that 'reasons' preceded and produced responses, while Evans' analysis and data suggested the reverse order.

Evans (1984, 1992) extended the notion of Type I and II processes and relabelled them as 'heuristic' and 'analytic' processes respectively. By 'heuristic' processes are meant rapid preattentive processes that select items from the problem present- ation for attention; 'analytic' processes can then operate on the selected information to draw inferences (not necessarily by means of logical rules).

When data from a number of studies of matching in the selection task with all combinations of affirmative and negative antecedents and consequents are put together (e.g. Evans *et al.* 1993, p.110) it would seem that the matching tendency is stronger in the case of the consequents than antecedents. To cope with this obser- vation two specific attentional heuristics, the 'if' heuristic and the 'not' heuristic are proposed. These heuristics derive from the linguistic functions of 'if' and 'not'. Evans' (1989) proposal is that the 'if' heuristic directs attention to the antecedent conditions of an implication (whether the antecedent is positive or negative), whereas the 'not' heuristic directs attention to the state of affairs that is negated and results in high 'q' choices whether the rule is in terms of 'q' or 'not-q'.

In Evans' two-process approach, typical selection task performance is explained by 'heuristic' processes that select cards as relevant. Since relevance is determined rapidly by preattentive processes and it is proposed that such cards are then chosen, it was predicted that the initial decisions would be 'select' decisions and later decisions would be 'do not select' decisions. Evans *et al.* (1987) found, as predicted, that there was a strong relationship between the order in which decisions were made and the nature of the decisions. 'Select' decisions were made before 'do not select' decisions. Evans (1992) extended this line of study by measuring total time spent considering each card before a 'select–do not select' decision was made. (This was done by having subjects point with a mouse on a computer screen at each card while they were considering it.) Subjects spent markedly longer considering the cards that they finally selected, whereas very little time was given to unselected cards. Evans hypothesized that subjects were thinking of justifications for the choices suggested by the relevance heuristics and some support came from a verbal protocol study (Evans, in press). There was a clear tendency to refer much more to the selected cards than to the unselected cards, and this held both for the facing and the hidden sides of the cards. A similar finding was also reported by Beattie and Baron (1988) for the facing sides. Evans concluded that subjects think only about some cards (those heuristically deemed relevant) and that their thoughts are directed to justifying selection of the deemed relevant cards. Thus, analytic processes do seem to take place but they do not affect the final choices, which are determined by heuristic preattentive relevance judgements.

F. Memory-cueing (availability) accounts

The rule that Johnson-Laird *et al.* (1972) used in their 'postal' study was a rule current in real life and so was well known to their subjects at the time of the experiment. However, the rule ceased to be operative in the UK some years ago and later studies, using young adult subjects, failed to find facilitating effects of the postal rule condition compared with the abstract condition (Griggs and Cox, 1982). Thus, it is possible that prior experience of specific counter-examples facilitates performance. Subjects for whom the rule was a real everyday rule would, because of their prior experience, be more likely to think of possible counter-examples than would be subjects to whom the rule was an arbitrary laboratory invention; in other words, falsifying possibilities would be more available to subjects familiar with the rule in real life.

Griggs and Cox (1982) found a similar effect to that of Johnson-Laird *et al.*'s postal study in an experiment involving the rule governing the legal drinking age in Florida (where the experiment was conducted). Subjects were to imagine they were police officers and they were to ensure that the regulation 'If a person is drinking beer, then the person must be over 19' was being followed. Four cards contained information about four people: on one side of each card was the person's age, and on the other side what they were drinking. Face up, the subjects saw the cards showing '16 years of age', '22 years of age', 'drinking beer', 'drinking coke'. The task was to turn over the cards that definitely needed to be turned over to determine whether the rule was being violated. Correct selections were made by 74.1 per cent of subjects. As with the postal task, a memory-cueing explanation was suggested.

A slightly different explanation seems to be called for the task variant devised by D'Andrade (see Rumelhart, 1980). In this version, subjects imagine that they are managers in a store (Sears) and are responsible for checking sales receipts to determine whether the rule 'If a purchase exceeds $30, then the receipt must be approved by the department manager' has been followed. If approved, the receipt is signed on the back. Four receipts are shown: one for $15, one for $45, one signed and one not signed. D'Andrade found approximately 70 per cent correct choices in this task. These results have been replicated by Griggs and Cox (1983). However, since none of the subjects had been Sears store managers, performance facilitation could not be due to specific memory cueing but may reflect experience with analogous materials, e.g. perhaps as customers having receipts authorized or not.

G. Pragmatic reasoning schemas

It is a reasonable conclusion, from the low levels of performance typical with abstract versions of the conditional rule testing task, that subjects do not bring to bear formal 'syntactic' rules of logical implication in these tasks. Data outlined in the preceding section raised the possibility of specific memory cueing. A third possibility was developed in Cheng and Holyoak's (1985) work on the notion of pragmatic reasoning schemas. Such schemas are quite abstract rule systems, in that they apply to a wide range of contents, but are not so wide and abstract as syntactic logical rules. A relevant schema in the context of the four-card problem is the 'permission schema'. The core content of the permission schema is, 'If one is to do X, then one must satisfy precondition Y'.

Cheng and Holyoak examined the possible rule of the permission schema in the following study. Subjects in Hong Kong and Michigan were instructed in a problem about checking passengers' forms at an airport. The rule to be checked was 'If the form says 'ENTERING' on one side, then the other side includes cholera among the list of diseases'. Four cases corresponding to p, q, not-p, and not-q were available for examination. Half the subjects were given a rationale for the 'cholera' rule by being told that the form listed diseases for which the passenger had been inoculated and that a cholera inoculation was needed to protect the entering passengers from the disease. It was expected that this explanation would invoke the 'permission schema' (which matches closely the logic of the conditional). The expectation was justified in that both Hong Kong and Michigan subjects showed a marked increase in correct performance when given the rationale. This result is not consistent with the memory-cueing explanation since subjects did not have relevant memories; nor is it consistent with the syntactic rule view, since the logical structure of the task is not affected by the rationale. The result is, however, consistent with the pragmatic reasoning schema approach.

Cheng and Holyoak (1985) found further facilitating results of permission schemas when subjects were given an abstract version of the selection task in which the rule to be tested was based on the permission schema ('If one is to take action A, then one must satisfy precondition P'). The abstract description was apparently sufficient to evoke the permission schema and so facilitate solution.

H. Social contract theory

Cosmides (1989) has argued that, as a result of evolutionary pressures, the human mind contains a number of special-purpose mechanisms to handle problems that have been critical to survival over many millenia. Specifically, she proposes that correct handling of social contracts between individuals and between individuals and groups has been of evolutionary significance for at least 2 million years and that special-purpose cognitive mechanisms have evolved to detect cheaters. In a social contract, individuals agree to take a benefit (e.g. eating deer meat) only if they have paid an agreed cost (e.g. gathered sufficient branches for a cooking fire). Cheats are those who eat the deer meat without having gathered the wood. Thus, possible cheats would be found amongst those who eat the deer meat (they may not have gathered wood) or those who have not gathered wood (they may illicitly eat the meat). Cosmides proposes that humans have evolved so that they possess a 'cheat-detecting algorithm' which will focus in on possible cases of cheating.

The relevance of these evolutionary arguments for the four-card task is that versions of the task that fit the social contract pattern produce high rates of correct (falsifying) answers. The 'drinking age problem' of Griggs and Cox (1982) and the 'postal problem', of Johnson-Laird et al. (1972) are good examples of facilitating problems where a cost has to be paid (in waiting to be old enough or in money) before a benefit can be taken (drinking beer or sending a sealed letter). Cosmides (1989) argues that the only reliable facilitations of the four-card task with thematic materials occur when the rule used is a social contract and is understood as such by the subjects.

In a series of experiments, Cosmides (1989) sought to test the rival claims of social contract theory, availability and pragmatic schema approaches. We will first outline the studies comparing social contract and availability explanations.

Problems were devised that concerned unfamiliar social contracts, unfamiliar descriptive rules, familiar descriptive rules and abstract rules. An example unfamiliar social contract is 'If a man eats cassava root, then he must have a tattoo on his face'. This rule was framed as a social contract by means of a background story according to which the rule holds among certain Pacific islanders; the cassava root is described as a powerful aphrodisiac available only to married men and only married men are tattooed. In the social contract condition the subject is to adopt the role of an enforcer of the rule that unmarried men are eager to break. The four cards indicate on one side whether a man is tattooed or not and on the other side whether he is eating cassava root or molo nuts. The task is to decide whether to turn over cards showing 'Tattooed', 'Not-Tattooed', 'Cassava root' or 'Molo nuts'. In the unfamiliar descriptive version the subject is to adopt the role of an anthropologist seeking to determine whether a proposed descriptive rule that eating cassava roots always goes with being tattooed is being broken. The familiar descriptive problem was a 'transport and towns' problem, using places and means of transport familiar to the subjects. The abstract version was similar to Wason's original problem. In all cases a 'detective' type of set was induced to seek possible violations of the rules.

The results of these studies were that subjects made a high rate of falsifying (p and ~q) choices in the unfamiliar social contract condition (70 per cent), a low rate with unfamiliar descriptive problems (23 per cent) and a medium rate with familiar descriptive problems (42 per cent). The unfamiliar abstract baseline condition yielded c. 27 per cent falsifying responses. Availability of relevant memories cannot explain the high correct rate with the unfamiliar social contract task (although there does seem to be an advantage for familiar descriptive tasks over baseline). Thus, social contracts produced a strong facilitation even when the material was unfamiliar and could not cue relevant memories. An effect of availability appears to be present but was of modest size compared with the social contract effect.

Further studies by Cosmides (1989) lend more support to her case. In particular, experiments involving so-called 'switched' social contracts produce unusual choices predicted by social contract theory. Consider the cassava root rule. In its normal form this is 'If a man eats cassava root then he must have a tattoo on his face'. In the switched version it is 'If a man has a tattoo on his face then he eats cassava root'. Simply taking the surface logic of the switched rule, a falsifying approach would predict choices of 'Tattoo' and 'Molo nuts'; however, on the social contract interpretation, subjects would choose 'Not-Tattooed' and 'Cassava root' (more abstractly, the ~p and q cards). This prediction arises because it is among the 'Non-Tattooed' and the 'Cassava root' eaters that cheats may be found. Subjects were tested with the switched social contract, unfamiliar descriptive rules, familiar descriptive rules and abstract descriptive rules. The results indicated a high rate of the ~p and q choices for the switched social contract (70 per cent) with a near zero rate of such responses in the other conditions. Thus, the social contract theory was again upheld and the data from these experiments cannot be explained in any obvious way by the availability or memory-cueing approach.

An alternative explanation might be found in the pragmatic permission schema approach of Cheng and Holyoak (1985). Pragmatic schemas, as discussed in the previous section, take the form of 'If action A is to be taken then precondition B must be met'. Social contracts meet this specification in that they say 'If benefit A is to be taken, then cost B must be met'. Cosmides (1989) points out that, although all social contracts are 'permissions', not all permissions are social contracts, since social contracts always involve costs and benefits while permissions as a class do not always do so. Cosmides argues that permission rules have been facilitating only when they have incorporated costs and benefits and hence have been social contracts. To test this notion, experiments were carried out in which the same rules were framed by means of background stories as either social contracts (in which the actions were taking benefits and the preconditions were costs to be met) or as

permissions where the same actions and preconditions were without costs or benefits to the individuals. For example, the cassava root rule was framed as a social
contract as previously, or as a permission in which there was no individual advantage
to eating cassava roots or molo nuts and being tattooed was not painful. The
permission rule was justified as balancing out the frequency with which the two
foods were eaten to conserve food supplies for the group. The outcome was that
falsifying choices (p and ~q) were more frequent for the social contract version than
for the permission version (80 *v.* 45 per cent). Switching the rule to 'If a man has a
tattoo on his face then he eats cassava root' produced a high rate of ~p and q choices
in the social contract version compared with the permission version (65 *v.* 0 per
cent), as predicted by social contract theory.

The social contract theory has been further developed and refined by Gigerenzer
and Hug (1992). As a first step, these workers established the robustness of
Cosmides' basic findings with American subjects by replicating her strong facilitatory findings with unfamiliar social contracts in a study involving German students.
(Perhaps due to training in logic at German high school level, the German subjects
displayed a relatively high base rate of 'logic' choices; however, the pattern of results
was the same as that of Cosmides.) Gigerenzer and Hug then addressed the question
of whether it is the nature of the rule as a social contract or the elicitation of the
cheat-detecting algorithm that causes facilitation. In Cosmides' studies, the social
contract rules were always linked to cheat-detecting instructions. Gigerenzer and
Hug explored social contract rules, using familiar materials, but with the subjects
either cued into the perspective of a rule enforcer or that of an observer trying to
determine whether a proposed rule is honoured. An example rule used is the
'overnight cabin' rule familiar to Alpine hikers. This rule states that 'If someone
stays overnight in the cabin, then that person must bring along a bundle of wood from
the valley'. Wood is burned to keep the cabin warm overnight and to have the benefit
of warmth each hiker should pay the cost of bringing wood to the cabin. In the
'cheating' condition, subjects are cued into the perspective of a guard who checks
whether any of four hikers have broken the rule. The four hikers are repre- sented by
cards showing 'stays overnight in the cabin', 'carried no wood', 'carried wood' and
'does not stay overnight in the cabin'. In the 'no cheating' condition, the subject is
cued into the perspective of an observer who is trying to learn how the cabin system
operates. The rule as above is suggested as possibly applying but it is also suggested
that perhaps non-overnight stayers actually supply the wood. The subject is asked to
check the above four cards to find out whether anyone had broken the proposed
overnight rule. The 'no cheating' condition here differs from Cosmides' unfamiliar
descriptive rule conditions in that the social contract nature of the rule was made
clear to the subjects whereas Cosmides' unfamiliar descriptive rules were explicitly
not social contracts. A high percentage of p and ~q responses (89 per cent) were
obtained for the 'cheating' condition, with markedly less for the 'no cheating'
condition (53 per cent). Thus, the status of the rule as a social contract is not
sufficient for a high degree of facilitation; a cheat-detecting perspective must be
adopted.

Gigerenzer and Hug (1992) pointed out that social contracts can be divided into those that may be called *social exchanges*, in which the parties exchange goods or services of some sort and both sides can cheat, and social contracts (e.g. the drinking-age rule) where an obligation must be met but only one side can cheat (e.g. buying beer when under age). With bilateral cheating possibilities, it was found that switching perspectives produced a sharp change in reponse tendencies from p and ˜q to ˜p and q. For example, with the rule 'If an employee works on the weekend, then that person gets a day off during the week', subjects were either cued in to the employers' perspective or the employees' perspective and asked to check four cards to determine whether the rule had been violated. The four cards showed 'worked on weekend' (p), 'did not get a day off'(˜q), 'did not work on the weekend' (˜p) and 'did get day off' (q). With the employee perspective, p and ˜q responses dominated (75 per cent), but with the employer perspective, ˜p and q responses predominated (61 per cent). Thus, Gigerenzer and Hug obtained a switch in response preferences by switching perspectives while keeping the rule the same; Cosmides (1989) obtained a similar change by switching the rule around while keeping the same 'enforcer' perspective. Switching perspectives is a 'cleaner' manipulation since rule switching raises problems with wording and with interpretation of the switched rule in relation to the original rule. It may also be noted here that essentially the same effects of perspective switching have been also reported by Manktelow and Over (1991) and by Politzer and Nguyen-Xuan (1992) using 'promise' rules and a variant of the 'Sears' rule respectively. The results, from both rule and perspective switching, however, are in line with social contract theory predictions.

Gigerenzer and Hug (1992) found further that, in the case of rules that were not social exchanges but rather permissions in which only one side could readily be said to have a cheating opportunity (e.g. the postal rule), the perspective of the party who might be cheated produces many p and ˜q responses (e.g., 'sealed' and 'low-price stamp') but a switch of perspective to the other side produces a mixture of p and ˜q, ˜p and q, and all four card choices. The perspective of the party who cannot be cheated does not allow the cheat-detecting algorithm to give the subject any guidance about which cards to select; hence it seems the more variable pattern observed in such cases.

Overall, it is clear that Cosmides' evolutionary argument has led to identification of a class of rules that will reliably produce response patterns matching falsification choices (p and ˜q) or, if switched, will produce choices unlikely to occur in the standard abstract version (˜p and q). Cosmides explained these patterns in terms of social contracts and cheat-detecting algorithms, which she argued were prewired by evolutionary pressures. Gigerenzer and Hug have refined the social contract approach by demonstrating that the social contract nature of the rule is not sufficient but must be accompanied by the elicitation of cheat detecting before facilitation is obtained in the normal case. They also demonstrated the importance of perspective in determining which possibilities are possible 'cheats' and therefore need to be examined. They sum up their results thus:

If a selection task (rule and context information) (1) cues a person into the perspective of one party engaged in a social contract, and (2) the other party has a cheating option, then a cheater-detection algorithm is activated that selects the conjunction of cards that define being cheated, that is, benefit taken and costs not paid (requirement not met) by the other party.

The research reviewed above on the social contract approach and on the pragmatic reasoning schemas approach has highlighted the facilitating effect of *deontic* rules, i.e. rules regarding what *may* or *must* be done. Special deontic systems of logic have been developed but the field is considerably less advanced than that of propositional logic and subject to more controversy (Over and Manktelow, 1993). The research suggests that subjects generally do have a good grasp of basic deontic rules expressing simple social contracts since their selection task choices are in line with such understanding. This high level of understanding may reflect some evolutionary pressure leading to special purpose mechanisms becoming hard-wired into human brains (Cosmides' proposal) or it may reflect the importance of such practical knowledge, which might be acquired through general-purpose learning mechanisms. Although research on deontic rules (social contracts, etc.) arose from studies of thematic effects on the four-card selection task, this work has departed considerably from Wason's (1966, 1968) initial concern with hypothetico-deductive reasoning aimed at determining the truth or falsity of a proposed conditional rule, rather than whether a contract has been violated. The work discussed in the next section (Oaksford and Chater, 1994) re-addresses the basic issues of inductive reasoning in the four-card selection task and pursues an interpretation of data that leads to a more sanguine conclusion about human rationality than is often drawn (e.g. Cohen, 1981).

I. The selection task as optimal data selection

Wason's initial studies of the selection task (1966, 1968) were informed by Popper's (1959) notion that falsification was the rational way to test scientific hypotheses and by extension any causal or indicative hypothesis. As we have seen repeatedly, few people spontaneously adopt a falsifying approach to the standard abstract selection task and this aversion to falsification has been seen as a sign of imperfect rationality. However, Oaksford and Chater (1994) have proposed an alternative normative approach which also has a strong claim to rationality. This is an approach in terms of comparative testing of hypotheses to reduce the tester's uncertainty between them and involves the use of Bayes' theorem.

A hypothesis is proposed, e.g. that 'if a card has p on one side then it has q on the other side'. Among other things this hypothesis implies that the probability of a card having not-q on it, given it has a p on it, is zero and that the probability of qs must be at least as great as the probability of ps. The obvious alternative hypothesis is the null hypothesis, that p and q are unrelated so the probability of not-q given p is non-zero and the probability of q could be less than the probability of p. Bayes' theorem allows the investigator to revise the probabilities of hypotheses in the light of data which are more or less likely if the hypotheses are true.

Oaksford and Chater (1994) showed that if the proposed rule and the alternative null hypothesis are viewed as equally likely initially, and the probabilities of ps and qs are seen as fairly low, then the best choices on Bayes' theorem to discriminate between the two hypotheses are the p card, the q card and the not-q card, in that order. The not-p card would yield no discriminating information. The predicted preference order of card choices then is p > q > not-q > not-p, and this was the order found in a review of 13 papers reporting a total of 34 abstract selection tasks.

Other more subtle aspects of the data also fit the optimal selection model. For example, choice frequencies of similarly signed cards (p and q, and not-p and not-q) tend to correlate positively (Evans, 1977) and this also is explicable on the optimal data selection approach.

The model was also shown to fit results from Kirby (1994), in which it was found that as probability of p was varied in the cover story from 0.001 to 0.90, the likelihood of subjects' choosing not-q increased, while the likelihood of choosing p or q decreased. By taking account of the utilities (gains and costs) of various outcomes, the model is also able to fit the thematic, deontic, rule results on per-spective switching from Gigerenzer and Hug (1992), discussed in the previous section. Kirby (1994) varied probabilities and utilities of different outcomes in the 'drinking age' rule, with an enforcer perspective. Here, varying the costs of false alarms and misses, and the benefits of hits, alters choice frequencies in line with an approach in terms of choosing to maximize expected utility. Again, the optimal data selection model fits the results well.

Although the optimal data selection model does give an impressive fit to a wide range of data (and is more flattering of human capabilities than many models in this area), the mechanisms by which selections are made are not specified. It seems unlikely that subjects are explicitly working through Bayesian calculations and the suggestion is that implicit processes have become optimized to yield adaptive behaviour. The model fits Anderson's (1991) rational analysis approach to cognition which stresses the value of considering what adaptive problems cognition is solving. The assumption is that cognition is adaptive and is optimized to its environment. Determining the nature of the environment and the nature of the goals suggests what will be optimal solutions and may narrow the search for a description of *what* subjects are accomplishing; however, the question of the mechanisms by which such optimal results are reached remains unanswered . The overall benefits of a problem-solving process must be calculated in such a way as to take into account the costs in effort of the process as well as the benefits obtained from the process. Further relevant discussion of optimal processing will be found in Chapter 8.

II. GENERATING AND TESTING HYPOTHESES

In studies of conditional rule testing, such as those discussed above, subjects are given a rule and possible sources of evidence which may or may not support or disconfirm the rule. Usually, in real-life research, one is not given a rule but must generate possible rules (hypotheses) which can then be tested.

The processes of generating and testing self-produced hypotheses have been subject to laboratory investigation in a number of ways. The three main approaches have involved the study of (1) concept learning tasks, (2) Wason's 'reversed 20 questions' task and (3) most realistically, performance in simulated research environments. As we shall see, somewhat similar points seem to emerge from these different lines of research.

A. Concept identification

In a concept identification task, a collection of stimuli has been classified by the experimenter into two or more categories on the basis of some rule. It is the subject's task to induce the rule on the basis of information about the category membership of individual stimuli. Normally, the stimuli are constructed by combining values on a small number of dimensions (e.g. *colour*: red/blue, *shape*: square/triangle, *size*: large/small). Information can be made available to the subject in two main ways. Either the stimuli and their classifications are presented to the subject in an order determined by the experimenter (reception paradigm) or the whole stimulus array is available and the subject chooses the stimuli to be informed about (selection paradigm).

As Bruner *et al.* (1956) put it in their classic study, in the reception paradigm the subject is like a researcher on the effects of human brain damage on language. He or she must wait for accident cases to turn up and these may not arrive in the 'best' sequence. In the selection paradigm, the subject is more in the position of a researcher on brain areas underlying pattern vision in monkeys. Such a researcher can choose which areas to remove in each study and can devise an optimum sequence of tests. Similarly, the selection paradigm subject can choose an optimum sequence of stimuli about which to receive classification information.

Bruner *et al.* had their subjects write down their hypotheses after each trial (stimulus followed by feedback on the correct answer) in reception paradigm studies. They found that people had difficulty in correctly handling information that falsified their current hypotheses. This was true whether their initial hypotheses were complex (based on all attributes) or simple (based on one or two attributes). In the selection paradigm, two main types of strategy were identified: focusing and scanning.

Focusers took a particular instance which was a positive example of the experimenter's rule and sought out stimuli that differed in just one attribute from the 'focus'. If the new stimulus was still 'positive', then the changed attribute was irrelevant and could be ignored; if the new stimulus was 'negative', then the changed attribute was at least part of the answer and should be held constant when choosing a further stimulus to test. The focuser could thus narrow down to the correct set of attributes with little strain on memory or inference. The scanning approach was less efficient and produced information relevant to the question of verification bias.

Scanners essentially picked on a particular hypothesis (e.g. 'two squares') and sought to test it against instances until it was falsified, whereupon another hypothesis would be selected. It was noticeable that subjects tended to pick stimuli that could verify their hypothesis rather than stimuli that could falsify it. For example, if the subject's hypothesis was 'red squares', he or she tended to enquire about red square stimuli, rather than checking green squares or red circles. (All red squares may be +, but the rule could be 'red' alone or 'square' alone or 'red or square' rather than 'red and square'.) Further data regarding 'verification bias' will be discussed below.

It should be mentioned that Bruner *et al.*'s (1956) pioneering work on the concept identification paradigm led to a flood of experiments over the following 20 years or so, particularly on the effects of varying parameters of the reception task. This work (e.g. Bourne, 1966) tended to focus on the overall effects of task variations on learning speeds rather than on particular theories of inference.

Recently, there has been considerable interest in more 'naturalistic' forms of concept learning, using less stylized stimuli. Such work tends to implicate unconscious learning and generalization processes (e.g. McClelland and Rumelhart, 1985) rather than the deliberate forms of inductive reasoning that are the focus of this chapter. Thus, the topic of concept learning has rather dropped out from the study of reasoning in current cognitive psychology.

B. Wason's reversed 20 questions task

1 Early results

Wason (1960) devised a special task in which subjects tended to generate overrestrictive hypotheses which would lead astray those with verifying tendencies. Subjects were given three numbers, (2, 4, 6) and told that these conformed to a rule that they had to discover. The means of discovery was to be by generating other three-number series that might match the rule or not. The experimenter gave feedback on each triplet produced by subject. Subjects were asked to announce their rule when they were highly confident that it was the correct answer. The correct rule was 'numbers in increasing order of magnitude'. As you might expect, subjects stuck to more restrictive hypotheses, e.g. 'intervals of 2 between increasing numbers', 'arithmetic series'. However, the main interest lay in how subjects tested their hypotheses. The overwhelming tendency (Wason, 1960) was for subjects simply to generate series consistent with their particular hypothesis and to keep on doing so until they felt sufficiently confident to announce the hypothesis as correct. Few subjects either tried out series that ran counter to their own hypotheses or spontaneously varied their hypotheses. About 20 per cent of subjects discovered the rule without any incorrect announcements, and these people had tended to vary their hypotheses spontaneously. Little evidence was found for a falsification strategy.

A number of task variations were attempted – with little effect. The material was varied from 'numbers' to a task in which the subject was given an instance of some very general class (e.g. 'microphone' as an instance of the class 'inanimate objects') and was instructed to find the class by trying out other possible instances.

This modification was ineffective in changing the prevalent 'verifying' strategy. Instructions to discover all the rules that could be correct had no effect. Also, imposing a charge of 12.5 pence for each incorrect rule announcement made subjects more cautious about claiming to know the answer but did not affect the apparent bias toward verification.

2 Positive and negative tests

Klayman and Ha (1987) carried out what amounts to a 'rational analysis' (Anderson, 1991) of the 2–4–6 task similar to that later carried out by Oaksford and Chater (1994) on the four-card selection task. Klayman and Ha argue that what subjects typically do is better characterized as a *positive test strategy* rather than as a confirming or verifying strategy. The positive test strategy for hypothesis testing involves examining instances in which the property or event of interest is expected to occur (to check whether it does occur) *or* in which the property or event of interest is known to have occurred (to see whether the hypothesized conditions hold). For example, if meteorologists have a hypothesis about when tornadoes will occur, on the positive test strategy they will look to see what happens when the hypothesized conditions hold and/or look at tornado records to see whether the hypothesized conditions held. Note that these positive tests could yield falsifying as well as confirming information. Discussions of this area have been hampered by a tendency to confuse positive tests with a verifying bias and negative testing with a falsifying strategy. A negative test in the tornado example would involve looking at calm weather days (to check that the hypothesized tornado conditions were not present) or examining what happens when the hypothesized conditions are not met (in the expectation that a tornado would not occur). Such negative tests might yield confirming or disconfirming information. However, when events of interest, such as tornadoes, are rare, Klayman and Ha (1987) show that the positive test strategy is more likely to yield falsifying results than is a negative test strategy. In general, then, the positive test strategy is adaptive in many real-life situations but not in the special conditions of the 2–4–6 task where typical hypotheses are over-restrictive and *require* negative testing to produce informative falsifications.

Consistent with this analysis, Gorman *et al.* (1984) found on a related task (a card game called 'New Eleusis') that training on a 'disconfirmatory' strategy (negative testing) markedly improved performance (15 of 16 solved), relative to training on a 'confirmatory' (positive testing) strategy (six of 16 solved). Tweney and colleagues (1980), however, found no facilitation with disconfirmatory (negative test) instructions in the 2–4–6 task. In contrast, Gorman and Gorman (1984) found a strong facilitating effect of negative test instructions in terms of numbers solving the 2–4–6 task.

The main reason for these differing results seems to be that in the Gormans' studies the subjects had to decide for themselves whether they had finally solved or not, but in the Tweney *et al.* study subjects could ask the experimenter whether they had solved or not. In other words, the experimenter would provide confirmation or disconfirmation on request; this was Wason's original procedure. Gorman (1992) argues that his version of the task is more similar to the position of real scientists, who cannot appeal to God to tell them whether they have cracked nature's secrets. Disconfirmation (negative testing) seems to be an effective instruction when subjects cannot appeal to an outside authority. If appeal to authority is allowed *ad lib*, then subjects seem to forego negative testing in favour of the less stressful procedure of checking with the experimenter (if not with God!).

Klayman and Ha (1989) followed up their theoretical analysis with a large-scale empirical study in which subjects had 18 trials on a variety of reversed 20 questions problems using a range of contents. An interesting manipulation was that the target rules were of three types so that typical initial hypotheses were 'embedded' in the target rule, 'overlapped' the target or 'surrounded' the target. For example, with the typical 2–4–6 hypothesis, 'increasing by 2', an embedded condition rule would be 'ascending numbers' (the standard case), an overlapping condition rule would be 'single-digit numbers' and a surrounded condition rule would be 'consecutive evens that end in 2, 4, 6' (such as 12, 14, 16).

On each trial, subjects stated their current hypothesis and generated an instance with a reason, and were given feedback on the instance as matching the target rule or not. Overall, positive tests predominated (67 per cent of trials). *Alternative tests*, in which a specific alternative to the prior hypothesis was proposed and tested in a way that would distinguish from the previous hypotheses, were next most common (22 per cent of trials). The more successful subjects made more use of alternative tests. However, alternative tests were less common in the 'surrounding' conditions, where the typical initial hypothesis was too broad; in such cases, the positive test strategy led to many falsifications and to consequent frequent changes of hypo- thesis. Alternative hypotheses tended to be tried only after one hypothesis had received a fair measure of confirmation. Tweney (1985) has pointed out that this pattern of initial confirmation followed by attempted disconfirmation by testing an alternative was a pattern observable in the work of the distinguished nineteenth century scientist, Michael Faraday.

3 Single v. dual rules

An interesting manipulation that has been found markedly to facilitate performance in the 2–4–6 task is to ask the subjects to discover both the normal target rule and the rule for the complementary set, i.e. those triples not conforming to the target rule (Wetherick, 1962; Tweney *et al.*, 1980; Tukey, 1986; Gorman *et al.* 1987; Farris and Revlin, 1989). Typically in this manipulation, subjects are told that the experimenter has two rules in mind, one for DAX triples and one for MED triples. The DAX triples correspond to the familiar 'ascending numbers' rule and the MED triples are the 'not-ascending numbers' complementary set. Subjects are given 2–4–6 as an example of DAX triples and then propose and test triples in the usual way. The percentage of subjects who make a correct first announcement of a hypothesis in the dual-rule condition is approximately twice that in single-rule conditions according to Wharton *et al.*'s (1993) survey.

On the basis of Klayman and Ha's positive test strategy analysis, Wharton and co-workers (1993) argued that positive testing of the complementary MED rule would lead to falsifications of MED hypotheses, and by implication of DAX hypotheses. For example, if the DAX hypothesis is 'ascending in 2s' then the MED hypothesis would be 'not ascending in 2s'; MED might be (positive) tested by proposing '5, 8, 11', which would be given feedback 'DAX' and so falsify both the current MED and DAX hypotheses. The proposed analysis of the benefits of dual-rule testing works, however, only if subjects understand that the rules are indeed complementary. Wharton *et al.*, found that subjects benefited from the dual-rule condition only if they were explicitly informed that the rules were complementary; otherwise, there was no advantage over the normal single-rule condition.

4 Hypothesis testing v. observing

Tukey (1986) argued that subjects in this task, without special instruction in 'ideal' methodologies, nevertheless behave in ways that are rational in terms of various alternative philosophies of science. The stress on falsification in many studies of inductive reasoning is derived from Popper's (1959) analysis of scientific method. Tukey points to alternative accounts of scientific inquiry by, for example, Mill (1875/1967), Lakatos (1970), Kuhn (1970) and bayesian theorists (Hesse, 1975). Subjects were asked during the task to describe their procedures, to select from a list of terms those that best characterized their methods and to state their preferred hypotheses and judgements of how likely their hypotheses were to be correct. Subjects had difficulty describing their methods of approach, but they could use the methodology terms in ways that were consistent with their performance. It emerged that subjects were not always testing particular hypotheses on each trial, but would quite often be examining instances 'at random' or just because they were 'different'. Certainly, subjects rarely reported attempting to 'disconfirm' their hypotheses. Attempts to confirm and simply to explore accounted for over half the trials, according to the labels given the trials by the subjects. Overall, Tukey's study indicates that possibly a rather narrow view, based on the Popperian philosophy of science, was applied to this task hitherto. When alternative philosophies are considered, much of the subjects' behaviour seems more rational and intelligible.

C. Simulated research environments

Although philosophers of science tend to stress the importance of falsification (Popper, 1959) and of considering more than one hypothesis at a time (Platt, 1964), the results of Wason and of Bruner *et al.* (1956), discussed above, suggest that naive subjects tend neither to consider alternative hypotheses nor to seek out potentially falsifying data. Studies by Mynatt *et al.* (1977, 1978) and Dunbar (1993) sought to investigate such tendencies in complex environments that intended to simulate real-life research.

In Mynatt *et al.*'s (1977) study, subjects saw computer-generated displays on a screen (see Fig. 7.1) showing various shapes (circles, squares, triangles) of varying degrees of brightness (dim or bright). A particle could be fired across the screen (from a fixed position) in any direction, and it would be stopped when it approached some objects but not others. The subject's overall task was to produce a hypothesis that would account for the behaviour of the particle. The correct answer was that the particle stopped on approaching dim shapes.

At first, subjects were allowed to formulate an initial hypothesis on the basis of the particle's behaviour with one particular configuration of objects (a configuration that favoured adoption of a wrong hypothesis in terms of object shape). They then chose between pairs of environments, in one of which they could make observations that would probably confirm the typical wrong hypothesis and in the other of which they would test alternative hypotheses. Evidence for a confirmation bias, involving failure to choose environments allowing tests of alternative hypotheses, was found. However, if subjects did obtain explicit falsifying information, they generally used this information to reject incorrect hypotheses. Behaviour in this task was not affected by instructions stressing confirmation or disconfirmation.

In Mynatt *et al.*'s 1978 study, subjects were allowed 10 hours to explore a complex

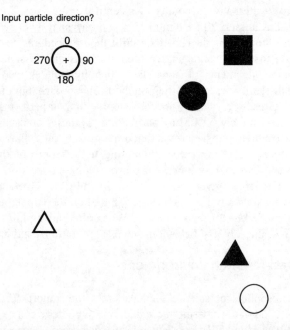

Fig 7.1 *Type of display used in study of confirmation bias. Textured features had 0.5 brightness levels. 'Particles' were fired from the grid in the upper left of the screen. The subject controlled the direction of the particle's motion. Reproduced with permission from Mynatt, C.R., Doherty, M.E. and Tweney, R.D. (1977). Confirmation bias in a simulated research environment: an experimental study of scientific inference.* Quarterly Journal of Experimental Psychology **29**, *85–95.*

environment of 27 objects, varying in shape, size and brightness, in which particles were deflected on approaching objects. The angles of deflection were governed by a formula involving parameters whose values were determined by the shape, size and brightness of the objects. No one solved and Mynatt *et al.* inferred a 'confirmation bias' from the subjects' reaction to observations that falsified their hypotheses but the interpretation of these results (Table 7.4) is debatable.

Mynatt *et al.* had two groups of subjects. One group was instructed in Platt's (1964) 'strong inference' approach to scientific methodology (this emphasizes developing and testing alternative hypotheses, especially with a view to falsification). A control group received no special instructions about scientific research strategy. No major differences emerged between the two groups' patterns of results, and so in Table 7.4 the data from two groups have been merged .

When falsifying data were obtained the subjects either abandoned or revised their hypotheses 67 per cent of the time. On 33 per cent of occasions the falsifying data do seem to have been discounted either immediately or after a delay during which forgetting could have intervened. So, if we allow hypothesis revision (as well as abandonment) to be a reasonable reaction to data that disconfirm a particular hypothesis, then subjects reacted in some appropriate way to 67 per cent of falsifications. It seems unfair, on these data, to class the majority of subjects as showing 'a strong tendency to discount or disregard falsification' (Mynatt *et al.*, 1978, p. 400). However, it was clear from the subjects' thinking-aloud records that deliberate attempts to falsify their own hypotheses almost never occurred. There was an overwhelming tendency to seek confirming data, but the subjects in the 1978 study do seem to have reacted appropriately, on the whole, to the occurrence of disconfirming evidence. Perhaps because the environment was much more complex in the 1978 study, there was less tendency to reject disconfirmed hypotheses totally and more of a tendency to modify than was evident in the 1977 results.

Dunbar (1993) devised a task environment which was a still closer simulation of real science than the artificial universes of Mynatt *et al.* In Dunbar's study subjects had to devise explanations of how genes are controlled by other genes using a simulated molecular genetics laboratory on a computer. The problem that the subjects were tackling was a real one, which had been solved by Jacob and Monod

Table 7.4 *Summary of reactions to hypothesis disconfirmation*

	Results of hypothesis tests	No. of cases
Responses following disconfirmation	Permanently abandoned hypothesis	26 (30)
	Temporarily abandoned hypothesis	11 (13)
	Revised hypothesis and retested	33 (37)
($n = 88$)	Retested hypotheses without revision	18 (20)

Value in parentheses are percentages. From Mynatt *et al.* (1978), with permission.

(1961) and for which they received the Nobel prize. Dunbar's subjects could make a creditable attempt at the problem in an hour or so because they were brought by pretraining to a state of knowledge similar to that of Jacob and Monod (1961) before their crucial studies, and because the subjects did not have to develop apparatus and methods which the Nobel prize-winning scientists had to do over a 20-year period. The problem concerned how certain genes in the bacterium *Escherichia coli* controlled the production of a crucial enzyme by other genes. Basically, two genes *inhibit* the producer genes until the enzyme is needed. If either of the inhibitory genes is absent, then enzyme production is continuous. The critical shift of hypothesis was from a hypothesis that the controlling genes *activated* the producing genes to the inhibitory control hypothesis.

In Dunbar's first experiment, subjects were pre-instructed in relevant parts of molecular genetics and were exposed to an example of gene control by activation and instructed in the experimental methods allowed in the simulated laboratory. Next, while 'set' for an activation explanation, subjects tackled the experimental task of discovering the inhibitory control mechanism. Only four of 20 succeeded. All subjects began with an activation hypothesis but differed in their reaction to disconfirming data. Some subjects set the goal of seeking data consistent with their hypothesis; none of these subjects solved. Other subjects set the goal of attempting to explain the discrepant findings; the solvers were in this group.

Dunbar proposed that if subjects achieved some corroboration of their first hypothesis they would be more likely then to attend to discrepant data and find alternative hypotheses. A second study was therefore carried out with a new group of 20 subjects; the procedure was as in the first study except that the solution to the main task involved both activation control by one gene and inhibitory control by two genes. Thus, one mechanism was consistent with the predominant activation hypothesis and one was inconsistent. Twice as many subjects reached the correct conclusion in study 2 as in study 1.

An interesting point which emerged from detailed analysis of verbal protocols in these studies is that hypotheses were hierarchically organized. Typically, subjects started with a general activation hypothesis, that activation was involved in control. This was then specialized to one particular gene being an activator. Confirmatory evidence was then sought. If discrepant evidence was obtained, then a different gene was hypothesized to be an activator, and so on. When all simple activation hypotheses were disconfirmed in study 1, some subjects would then set a new goal of explaining the data inconsistent with activation. Other subjects would persist in seeking confirmatory evidence. It was only when subjects changed goals from seeking to confirm their initial broad hypothesis, to seeking to account for discrepant data, that other broad or over-arching hypotheses would be considered. In study 2, the initial goal of seeking confirmation of the activation hypothesis is met and most subjects then adopt the new goal of accounting for the discrepant data, which leads them to the inhibitory part of the solution.

D. Real research environments

Studies of real-life hypothesis testing in the sciences (Mitroff, 1974; Chalmers, 1978) are consistent with many laboratory studies in that scientists do not seem overly disposed to seek falsifying data or to accept that favoured theories require revision or abandonment in the face of apparently falsifying results.

For example, Galileo ignored much data that was apparently inconsistent with copernican theory, and protagonists of Newton's theory did not abandon it in view of the 'misbehaviour' of certain planets, such as Uranus. The typical reaction to observations inconsistent with a favoured theory is to seek an explanation that preserves the theory. In the case of Uranus' orbit, a new undiscovered planet was postulated and in due course the theory received spectacular support from the discovery of Neptune in the predicted place. Other anomalies in newtonian theory were never resolved, but the theory was not abandoned.

In more recent times, Mitroff (1974) closely surveyed the attitudes and beliefs about scientific practice of a group of 43 geologists engaged in the study of lunar geology under the auspices of the Apollo space research programme. These well established scientists saw their aim as (mainly) confirming rather than falsifying hypotheses. The only hypotheses that they were interested in falsifying were the hypotheses of rival scientists! As Mitroff puts it, these scientists differed markedly from the 'story-book scientist' who is supposed to be completely disinterested and uncommitted to any particular hypothesis. The real scientists tended to be strongly committed to particular points of view and would abandon their views only reluctantly in the face of contrary evidence – rather than immediately, as a naive falsificationist position would suppose.

Perhaps then, the laboratory subjects in Mynatt et al.'s studies are not untypical, in seeking confirmation rather than falsification. Indeed, the relatively high rate of appropriate reactions to falsifying data in the studies of Mynatt et al. (1977, 1978) and Dunbar (1993) may reflect the artificiality of the environments, e.g. subjects could not doubt their 'instruments' in the way that real scientists might. [Gorman (1986) has shown in a laboratory task that the possibility of error in feedback 'insulates' hypotheses from rejection.] Mitroff's moon scientists pointed out that 'commitment' was valuable from the point of view of motivating individual scientists. Also, since there would always be scientists with opposing commitments, the 'scientific community' would not be biased as a whole and the rivalry of competing factions would ensure that opposing views would be tested thoroughly by the opposition. Even a few cases of extreme commitment or outright bias could be useful to have around, because those biased individuals would keep alive ideas that might prove useful again at a later date after having been abandoned by most researchers in a given area. These analyses of actual scientific practice suggest that the 'simulated research environments' of Mynatt et al. have, so far, lacked the social–psychological dimension that appears to be crucial in real-life environments.

III. SUMMARY AND CONCLUDING COMMENTS

What conclusions, if any, can be drawn from the review of research in inductive reasoning presented above? A few themes seem to emerge consistently. These are: (1) a tendency to ignore sources of potentially falsifying information; (2) a preference for 'direct tests' of hypotheses using potentially confirming data; but also (3) a generally saving ability to take some appropriate action (abandonment or revision) when clear falsifying data are obtained. Let us now consider these points in more detail.

Available potentially falsifying information was generally not used in either the abstract version of Wason's four-card task or in the more realistic settings of Mynatt *et al.*'s simulated research environments. Preference for direct tests of hypotheses emerged in Wason's (1960) reversed 20 questions task, in Mynatt *et al.*'s studies and in Bruner *et al.*'s studies of concept learning. Appropriate reactions to falsification were often (if not always) observed in both Bruner *et al.*'s, Mynatt *et al.*'s and Dunbar's studies. The preference for direct tests of hypotheses is the best established of the three conclusions and a plausible explanation was suggested by Bruner *et al.* (1956, p. 86) in terms of minimizing cognitive strain. The hypotheses being tested by the subjects in the relevant studies could be phrased as 'equivalences', e.g. 'if and only if the figure is red, is it a positive example of the rule' or 'if and only if the series is arithmetic, is it an instance of the experimenter's category' or 'if and only if the particle approaches a triangle will it stop'. The general form is 'if and only if p then q'. To make a direct test, one has only to seek or generate instances of p and check whether they are also q's. To make an indirect test on the other hand, one would have to decide which of the possible vast range of instances of not-p to examine to check whether it was also not-q. Thus, it appears to be simpler to rely on direct tests. Such tests also have the benefit that they will usually succeed eventually (Klayman and Ha,1987) and will be seriously misleading only if the hypothesis being directly tested is included completely in the correct hypothesis, e.g. in concept learning, if the hypothesis 'red' was tried when the correct answer was 'red or square', or in the reversed 20 questions task if 'arithmetic series' is tried when the correct answer is simply 'increasing magnitude'. Direct testing, which involves not deliberately seeking falsifying data, would thus usually be a reasonable cognitive strategy that would often succeed with low cognitive strain in real life. Ignoring available but potentially falsifying data may also arise from customary habits of hypothesis testing. In the case of the four-card task, Wetherick (1970; 1971; see also Shapiro, 1971) has pointed out that it is 'unrepresentative' of real-life hypothesis testing. Wetherick argued that outside the thinking and problem-solving laboratory a hypothesis of the 'if p then q' variety would be formulated in order to facilitate prediction of 'q' from 'p' (e.g. predicting success at a particular job from test score). Thus, the normal procedure would be to seek 'p's' and then check to see whether they did later display 'q' or not. The suggestion is that, if subjects treat the four-card task as representative of real-life hypothesis testing, they will tend to focus on the 'p' card to see whether 'p' predicts 'q' and will ignore the 'q' and '~q' cards as irrelevant to prediction.

Rule content emerged as an important factor in the four-card task. Particularly facilitatory results have been found where the rule states an obligation or contract and the subject has the perspective of an enforcer (Cheng and Holyoak, 1985; Cosmides, 1989; Gigerenzer and Hug, 1992). Change of perspective produces marked switches in card choices. Such rules are well understood, with clear cost–benefit relationships, and the subjects' choices seem intelligible as a form of decision making to maximize information and/or utilities (Kirby, 1994; Oaksford and Chater, 1994).

Overall, the general run of results and ideas outlined in this review are consistent with the usual information-processing assumptions made in previous chapters, of small working memory, vast long-term memory and serial processing. Finally, it may be noted here that Evans, in the course of developing the notions of Type I and II (later, heuristic and analytic thinking), criticized the use of subjects' reports as a source of evidence about information processing (since the reports may be misleading rationalizations, rather than accurate accounts). This point raises important questions, concerning the meaning and utility of subjects' reports (whether 'thinking aloud' or retrospectively justifying behaviour), which will be discussed further in Chapter 11, when we have a broader range of background information on which to draw.

IV. FURTHER READING

Mitroff, I.I. (1974). *The subjective side of science*. Amsterdam: Elsevier. An intriguing empirical account of real life 'inductive reasoning' among lunar research scientists.

Wason, P.C. (1983). Realism and rationality in the selection task. In J.St.B.T. Evans (Ed.). *Thinking and reasoning*, pp. 44–75. London: Routledge and Kegan Paul. A useful overview and a unique historical account of the origins of the selection task by its deviser.

8

Decision making

Decision making and problem solving are closely intertwined activities. Problem solving always involves some decision making, such as deciding whether a possible solution is acceptable or which alternative line of search or of problem reduction should be developed first. Decision tasks can be seen as a special form of problem in which the goal is to make a good selection from the available options. It may be necessary to think ahead to possible consequences of the alternative choices given different states of the world. Thus, deciding may require extensive mental exploration of tree-like mazes of possible sequences of events. Although decision making and problem solving are closely interrelated, the main foci of the two activities are different.

In problem solving the focus is on generating possible actions, whereas in decision making the focus is on selecting among possible actions. Indeed, in typical laboratory studies of decision making the options are presented and subjects choose among them without the load of option-generation.

Decision problems can be characterized on a number of dimensions. One important distinction is between risky and riskless decisions. In a risky decision there is some element of uncertainty about the outcome of the choices available. Choosing between gambles is a classical case of risky decision making. In a riskless decision there is no such uncertainty. (An example of a riskless decision might be choosing between two pairs of socks or similar reliable consumer goods. Unfortunately, in real life, even this choice may involve a perceived gamble. How likely are the socks to last a period? How likely are the socks to remain acceptably fashionable?)

Furthermore, decisions may involve *single-attribute* or *multi-attribute* alternatives. Choosing between single-attribute objects is simple enough, but most choices are between multi-attribute objects (e.g. between cars varying in cost, maximum speeds, reliability, economy, servicing intervals, colours, etc.). Such choices require weighting of the attributes and an integration of information over the attributes to reach a decision.

Another useful distinction is between *single-stage* and *multi-stage* decisions. In multi-stage decisions, sequence of decisions is involved, such that each choice leads to one of a number of alternative choices. Such multi-stage decision making is probably more typical of real life than the 'one-off', isolated, single-stage decisions most often studied in the laboratory.

Decision making has long been studied in a *normative* way, with the aim of recommending to decision makers what they should rationally do. This approach leads to descriptions of how an idealized rational decision maker would make choices. Although no one individual is likely to be perfectly rational at all times, normative decision theory has provided a basis for economic theory in its attempt to understand and predict aggregate behaviour (e.g. of stock markets). From the psychological point of view, normative models can provide a starting point for empirical research and for empirically oriented theory. To what extent do people approximate to normative models? Can normative models be modified from empirical models that will fit individual decision-making behaviour? More recently, psychological efforts have begun to focus on developing *process* models that try to capture the cognitive processes underlying decision making.

I. NORMATIVE MODELS FOR RISKY DECISION MAKING

A. Values, utilities and probabilities

In real life one often has to choose between alternative courses of action without being completely certain what consequences the alternatives will have. Choosing between gambles provides simplified risky decisions, and the basic ideas of the normative approach to risky choices can be best explained by using gambling examples.

Suppose two horses, called Alpha and Beta, are racing each other. Alpha will win with probability of 0.8 and Beta with a probability of 0.2. (Assume that probabilities may have been established over hundreds of races and can be taken to be accurate.) You have a choice of betting 50 units of money on Alpha to win or 10 money units on Beta. If Alpha wins, you will gain 100 units. If Beta wins, you will gain 400 units. Which should you choose?

The basic notion of the normative approach to decision making is that the decision maker should choose in such a way as to maximize a measure of expected return. The main variations hinge on the degree to which the measure to be maximized is derived from objective or subjective elements. In the present simple example, the objectively expected value in money terms of each course of action can be readily obtained. The *expected value* (EV) of betting 50 units on Alpha, given it has a 0.8 probability of winning you 100 units, is determined as follows:

EV (Betting on Alpha) = $(0.8 \times 100) - (0.2 \times 50) = +70$

While the EV of betting 10 units on Beta, given it has a 0.2 probability of winning you 400 units is:

EV (Betting on Beta) = (0.2 × 400) – (0.8 × 10) = +72

Therefore, EV maximization would lead to a choice of the bet on Beta. Note that EV maximization implies that choice of either bet would be preferable to not taking one of the gambles at all. The EV of not accepting either gamble is simply zero, neither a gain nor a loss. The EV of a course of action is essentially the average value which would be obtained if that course of action was always chosen on a large number of repeated occasions. Thus, while the EV of betting 10 units on Beta is a gain of 72 units, on any one occasion you would either win 400 or lose 10 units. However, if this gamble were offered and accepted over many trials, your average gain per trial would be +72 units.

To make use of EV analysis in decision making you must (a) know the objective probabilities involved and (b) assume that the worth of money to you is equatable with objective value (or is at least a *linear* function of objective value). In practice, objective probabilities (e.g. derived from frequency counts over many trials) are not always known. In such cases, a modified version of EV can be followed, in which objective probabilities are replaced by *subjective* probabilities representing an individual's degree of belief in the possible outcomes of each choice. Substituting subjective probabilities in the EV model leads to the *subjectively expected value* (SEV) model. Clearly, the subjective assessment of probabilities is very relevant to decision making and will be the focus of a later section in this chapter.

It is not immediately clear whether the subjective values (utilities) of money amounts do equate with objective amounts or even with linear functions of money amounts. However, a number of considerations strongly indicate that the utility of money is not a linear function of cash value. For example, it is generally accepted that the worth of an extra dollar or pound is greater for a pauper than for a billionaire. We would be confident that the pauper would cross a busy road to pick up a dollar bill or pound coin lying on the opposite side; a billionaire seems less likely to do so for the same sum of money. Thus, it seems from this example that the utility of a unit of money for any individual is dependent on how much that person already has. Also, if money value was the criterion, it would be irrational to take out insurance (e.g. against loss of property) since, to survive, the insurance company must pay out less than it takes in and, therefore, most subscribers must lose and the expected value of insurance must be negative for the insured. Similarly, if money value is the criterion, it is irrational to buy lottery tickets. The lottery has to arrange the 'odds' offered so that the average customer is a loser.

On the basis of similar considerations it was argued over two centuries ago by Bernoulli (1738; 1954; also see, Savage, 1954) that a fixed increment of cash wealth results in an ever smaller increment in utility as the basic cash wealth to which the increment applies is increased, i.e. the Law of Diminishing Marginal Utility. Other features of the utility function for money gains and losses may be inferred from people's choices among gambles and certainties. For example, Kahneman and Tversky (1984) have found that most respondents in a sample of undergraduate students refused to wager $10 on the toss of a coin unless they stood to win at least

$30 (expected value +$10). Only a far from even bet was acceptable to these subjects. This is interpreted as reflecting loss aversion, i.e. that a loss of $x is more aversive than a gain of $x is attractive. Further, Kahneman and Tversky found that most subjects would prefer an alternative of $800 for certain, as against a 0.85 chance to win $1000 (with a 0.15 chance of winning nothing). This preference holds despite the fact that the expected value of the sure thing ($800) is less than the expected value of the gamble (+ $850). Kahneman and Tversky class preferences for sure outcomes over gambles with higher expected values, as cases of *risk aversion*.

These various intuitions and empirical results regarding risky choices led Kahneman and Tversky (1984) to a plausible function relating utility (or *value*, in their terminology) to gains and losses of money amounts.

They assume that decisions are basically about possible gains or losses relative to the individual's status quo and propose a function that is concave in the area of gains (diminishing marginal utility), but convex in the area of losses, and steeper for losses than gains (see Fig. 8.1) This last feature explains loss aversion (e.g. avoidance of fair gambles).

Kahneman and Tversky point out that, although the notion of risk aversion in the area of gains has been long recognized in normative decision theory (i.e. preference for a sure thing over a gamble with a higher EV), the opposite phenomenon of *risk seeking* in the area of losses has been less discussed. An example of such risk seeking would be a preference for a 0.85 chance of losing $1000 (with a 0.15 chance of losing nothing) over a sure loss of $800. Most people, it seems, would prefer the gamble to the sure loss. This example is the mirror image of a problem already described in the domain of gains: when the problem is in the area of gains, subjects nearly always prefer the sure choice and avoid the gamble (risk aversion). The phenomenon of risk seeking in the area of losses has been upheld in a number of studies (e.g. Slovic *et al.*, 1982; Tversky and Kahneman, 1981). Risk seeking in losses and risk aversion in gains follow from the S-shaped value (utility) function shown in Fig. 8.1.

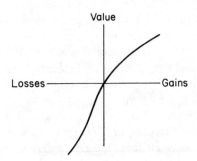

Fig. 8.1 *A hypothetical value function. Reproduced with permission from Kahneman, D. and Tversky, A. (1984). Choices, values, and frames.* American Psychologist 39, 341–350.

B. Normative theory and framing effects

Given a utility or value function and some means of estimating subjective probabilities, it may be argued that people would (or should) act so as to maximize their *subjectively expected utility* (SEU). If such rational behaviour is to be forthcoming, then certain principles, which seem intuitively clear, must hold. Two such principles or axioms of rational choice are (a) dominance and (b) invariance. The dominance principle states that if option A is at least as good as option B in all respects and better than B in at least one respect, then A should be preferred to B. Invariance requires that an individual's preference between two options should not be affected in the way in which the options are described.

Tversky and Kahneman (1981) examined the degree to which subjects respected the invariance principle when given the following pair of problems:

"*Problem 1*: Imagine that the US is preparing for the outbreak of an unusual Asian disease, which is expected to kill 600 people. Two alternative programs to combat the disease have been proposed. Assume that the exact scientific estimates of the consequences of the programs are as follows:

If Program A is adopted, 200 people will be saved. If Program B is adopted, there is a one-third probability that 600 people will be saved and a two-thirds probability that no people will be saved. Which of the two programs would you favour?"

The reader may care to decide which programme he or she would favour.

Now consider Problem 2. The same introduction is followed by a choice between two programmes C and D:

"*Problem 2*: If Program C is adopted, 400 people will die. If Program D is adopted, there is a one-third probability that nobody will die and a two-thirds probability that 600 people will die. Which of Programs C and D would you choose?"

Tversky and Kahneman found that there was a strong preference in a large group of subjects (*n* = 152) for Programme A over Programme B (72 *v.* 28 per cent). In a similarly large group of subjects there was a strong preference for Programme D over Programme C (78 *v.* 22 per cent). The intriguing point of these results is that Programme A is completely equivalent to Programme C (in both, 200 live and 400 die) and Programmes B and D are also completely equivalent to each other (in both, there is a one-third chance that 600 will live and a two-thirds chance that 600 will die). Tversky and Kahneman explain these results by saying that subjects 'frame' or construe the problems in different terms. In Problem 1, subjects are working in a 'gains' frame, i.e. in terms of lives *saved*. The majority choice of the sure option is typical of *risk aversion* in the domain of gains. On the other hand, in Problem 2, subjects are working in a 'losses' frame, i.e. in terms of lives *lost*. The choices here of the gamble reflect typical *risk seeking behaviour* in the domain of losses.

Thus, Tversky and Kahneman have induced subjects to show a striking departure from one of the major axioms of normative decision theory. Subjects have violated the invariance principle and are clearly affected by the way the problem is described. (The result has been demonstrated within individuals as well as between individuals.) As in many areas of problem solving, then, the way a decision problem is presented, and, consequently, internally represented – is extremely important.

What of the dominance principle? It appears that the tendency to risk aversion in the domain of gains and to risk seeking in the domain of losses can lead to violations of the dominance principle. Kahneman and Tversky (1984) demonstrated such violations in the following tasks. A total of 150 subjects were tested. The percentage of subjects choosing each option are indicated in parentheses.

> Imagine that you face the following pair of concurrent decisions. First examine both decisions, then indicate the options you prefer.
>
> Decision (i) Choose between:
> A. A sure gain of $240   (84%)
> B. 25% chance to gain $1000 and 75% chance to gain nothing   (16%)
>
> Decision (ii) Choose between:
> C. A sure loss of $750   (13%)
> D. 75% chance to lose $1000 and 25% chance to lose nothing   (87%)

Clearly, A is preferred to B, and D is preferred to C. In fact 73 per cent chose A *and* D and only 3 per cent chose B *and* C.

However, the preferred choice (A and D) is actually *dominated* by the rejected choice (B and C). Adding the sure gain of $240 (option A) to option D gives a 25 per cent chance to gain $240 and a 75 per cent chance to lose $760, whereas adding the sure loss of $750 (Option C) to option B gives a 25 per cent chance to gain $250 and a 75 per cent chance of losing $750. In choosing the B and C combination, one has the same chances of winning and losing as in the A and D combination, but one stands to win more and lose less from the B and C combination. Thus, B and C dominate A and D and, rationally, should be chosen. Indeed, when the combined options were shown to subjects ($n = 86$), they unanimously chose in accord with the dominance principle. The failure to conform to dominance in the 'distributed' version of the task is attributed by Kahneman and Tversky (1984) to risk aversion and risk seeking in the domains of gains and losses respectively.

C. Interim conclusions on framing effects and rationality

Kahneman and Tversky's demonstrations of framing effects and consequent violations of basic principles of rational decision making, such as invariance and dominance, seem to have 'bleak implications' for human rationality. In that regard, these results are in line with the findings from studies of human deductive and inductive reasoning. However, as Kahneman and Tversky point out, being aware of likely sources of non-rational decision making may help us to avoid such behaviour and make us more thorough in examining our decisions for consistency and rationality.

II. RISKLESS DECISION MAKING

A. Framing, mental accounting and riskless choices

Consider the following problem:

> Imagine that you are about to purchase a jacket for $125 and a calculator for $15. The calculator salesperson informs you that the calculator you wish to buy is on sale for $10 at the other branch of the store, located 20 minutes' drive away. Would you make a trip to the other store?

Note there is no element of risk in this problem. The choice is between paying $15 for the calculator and not driving for 20 minutes or paying $10 for the calculator and having a 20-minute drive.

Kahneman and Tversky (1984) argue that this problem can be framed in terms of a *minimal, topical* or *comprehensive* account. In a minimal account only the straight financial difference is considered; so, driving to the other store is framed as a gain of $5. On a topical account the value of the trip is the saving made relative to the initial price, i.e. a saving of $5 on a $15 item. The price of the jacket is irrelevant in the topical and in the minimal account. A comprehensive account, however, also takes in the individual's total expenses, including the jacket and other costs, over a period.

Together with the usual assumptions about the shape of the utility function for money, topical accounting would predict that, as the cost of the calculator rises, so the willingness to travel for 20 minutes to save $5 would diminish. Topical accounting also predicts that the cost of the jacket is irrelevant in this problem. In line with these predictions, Kahneman and Tversky (1984) reported that in the version of the problem with a $15 calculator (and a $125 jacket) 68 per cent of respondents (*n* = 88) were willing to drive for 20 minutes to save $5; but, when the calculator was priced at $125 (and the jacket at $15) only 29 per cent (*n* = 93) were willing to make the 20-minute. trip to save $5 on the calculator. Since both minimal and comprehensive accounts would predict no difference between these two versions, the topical account hypothesis is upheld.

Similar support for the notion of topical accounts comes from a set of 'ticket' problems, which are as follows:

> Imagine that you have decided to see a play and paid the admission price of $10 per ticket. As you enter the theatre, you discover that you have lost the ticket. The seat was not marked, and the ticket cannot be recovered. Would you pay $10 for another ticket?

Of 200 subjects, 46 per cent replied 'yes' and 54 per cent replied 'no' to this question. Consider now this second 'ticket' problem:

> Imagine that you have decided to see a play where admission is $10 per ticket. As you enter the theatre, you discover that you have lost a $10 bill. Would you still pay $10 for a ticket for the play?

To this problem 88 per cent of a sample of 183 answered 'yes' and 12 per cent answered 'no'.

In both 'ticket' problems the impact of buying a $10 ticket (after losing $10 or after losing a $10 ticket) is identical on the individual's total wealth. The main difference appears to lie in the topical account to which the loss is assigned.

B. Multi-attribute choices

1 Multi-attribute utility theory

Even when no risk is involved, making a choice among items that differ on many attributes can be demanding. A normative approach, known as *multi-attribute utility theory* (MAUT), suggests that the decision maker should (1) identify the relevant dimensions or attributes, (2) decide on weights to be assigned to the attributes, (3) obtain a total utility for each object by summing the weighted attribute values and (4) choose the object with the highest weighted total (Wright, 1984). For example, if the decision maker has to choose between a number of houses, he or she might identify buying price, distance from work, number of rooms, garden size, privacy and distance from services (shops, schools, etc.) as relevant attributes. Then the relative importance of the attributes would have to be considered. Is price a more important consideration than distance from services? Each alternative must then be scored on the attribute dimensions. The same scale length should be used for all attributes (e.g. from 0 to 100). So a given house may be assessed at '50' in terms of cost and '90' in terms of garden space, but at '10' on distance from work. Clearly all the scales have to be used in such a way that a higher score is 'more desirable' than a lower score. Having obtained the scores on each house for each attribute, overall utilities for each house can be obtained and the 'best' chosen.

Needless to say, there are difficulties with this approach in practice. The decision maker may not be certain what the relevant dimensions are, and the attribute weightings and scorings may suffer from unreliability over time. Goldstein (1990) has found evidence that attribute weights tend to vary with the range of values of the attribute in the set of choices. Some attributes such as safety, however, are weighted high relative to costs without much impact of ranges in the choice set (Beattie and Baron, 1991). Humphreys and Humphreys (1975) and Edwards (1977) have discussed some of the practical aspects of using MAUT.

A simplified version of MAUT has been labelled the Equal Weights heuristic (EQW) by Payne *et al.* (1993) and involves ignoring information on the relative importance of attributes. Instead, the decision maker simply sums attribute values for each alternative (assuming a common scale for all attributes) without weighting the attributes differentially, and then chooses the alternative with the highest total. This has been proposed as a good simplified model of decision making (Einhorn and Hogarth, 1975; Dawes, 1979).

The full version of MAUT is a normative model and so may or may not be descriptive of unaided decision making. Given the limited capacity of working memory, it would seem unlikely that MAUT could be followed except in fairly simple cases with just a few attributes being considered. Before discussing relevant data, some alternative strategies will be outlined.

2 Majority of confirming dimensions

This method (Russo and Dosher, 1983) takes alternatives one pair at a time. The two alternatives are compared on each attribute to see which is better on each attribute. The alternative that 'wins' the most such comparisons is retained and the 'losing' item is discarded. The retained item is then compared in the same way with another alternative, and so on, until all alternatives except the overall winner have been discarded.

3 Frequency of good and bad features

In this method (Alba and Marmorstein, 1987), alternatives are assessed on the basis of counts of 'good' and 'bad' features. This assumes that the decision maker has chosen cut-offs on the attributes corresponding to 'good' and 'bad' values.

4 Elimination by aspects

A less demanding procedure than MAUT was described by Tversky (1972) as a possible strategy that individuals might use to reduce processing load. This procedure is known as *elimination by aspects* (EBA). In an EBA process, the chooser would first select an attribute and eliminate all options that did not meet some criterion level on that attribute. In the example of house purchasing, for instance, 'price' is usually a critical attribute. The chooser will often have determined a ceiling price and so all houses over that ceiling price could be eliminated from consideration (irrespective of their other desirable qualities). Then, 'distance from work' might be taken as the next important consideration and all houses more than a certain journey time from work could be eliminated. If the chooser continues in this way to eliminate alternatives, sooner or later only one option will be left, and so the decision will effectively be made. EBA is clearly a less demanding procedure than that proposed by MAUT. Very different choices can arise depending on the order in which aspects are used to eliminate alternatives. Tversky suggests that the importance or weighting of attributes will influence the order of elimination.

5 Satisficing

A further simplifying technique that might be used in decision making, known as 'satisficing', has been described by Simon (1978). The fundamental idea is that, rather than expend time and effort in a bid to maximize utility, people are generally content to set a minimum acceptable level that will satisfy them but be short of the maximum. This may apply especially in the case of sequential decisions. For example, in buying a house, houses come on to the market continually and it would be difficult to establish that a given house was actually the optimum choice, since a better one might appear the next day. Thus buyers may set acceptable levels, either for a total utility or on key aspects of the properties, and choose the first property that meets all their minimum requirements. Should the initial minimum requirements prove too ambitious, Simon (1978) suggests that the satisficing level is gradually adjusted in the light of the average values present in the market, so that the decision maker may become more realistic about his or her criteria in the light of experience.

6 The Lexicographic method

This procedure, described by Tversky (1969), starts with the most important attribute and determines the values of all alternatives on that attribute. The alternative with the best value on the most important attribute is then chosen. If there is a tie, the next most important attribute is examined for all alternatives, and so on, until a choice emerges.

C. Testing multi-attribute choice models

To determine which (if any) of the main models for multi-attribute choice are reasonably descriptive of behaviour one needs to be able to infer how subjects process information during decision making. Payne (1976) pioneered a technique that has proven useful in the study of choice processes. In Payne's study subjects were presented with information on cards about aspects of a number of apartments. Each card was face down and gave information about one aspect of one apartment (e.g. Apartment A has two rooms). The cards were arranged in an Apartment × Attribute array so that subjects could easily obtain information either apartment by apartment or attribute by attribute (e.g. check all apartments for 'number of rooms', then for 'cost', etc.). Subjects were free to examine the cards in any order they wished. Payne distinguished two classes of strategies. One class was labelled 'compensatory' and the other 'non-compensatory'. The MAUT approach, the majority of confirming dimensions method and the frequency of good and bad feature method, described above, are examples of compensatory strategies in which an overall assessment is arrived at for each alternative by summing over all attribute values (a good rating on one attribute can compensate for a poor rating on another). EBA, lexicographic and satisficing methods are non-compensatory strategies. On the basis of the information searches used by his subjects, Payne reported a variety of different compensatory and non-compensatory strategies. Interestingly, subjects often used both within the same task, for example by using non-compensatory strategies to reduce the number of choices to a small number and then using a compensatory strategy to make the final choice. Payne also observed that non-compensatory strategies increased in frequency as task complexity was increased by manipulating the number of alternative apartments and the number of attributes per alternative. Similar changes in decision strategy with task complexity have also been reported in a study of decision making in 12-year-old children (Klayman, 1985).

Time pressure has also been found to shift preferred decision strategies. For example, Zakay (1985) reported that use of lexicographic strategies increased with time pressure. Payne, Bettman and Johnson (1988) found that processing accelerated, focused on a narrower subset of information and became more attribute-based (i.e. more non-compensatory) under severe time pressure.

The data, then, indicate that no single decision strategy is always used. Rather, it seems strategies are adopted that tend to compromise between minimizing cognitive load and maximizing the utility of the outcome chosen. As Payne *et al.* (1993) put it, decision-making processes are *contingent* and reflect conflicting goals of accuracy maximizing and effort minimizing in particular task conditions. Generally, cognitive load would be minimized by simply choosing at random, but the resulting decisions would be poor. Utility or value would be maximized by assessing all alternatives on all relevant dimensions, integrating the resulting information for all alternatives and selecting the best, but the information processing required would be demanding. Subjects generally exhibit a compromise solution and may change method during a task; for example, in Payne's (1976) study subjects used simple (non-compensatory) techniques to reduce the choice set and then analysed the remaining few options more exhaustively with compensatory methods.

Bettman *et al.* (1990) have examined the effortfulness of the major decision strategies. First, they analysed the strategies in terms of the number of *elementary information processes* (Newell and Simon, 1972) required to execute the strategies on a number of example tasks. Elementary information processes are basic operations such as *reading* an alternative's value on an attribute into working memory, *comparing* two alternatives on an attribute and *adding* the values of an attribute in working memory. A total of eight such elementary processes were identified. Comparison of strategies indicated that, for example, MAUT was indeed more costly in terms of elementary processes than EBA. Subjects were then trained in six different decision methods, including MAUT, EBA, satisficing and lexicographic methods. Each subject applied each rule to 20 decisions with varying numbers of attributes and alternatives. Times to decision increased with problem size, as did rated effortfulness; further, decision times and rated effortfulness also increased with theoretical number of elementary information processes per decision method.

How do subjects decide which decision method to use to decide between alternatives? The cost–benefit approach suggests that for a particular task the methods are compared in terms of the attributes of effort and accuracy. However, there is clearly a danger of an infinite regress developing. To choose among methods should one use MAUT, EBA, satisficing or some other method? That higher level choice in turn requires a choice among decision methods . . . and so on. Payne *et al.* (1993) suggest that the infinite regress is prevented by meta-rules that people develop with experience. An example would be "If the number of alternatives is greater than six, then screen on the most important attribute (by EBA)."

III. PROCESSING PROBABILITY INFORMATION

To choose effectively between options the decision maker often has to reach judgements about the probability of certain outcomes. For instance, a business executive in the US might have to decide whether or not to fly to Europe in a given month. What outcomes might be considered and the probabilities ascribed to those outcomes will be critical in determining whether a 'go' or a 'no-go' decision is made. If a US plane bound for Europe has recently been hijacked by terrorists, this possible outcome will likely be salient and may deter the executive from the 'go' choice. Since the perceived probability of outcomes is critical in decision making, much research has been aimed at unravelling some of the processes involved in probability judgements. Tversky and Kahneman have been particularly influential in this area and have proposed two major heuristics, *availability* and *representativeness*, which they argue are often used in making probability judgements.

A. Availability

Consider the following question:

> If a word of three letters or more is sampled at random from an English text, is it more likely that the word starts with 'r' or has 'r' as its third letter?

Tversky and Kahneman (1974) found a strong tendency for subjects to report that a word beginning with 'r' was more likely to be picked out by random sampling than a word with 'r' in the third position. However, in fact the reverse is true. Tversky and Kahneman suggest that people tackle this question by comparing how easy they find it to think of words beginning with 'r' as against words with 'r' as the third letter. Since starting letters usually provide the best cues for word retrieval, subjects are able to think of more words that start with 'r' than they do having 'r' in third place. Therefore, they misjudge the relative frequency of the two types of words.

Reliance on availability of examples to judge frequency is quite reasonable since frequency does affect availability (e.g. subjects can readily judge which of two words markedly different in frequency of occurrence are more likely to be selected by chance from a text). However, since availability can also be affected by recency and emotional impact, among other factors, availability is not always a valid guide to objective frequency or probability. Thus a single vivid terrorist incident can deter possible travellers from crossing the Atlantic, say, because it makes a highly unlikely outcome very available when the person contemplates travelling. Lichtenstein *et al.* (1978) have shown how causes of death that have more publicity (e.g. murder) are judged more likely than those with less publicity (e.g. suicide), contrary to the true state of affairs.

The availability heuristic can lead to contradictions of basic laws of probability as well as to the simple inaccuracies indicated above. Tversky and Kahneman (1983) reported that when subjects were given 60 seconds to list seven-letter words of the form '----ing', more words were reported than when they were given the same time to list seven-letter words of the form '-----n-.' This result reflects a difference in availability since, of course, the set of '-----n-.' words includes the set of '----ing' words, and so is considerably larger. Interestingly, Tversky and Kahneman also found that when subjects were asked to rate the frequency (in a sample of 2000 words from a novel) with which they would expect '----ing' and '-----n-.' words to occur, they rated the former much more frequent than the latter. Comparable results were found in a comparison of frequency judgements for words of the forms '-----ly' and '-----l-'. Those judgements, based on availability, violate a fundamental law of probability, known as the 'extension rule'. If the extension of a set, A, includes the extension of a set, B, then the probability of A must be greater than or equal to the probability of B.

So, use of the availability heuristic can lead to rather gross errors, which decision makers should strive to avoid.

B. Representativeness

A second heuristic which Tversky and Kahneman (1983) have identified is that of representativeness. Representativeness is an assessment of the degree of correspondence between an instance and a category. For example, how representative is a particular individual of the category 'Hollywood actresses' or a particular act (e.g. 'murder') of the behaviour of a category of people (e.g. 'law officers')? In the study of conceptual structures (Rosch, 1978) it is well established that judgements of the representativeness of instances of categories can be made reliably and with high agreement among subjects (e.g. that 'robins' are representative instances of 'birds' but 'penguins' are not). Tversky and Kahneman proposed that representative instances tend to be judged more likely to occur than unrepresentative instances and that such judgements can lead to error.

A particular form of error attributed to the representativeness heuristic is that known as the 'conjunction fallacy'. A form of task used by Tversky and Kahneman (1983) to demonstrate the conjunction fallacy is as follows. Subjects were first presented with a personality sketch of an imaginary individual and then asked to rate or otherwise judge the likelihood of a number of statements about that individual. Consider the following example:

> Linda is 31 years old, single, outspoken and very bright. She majored in philosophy. As a student, she was deeply concerned with issues of discrimination and social justice, and also participated in anti-nuclear demonstrations.

> Linda is a teacher in elementary school
> Linda works in a bookstore and takes Yoga classes
> Linda is active in the feminist movement (F)
> Linda is a psychiatric social worker
> Linda is a member of the League of Women Voters
> Linda is a bank teller (T)
> Linda is an insurance salesperson
> Linda is a bank teller and active in the feminist movement (T and F)

The description of Linda was intended to be representative of a feminist (F) and unrepresentative of a bank teller (T). A group of 88 undergraduates ranked the eight statements by 'the degree to which Linda resembles the typical member of that class'. The overwhelmingly chosen order of typicalities for the key statements (F, T, and T and F) was: F most typical, then T and F, then T. Thus Linda was seen as highly typical of the class 'feminist', moderately typical of the class 'feminist bank tellers' and untypical of the class 'bank tellers'. More surprising, and in violation of the extension law of probability, was that nearly all subjects ranked the conjunction 'T and F' as more probable than either T or F alone. Since the set T includes the set T and F, the probability of T must be greater than the probability of T and F; similarly, the probability of F must be greater than the probability of T and F. Thus, it seems that the representativeness heuristic has led to an error (violation of the extension law), just as the availability heuristic was shown to when subjects judged the probabilities of words ending 'ing' or '-n-'.

The conjunction fallacy has proved to be a robust phenomenon and has been replicated under many variations of the task, described by Tversky and Kahneman (1983). Even medically trained subjects were affected by the fallacy when given a brief case history and asked to then say whether the patient was more likely to develop one particular (unusual) symptom (B) or a combination of the unusual symptom (B) and a typical symptom (A). The expert subjects overwhelmingly judged the conjunction A and B to be more likely than the single symptom B. Again, this judgement violates the extension law of probability.

Interestingly, use of *extensional* cues, by stating the task in terms of frequencies rather than probabilities, seems to virtually remove the fallacy. Consider the following:

> A health survey was conducted on a sample of 100 adult males in British Columbia, of all ages and occupations. Please give your best estimate of the following values.
>
> How many of the 100 participants have had one or more heart attacks?
>
> How many of the 100 participants both are over 55 years old and have had one or more heart attacks?

Only 25 per cent of 117 statistically naive subjects gave a higher estimate for the second question (Tversky and Kahneman, 1983). When 147 similar subjects were given the same problem but asked to estimate percentages rather then absolute numbers, a clear majority gave higher estimates. Using frequencies rather than percentages seems to facilitate correct extensional thinking.

Fiedler (1988) found the same facilitating effect in a frequency version of the Linda problem in which it was stated after the standard Linda description that 100 people fitted her description. Subjects were then asked to say how many of the 100 fitting Linda's description were bank tellers and how many were bank tellers and active feminists. Fiedler found that the rate of conjunction violations fell from 91 per cent in the original version to 22 per cent in the frequency version.

Speculatively, it might be that extensional (frequency) cues lead subjects into forming mental models, similar to those proposed by Johnson-Laird for reasoning tasks, and that such models help to rule out wrong answers and suggest correct ones.

C. Base rates

In considering the extent to which evidence affects the probability of a hypothesis, one should generally take into account the probability that the hypothesis is true when the evidence is *not* taken into account (i.e. the base rate). A number of studies have found a tendency to ignore base rates. However, as we shall see, whether base rates are used varies with task conditions. A striking example study is that of Casscells *et al.* (1978). They presented 60 staff and medical staff at Harvard Medical School with the following problem:

> If a test to detect a disease whose prevalence is 1/1000 has a false-positive rate of 5 per cent, what is the chance that a person found to have a positive result actually has the disease, assuming you know nothing about the person's symptoms or signs?

If you are inclined to say '95 per cent' then you are in agreement with most of the medical subjects in the study. Unfortunately, the correct answer is 2 per cent. Most subjects answer on the basis of the false-positive rate and the inferred true positive rate of 95 per cent. However, the base rate of the disease is very low and must be taken into account. The relevant normative formula for revising the probabilities of hypotheses is given by Bayes' theorem [see Garnham and Oakhill (1994, pp. 166–168) for a mathematical explanation of this important theorem]. However, the rationale of the correct approach is perhaps most clearly conveyed for the non-mathematically keen by considering frequencies as follows. Of 1000 patients only one will have the disease and 999 will not. Of the 999 healthy patients the test will report that approximately 50 have the disease. So, even assuming the test correctly diagnoses the one sufferer, it will misdiagnose as ill 50 who are not. Thus, of the 51 who are diagnosed ill, only one will actually be ill, giving the probability that a person with a positive result is ill as 1/51 = 2 per cent. Of course, this is an increase over the base rate of 0.01 per cent, but still quite a low probability in absolute terms.

Tversky and Kahneman (1980) also found a tendency to ignore base rates in the following problem:

> A taxi-cab was involved in a hit-and-run accident one night. Two cab companies, the Green and the Blue, operate in the city. You are given the following data:
>
> (i)   85 per cent of the cabs in the city are Green, and 15 per cent are Blue.
> (ii) in court, a witness identified the cab as a *Blue* cab.
>
> The Court tested his ability to identify cabs under appropriate visibility conditions. When presented with a series of cabs, half of which were Blue and half of which were Green, the witness made correct identifications in 80 per cent of the cases, and was wrong in 20 per cent.
> What was the probability that the cab involved in the accident was Blue rather than Green? (___ per cent)

Tversky and Kahneman found a median response of 80 per cent which indicates that the base rate information was ignored and the response based only on the probability of the witness saying Blue if the cab was Blue. Taking account of the low base rate of Blue cabs (15 per cent) the correct answer should be 41 per cent – a marked increase over the base rate certainly, but well short of the typical answer. The correct answer may perhaps be more understandable if one imagines the accident being staged and witnessed repeatedly, using all the cabs in the city. Out of the 85 Green cabs the witness would wrongly report 17 (20 per cent) as Blue and would correctly report 12 of the 15 Blue cabs as Blue (80 per cent). Thus, of the 29 reported to be Blue, 12 would actually be Blue; hence, the probability that a cab was Blue given that it was reported to be Blue is $12/29 = 0.41 = 41$ per cent.

While many studies have reported ignoring of base rates, a significant number have found at least some effect of base rates, and Koehler (in press) has argued that the extent of the base rate fallacy has been exaggerated. One type of manipulation which seems to remove the base rate fallacy is to state the problem in terms of frequencies. For example, Cosmides and Tooby (in press) developed a frequency version of the Harvard Medical School problem which reads as follows:

One out of 1000 Americans has disease X. A test has been developed to detect when a person has disease X. Every time the test is given to a person who has the disease, the test comes out positive. But sometimes the test also comes out positive when it is given to a person who is completely healthy. Specifically, out of every 1000 people who are perfectly healthy, 50 of them test positive for the disease. Imagine that we have assembled a random sample of 1000 Americans. They were selected by a lottery. Those who conducted the lottery had no information about the health status of any of these people. How many people who test positive for the disease will actually have the disease? (__ out of __)

With this version the proportion of correct answers rises from 12 per cent with the original Casscells *et al.* (1978) wording to 76 per cent. Thus, expressing base rate problems in frequency terms helps considerably (as was also the case with conjunction effect problems). The reader may also have noticed that the explanations given of the cab problem and of the original Harvard Medical problem were in frequency terms for ease of understanding. Gigerenzer (1993) suggests that thinking in frequencies is developmentally (and evolutionarily) earlier than thinking in probabilities or percentages, which requires specific training. Posing problems in terms of frequencies may evoke quite concrete mental models of the situations described and hence provide guidance for inferences and checks on erroneous inferences.

IV. CONSEQUENTIALISM AND NON-CONSEQUENTIALISM

In the discussion so far in this chapter, it has been assumed that decisions are made on the basis of the consequences expected to follow from each of the choices available (*consequentialism*). Baron (1994) argues that the best decisions are those that yield the best consequences for the achievement of the decision maker's goals. Although such a proposal would surely be widely accepted, Baron points to numerous examples of *non-consequentialist* decision making, particularly concerning ethical and policy decisions; a selection of these are outlined in the following sections. Baron (1994) argued that the breaches of consequentialism reflect the use by subjects of less demanding heuristics, which often do work well (i.e. match consequentialist recommendations) but fail in certain circumstances. Example heuristics would be: "Do no harm", "Avoid unfairness", "Don't breach people's rights".

A. Omission and status quo bias

Ritov and Baron (1990) asked subjects to make decisions about vaccinations where omission (not giving vaccine) and commission (giving vaccine) were options. In one study, subjects were to imagine that their child had ten chances in 10,000 of dying from flu in an epidemic if the child was not vaccinated. The vaccine would prevent flu but would itself kill a certain number of children. Subjects were asked to state the maximum death rate due to the vaccine at which they would still give their child the vaccine. From the consequentialist point of view, a rate of vaccine-induced deaths up to nine out of 10,000 should be acceptable as it is an improvement over the unvaccinated rate of ten out of 10,000. The mean acceptable risk reported was considerably lower at five deaths per 10,000. Subjects tended to state that they would feel more responsible for deaths caused by their action (of vaccinating) than by their omission (not vaccinating). Other studies have also found a tendency to judge consequences less bad when the consequences are due to omissions rather than commissions. For example, Spranca *et al.* (1991) gave subjects scenarios in which one tennis player knowingly *allows* his rival to eat an allergy-producing substance before a match (omitting to warn him) or *deliberately causes* the rival to eat the allergen (commission). In terms of consequences, the omission and commission have the same effect, yet subjects tend to judge the commission worse. Thus, there seems to be a bias to downplaying the negative consequences of omissions as against commissions that have the same effects.

Inaction tends to maintain the status quo, and other studies have also found a bias toward the status quo in its own right. So, for example, people will ask for more money to give up something which they have than they are willing to pay for the same thing (Samuelson and Zeckhauser, 1988).

B. Punishment

From the consequentialist point of view, punishment is valuable only if it has a deterrent effect and prevents the undesired acts being repeated by the perpetrator or others. However, it seems that many people believe that retribution is the main function of punishment and are little swayed by the consequences of punishment. Baron and Ritov (1993) had subjects assess penalties for makers of vaccines and birth control pills that had caused harm. In one scenario, subjects were told that a high penalty would make the company try harder to make a safer product. In a contrasting case, subjects were told that a high penalty would make the company stop making the drug, leaving only more dangerous products on the market. Most subjects, including a group of judges, gave the same penalties in both cases despite the very different consequences of the penalties in the two situations. These results suggest a bias toward retribution in making decisions about punishment.

A second bias is to wish injurers to undo the harm they have done, even if other penalties would have more beneficial consequences. For example, Baron *et al.* (1993) found that subjects would prefer to have companies clean up waste they had themselves generated rather than to clean up more dangerous waste produced by a different firm that had gone out of business.

C. Resistance to coerced reform

Although subjects will often endorse certain reforms as having desirable consequences for society or even the planet, the same subjects will often say that they would not vote for the consequentially desirable reforms. For example, most of Baron and Jurney's (1993) subjects in the US agreed that a 100 per cent tax on gasoline (petrol in UK) would be a good measure on the whole (to reduce global warming), yet many of the same subjects would not vote for such a tax. The main reasons given for this inconsistency were (1) that the tax would be unfair and harm some more than others, (2) that harm would be caused to some and (3) that the tax would impair a right of people to choose for themselves. Similar results were found when the proposed reforms involved abolition of television advertising during political campaigns, compulsory vaccination for a dangerous flu virus, compulsory treatment for a highly contagious disease, and elimination of law-suits against obstetricians. In all cases, consequentialism was breached.

V. SUMMARY AND CONCLUDING COMMENTS

A. Overview

In this chapter we have reviewed some of the major concepts and research findings in the area of decision making. Although decision making and problem solving are closely intertwined, the foci of the two activities differ. In decision making the focus is on *selecting* between options; in problem solving the focus is on *generating* options.

Decision problems were characterized in terms of a number of dimensions: risky *v.* riskless, single attitude *v.* multi-attitude and single-stage *v.* multi-stage. Approaches in decision making were divided into normative and process approaches. Normative models seek to characterize the behaviour of an ideally rational decision maker and vary in the extent to which selective assessments of value and probability are incorporated. The simplest normative model, the expected value maximization model, clearly does not fit individual behaviour. This is partly because the subjective value (utility) of money, say, is not a simple linear function of money amounts. The rather more plausible subjectively expected utility models fail to handle effects of framing which lead to violation of basic axioms of rationality such as dominance and invariance (Tversky and Kahneman, 1981), in both risky and riskless decision making.

In the case of multi-attribute decision making, the load of processing differing attributes into an overall value measure leads to suboptimal but simple strategies such as elimination by aspects (Tversky, 1972), satisficing (Simon, 1978) and majority of confirming dimensions (Russo and Dosher, 1983). Use of elimination by aspects, at least as an initial stage in multi-attribute decision problems, has been shown by Payne (1976; Payne *et al.* 1993).

Since risky decisions require that decision makers take account of probabilities, the question of how people handle probability information has been the object of a number of studies. Tversky and Kahneman (1974, 1983) have provided many demonstrations of inappropriate usage of heuristics, such as availability, representativeness and ignoring of base rates, which can lead to misjudgements of likelihood and to violations of laws of probability, such as the extension rule. However, if problems are posed in terms of frequencies rather than probabilities, most responses are quite accurate (Fiedler, 1988; Gigerenzer, 1993). Perhaps frequency cues facilitate development of appropriate mental models that help rule out wrong answers.

B. Rationality and decision making

Are people rational decision makers? Clearly people do not always behave in accord with a simple expected value maximizing model of rationality, even in situations that are completely well defined (e.g. simple gambles). To some extent decision behaviour is better explained by models that take subjective values and subjectively assessed probabilities into account (i.e. subjectively expected utility maximizing models).

However, from Tversky and Kahneman's results there are some striking departures from the axioms of subjectively expected utility theory. Examples of such departures occur in problems susceptible to framing effects, in which the invariance and dominance assumptions of rational choice are violated. Furthermore, conjunction effects in the handling of probabilities suggest that typical heuristics lead subjects into error. In the area of multi-attribute decision making, strategies that reduce cognitive load such as eliminating by aspects and satisficing lead to suboptimal and unreliable choices. In less well defined 'moral' decisions, it appears that giving weight to consequences is often replaced by various biases (Baron, 1994).

As in the study of deductive and inductive inference then, it often appears that research on decison making has 'bleak implications for human rationality' (Nisbett and Borgida, 1975). However, Cohen (1981) has urged caution in drawing any sweeping conclusions. First, he points out that the normative theories (e.g. of probability) against which subjects' judgements are compared are themselves founded on human intuitions about assumptions taken to be true (axioms). He argues for a competence–performance distinction in the area of rationality, according to which normal adults are assumed to have some basic competence in reasoning (and this backs up the intuitions underlying normative theories) but their competence is often overshadowed by performance factors (distractions, memory limitations, etc.).

Also, he makes the point that when performance is compared against a normative theory, it is not always clear what normative theory applies; there is often more than one applicable normative theory. MacDonald (1986) also points to difficulties in determining which normative theory best applies to a given problem, and in addition argues that the ordinary assumptions of conversational logic may justify apparent fallacies. For example, in the 'Linda' problem, merely asking how likely Linda is to be a bank teller may raise the credibility of that possibility, since the question would not normally be raised of an individual, unless there were some reason for believing it might be true. Gigerenzer (1993) points out that accuracy is generally greater when people deal with frequencies rather than probabilities, and this is more typical of everyday decision making.

Overall, then, the issue of rationality is a complex one. Simon's (1957) notion of 'bounded' rationality still seems to be a useful compromise between the extremes of imputing complete rationality or irrationality to humans. Simon argued against the notion of 'rational man' as used in economic theory, since such a notion implied an infinite capacity for correct information processing, and instead he posited that people would be rational but within the limits imposed by constraints on memory, speed of processing and available knowledge.

VI. FURTHER READING

Kahneman, D., Slovic, P. and Tversky, A. (1982). *Judgement under uncertainty: heuristics and biases*. Cambridge: Cambridge University Press. This is a classic collection of readings which give further detail on the main paradigms used in casting doubt on human rationality.

Manktelow, K.I. and Over, D.E. (Eds) (1993). *Rationality: psychological and philosophical perspectives*. London: Routledge. A useful collection on rationality in general.

Payne, J.W., Bettman, J.R. and Johnson, E.J. (1993). *The adaptive decision maker*. Cambridge: Cambridge University Press.

9

Daydreaming

From early times a distinction has been made between two broad kinds of thinking. According to this distinction, on the one hand we have thought directed toward some end or goal, and on the other hand undirected thought, such as occurs in day-dreaming. The English philosopher Thomas Hobbes (1651/1919, p. 9) expressed the difference over three centuries ago as follows:

> This train of thoughts, or mental discourse, is of two sorts. The first is unguided, without design, and inconstant . . . In which case the thoughts are said to wander, and seem impertinent (unrelated) one to another, as in a dream . . . And yet, in this wild ranging of the mind, a man may oft times perceive the way of it, and the dependence of one thought upon another . . . the second is more constant, as being regulated by some desire, and design.

Much later, a related influential distinction was made by Freud (1900), between primary and secondary process thinking. Primary process thinking is characterized as wish fulfilling, unfettered by logic or reality, and operating in accord with the *pleasure principle* of immediate gratification (though the gratification obtained may be in imagination only). This is the earliest form of thought in Freud's view. Secondary process thinking, in contrast, is reality respecting, seeks real rather than imaginary satisfaction and is governed by logic. Secondary process thinking also ultimately serves the pleasure principle but does so with due respect to the *reality principle* of obtaining what is possible and safe, deferring gratification when necessary. In Freud's theory, night dreams are nearly pure representatives of primary process thinking and daydreams predominantly so, while real problem solving would predominantly involve secondary process thinking.

As one might expect, similar distinctions have been made by many writers. A selection appears in Table 9.1.

Early in the development of psychology as an independent subject there was strong interest in the naturally occurring stream of consciousness, including its undirected flow (e.g. James, 1890). However, post-Watson experimental psychology, in so far as it dealt with thinking at all, focused on directed thought as exemplified in studies of problem solving and logical reasoning tasks. Perhaps this was because directed thinking seemed technically easier to investigate behaviourally or perhaps because directed thought was believed to be more educationally and socially useful than undirected daydreaming, which might be judged time-wasting and foolish, if not actually pathological. Interest in daydreams and fantasy generally was kept alive in clinical rather than in experimental psychology until the early 1960s. At that point many psychologists felt ready, technically and theoretically, to try to make sense of daydreaming, which, after all, is a very common and familiar mental activity. Much of the credit for the revival of scientific interest in this topic must go to Jerome Singer and his colleagues (see Singer, 1975a,b; 1978).

In the next sections of this chapter the empirical work on daydreaming will be reviewed and its theoretical significance considered.

I. PSYCHOMETRIC APPROACHES

A. Descriptive studies

The most basic questions concern the frequency and content of daydreams in the general population. Does everybody daydream? About how often? Are there differences in frequency or in content, depending on age, sex, cultural and personality factors? Some answers can be obtained by questionnaire methods (also called psychometric studies).

First, you may be relieved to learn that daydreaming is extremely widespread. An early survey by Singer and McCraven (1961) sampled 240 normal adults in the US, of whom 96 per cent reported some form of daydream activity every day. This investigation involved a General Daydream Questionnaire in which respondents indicate the frequency on a six-point scale with which they have experienced each of

Table 9.1 *Classifying thought: a sample of distinctions*

Distinction	By whom proposed
Undirected *v.* directed	Many
Passive *v.* active reason	Aristotle
Unregulated *v.* regulated thought	Hobbes (1651)
Primary *v.* secondary process	Freud (1900)
Foreconscious *v.* conscious	Varendonck (1921)
Autistic *v.* reality	McKellar (1957)
Impulsive *v.* realistic	Hilgard (1962)
Autistic *v.* directed	Berlyne (1965)
Multiple *v.* sequential	Neisser (1963b)
Respondent *v.* operant	Klinger (1971)
Type I *v.* Type II	Evans (1980a)

a series of about 100 daydreams, e.g. 'As a child, I imagined myself as a great detective'; 'I suddenly find I can fly – to the amazement of passers by'; 'I picture an atomic bombing of the town I live in'. The results of this study indicated that daydreams took the form of fairly clear images, mainly of people, objects or events. Items dealing with *planning* for future actions, particularly interpersonal actions, were high in frequency. Daydreaming generally occurred, it was reported, when the person was alone and in a restful state. In addition to such environmental factors it may be noted that studies by Kripke and Sonnenschein (1978), in which subjects were asked to report their thoughts at intervals throughout the day, have suggested the existence of an intrinsic cycle, in which daydreaming peaks about every 90 minutes and is associated with heightened alpha waves in electroencephalogram and reduced eye movements. This cycle seems to hold both in laboratory studies and in real-life settings.

Most people's high-frequency daydreams involve practical, immediate concerns, with daydreams about sex and unusual good luck also common. Singer (1975a) has suggested that the range of items that have a high frequency do not exactly tally with the notion that daydreaming is purely unrealistic wish fulfilling. Rather, day-dreaming often reflects attempts at anticipating possible future events and it is oversimplifying to say that 'daydreams are unrealistic'. It seems that daydreams vary in reality orientation from the practical and plausible through to true fantasies.

Singer and Antrobus (1972) have developed a lengthy questionnaire known as the Imaginal Processes Inventory. This involves 400 items that are to be rated on five-point scales. Example items are 'The pictures in my mind are as clear as photographs'; 'I often have the same daydream over and over'; 'My daydreams have such an emotional effect that I often react with fear'. The items fall into 29 groups of sub-scales dealing with different aspects, such as frequency of daydreaming, degree of acceptance of daydreaming, fear of failure, sex and hostile–aggressive content, guilty daydreams, visual imagery in daydreams and distractability associated with daydreams, among others.

Using large US student samples, factor analysis of these scales produced three factors, suggesting three different styles of daydreaming. Factor 1 (guilty–dysphoric) high scorers are inclined to 'tortured self examination', have strong achievement drives and negative fantasies. Subjects high on Factor 2 (anxious–distractable) seem to be very anxious, self-doubting, rather disorganized in thought and lack clear and elaborate daydreams. They are not oriented toward achievement and persistence. The high scorers on Factor 3 have a positive attitude to daydreaming and fantasy, and show a high level of 'thoughtfulness'. It appears that Factor 1 and 2 scores decline with age but Factor 3 scores remain steady. Future-oriented and sexual daydreams also seem to decline with age.

B. Validity of daydreaming questionnaires

Daydreaming questionnaires, of the type discussed above, exhibit high degrees of test–retest *reliability*. The question of the extent to which they measure something outside of themselves (i.e. the question of their *validity*) has also been investigated, with promising results.

One way of validating daydream questionnaires is to see whether subjects whose questionnaire scores put them in high or low daydream frequency categories, differ from one another in various experimental tasks. For such research purposes, day-dreaming has often been operationally defined as the report of "thoughts that involve a shift of attention away from an immediately demanding task" (Singer, 1975a, p. 730). An example experiment is that by Antrobus *et al.* (1967) in which subjects who reported themselves to be high or low daydreamers were given a monotonous signal task. The high daydreamers indeed reported more thoughts unrelated to the task when 'probed' at intervals throughout. Also, although high and low daydreamers did not differ in efficiency of initial performance, the high daydreamers missed more signals and reported more task-irrelevant thoughts as time went on. It is notable that, even though this task involved monetary pay-offs for correct detections, much of the time subjects daydreamed rather than attend to the external stimuli.

An interesting correlation that has turned up is that obese students have signifi-cantly lower scores than normal-weight students on daydream vividness as measured by the Imaginal Processes Inventory. Singer (1975a) suggested that this result is consistent with the theory about obesity put forward by Schachter (1968), which says that obese individuals are dominated by external stimulus cues and so, given any amount of food, will continue to eat as long as some food remains. If there is indeed a general tendency on the part of obese individuals to attend to external stimuli rather than to internal stimuli, then lower vividness ratings of daydreams would be ex-pected from such subjects.

During daydreaming, a fixed leftward gaze is often adopted. This leftward orientation of the eyes indicates a predominance of activity in the right cortical hemisphere during daydreaming. Further evidence for the validity of the Imaginal Processes Inventory, then, comes from Meskin and Singer's (1974) observation that high scorers on the inventory showed more leftward eye-shifts in response to imagery-evoking questions than did low scorers.

Overall, it appears that there is a reasonable amount of evidence for the validity of daydreaming questionnaires as indices of a style of thinking. Further supporting evidence also emerges in later sections of this chapter.

II. EXPERIMENTAL APPROACHES TO DAYDREAMING

A. Task demands

As well as individual differences in frequency and style of daydreaming, situational factors also play a role. Roughly speaking, the more important it is to attend to the outer environment, the less likely one is to engage in daydreaming. A number of experimental studies support this generalization.

Singer and his colleagues have generally used signal detection tasks. These have the advantage that the task load can easily be varied in a number of ways. For example, rate of occurrence of signals (fast *v.* slow) and complexity of judgement (judge tone to be high or low *v.* judge tone to be same or different to preceding one) were varied in a study by Antrobus *et al.* (1966). As dependent measures, in addition to signal detection performance, they had subjects rate their frequency of task-irrelevant thoughts and obtained ratings of degree of verbal thinking, visual imagery and auditory imagery at intervals throughout the task. The major effects were as one might expect. Task-irrelevant thought declined with increase in speed of signals and with increase in complexity of judgement. Overall, the correct response rate was quite high (92.4 per cent) and there was no particular correlation, in this experiment, between daydreaming frequency and signal detection performance. Subjects seemed to maintain a fairly stable rate of correct responses and varied daydreaming up or down depending on the amount of 'spare mental capacity' left by the demands of the main task.

A second experiment in the same paper concerned the rate of daydreaming (i.e. task-irrelevant thought) depending on the rewards and costs of 'hits' and 'misses' in signal detection.

There were four groups of subjects and each group started off with $3, but the groups differed in the penalties for errors, these being 0¢, 2¢, 4¢ or 8¢ respectively. After each block of 15 trials, the subjects had to make a simple yes/no report of whether they had had task-irrelevant thoughts or not. The probability of task-irrelevant thought being reported declined as the penalty for missing signals increased (see Fig. 9.1). So, it can be shown experimentally that the complexity and importance of a current task affects levels of daydreaming during performance.

B. 'Bad news'

It was mentioned above that, according to survey data, much daydreaming is concerned with anticipating or planning for future events. Antrobus *et al.* (1966) explored this experimentally by giving a group of subjects some information, which, if true, would have seriously affected their futures. This experimental group was then compared with controls in the amount of task-irrelevant thinking they reported during a signal detection task.

The 'information' was given in the form of a special radio news bulletin that the experimental subjects overheard while in a waiting room before the signal detection task got under way. Imagine you were an American male student in June 1965 and you heard the following:

> High military aides in Saigon have conceded that heavy damage has been inflicted upon our air base at Da Nang after the surprise massive air and ground attack earlier today. This action, in addition to last night's sinking of two Navy aircraft carriers by Chinese jets, has served to weaken seriously our offensive air postures in Southeast Asia . . . Meanwhile, the Associated Press reports that Defense Secretary McNamara has placed all active military units on emergency alert status . . . Allegedly, the communique also instructed the local (draft) boards to call in for physical examination as soon as possible, all unemployed youths over 18 and all eligible college graduates.[a]

Fig. 9.1 *Probability of reporting task-irrelevant thoughts during signal detection task as a function of penalty for missing signals. Reprinted with permission from Antrobus, J.S., Singer, J.L. and Greenberg, S. (1966). Studies in the stream of consciousness: experimental enhancement and suppression of spontaneous cognitive process.* Perceptual and Motor Skills **23**, 399–417.

As might be expected the experimental group reported much higher levels of task-irrelevant thought throughout the 150 signal detection trials (see Fig. 9.2). Experimental subjects were also more likely to miss signals.

After the experiments the subjects wrote down examples of their task-irrelevant thoughts. These generally concerned implications of the news for their future, e.g. possibility of themselves or their friends being drafted, possibility of escaping to Canada, etc. Another class of thoughts concerned images of the Vietnam war or war in general. Thus, by introducing a rather drastic change in subjects' expectancies about the future, the 'stream of thought' was diverted toward making adjustments

[a] Reprinted with permission of the authors and publisher from Antrobus, J.S., Singer, J.L. and Greenberg, S. (1966). Studies in the stream of consciousness: experimental enhancement and suppression of spontaneous cognitive processes. *Perceptual and Motor Skills* 1966, **23**, 399–417.

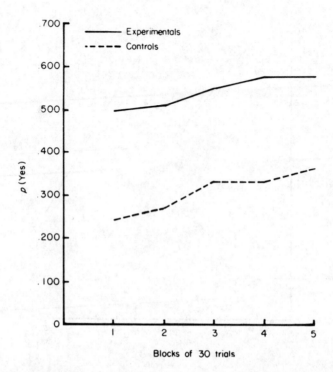

Fig. 9.2 *Probability of reporting task-irrelevant thinking as a function of time within the detection session for experimental ('bad news') and control subjects. Reprinted with permission from Antrobus, J.S., Singer, J.L. and Greenberg, S. (1966) Studies in the stream of consciousness: experimental enhancement and suppression of spontaneous cognitive processes.* Perceptual and Motor Skills **23**, 399–417.

and anticipations in order to deal with the change. Of course, the subjects were 'debriefed' after the experiment – no doubt to their relief.

C. Stress effects

Becker *et al.* (1973) reported a number of experiments concerning the effects of stress on cognitive responses (as contrasted with physiological responses). The clinical literature suggested that, after traumatic stress, 'intrusive' thoughts that involve 'stimulus repetition' are common reactions. These reactions are sometimes labelled 'repetition compulsion' and involve repeated thoughts about the traumatic experience despite attempts to avoid such thoughts. Horowitz hypothesized that this 'repetition compulsion' was an extreme version of a general tendency that occurs in normal populations even after relatively mild stress.

In the study carried out by Becker *et al.* (1973), subjects did signal detection tasks after seeing a 6-minute stressful film and after a 6-minute neutral film. The signal detection tasks were split into three periods between which the subjects wrote down what they could recall of their mental contents during the preceding task period. It was expected that the stressful film would produce more signs of repetition compulsion than the neutral film. The stressful film was entitled *Subincision*. It showed repeated scenes of circumcision rites among Australian bushmen and it features old men inflicting pain on young adolescents, nudity, injury, blood and anguished expressions. Prior studies have shown that this film is indeed stressful in terms of physiological measures. The neutral film was entitled *The Runner* and consisted of a man running through the town he grew up in, having flashbacks along the way. It is said to be quietly interesting without being very exciting.

After the experiment, the subjects' mental reports were content-analysed by three independent judges for intrusions, film references and task-irrelevant thoughts. Inter-judge reliability correlations were high ($r = 0.94$). An intrusive thought was defined as "any thought the subject experiences as (a) non-volitional; (b) hard to dispel; (c) something to be avoided, or (d) a repetition of the identical thought." (The other thought categories are self-evident.) The main results were that the stressful film significantly increased the number of intrusive thoughts and film references but did not significantly affect the total number of task-irrelevant thoughts compared with the neutral film. Both films increased the number of irrelevant thoughts above a baseline level established before the films were shown.

It is interesting that in this experiment the stressful material did not have any direction implications for the subjects' futures, unlike Antrobus *et al.*'s (1966) 'bad news' study, and yet similar effects were obtained. Perhaps because *Subincision* presented material very discrepant from the subjects' prior conceptions about human behaviour, cognitive work had to be done to adjust existing schemata to accommodate such events.

Whatever the explanation, it would seem that Singer, Becker and their colleagues have produced experimental analogues of certain real-life experiences *viz.* compulsive mulling over of 'bad news' in the Antrobus *et al.* experiment and mental replaying of disturbing scenes from films or television (even if they do not have any personal relevance) in the Becker *et al.* study.

D. "Do not think of a white bear!" *or* Paradoxical effects of thought suppression

The studies of Antrobus *et al.* (1966) and of Becker *et al.* (1973) outlined above showed that intrusive thoughts can be provoked by 'bad news' or by witnessing disturbing scenes in film or other media. Real-life traumas often induce post traumatic stress disorder, part of which involves intrusive thoughts of the precipitating incident. People generally find it very difficult to control or suppress such intrusive thoughts. Similarly, a person trying to cut calories, or give up tobacco, alcohol or other drugs, will typically be troubled by thoughts of the 'forbidden' substance which they would wish to suppress. Wegner and colleagues (Wegner *et al.* 1987, 1990; Wegner, 1994) have specifically explored the topic of thought suppression, with intriguing results.

In an initial study (Wegner *et al.*, 1987), subjects were asked to think aloud for 5 minutes while not thinking of a white bear during that period. If they did think of a white bear they were to ring a bell. Subjects were unable to suppress the thought of white bears and reported such thoughts on average more than once per minute. Interestingly, when subjects were asked to think about a white bear for 5 minutes following attempted suppression, they produced significantly more thoughts about white bears (22.06 on average) than did subjects instructed to think about a white bear without an initial suppression period (16.38 on average). This result suggests that trying to suppress thoughts has a paradoxical ('rebound') effect in which such thoughts become more likely after the suppression attempt than they were before. A further experiment in the same paper found that when subjects were given a specific distractor ("If you do happen to think of a white bear, please try to think of a red Volkswagen instead"), the rebound effect was markedly reduced.

Processes, such as thought suppression, which have a tendency to produce effects opposite to those intended may be called *ironic*. Wegner (1994) proposed a theory of *ironic processes of mental control*. This theory suggests that attempts to control thought content involve two processes: (a) an operating process that seeks to bring about the intended change and (b) a monitoring process that tests whether the operating process is needed by examining current thought content for departures from the intended state. Operating processes function by searching for contents (typically in long-term memory) consistent within the intended state, e.g. 'happy thoughts', 'not-sad thoughts', 'not white bear thoughts'; in this example, the monitor meanwhile would check thought contents for signs of 'not-happy thoughts', 'sad thoughts' and 'white bear thoughts'. If the monitor finds that its trigger conditions are met, the operating process is invoked.

Wegner argues that mental control is dependent on *mental capacity*. The operating processes require more capacity than the monitoring processes and so, if capacity available for control is reduced due to stress, drugs or additional tasks, then the operating process may fail, allowing the monitoring process to arouse thoughts consistent with its triggering conditions (which, ironically, are the opposite of the goals of the operating processes). Thus, under extra task loads, someone trying to think 'not-sad thoughts' may be overwhelmed by sad thoughts, and similarly the person trying not to think of white bears under stress will find it difficult to think of anything else. Experimentally, Wegner and Erber (1992) found that subjects instructed not to think about a target word (e.g. house) were much more likely to respond with the target when under time pressure during a word association task than when not under pressure. Even more strikingly, subjects trying to suppress the target during word association produced it more under time pressure than did subjects also under time pressure who were trying to think about the target. Similar ironic effects of mental load have been found in a range of other studies: for example, when subjects tried to change their mood under load conditions (Wegner *et al.* 1993b), changes opposite to those intended occurred; when subjects tried to lie convincingly under load, they were detected more than when not under load (De Paulo *et al.*, 1991); when subjects under load tried to avoid sexist completions of sexism-relevant sentences they were *more* sexist than when no instruction was given, but with low load conditions the instruction to be non-sexist produced a reduction in sexist completions (Wegner *et al.*, 1993a). Thus, it seems well established that concurrent loading when mental control is sought will tend to produce frequent ironic effects, as the operating process is impaired and the less demanding monitor arouses contrary thoughts into consciousness.

The nature of the target state is theoretically relevant to the effortfulness of the control and monitoring processes. The operating and monitoring processes search for complementary ranges of contents in that what is not the target of the operating process indicates a failure that should be recognized by the monitor. Thus, one search will be 'feature-positive' (e.g. searching for X) and the other will be 'feature-negative' (e.g. searching for not-X); feature-positive searches are known to be easier than are feature-negative searches (Newman *et al.*, 1980). So, suppression of a thought (e.g. white bears) will involve the operating process in a relatively difficult feature-negative task (generate thoughts that are not white bears), whereas the monitor has the easier feature-positive task (detect any thoughts that are of white bears). In such a situation ironic effects should be plentiful. In concentration tasks (e.g. think of white bears), the relative difficulties of the monitoring and operating processes are reversed and ironic effects are less common. Concentration is generally more successful than suppression. Hence, it is more advisable to frame one's mental control goals in terms of some positive state (e.g. happy thoughts) rather than a negative state (e.g. not-sad thoughts).

E. Analysing daydream protocols

The daydreaming reports obtained in the many of the earlier studies of daydreaming, discussed above, were typically retrospective and/or incomplete. Fuller report methods should produce finer-grain information on the structure of daydreaming sequences. Klinger (1971, 1978) at the University of Minnesota has experimented with a variety of thought-sampling methods. One of these methods, 'thinking out loud', requires the subject to talk continuously for a period of 5–30 minutes. The subject is seated in a chair and simply asked to keep talking aloud. The utterances are tape recorded for further analysis. An example 2-minute protocol is given below (from Klinger, 1971, p. 97; reprinted by permission of author and publisher):

> Oh, I also think about how I wanted to die. I don't want to die you know, like ahm, by living in a hospital for six months, kept on by drugs. I don't want to die, um, on the golf course on the 9th hole, being struck by lightning or doing my daily jogging – Ahh, being hit by a car or something like that just being free . . . and be still young at heart. I don't know, I don't want to have to sit in a room like that, seeing my family watch me die, I don't know, that's, it's ridiculous. Isn't there some way we can say hell and let me die? How can people do that to other people? It's just like an old folks home. Can't stand to go there and watch. It scares me half to death seeing people like that. Usually . . . Almost like . . . T. and another

couple, they're ahm just look at them and you could almost get hypnotized. I think one of the major things is . . . No, that's, where did I hear that? Oh. D. told me. Told him to quit smoking all you have to do is to go and get hypnotized for a cost of $50 or something but completely, completely quit smoking. No desire to smoke. All you do is get hypnotized. Hmm, my stomach's growling. Ha I think mmm . . . You know that one little dot right there seems so funny. Reminds me of a graba I saw in a, from a horror movie. Yeah, creepy films series again for this fall going to be. Consists of um, Frankenstein, King Kong, oh, all those really goodies, man.

Klinger has found that coders can reliably analyse such sequences into 'main routines' or 'themes' (e.g. 'dying' in the above protocol), and further into 'sub-routines' or 'sub-themes' (e.g. 'Dying on golf course' in above). Main routines define an area of concern, while sub-routines either go to finer and finer levels, drift from one sub-topic to another within a given level, return to the main theme or apparently stimulate new themes. Most routines are fragmented and are interrupted before a natural conclusion is reached by some new routine.

Klinger (1974) compared thinking-aloud protocols from problem-solving sessions with thinking-aloud protocols obtained under daydreaming instructions. In the problem-solving protocols there were many more utterances containing progress evaluations (e.g. 'yep', 'Dammit', 'Now wait . . . '). At the least, these results indicate that the general method of obtaining and analysing thinking-aloud records has some validity.

However, it must be acknowledged that the 'thinking aloud' method has some possible drawbacks. The requirement to verbalize may slow down the apparent rate of flow of thought and may make thinking seem more verbal than it is. A study discussed by Pope and Singer (1978) indicates that verbalization does affect the apparent nature of the stream of consciousness. Subjects were asked to report on shifts in thought by releasing a key each time a change in topic or direction of thinking occurred. These data suggested that thought shifts occurred every 5 or 6 seconds on average. In contrast, data from subjects who had been thinking aloud produced an average rate of one shift per 30 seconds. Thus, thinking-aloud methods may produce a biased picture. In view of this point, *thought-sampling* methods may be a useful option, in that they can yield fairly detailed data without affecting the flow as much as continuous verbalization. In thought-sampling methods the subjects are cued at irregular intervals and describe their most recent thoughts, often by means of rating scales that can be completed quickly. This technique has been used to good effect by Klinger in some studies outlined below.

F. Thought-sampling studies

1 Normal thought flow

Klinger (1978) reported a large-scale quantitative study of normal conscious thought that used thought-sampling techniques both in and out of the laboratory. In both settings, subjects were periodically interrupted and asked to report their thoughts in terms of the 15 scales that comprise the 'Thought Sampling Questionnaire'. The scales were as follows:

(1)   Estimated duration of the latest thought segment.
(2)   Estimated duration of the previous segment.
(3)   Vagueness *v.* specificity of the imagery.
(4)   Amount of directed thought.
(5)   Amount of undirected thought.
(6)   Amount of detail in imagery.
(7)   Number of things going on simultaneously.
(8)   Visualness of imagery.
(9)   Auditoriness of imagery.
(10) Attentiveness to external stimuli.
(11) Recall of recent stimuli.
(12) Degree to which imagery felt controllable.
(13) Degree of trust in accuracy of memory.
(14) Familiarity *v.* unfamiliarity or bizarreness of the latest experience.
(15) Time of life associated with the experience.

In the out-of-the-laboratory setting, scale 14 was divided into Usualness and Distortedness scales.

In the study conducted in the laboratory the subjects listened to dichotic tapes and were required to indicate by means of a toggle switch the channel that they were attending to. The tapes were interrupted at irregular intervals by a tone that signalled the subjects to report on their thoughts using the questionnaire. A total of 936 thought samples were obtained in the laboratory setting from a sample of 20 subjects.

Outside the laboratory, the subjects carried with them an alarm device (a 'beeper') that emitted a soft tone at random intervals having a mean of 40 minutes. On hearing the tone, the subjects filled in a similar thought-sampling questionnaire to that used in the laboratory studies. (The beeper could be switched off, if the subject felt that its activation might prove embarrassing.) This study yielded a total of 285 real-life thought samples from 12 subjects.

Klinger proposed certain *a priori* dimensions in terms of which thoughts could be characterized, and used these in interpreting his thought-sampling data. The first dimension is the familiar one of 'directed *v.* undirected'. The second is that of 'stimulus independent *v.* stimulus bound'. As Klinger points out, these two dimensions are conceptually independent. A person may think in a very directed way about a problem that does not relate to his or her current stimulus field (e.g. a student trying to solve a maths problem mentally while riding in a bus). At the other extreme, a person might free-associate to stimuli in the immediate environment. Some of the earlier studies of daydreaming assumed that 'stimulus independent' equalled 'undirected', but this is not necessarily true. A further dimension is that of 'fanciful–realistic'. Again, fanciful thinking about improbable events may or may not be directed. In some problem-solving techniques (e.g. brainstorming, discussed in Chapter 10), the person deliberately tries to think of fanciful combinations and events. A fourth dimension is that of 'integrated *v.* fused or degenerate'. In normal waking thought, images and ideas remain as intact, separate wholes, while in dream-like thought images tend to flow together and merge. This latter sort of thinking can also occur in the waking state, especially under the influence of some drugs and during sleep deprivation. Nor are such thoughts at all uncommon, at least fleetingly, during normal waking states.

The main results from Klinger's thought-sampling study may be summarized as follows:

(1) The median judged duration of thought segments was 5 seconds and the mean was around 10 seconds. These results agree quite well with those of other studies that have used toggle-switching to indicate change of thought topic.

(2) Thoughts rated as 'directed' were also rated as more specific, more related to external cues and more controllable than undirected thoughts. 'Directedness' was not related to duration of the thought segment, amount of detail, presence of visual or auditory imagery, familiarity or time of life associated with the thoughts.

(3) Stimulus-bound thoughts tended to be 'directed' but the connection was not a strong one. Degree of fancifulness of thought segments was not strongly related to their directedness (presumably because undirected thought can easily be either fanciful or realistic).

(4) There was a detectable baseline of 'strange' or 'degenerate' thoughts; indeed 22 per cent of out-of-laboratory thoughts were so rated. 'Strangeness' was negatively related to thought specificity, to relatedness to external cues and to controllability. 'Strange' thoughts did occur during both directed and undirected segments.

(5) In general, compared with in-laboratory thoughts, out-of-laboratory thoughts were more specific, more directed, more related to external cues, more oriented to the present and led to better recall of external cues.

(6) Visual imagery was reported considerably more frequently than auditory imagery in both in- and out-of-laboratory settings.

These results, especially those obtained outside the laboratory, give a broad picture of the normal thought stream and indicate that thought sampling is a useful technique.

A further thought-sampling study of 29 subjects in out-of-laboratory settings generated a total of 1425 thought samples (Klinger and Cox 1988). Analysis of ratings of these samples corroborated the findings of Klinger (1978) and confirmed the independence of the dimensions of directedness, stimulus independence and fancifulness.

2 The induction principle

It seems apparent from the thought-sampling and protocol studies that the topic of thought changes quite rapidly in the normal course of events. What determines which topic will be taken up next?

Psychologists have generally assumed that moment-to-moment thoughts are determined by a combination of motivational factors and cues interacting with memory contents.

The motivational concept of a 'current concern' has been found useful in considering the determinants of thought content. A 'current concern' is defined as the state of an organism between the time it becomes committed to pursuing a goal and the time it either obtains the goal or abandons it. Another label for essentially the same concept as 'current concern' is 'unfinished business'. Any individual is typically beset by many current concerns, most of which will not be in consciousness at a given time. However, it is proposed that the contents of consciousness at a particular time will tend to reflect one or other current concerns or pieces of unfinished business.

As well as current concerns, cues related to these concerns are also likely to play a role in steering thought. Klinger (1978, p. 250) proposed an 'induction principle' as follows:

> At any given moment, the next thematic content of thought is determined by the combination of a current concern and a cue related to that concern.

The cue may be of external origin or be a symbolic event in the individual's own stream of thought. Also it is surmised that people may be more perceptually sensitive to cues bearing on current concerns. Such 'attention tuning' would be of obvious utility.

Taking the induction principle as a starting point, Klinger (1978) carried out the following experiment. First, subjects were interviewed and from these interviews four current concerns were extracted for each subject. One or two days later the subjects were presented with dichotic tape messages. These consisted of literary extracts in which, at intervals, material relating to a current concern was introduced on one channel while material relating to a non-current concern was introduced into the other channel. The inserted passages lasted for 25 seconds. Throughout the experiment, the subjects indicated by means of a switch the channel to which they were attending. Ten seconds after each inserted passage, a signal was given, whereupon the tape stopped and the subjects reported their latest thoughts in accordance with the Thought Sampling Questionnaire. They also reported their recollections of the most recent taped passages.

As would be predicted on the induction principle, the concern-related passages received more attention than the non-concern passages. The subjects switched to them sooner and spent longer listening to them. Furthermore, the concern-related passages had more effect on subsequent thought content and were recalled better. It seems, then, that people's current concerns dispose them to attend to, and to retain and reflect in their thoughts, cues related to those concerns, as the induction principle predicts.

Further research (Hoelscher et al. 1981) indicates that the induction principle operates on thought content even during sleep. Subjects were presented with concern- and non-concern-related words at low volumes during rapid eye movement

(REM) sleep. There was significantly more incorporation of concern stimuli than of non-concern stimuli in dream reports obtained shortly after stimulus presentation. Since people might be expected to dream more about concern than non-concern topics irrespective of any cues, the authors checked that the probability of a dream related to a particular concern was indeed higher immediately after the concern stimulus than after other stimuli. These results suggest that the induction principle is descriptive of a powerful tendency than affects cognitive processes both in waking and sleeping.

As it has been described so far, the induction principle is non-committal with respect to the degree of influence that a person's various current concerns will have on thought flow. Most of the research has dealt with the role of cues rather than with the effects of concern attributes. Klinger *et al.* (1980) have remedied this deficiency to some extent. Questionnaires were used to elicit topics thought about with varying degrees of frequency and the resulting topics were then rated by the subjects on a variety of scales (such as positive value of thing thought of; negative value; antici-pated future effort; nearness in time; and so on). Real-life thought sampling (beeper studies) supported the validity of the questionnaires as measures of topic frequency in thought.

The main results may be summarized as follows. The frequency of thoughts about particular goals was predicted best by the person's self-reported commitment to the goal, the value of the goal, the subjective probability of achieving the goal and the time left before action was required. Thoughts related to threatened personal rela-tionships and unexpected difficulties were notably high in frequency. Although the particular thought contents reported in this study probably largely reflect the concerns of undergraduate students, the general conclusions should be widely applicable.

G. Functions of daydreaming

Given the frequency of daydreaming in everyday thought, an obvious question to ask is "What functions does this activity serve?"

As Singer (1975b, Ch. 5) points out, on Freud's psychoanalytic theory daydreams are always connected, although sometimes indirectly, to drives considered to be basic (such as sex and aggression) and serve a temporary drive-reducing function. The psychoanalytic theory proposes that daydreaming starts in infancy, when the hungry baby in the absence of immediate gratification, automatically engages in 'primary process' thinking and hallucinates an image of breast or bottle. These images are presumed to have temporary drive-reducing effects.

A label used for such drive reduction brought about by imagery, fantasy or vicarious means is catharsis. Freud borrowed this term from Aristotle's theory of tragedy. Watching a play in which a character (Oedipus) discovers that he has murdered his father and married his mother is considered, on the psychoanalytic view, to help the audience to discharge repressed sexual and aggressive tendencies relating to their parents. On this approach then, daydreams act as safety valves, permitting the partial reduction of drives whose overt expression would be unacceptable.

According to this catharsis view, the regular presentation of sex and violence in the mass media should be encouraged in order to help reduce the rates of actual rape and murder.

Alternatively, it can be argued that the witnessing of 'pre-packaged fantasies' on television or films has a stimulating effect on the relevant drives and that such stimulating effects might also hold for self-generated fantasies in daydreaming. Indeed, it seems from the general run of results from a number of studies by Berkowitz (1969), in which subjects were shown aggressive film scenes and then given opportunities to act aggressively, that those who witnessed the aggressive scenes showed an increase in aggressive activity, rather than the decrease that catharsis would suggest.

More directly related to daydreaming is a complex study by Paton, reported by Singer (1975b, pp. 113–114). A group of college student subjects took the Imaginal Processes Inventory and then later in the session were insulted while performing a task. Immediately after the insulting episode, one group was given pictures of aggressive material (such as battle scenes) to look at. A second group that had also been insulted were shown interesting non-violent pictures. Both groups then daydreamed and reported their thoughts. Next, they were given questionnaires which yielded measures of how angry and aggressive they felt about the person who had insulted them. There were also two control groups. One control group had no opportunity for fantasy activity after being insulted, and the other control group was not insulted at all. These control groups made it possible to show that the insults really did anger the subjects. The insulted group without an opportunity to daydream showed a higher level of subsequent anger than did the group that had not been insulted.

The main question in this experiment was whether the opportunity to daydream after becoming angry would lead to a reduction in the amount of anger felt about the insulter. If there is an aggressive drive that is aroused, and if daydreams related to the aggressive drive reduce that drive, then one would expect the greatest drop in aggression to occur if the subject has produced angry and hostile thoughts rather than non-violent thoughts. Alternatively, it might be that the effect of daydreaming after being insulted would be mainly to divert the subject and produce an alternative mood that would reduce anger. In that case, one would expect that the subjects who produced non-violent daydreams would show a greater drop in subsequent aggressive tendencies toward the insulter than would those who produced aggressive fantasies. It would also be consistent with this view if both kinds of daydreams produced a greater reduction in anger than did no opportunity for daydreaming.

The results supported the 'diversion' hypothesis. Both groups who daydreamed showed less anger toward the insulter than the group who had no daydream opportunity. However, there was a large difference in the effect between the conditions. Subjects who produced mainly neutral daydreams showed a greater drop in anger than those whose daydreams were aggressive. From this study it seems, then, that the motivational effect of daydreaming is mainly one of diversion and mood shifting. The view that daydreaming brings about an automatic reduction of the relevant drives was not supported.

If daydreams do not serve as simple drive-reducing safety valves, what functions might they serve? On the basis of the existing literature, Singer (1975b; 1978) has suggested that daydreams may serve functions of (1) anticipation and planning, (2) reminding us of 'unfinished business' which we may be trying to suppress, and (3) maintaining arousal in dull environments.

Whatever functions daydreams may serve, Singer suggests that their occurrence follows from widespread and continuous activity in the brain. His model is described below.

III. CONCEPTUAL MODELS OF DAYDREAMING

A. Singer's model

Singer (1975a; Pope and Singer, 1978) has proposed a simple model that can handle much of the data regarding daydreaming. This model claims that (a) there are two continuously available sources of stimulation, one internal and one external, and (b) there is a limited-capacity central processor that attends to only one of these sources at a time. The external source is the outside environment. The internal source that Singer proposes is a continuously active long-term memory in which information is not stored in some inert form but rather through continuous representational activity. Similar notions of an active long-term memory have also been put forward by other authors (e.g. Neisser, 1963a,b; Reitman, 1965). Daydreaming, Singer suggests, involves attending to the normally unnoticed ('underground') flows of activity in long-term memory. Some support for the notion of continuous unconscious activity can be drawn from the occurrence of intrusive thoughts (as in Becker *et al.*, 1973) and from personal reports by scientists and artists of incubation and inspirational experiences (see Chapter 10). These phenomena suggest the existence of internal parallel processes than can occasionally 'sieze' attention. Of course, the existence of such processes would be contrary to the serial activity assumption of the standard information-processing approach to thinking.

Whatever the merits and problems of the 'active long-term memory' notion, there is much support for the view that daydreaming and external attending are incompatible and that a selection of one or the other form of activity has to be made on the basis of task demands. Daydreaming frequency drops as task complexity and the costs of errors go up (Antrobus *et al.*, 1966). On the other hand, if external inputs are severely restricted, as in sensory deprivation experiments, then daydreaming increases markedly. Increased daydreaming could serve useful arousing functions in dull environments.

As a final point, this model suggests that individual differences in self-reported daydreaming frequency may be due to differences either in dominant attention strategies or in the amount of unconscious mental activity. Whether these two possibilities could be operationally separated is an open question.

B. Working memory and daydreaming

Singer's model for daydreaming was based on the assumption of a single general-purpose limited-capacity processor. More recent theories of human cognitive architecture have proposed a number of separate modular systems that permit simultaneous performance of tasks that do not compete for the same resources. Baddeley's (1992; Baddeley and Hitch, 1974) working memory theory, which proposes separate verbal, visuospatial and central executive systems, has been applied to stimulus-independent thought by Teasdale (1989; Teasdale and Barnard, 1993, Ch. 13). Teasdale and colleagues found that when subjects were practised at a pursuit rotor task, they reported more stimulus-independent thoughts than did less practised subjects at the same or worse levels of performance. This result is not consistent with Singer's single limited resource model, which stressed the simple amount of information processed (which would be the same at the same levels of performance, irrespective of practice levels). However, the result is consistent with the working memory model, according to which the central executive would be less involved in a practised skill and so capacity would be available for daydreaming.

A related finding in another of Teasdale's studies (cited in Teasdale and Barnard, 1993, Ch. 13) was that a task of random number generation, which loads the central executive, greatly reduced stimulus-independent thought revealed by probes. Furthermore, random generation during periods in which stimulus-independent thought had occurred was less random than in periods without such task-irrelevant thought. Thus, central executive capacity would seem to be involved in daydreaming.

IV. SUMMARY AND CONCLUDING COMMENTS

The material reviewed in this chapter shows that undirected thinking can be success-fully studied, although it has not been given the same degree of research attention as directed thought. The question of a definition of 'daydreaming' was largely bypassed in the foregoing review and deserves some consideration at this point.

As Klinger (1978) has argued, thoughts may be independently, directed or not, realistic or not, related to current external stimuli or not, and so on. Of these characteristics the major feature of daydreaming seems to be a lack of persistent direction. Daydreams are not necessarily unrealistic but tend to drift from one topic to another, whereas thinking in problem solving is checked against feedback con-cerning progress toward the current goal and attention is 'locked' on to the problem materials (Klinger, 1971). Daydreams are often concerned with anticipating future problems. So, for instance, in anticipating a dinner date with a girl, a boy may be seen as setting up an internal symbolic model representing the meeting, which he then runs in order to anticipate possible outcomes of going to alternative restaurants. To be classed as daydreaming, as against problem solving, we would have to suppose a loose degree of control over the model running process – permitting departures from reality and switches to different, if associated, topics.

From the studies discussed above, daydreaming is a widespread and frequently occurring phenomenon, whose incidence varies with personal characteristics (e.g. obesity) and with external demands (e.g. sitting in a drab waiting room *v.* descending a sheer rock face or carrying out a central executive loading task). The moment-to-moment contents of daydreams seem to reflect both immediate and recent internal or external stimuli and the person's list of 'current concerns'. In terms of functions, daydreaming resists attempts to reduce it to a freudian safety valve. Rather, it seems to serve functions of anticipating, reminding about outstanding concerns and maintaining arousal in uninteresting environments.

The model for daydreaming put forward by Singer (1975a; Pope and Singer, 1978) clashes with the 'seriality' assumption intrinsic to the modal information-processing approach to thought (e.g. Newell and Simon, 1972). Singer suggests that there is continuous activity within the long-term memory and that this activity is the source of daydreams. From the data discussed so far, the case for parallel processes in conjunction with the conscious mainstream of thought is perhaps most strongly supported by the occurrence of intrusive and unwelcome thoughts (Becker *et al.*, 1973). [Attempts to suppress such thoughts seem to involve monitoring processes, which can have ironic effects counter to those intended, particularly when cognitive capacity is under stress (Wegner, 1994)].

A possible 'serialist' argument against Singer's parallel approach would be that the mainstream of thought could be halted every so often and the list of current concerns scanned. This might lead to a switch in the thought stream in order to deal with one of those concerns (e.g. adjust concept of range of human behaviour to incorporate data from *Subincision* film in the case of Horowitz *et al.*'s subjects). The issue of serial *v.* parallel models for thinking will arise again in Chapter 10, which deals with creative processes, and will also be discussed in Chapter 11 in the broad context of human information processing.

V. FURTHER READING

Teasdale, J.D. and Barnard, P.J. (1993). *Affect, cognition and change.* Hove: Lawrence Erlbaum Associates. Working memory and daydreaming set in the context of a general cognitive model.

Wegner, D.M. (1994). *White bears and other unwanted thoughts: suppression, obsession and the psychology of mental control.* New York: Guilford Press. A very readable account of Wegner's ironic control of cognition theory.

10

Creative processes

Before discussing creative processes, it is necessary to consider briefly what is meant by the term 'creative' and its associate 'creativity'. It is perhaps easiest to start by defining creative products. Creative products, whether they are poems, scientific theories, paintings or technological advances, are both novel and acknowledged to be valuable or useful in some way. Whether a product is novel or not is relatively easy to determine, although an element of judgement does enter, in that some products are more obviously derived from previous developments than others. Objective measurement of novelty is possible in laboratory settings, since the same task can be given to a large number of people (e.g. "think of ways of improving a doorknob"), and the degree of novelty of proposed solutions can be readily assessed by counting their frequency of occurrence. In real life, however, only the 'creator' may be working on a given self-set problem [e.g. an author seeking to represent the stream of consciousness of a Stone Age person, as in W. Golding's (1955) *The Inheritors*], and so frequency of production is not always available as a criterion. When we turn to the quality of a product, subjective judgement looms still larger than in the case of judging novelty. In science and technology the criteria for quality are clearer than in the arts. A new theory or gadget can be seen to 'work' if it covers more phenomena with no more assumptions than its predecessors (e.g. Einstein's theory compared with Newton's) or meets the function for which it was devised (e.g. the first telephone). Notoriously, there is usually less agreement about the merits of artistic productions, both at the time of their emergence and over history. Initial reactions may well be negative to artistic products that either depart too far from established styles or, at the other extreme, are too conventional. Later generations are more likely to appreciate the boldness of developments that their ancestors decried as 'insane', e.g. Surrealism, Cubism, Expressionism, etc.

It may also be suggested here that judgements of 'novelty' or 'unusualness' will presumably relate to the degree to which the product can be fitted into an established style (in the arts) or 'paradigm' (in the sciences). Highly creative products signal and exemplify a new style or paradigm. Subsequent work within a given style or paradigm would generally be regarded as less creative than the initial style-defining work.

213

The above comments should serve to indicate what is meant here by a creative product. What of 'creative processes' and persons blessed with 'creativity'? Although it is a starting point, it is not very informative to say that creative processes are those processes that result in creative products. Later on, I will be reviewing some attempts to be more detailed about such processes. At this stage, though, it may be noted that psychologists hold to the belief that creative processes are composed of similar ingredients to less exalted forms of thinking. It is assumed that creative products result from multitudinous small steps carried out by limited-capacity cognitive systems that suffer from all the normal limitations of cramped working memory and imperfect retrieval from long-term memory. Indeed, most of the approaches to 'small-scale' problem solving (e.g. behaviourist, associationist and information processing) have something to say about creative thinking. It is an article of faith for theories of thinking that creative processes can be explained in terms of their basic processes (whatever the basic processes may be for any particular theory, e.g. associations or production rules) and that supernatural interventions in the form of 'demons' or 'divine sparks' are ruled out. Turning now to 'creativity', this is an attribute ascribed to those individuals who show a long-term tendency to generate novel products that are also influential (Albert, 1975). With a few extremely rare exceptions (such as Leonardo Da Vinci) most 'creatives' display their valued characteristic within a particular speciality – but within that speciality they are marked for their combination of productivity (e.g. Picasso) and high quality of work (as indexed by its influence). Of course, in real life, for someone to be acknowledged as displaying 'creativity' involves social processes, as well as purely within-individual cognitive processes. To become known, creative individuals must 'promote' their products and convince a sufficient number of those who control the communication media that these products should be presented to a larger audience (Stein, 1974). Given that wider presentation, further social processes leading to widespread acceptance and influence, or to apathy or rejection, can begin. A similar point is made by Simonton (1988), who argues that creativity is a form of *leadership* in that it entails personal influence over others. Just as a leader must have followers to be classed as a leader, so a creator must have appreciators to be classed as an effective creator.

In the rest of this chapter, I will discuss some of the main approaches and topics that have arisen in the study of creative processes. First, there is the individual differences approach, which considers in what ways individuals acknowledged to be creative might differ in cognitive, personality or biographical characteristics from others. Second, there is the approach via personal accounts by artists and scientists of how the process seemed to them, and this leads on to stage models for creative thinking based on personal accounts. Next, we turn to laboratory-based approaches that have examined ways of stimulating idea production. Then, there is a discussion of theoretical approaches and, finally, a summing up.

I. STUDIES OF CREATIVE INDIVIDUALS

A. Individual difference studies

A number of studies have been made of people acknowledged to be creative [e.g. Roe's (1952) study of scientists, MacKinnon (1962) on architects, and Barron (1955) on writers and artists]. These studies were aimed at uncovering any common background or personality characteristics of these unusual groups of people.

1 Scientists

In one of the earliest investigations of its kind, Roe (1952) studied 64 American scientists who had been rated as eminent in their fields by expert panels. The 64 were roughly evenly split amongst physicists, biologists and social scientists. Each individual was subjected to long interviews, projective personality tests (TAT and Rorschach) and a conventional intelligence test. On the basis of this investigation Roe gave the following composite picture of the average eminent scientist.

The average eminent scientist was a first-born son in a middle-class Protestant family, with a professional man as a father. He was likely to have been ill often in childhood or to have lost a parent early. He had a very high IQ and began reading avidly at an early age. He felt 'lonely' and different from his school mates, did not have much interest in girls and married late (27 years old on average). He usually decided on his career as a professional scientist as a result of a student project involving individual research. He worked hard and persistently, often for 7 days a week with few holidays.

This general picture seems to have held best for the physicists. The social scientists were on average somewhat more extroverted, and showed more concern for personal relationships. They displayed more aggression in the projective tests than members of the other scientific groups. A large proportion of social scientists came from homes with a dominant mother and social scientists had a very high divorce rate (41 per cent). Though different in these ways, they were also totally absorbed by their work and worked very long hours, as did the other groups of scientists.

Similar evidence on personality characteristics of creative people was gathered by Cattell and his colleagues. Before actually testing any 'live' scientists, Cattell (1959) scanned the biographies of many famous scientists and noted that the typical eminent scientists seemed to be introverted and stable. Although introverted, they were generally independent and self-sufficient. They also tended to be solemn or restrained, and rather dominant in personal relationships.

Cattell and Drevdahl (1955) selected groups of about 45 eminent researchers in physics, biology and psychology and had them complete the 16 Personality Factors (PF) test. Compared with the general population, the eminent researchers were more introverted, intelligent, dominant and inhibited; they were also more sensitive emotionally and more radical. These findings are in line with the suggestion of biographies and with the results of Roe's (1952) investigation.

Also relevant is Mitroff's (1974) study of scientists engaged in the analysis of lunar samples as part of the Apollo moon project. Mitroff noted a strong tendency toward a style of thinking often labelled as 'convergent' (Hudson, 1966). Any open-ended question put to the scientists would be quickly transformed into a narrower, more tightly defined, one. This tendency fits in with Hudson's finding that those boys who performed better on convergent (one-answer) test questions than on divergent items (multiple possible answers) tended to specialize in science subjects. It was also noted that the lunar scientists strongly identified with the traditionally conceived 'masculine' characteristics. They believed in hard work, dedication, striving, and did not disapprove of a touch of ruthlessness. Intriguingly, and contrary to earlier reports, Mitroff found evidence in his interviews of strongly aggressive tendencies. In discussing other scientists and rival groups, the desire to win glory at the expense of others and a fear of their rivals' over-aggressive tactics (e.g. idea stealing) were evident. Aggressiveness was also clear in their attitude towards promoting their own ideas. As one scientist remarked:

> If you want to get anybody to believe your hypothesis, you've got to beat them down with numbers: you've got to hit them again and again over the head with hard data until they're stupefied into believing it (Mitroff, 1974, p. 144).

Possibly, aggressiveness in scientists was not evident in previous studies that had relied on projective tests (e.g. TAT), because such tests are uncongenial to the scientists' preferred convergent style. McLelland (1962) noted the extreme dislike of scientists for the TAT and their tendency to analyse portions of the picture rather than to empathize with the characters and tell a story. In Mitroff's study, with material close to their hearts, few inhibitions were evident regarding aggression. Mitroff suggested that the scientists were somewhat one-sided in emotional expression and he found that they were far less free in displaying soft emotions compared with harsh or aggressive ones. The notion that science is an aggressive activity was also expressed in Freud's self description. He wrote:

> I am not really a man of science, not an observer, not an experimenter, and not a thinker. I am nothing but by temperament a *conquistador* – an adventurer, . . . with the curiosity, the boldness, and the tenacity that belong to that type of being (Jones, 1961, p. 227).

2 Artists and writers

A study of artists and writers (Drevdahl and Cattell, 1958) using Cattell's 16 PF test yielded a profile rather similar to that of the scientists (Cattell and Drevdahl, 1955). The artistic group was emotionally more sensitive than the scientists and exhibited more inner tension, but was otherwise similar.

More recent studies have pointed to a dark side of artistic creativity in a higher incidence than normal of manic-depressive and depressive pathology (Andreasen, 1987; Ludwig, 1992; Jamison, 1995). Jamison reviewed seven studies of acknowledged creative writers and artists, which have found rates of depression 8–10 times, of manic depression 10–20 times and of suicide up to 18 times those found in the general population. These studies included both living and dead artists and writers. For the latter, pathology is inferred from their biographies or from records of medical treatment while alive.

Although the association should not be over-interpreted – not all artists and writers display pathology and not all sufferers from depression or manic depression are highly creative – none the less a statistically significant association is present. Could such mood disorders conceivably be of aid in artistic endeavours? Mania and especially its mild form, hypomania, do have features that are plausibly conducive to creative thinking. Indeed, one of the diagnostic criteria for hypomania is 'sharpened and unusually creative thinking and increased productivity'. Hypomanic subjects tend to use rhyme, other sound associations and unusual words in their speech far more than do normal subjects. Also, hypomanic individuals are markedly faster at giving synonyms and word associations than normals. The condition, then, seems to involve a speeding of thought and a tendency to use uncommon associations and ideas. These tendencies could well be helpful in creatively bringing together unusual combinations of ideas. During manic periods the person tends to be extremely confident and filled with energy, which would also facilitate the production of creative work. While little overt progress is normally made during periods of pathological depression, it is conceivable that experience of such states gives a broader range of contrasting experiences to draw on in normal periods than would be otherwise available.

3 Age trends in productivity

An interesting point emerges from a study of the ages at which creative accomplishments tend to occur. Data gathered by Lehman (1953) revealed that in many fields the most highly regarded contributions are produced between 30 and 40 years of age. The average age is younger in some subjects, e.g. in chemistry it is 25–30 years, and it is older in others such as psychology, philosophy, novel writing and architecture. Although these age trends were detectable it should be noted that good work was evident in all fields at a very wide range of ages. The 32-year-old chemist is not necessarily 'finished' as far as creative work is concerned. The declines from peak productivity tend to be gradual and to remain well above initial levels even late in life. These data will be discussed further in connection with Simonton's (1988) chance configuration model of creative processes.

B. Personal accounts of creative problem solving

Many scientists and artists have provided accounts of their experiences in solving complex problems (see, for example, Ghiselin, 1952; Koestler, 1964; Vernon, 1970). These personal accounts are of interest for evidence they may contain about features common to the creative process in a wide range of difficult tasks. Fairly consistent patterns do seem to emerge and these patterns have served as the bases for various analyses into stages of both creative thinking and more routine problem solving.

It is worth noting that some well-known thinkers have disclaimed any ability to tell us how they solved problems or thought creatively. For example, Bertrand Russell was once asked to contribute to a book on how to think clearly. He replied that he could not help because, for him, thinking was instinctive, like digestion. He said that he simply filled up with relevant information, went about his business doing other things and later, with time and good luck, he found that the work had been done. Perhaps Russell was too modest on this occasion. His brief account broadly matches those of others who have tried to be more detailed. It is possible to consider only a small number of these more detailed reports here, and I have selected accounts by Poincaré, Helmholtz and Tchaikovsky.

1 Poincaré's account

Henri Poincaré was a prominent French mathematician of the nineteenth century. He reported (1908) once struggling for a long time to prove a certain theorem without getting any results. One evening he drank black coffee before going to bed and it seemed to him that ideas of possible ways of solving the problem combined and recombined in one way after another before he finally got to sleep. In the morning, he clearly saw how the problem was to be solved, and after 2 hours had completed the detailed proof. The solution to the initial problem raised further problems and Poincaré noted that these problems were solved as a result of ideas that occurred while he was not actively engaged on them, e.g. while riding in a bus, walking along a street or beach.

2 Helmholtz's account

The nineteenth century scientist Herman Helmholtz, who contributed to physics, neurology and psychology, volunteered the following report of his problem-solving experience in a speech made at a dinner in honour of his 70th birthday in 1896 (Woodworth and Schlosberg, 1954, p. 838):

> So far as my experience goes, 'happy thoughts' never came to a fatigued brain and never at the writing desk. It was always necessary, first of all, that I should have turned my problem over on all sides to such an extent that I had all its angles and complexities 'in my head' and could run through them freely without writing. To bring the matter to that point is usually impossible without long preliminary labour. Then, after the fatigue resulting from this labour had passed away, there must come an hour of complete physical freshness and quiet well being, before the good ideas arrived. Often they were there in the morning when I awoke, just according to Goethe's oft cited verses, and as Gauss also once noted. But they especially liked to make their appearance while I was taking an easy walk over wooded hills in sunny weather.

3 Tchaikovsky's account

Peter Ilich Tchaikovsky attempted to describe his experience of composing in a series of letters [extracts of which are reprinted in Vernon (1970, pp. 57–60)]. Here are three examples:

Do not believe those who try to persuade you that composition is only a cold exercise of the intellect. The only music capable of moving and touching us is that which flows from the depths of a composer's soul when he is stirred by inspiration. There is no doubt that even the greatest musical geniuses have sometimes worked without inspiration. This guest does not always respond to the first invitation. We must always work, and a self respecting artist must not fold his hands on the pretext that he is not in the mood. If we wait for the mood without endeavouring to meet it half way, we easily become indolent and apathetic. We must be patient, and believe that inspiration will come to those who can master their disclination.

Generally speaking, the germ of a future composition comes suddenly and unexpectedly. If the soil is ready – that is to say, if the disposition for work is there – it takes root with extraordinary force and rapidity, shoots up through the earth, puts forth branches, leaves and, finally blossoms. I cannot define the creative process in any other way than by this simile. The great difficulty is that the germ must appear at a favourable moment, the rest goes of itself. It would be vain to try to put into words that immeasurable sense of bliss which comes over me directly a new idea awakens in me and begins to assume a definite form. I forget everything and behave like a madman. Everything within me starts pulsing and quivering; hardly have I begun the sketch ere one thought follows another.

Yesterday, when I wrote to you about methods of composing, I did not sufficiently enter into that phase of work which relates to the working out of the sketch. This phase is of primary importance. What has been set down in a moment of ardour must now be critically examined, improved, extended, or condensed, as the form requires. Sometimes one must do oneself violence, must sternly and pitilessly take part against oneself, before one can mercilessly erase things thought out with love and enthusiasm.

II. STAGE ANALYSIS

A. Wallas's stage analysis

On the basis of reports such as those of Poincaré, Helmholtz and others, and on the basis of his own experiences as a university teacher, administrator and writer, Graham Wallas (1926) proposed a four-stage analysis of creative problem solving in a book entitled *The art of thought*. In this book Wallas was concerned with the natural course of thought and with how thinking might be made more effective. So, in addition to proposing certain typical stages, he also offered advice on how these stages could be made more fruitful. The stages extracted by Wallas were as follows.

1 Preparation

In this stage the problem solver familiarizes themself with the problem and engages in conscious, effortful, systematic and usually fruitless work on the problem. Although this stage may well not lead to solution in itself, it is widely believed to be very important in influencing the likelihood that the next stage will result in a useful idea. Much personal testimony indicates that inspiration will not be forthcoming without this preliminary labour or, as Edison, the prolific inventor, is reported to have said, "No inspiration without perspiration".

2 Incubation

This is a period during which the task is set aside. No conscious work is done on the problem during this stage. Poincaré and others have hypothesized that unconscious work is carried out during this phase. On the other hand, it may be that this is simply a necessary rest period which enables a later period of conscious work to proceed more effectively than it would have without the break. Wallas suggested that this phase could be made more or less effective, depending on the intervening activity. Light work on minor problems or duties could be beneficial. Better still, he thought, was complete mental rest, coupled with mild exercise. He felt that the habit of filling every spare minute with reading was especially detrimental.

3 Illumination or inspiration

This is the point when a fruitful idea, or 'happy thought' in Helmholtz's phrase, occurs to us. The inspiration is not usually a complete solution to the problem but points to the direction in which the complete solution may be found.

This phase may be preceded by a vague feeling of 'intimation', a feeling that the solution is nigh. Wallas suggests that if thinkers can recognize this feeling, then they should relax, cut out possible distractions and let the inspiration come. If the intimation feeling is not recognized, then the possible inspiration may be lost as a result of distracting stimuli.

4 Verification

This stage is much like preparation, in that conscious work must be done to develop and test the inspiration.

These four stages are visible in the personal reports of Helmholtz, Poincaré and Tchaikovsky. Their reports, however, do not stress 'intimation' and rather suggest that inspiration comes suddenly and without warning. Wallas suggests that the 'intimation' experience is easily forgotten in the excitement of inspiration. It may also be noted that Poincaré proposed a four-stage view like Wallas's but with the omission of 'intimation'.

Wallas's stage analysis could be interpreted as proposing a strict 1, 2, 3, 4 order that is gone through once and once only in solving a problem. Such a formulation is open to the criticism of being overly rigid. However, Wallas (1926, p. 81) did not intend such a rigid interpretation. He wrote:

> In the daily stream of thought these four different stages constantly overlap each other as we explore different problems. An economist reading a Blue Book, a physiologist watching an experiment, or a business man going through his morning's letters, may at the same time be 'incubating' on a problem which he proposed to himself a few days ago, be accumulating knowledge in 'preparation' for a second problem, and be 'verifying' his conclusions to a third problem. Even in exploring the same problem, the mind may be unconsciously incubating on one aspect of it, while it is consciously employed in preparing for or verifying another aspect.

Some attempts have been made to bring Wallas's stages into the laboratory, notably by Patrick (1935, 1937) whose work is reviewed below. The incubation stage has been singled out as the specific focus of some laboratory studies that will be discussed in a later section.

B. Patrick's laboratory studies of stages

In the 1930s Catherine Patrick attempted to gather more systematic data on the stages of creative problem solving than were available in retrospective reports. Her method involved having subjects produce poems in response to a painting (1935) and sketches in response to a poem (1937). In each case, Patrick recorded all that the subject said and did between presentation and completion of the task. I will discuss here the 1937 study of the sketching task. The 1935 study of poetic composition was similar in method and results.

Two groups of subjects were tested. One group consisted of 50 experienced painters, all of whom had exhibited their paintings publicly. A comparison or control group consisted of 50 non-artist subjects who had no or only very slight experience of art work. The two groups were similar in ages, sex distribution and intelligence test scores.

The subjects were tested in their own homes. After a brief conversation period to put subjects at their ease and to accustom them to having their words noted down, they were presented with an extract from Milton's poem *L'Allegro* and asked to draw a sketch about the poem or anything it suggested to them. There was no time limit and subjects were encouraged to 'think aloud' throughout. When the sketch was finished the artist subjects were questioned about their normal working methods.

To obtain objective evidence on stages of thinking, Patrick divided each thinking aloud record (protocol) into four equal time quarters. The protocol quarters were then analysed for (a) the number of *thought changes*, (b) the number of *general shapes drawn for the first time* and (c) the number of instances of *revision* in each quarter.

Thought changes were taken to indicate *preparation* stage thinking and 75 per cent of thought changes occurred in the first quarter. *Illumination* was taken to be indexed by drawing a general shape for the first time; 66 per cent of such events occurred in the second and third quarters. Revisions were taken to indicate a *verification* stage and 75 per cent of revisions occurred in the third and fourth time quarters. The incidences of these types of events, then, were in accord with Wallas's stage analysis.

Incubation was taken to be indicated if an idea occurred early in the protocol, recurred one or more times while the subject spoke of other things and, finally, appeared as the chief topic of the picture. Approximately 85 per cent of the protocols showed such evidence of incubation.

According to the questionnaire given to the artists after the experiment, 94 per cent reported using incubation at least some of the time in their *normal* work (76 per cent usually, 18 per cent sometimes). The reported time periods of real-life incubation ranged from days to years.

In the experimental data, there were no differences between the artist and the control subjects in the amount of incubation. In fact, there were no differences between artist and non-artist groups in any of the performance measures, except in the rated quality of the sketches. The artist's sketches were rated far higher than those of the control subjects, as one would hope.

Patrick's data are in accord with Wallas's four-stage analysis. However, any incubation that occurred in this study was very brief compared with the retrospective reports by noted thinkers. Furthermore, the main problem was never wholly put aside but, rather, was worked on continuously for an average of 18 minutes. In typical reports by artists and scientists of incubation phenomena, the problem is often set aside for lengthy periods. The one example of incubation that Patrick gives in detail (1937, pp. 55–56) might be explained by the problem-solving strategy of scanning a number of possibilities first, before returning to the most promising one to develop it further. This 'progressive deepening' (see Chapter 2) strategy has emerged in other protocol studies of problem solving (De Groot, 1965) and could account for the effect that Patrick attributed to incubation. The difficulty here seems to be that the criterion used by Patrick for incubation effects was too weak.

To sum up, Patrick's data are certainly of interest and support the broad stages of preparation (in which possible directions are surveyed), illumination (in which one possiblity is decided on) and verification (in which revisions occur). The protocol data are less convincing on incubation effects, since at no time was the main task set aside during the average 18 minutes spent on it. However, the artists' questionnaire reports did support incubation as a real-life phenomenon, despite the difficulty of trapping it in the confines of the sketching task. Finally, Patrick notes, as did Wallas, that the stages appear to overlap and recur.

C. Laboratory studies of incubation

As we have seen, the notion of incubation plays a prominent role in the recollections of artists and scientists. Despite its importance in personal accounts of creative thinking, incubation has not attracted much experimental study. However, some data are available and will now be discussed.

Murray and Denny (1969) investigated the effects of incubation opportunity on subjects of high and low problem-solving ability. Subjects were divided into high and low ability on the basis of the Gestalt Transformation Test. This test requires the selection of objects for unusual uses, e.g. "From which object could you make a hose: a tree, cigarette, shirt, bicycle, eye glasses?".

Subjects were also divided into control and experimental groups. Both were given a rather complicated problem devised by Saugstad, in which the subject is given a nail, pliers, a length of string, a pulley, some elastic bands and several newspapers.

A glass containing metal balls and standing on a movable frame was situated 8 feet from the subject. Next to the glass was a steel cylinder. The subject had to find a way of transferring the steel balls from the glass to the cylinder without going nearer than 8 feet to the glass or the cylinder.

The solution involves two stages. First, bend the nail into a hook, attach the hook to the string and throw it into the frame. The frame can then be dragged back to the line and the balls removed. The second stage is to construct a long hollow tube by rolling up the newspapers and connecting them in telescopic fashion by elastic bands, and then to roll the balls down the tube to the steel cylinder.

Control subjects were given 20 minutes continuously to solve the problem, whereas the experimental subjects worked for 5 minutes on the task, then had 5 minutes on an unrelated pencil and paper task, and were then given a further 15 minutes on the main task.

Neither incubation nor ability level significantly affected the frequency of solutions, but there was a significant interaction in that high-ability solvers were hindered by incubation opportunity while low-ability solvers were aided by an incubation opportunity. Murray and Denny interpreted these results by suggesting that low-ability subjects quickly became fixated, and incubation allowed their inappropriate sets to die out, while the high-ability subjects may have been working more systematically through various possibilities, without fixation, but this orderly process was disrupted by an incubation opportunity.

Murray and Denny suggest, then, that incubation will be most effective when the problem is very difficult for the solver – as for their low-ability subjects tackling the tube and balls problem and, presumably, for famous scientists and artists tackling major problems and projects.

Incubation effects appear to be difficult to obtain in the laboratory. Dominowski and Jenrick (1972) carried out a follow-up of Murray and Denny's findings using a different problem involving manipulation of objects, but found no significant effect of incubation. However, on a divergent task, Fulgosi and Guilford (1968) found significant effects of 20 minutes' incubation on the quantity of solutions provided, but no effect on the quality of solutions. Clearly, research remains to be done, for example varying problem types, preparation time and length of incubation period. Olton and Johnson (1976) examined possible incubation effects on the solving of chess problems by expert players. Thus, the problems were realistic and familiar for the subjects (unlike the situation in previous studies that used unfamiliar puzzles). However, the chess-playing subjects given an incubation opportunity showed no advantage over subjects who worked continuously on the task. Assuming that incubation opportunities are sometimes useful, how might any benefits be brought about?

Three main ideas that have been put forward are those of (a) unconscious work, (b) the decay of inappropriate sets and (c) spreading activation during incubation.

Poincaré (1908) provided a graphic attempt at describing possible unconscious work during incubation periods. He proposed that the course of unconscious activity would be influenced by prior preparation or conscious work. Imagine ideas to be like hooked atoms, then, Poincaré says, conscious work selects certain atoms or ideas as relevant to the problem and tries to organize them to reach a solution. When the problem is put aside, the atoms continue to move about, hooking up with each other and with other atoms not activated during conscious work. Eventually, a solution combination may be reached, but it will generally involve at least one of the atoms or ideas that were selected during conscious work.

In contrast, Woodworth and Schlosberg (1954) suggested that incubation simply involves a decay in misleading tendencies that interfere with solution of the problem. Yaniv and Meyer (1987) proposed that, when an unsuccessful attempt is made at a problem, activation spreads from information activated by the problem statement and eventually may weakly activate solution-relevant information in long-term memory. If a hint or relevant accidental cue arises, then the weakly activated solution information may be activated above threshold and an 'insight' will be experienced. At present, the 'decay', 'unconscious work' and 'spreading activation' hypotheses remain open and await creative experimentation.

III. INCREASING IDEA PRODUCTION

Are there any ways of increasing the production of novel ideas? Numerous proposals have been put forward (see Stein, 1974, 1975) for stimulating the idea production stage of creative thinking. Probably the most famous, and certainly the most re-searched, method is that known as 'brainstorming'.

A. Brainstorming

1 Basic results

In the 1940s and 1950s a practical businessman, Alex Osborn, developed a package of recommendations known as the brainstorming method. This was intended mainly for use in group problem solving and as a means of increasing idea production. The method can be adapted for individual use and is described in Osborn's (1953) book *Applied imagination*. Brainstorming has been taken up quite widely in a variety of organizations and has also been investigated extensively in laboratory settings.

Osborn adopts the standard view that problem solving and creative thinking involve (1) problem formulation, (2) idea finding and (3) evaluation of ideas to find a likely solution. Brainstorming aims at facilitating the middle – idea finding – stage and it can be summarized as involving two main principles and four rules.

Principles
(1) Deferment of judgement.
(2) Quantity breeds quality.

Rules
(1) Criticism is ruled out.
(2) Free-wheeling is welcomed.
(3) Quantity wanted.
(4) Combination and improvement sought.

The 'deferment of judgement' principle meant that evaluation of ideas was to be postponed until a set period of idea production had elapsed. The untutored thinker will tend to evaluate each idea as it is produced. Osborn suggests that this can be inhibiting and may lead to premature abandonment of ideas that, although not useful in themselves, may lead on to possible solutions. The 'quantity breeds quality' principle states that the more ideas produced the larger the absolute number of useful ones there are likely to be, even if the proportion is very low. The rules listed above remind 'brainstormers' not to criticize their own ideas or those of others, to free-associate to ideas already produced, to aim for quantity, and to combine and improve already generated suggestions.

The method was originally devised for group use but can be adapted for individual applications. A number of questions arise; for example, does the method lead to better productivity (a) for groups and (b) for individuals? Does group brainstorming lead to better results than would be obtained by pooling the ideas produced by the appropriate number of individual brainstormers?

Numerous studies support the hypothesis that groups using brainstorming produce more ideas than similar groups working along conventional lines. Brainstorming instructions strongly affect the quality of ideas produced and, although effects on average quality are not so evident, reports of more high-quality ideas have been obtained (as would be expected by virtue of the 'quantity effect'). An example study is the following by Meadow *et al.* (1959). They compared the effects of brainstorming instructions with the effects of instructions that stressed the quality of ideas produced. The tasks set the subjects were to think of as many uses as they could for a broom and a coathanger. Ideas were rated independently for uniqueness (the degree to which the suggested use differed from normal use) and for value (social, economic or aesthetic). 'Good' ideas were defined as those rated highly on both uniqueness and value. The results indicated that significantly more good ideas were produced with the brainstorming than with the non-brainstorming instructions.

Favourable results on individual brainstorming have also been reported by Parnes and Meadow (1963). In one study, subjects were individually required to think up possible solutions to problems for 5 minutes. On one problem they operated conventionally, evaluating ideas as they thought of them; on the other problem, they used deferred judgement. The first method produced an average of 2.5 'good' ideas, while the second produced an average of 4.3 'good' ideas. Parnes estimated that in this case 72 per cent better productivity resulted from deliberate deferment of judgement during idea production.

2 Brainstorming: real v. nominal groups

Given that both individual and group brainstorming seem to be effective, the question arises whether brainstorming in a group produces better results than would be obtained by pooling results from individual brainstormers. It could be argued either that the group procedure would lead to beneficial mutual stimulation or, alternatively, that participants would be inhibited by fear of implicit criticism even although overt criticism is not permitted.

Taylor *et al.* (1958) tackled this question with an experiment in which 12 groups of four men and 48 individuals followed the basic rules of brainstorming while working on the same three problems. The problems were (a) 'Think of as many ways as possible of encouraging European tourists to visit the USA'; (b) 'What would be the consequences if all future children were born with an extra thumb on each hand?' (a diagram of the new hand structure was provided); and (c) 'How could the education system cope with the effects of a 'bulge' in the school age population?' (as was being experienced at the time of the study).

After the idea production stage, the 48 individual subjects' data were assigned to 12 *nominal* groups of size four. The performance of each such nominal group was then scored as though the members had in fact worked together. The achievement of such nominal groups provided a baseline level of performance which would be achieved if group work were neither facilitating nor inhibiting. The nominal groups produced (a) more unique ideas than the real groups and (b) more distinctly 'good' ideas – largely by virtue of a quantity effect.

It was concluded from these data that group participation in brainstorming inhibited creative thinking relative to individual brainstorming. Perhaps, then, individuals feared implicit criticism even when open criticism was not permitted. Also, individuals working in a real group are more likely to develop the same set or direction in their thinking than the same number of individuals working alone. Individuals working alone will probably develop 'sets', but these sets are likely to differ from person to person.

The 'nominal group superiority effect', first revealed in Taylor *et al.*'s experiment, has held up over a number of procedural variations. For example, Dunnette *et al.* (1963) used a similar design to that of Taylor *et al.*, but their subjects were research scientists and advertising people who had extensive prior experience of working with each other. Thus the groups were more like real groups in a working environment than were Taylor *et al.*'s student groups. The same three problems as those in the Taylor *et al.* study were used, plus the so-called 'People' problem (i.e. "What adjustments and consequences would follow if people's average height increased to 80 inches and their average weight doubled?"). The performance of real brainstorming groups of size four was compared with that of nominal brainstorming groups of four. Again, the nominal groups produced more ideas and more good ideas than the real group. This led Dunnette *et al.* to conclude that brainstorming is most effective when undertaken by individuals working alone in an atmosphere free from the apparently inhibiting influence of group interaction.

Four-person groups, as in the above two studies, are at the low end of group size. Perhaps larger groups would show an advantage over nominal groups? Bouchard and Hare (1970) addressed this possibility in a study in which 84 male students individually brainstormed the 'thumbs' problem while a further 84 were assigned to groups of five, seven or nine persons. The results indicated that, as group size increased, the advantage of the nominal groups also increased, both in terms of quantity and quality.

The problems used in the foregoing studies were rather artificial, or unreal, and possibly not very involving for the subjects. Dillon *et al.* (1972) used a topic that was both real-life and 'hot' at the time. This was, "How might people influence US foreign policy as a result of the US invasion of Cambodia in 1970?" Once more, nominal groups out-scored real groups on quantity of ideas for dealing with this question.

The nominal group superiority effect seems to be very robust and, in addition to the manipulations already described, has withstood variations in sex of experimenter, presence of experimenter, and written v. tape-recorded responses (see Stein, 1975, Ch. XIII, for further details).

3 Deferment v. separation of judgement

Whether undertaken by individuals or groups, deferment of judgement is a key tenet of Osborn's description of brainstorming. Some research has considered whether it is really the deferment of judgement or simply the separation of judgement from production that is the effective feature. Brilhart and Jochem (1964) compared three different patterns of stages in problem solving. Pattern A was labelled 'ideas–criteria' and conformed to the normal brainstorming sequence of events, i.e. (1) analysis of problem, (2) brainstorming production of ideas, (3) consideration of criteria, (4) evaluation and (5) report of best idea. Pattern B ('criteria–ideas') reversed the order of steps 3 (criteria consideration) and 2 (ideas production) but was otherwise the same as Pattern A. In Pattern C ('problem–solution') the following three steps were followed: (1) analysis, (2) simultaneous generation and evaluation of ideas, and (3) selection of best solution.

Five-person groups worked on three problems using three different patterns of steps, and all group results were scored for quantity and quality of ideas produced. Patterns A and B resulted in many more ideas than Pattern C, and Pattern A was best in terms of numbers of good ideas. So, it seems that separation of idea producing and criteria considering is useful in terms of quantity irrespective of the order of these two steps. However, the standard order used in brainstorming (i.e. 'ideas–criteria') seems most effective in terms of quality of ideas, compared with the other two patterns.

B. Checklists and morphological synthesis

The brainstorming technique was not very explicit on how to generate ideas, apart from urging free association. Warren and Davis (1969) compared three more specific methods that are suitable for individual use. Subjects were set the task of thinking of ideas for changing or improving a particular object – a doorknob. One group of subjects was given a short checklist of general 'idea-spurring' suggestions (e.g. add something, subtract something, change colour, change materials, etc.). A second group was given a long checklist of 73 idea-spurring questions organized into nine categories [e.g. *magnify?* (add what?, time frequency, strength, etc.) *modify?* (meaning, colour, motion, etc.)]. The third group was instructed in a technique known as *morphological synthesis* (Zwicky, 1969). This technique requires the problem solver to list ideas for one aspect of the object in question along one axis and ideas for another aspect of the problem along a second axis. Novel ideas would then be found in the matrix formed by combining the two axes. For example, if the problem was to invent a new type of vehicle, this could be tackled by creating a matrix with ideas for power sources along one dimension (axis) and ideas for the medium of transport along the other dimension (see Fig. 10.1 for a possible morphological synthesis of the 'new vehicle' problem).

Each point in the matrix (Fig. 10.1) represents some combination of power source and medium. Some are familiar, and some impossible; but others may be new and useful. Evidently the number of combinations increases rapidly with the number of ideas per dimension. More than two dimensions may be used, leading to further increases in the number of combinations.

A fourth, control, group was given no particular instructions in problem-solving methods. Of the four groups, the short checklist and morphological synthesis groups produced the highest number of ideas and the greatest number of high-quality ideas. Surprisingly, perhaps, the long checklist produced no improvement over the control conditions. The morphological synthesis instructions produced the greatest number of ideas and had the highest rate of production; and so, when time is taken into account, this method appeared to be the most effective of those studied.

C. Synectics

A method that has been extensively taken up, especially in the US, by industrial and other organizations that have practical and pressing needs for innovative ideas is known as synectics (Gordon, 1961). Despite its wide use in practice, synectics does not seem to have attracted much laboratory investigation. Thus data on its utility are largely in the form of anecdotes. However, it is an interesting and plausible technique and is worth describing here, albeit briefly.

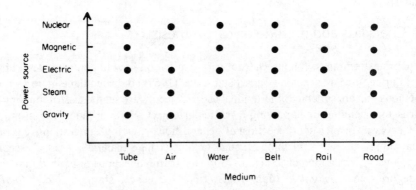

Fig. 10.1 *Morphological synthesis applied to the 'new vehicles' problem.*

Synectics involves the joining together of different and apparently irrelevant elements by the use of metaphors and analogies. An unfamiliar problem may be better understood when it can be represented by an analogy with something familiar (i.e. 'making the strange familiar'). Conversely, a problem that is overfamiliar, and about which we have difficulty in generating fresh ideas, can often be usefully handled by means of an unusual metaphor ('making the familiar strange'). These two uses of metaphor are helpful in developing formulations of problems. Four types of analogy are proposed for use in generating further ideas toward solutions: (1) personal analogy, (2) direct analogy, (3) symbolic analogy, and (4) fantasy analogy. The personal analogy requires that the problem solver identify him or herself with part or all of the problem and its solution (e.g. imagine how it would feel to be a zip fastener, if the problem was to improve on such a device). Direct analogy attempts to find parallel facts in other fields (e.g. considering biological examples of apertures that close up tightly in the zip fastener problem). The symbolic analogy involves a compressed description of the problem or of a possible solution, and may be verbal or in the form of an image. For example, according to Stein (1974, p. 189), one group used the Indian rope trick as a symbolic analogy in developing a new jacking mechanism. Fantasy analogy allows purely wish-fulfilling and unrealistic proposals to be put forward. For example, on the problem of making a vapour-proof closure for space suits (earlier referred to as the zip fastener problem), one participant expressed a fantasy analogy as follows: " . . . wish fulfilment. Childhood dream . . . you wish it closed, and invisible microbes, working for you, cross hands across the opening and *pull* it tight".

Little work appears to have been published evaluating synectics, apart from anecdotal accounts of successes. However, Bouchard (1972) did find that use of the personal analogy technique led to improved performance in brainstorming as compared to brainstorming without the use of personal analogy. This result, then, lends some laboratory support to the use of synectics.

D. Lateral thinking

De Bono (1983) has popularized the notion of lateral thinking as an aid to effective creativity and has developed instructional materials aimed at teaching lateral thinking skills. Lateral thinking involves re-representing a problem while, in contrast, normal ('vertical') thinking involves working *within* a given problem representation. Vertical thinking is seen as logical, sequential, predictable and habit-bound, while lateral thinking would be characterized by the opposite attributes. De Bono has devised a set of instructional materials known as the CoRT programme (named after de Bono's Cognitive Research Trust). These materials are intended to increase individuals' skills in lateral thinking. The programme involves six units each consisting of ten 35-minute lessons. The six units are outlined in de Bono (1983) and may be summarized as follows:

(1) CoRT1: *Breadth* – stresses thinking about problems in different ways.

(2) CoRT2: *Organization* – aims at effective control of attention.
(3) CoRT3: *Interaction* – focuses on questions of evidence and arguments.
(4) CoRT4: *Creativity* – provides strategies for producing unusual ideas.
(5) CoRT5: *Information and Feeling* – considers affective factors related to thinking.
(6) CoRT6: *Action* – presents a general framework for tackling problems.

De Bono suggests that CoRT1 should be taught first, after which the other units can be used in any order. Broadly speaking, the CoRT lessons involve using 'operators', which are given to help students retrieve and apply the operators when needed. Sample operators are 'consider all factors (CAF)' and 'positive, negative and interesting points (PNI)'.

De Bono (1976) reported studies in which students who had undergone CoRT instructions produced more ideas than those in control groups. This certainly suggests a 'quantity' effect; whether average quality was improved is unclear. The test questions were similar to the exercises in the training material and so the extent of transfer of training is also unclear. Edwards and Baldauf (1983) carried out an instructional study using CoRT1 and found that various measures of quantity and quality of divergent thinking improved after the CoRT1 course. Transfer of training in CoRT1 to performance in high-school physics was investigated, but no clear indication of transfer emerged.

Rather stronger evidence supporting the CoRT programme comes from a Venezuelan study (de Sanchez and Astorga, 1983). Large groups of children received training in a version of the CoRT programme for periods of 1–3 years. Control subjects of similar background did not receive these lessons. Pre- and post-tests with divergent problems similar to those used in training showed significantly larger gains on quantity and quality measures for the experimental subjects compared with the controls. Interestingly, the relative gains increased with the number of years of training.

The results, particularly those of the Venezuelan study, are quite encouraging for the CoRT programme. However, questions regarding transfer to dissimilar tasks and long-term beneficial effects remain open.

IV. THEORETICAL APPROACHES

So far, our discussion of research on creative processes has been somewhat atheoretical. In this section I will consider some attempts to explain creative processes within the frameworks of theoretical approaches established in other areas. The approaches dealt with here are those of associative, piagetian and information-processing theory.

A. Associative theories

1 Mednick

Mednick (1962, p. 221) defined the creative thinking process as the "forming of associative elements into new combinations which either meet specified requirements or are in some way useful". On this view, then, the creative thinker comes up with useful combinations of ideas that are already in the thinker's repertoire but which have not been previously brought together (e.g. Salvador Dali combining the idea of a 'watch' with that of 'softness', producing the novel combination 'a soft watch'). In accord with the standard associative approach, ideas are assumed to be linked to each other, more or less directly and with varying degrees of strength, in a vast associative network. Thus 'watch' and 'clock' would tend to be strongly associated, while 'watch' and 'soft' would not be. Mednick suggested that the more weakly or indirectly connected two combined ideas are, the more original is their combination. As he puts it, "The more mutually remote the elements of the new combination, the more creative the process of solution" (1962, p. 221). Three ways are suggested in which 'mutually remote' ideas could be brought together.

Serendipity This is the accidental occurrence of environmental stimuli that evoke the requisite ideas in close proximity. Accidental events do seem to have played a role in a number of scientific discoveries and inventions, e.g. discovering the vulcanization of rubber, X-rays and penicillin.

Deliberate use of serendipity is not unknown in the arts and sciences. Mednick cites a physicist who keeps in a fishbowl large numbers of slips of paper, each with some physical fact written on it. Every so often, he randomly draws pairs of facts from the bowl in the hope of finding new and useful combinations. The avant-garde author William Burroughs made good use of his 'cut up' method, which involved snipping portions from newspapers and randomly arranging and rearranging them until a suitable effect was obtained. Similarly, in painting, collages and *objets trouvés* deliberately involve chance elements.

Similarity The required elements may be evoked close together by similarity on some dimension. Examples would include rhymes, alliterations and homonyms.

Mediation The required ideas may be evoked through the mediation of associates that they have in common. For example, the idea of using a vacuum cleaner to remove a cloud of small flies that has settled on the ceiling may come about through an associative sequence such as 'ceiling–floor–vacuum cleaner' where the 'ceiling–vacuum cleaner' connection is mediated by their common associate 'floor'.

Given this view, Mednick proposes explanations of individual differences in creativity principally in terms of differences in associative organization. In particular, it is suggested that individuals may be characterized by the 'steepness' of their 'associative hierarchies'. Take the word 'table'. Two individuals may have the same set of associates to table, ordered in the same way, but one may have a steep hierarchy in which the most associated word ('chair') is much more strongly associated with 'table' than is the second associate ('cloth'). The other person may have a much flatter hierarchy in which the differences in strength between successive associates to 'table' are much less. Figure 10.2 represents two such hierarchies.

Mednick suggests that creative individuals may be characterized by relatively flat associative hierarchies which enable them to connect together remote ideas more readily than people with steep hierarchies. On the basis of this theory, Mednick devised the Remote Associates Test (RAT). In this test each of the 30 items consists of three words, known to be mutually remote. The subject's task is to produce a fourth word which is a common associate of all three remote words. An example item is 'surprise, line, birthday', and the answer is 'party'. People with 'flat' hierarchies should find this test easier than those with 'steep' hierarchies. The test displays satisfactory levels of reliability (around 0.91) and validation studies have been quite encouraging. Mednick reported a correlation of 0.7 between RAT score and rated creativity of design students. Other, weaker, but statistically significant connections were reported between RAT scores and creativity ratings of psychology graduate students, originality assessments of eminent architects and 'non-conformist' tendencies among students. Furthermore, high scorers on the RAT have been found to detect and use incidentally presented information to a greater degree than low RAT scorers (Mendelsohn and Griswold, 1964; Laughlin *et al.*, 1968). This suggests that a broad, less focused, attentional style may underlie the development of the presumed flatter hierarchies of high RAT scorers.

Despite the plausibility of Mednick's theory and the early promise of the RAT, little further development seems to have occurred in this approach since the late 1960s. This may reflect a general disenchantment with simple associative theories of

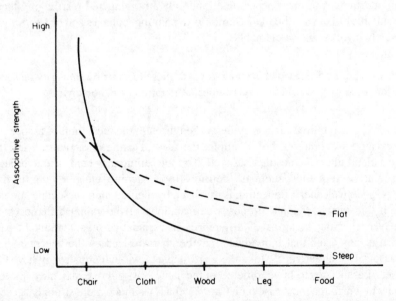

Fig. 10.2 *Steep and flat associative hierarchies to the word 'table'. After Mednick (1962).*

memory and thought. Before moving on to consider some approaches that allow more to mental organization than purely associative links, a quite influential associative theory due to Koestler (1964) will be briefly discussed.

2 Koestler

Arthur Koestler (1964) has put forward a somewhat more sophisticated associative theory than Mednick's. However, perhaps because it derives largely from case studies of numerous 'acts of creation' and has not led to laboratory tests, this theory has had little impact on psychology, although it has been well received by the lay public. Koestler's *bisociative* theory claims that a creative act involves linking together two previously unconnected 'frames of reference' (also known as 'associative contexts', 'universes of discourse' or 'matrices'). Koestler proposes that, in given associative contexts, ideas are connected by fixed rules, and that normal problem solving involves working with the established rules within one context (e.g. applying rules of chess, exploring permissable moves in an eight-puzzle problem, etc.) The (possibly apocryphal) case of Archimedes solving the problem of measuring the volume of an irregular object (a crown) serves to illustrate the bisociation of different associative contexts. None of the rules in Archimedes' habitual 'frame of reference' for measuring volume would yield the volume of a valuable crown without damaging it (e.g. by melting it down or by hammering it into a regular shape). Presumably, all the time, Archimedes also had rules relating to the 'bathing' context. One of the bathing rules would be that if one got into a full bath, the water would spill out. The volume-measuring 'frame of reference' and the bathing 'frame of reference' were suddenly linked when Archimedes noticed the water level rise as he stepped into a bath after thinking about the volume problem for a considerable time. It became clear that immersion of a body in a full container (as in bathing) would displace liquid whose volume could then be measured by the rules already well established in the volume-measuring 'frame of reference'.

Koestler interpreted as cases of bisociation numerous other examples of scientific creativity (e.g. the discovery or invention of vaccination, printing, the notions of elliptical planetary orbits and evolution by natural selection). However, no predictions that could be tested in laboratory settings, or possible measures of individual differences that might be relevant to predicting creativity, have arisen from this theory. Indeed, Perkins (1981) has argued that Koesler's 'theory' of bisociation is essentially a redescription of creative products rather than a process explanation. Perkins' point is that a creative product is bound to involve a novel combination of ideas and thus can be described as 'bisociative'. It is not, then, helpful to say that there is a special process of bisociation that results in bisociative products. On this argument, Koestler's 'theory' is not a testable theory.

3 Simonton's chance configuration theory

Simonton (1988) builds on Campbell's (1960) earlier blind variation and selective retention model of creative processes. Campbell's model involved the following three basic propositions:

(1) The solution of novel problems requires some means of generating *ideational variation*. This process is 'blind' in that the problem tackler cannot know in advance of testing a new idea whether it will help or not.
(2) The idea variations are subject to a fixed *selection process* that retains advances and rejects non-advances.
(3) The selected variations must be *retained*.

Campbell's model of idea generation, selection and retention is clearly analogous to darwinian evolutionary theory. Simonton builds on this model in his chance configuration theory by introducing concepts of (a) the chance permutation of mental elements, (b) the formation of stable configurations and (c) the communication and acceptance of those configurations.

Simonton proposes that the creative process operates on mental elements, which are unitary ideas that are free to enter into combinations with other elements. The basic mechanism is *chance permutation* of these elements. The use of the term 'permutation' (rather than the more often used term 'combination') draws attention to the order in which elements are combined. The same elements (e.g. musical notes) will have very different effects depending on the order in which they are combined. Once a chance permutation has occurred, some selection must be introduced. Most chance permutations are unstable in that the elements do not cohere; the few that form an interrelated whole are highly stable and Simonton labels these *configurations*. Stable configurations are retained and become new 'chunks' which function as a single element and can thus enter into further permutations. Bringing together configurations to form new configurations is similar to Koestler's bisociation notion of bringing together different conceptual matrices. Hierarchical combining of configurations (as in taxonomies) is an especially useful mode of combination for cognitive efficiency and is pervasive across many domains.

A new configuration which seems useful has to be further developed into a *communication configuration* before the creative process is complete. The initial chance configuration then is a starting point, e.g. a sketch, an outline, a germinal idea, which must be the basis for a publicly available product, e.g. a painting, a symphony, a scientific paper, and so on. Finally, the product must be perceived as meeting a need by an audience.

Particular support for the chance configuration theory can be drawn from data on the distribution of creative productivity over contributors to particular fields, the relation between age and creativity, and the quantity–quality relationship.

In many fields the distribution of outputs is such that a few contributors account for a majority of products. Dennis (1955) found that the top 10 per cent produced around 50 per cent of contributions, while the bottom 50 per cent produced about 15 per cent of the contributions over many disciplines. Thus, the distribution of number of products per contributor is highly skewed. Simonton (1988) argues that even if the number of mental elements (n) available for chance permutation is normally distributed, as seems plausible, the number of possible chance permutations (e to the power n) is a highly skewed distribution. Thus, contributors with more elements will produce disproportionately more configurations, and so the observed productivity distributions are consistent with the chance configuration theory.

The relationships between age and output reported by Lehman (1953) have been supported by more recent research (Simonton, 1984). The main patterns are that productivity in all fields tends to increase initially with age, reach a peak and then decline more slowly than the initial rise; the onset, peak and rate of decline vary from field to field; and, finally, exceptional output is associated with precocity, longevity and high productivity rates. Simonton (1988) argues that the typical age–productivity curve reflects the operation of two processes: production of chance configurations (*ideation*) and elaboration of chance configurations into creative communications (communication configurations). Ideation is held to occur at a rate proportional to the size of the set of free mental elements that have not yet been combined, while elaboration rate depends in a similar way on the quantity of ideations awaiting conversion into communicable form. Simonton shows that by varying these two rates the typical age – productivity curves can be produced. In relatively formal disciplines (e.g. mathematics), the rates of ideation and elaboration are high, leading to early peaks; but in less formalized domains (e.g. history), the rates of ideation and elaboration are low, leading to late peaks and slow declines. Total productivity should be governed by the total number of possible chance configurations of the mental elements that a person brings to the domain. On Simonton's model it can be shown that the greater the number of such combinations that are theoretically possible, the earlier the person will begin to contribute (precocity) and the higher the rate of production will be. The longer the lifespan (longevity), the greater the total contribution (assuming reasonable health).

There appears to be a fairly consistent link between quantity and quality in that the longer the list of products a person has contributed, generally the longer will be that person's list of high-quality products. Over a creator's working life the quality ratio of major to minor works tends to be constant (Simonton, 1977). The 'constant-probability-of-success' rule follows from Campbell's blind variation model and from Simonton's chance configuration theory. The stability of creative reputations may depend partly on the existence of multiple high-quality products that can support the reputation even when individual product's perceived worth may fluctuate with time. Equally, it is notable that high creatives often have a 'tail' of work that is less highly regarded than the best work of their generally lower-ranked contemporaries. As W.H. Auden said, " . . . the major poet will write more bad poems than the minor", but only because the major poet will tend to write much more than the minor poet (Bennet, 1980).

Overall, Simonton's theory is consistent with a broad range of historical data on productivity and is broadly applicable over a range of artistic and scientific areas.

However, as with Darwin's original theory of evolution, further specification of the means of variation and retention are needed to complete the chance configuration theory.

B. Gruber's evolving systems approach

Gruber (1980) has painstakingly analysed the case of Charles Darwin's development of evolutionary theory in terms of evolving systems of ideas. To understand the evolution of ideas, Gruber has drawn on piagetian theory, which is, of course, concerned mainly with the development of concepts (e.g. that of the conservation of mass) in children; however, Gruber shows that the approach can be usefully applied to conceptual growth in adults. Gruber points to the long time periods involved in developing significant new ideas. The emphasis on 'acts of creation' and 'moments of insight' has, perhaps, been misleading and diverted attention from the long-term growth-like processes in which moments of insight are embedded. Analysis of Darwin's notebooks indicates a series of changes in his 'system of ideas' concerning the relationship of biological and geological phenomena.

Initially, the dominant conceptual scheme was that the physical world and the species inhabiting it were fixed at creation. However, evidence from geology more and more indicated a changing physical world. This led to a conceptual conflict. How could species fixed at creation remain adapted to changing environments? Darwin's first theory – the monad theory – suggested that simple living forms (monads) appeared through spontaneous generation from inanimate matter and then evolved to match the environment. This was fairly quickly abandoned and Darwin then sought other ways in which species could change. Hybridization seemed possible and led Darwin to a study of plant and animal breeding which increased his knowledge of artificial selection. The transmission of acquired characteristics was another possible solution and led Darwin into a study of mental processes and behaviour in animals and humans. Although this approach did not produce the desired answer to the question of heritable variation, it produced much evidence that would influence the final theory. Studying the evolution of mental processes also raised forcibly the issue of materialism. This was a somewhat suspect and dangerous idea at the time and Darwin expressed fear of persecution on account of his materialist notions. After many years of prior study and experience, Darwin read Malthus's *Essay on Population* on 28 September 1838, and this seems to have led him to realize that natural selection could work in favour of variants that were better suited to their environment than their ancestors had been. The idea of natural selection as a 'conservative' force, weeding out weak or maladapted variants, was well known but the positive aspects of natural selection, favouring the best adapted variants, had not been emphasized before Darwin's insight.

Darwin was not quite satisfied with the theory because it did not explain variation but rather took variation and heredity as unexplained assumptions. A further 20 years' work and the stimulus of Wallace's independent conception of 'evolution by natural selection' were required before Darwin finally published his evolutionary theory.

Gruber emphasizes the slowness of the changes in Darwin's system of ideas and he interprets the process of change in terms of Piaget's notions of 'assimilation' and 'accommodation'. 'Assimilation' involves the incorporation of new information into existing conceptual structures, while 'accommodation' involves changes in conceptual structure brought about by new information. Gruber argues that what appear to be dramatic breaks with the past can also be seen as the culmination of numerous small changes. This approach then, places 'moments of insight' within their long-term context and would suggest that little understanding of high-order creativity will result from laboratory studies of small-scale problem solving.

Gruber and his colleagues (e.g. Gruber and Davis, 1988) have applied their evolving-systems approach to case studies of the work of a number of other creative individuals in addition to Darwin, in a range of domains, including the scientist Benjamin Franklin, the psychologist William James, the philosopher John Locke, the novelist Dorothy Richardson and the poet William Wordsworth. Overall, these studies have supported the view that creative work in real life takes a long time – months, years or even decades. The spread of work over long time periods means that considerable organization of effort is needed. Sub-goals and sub-sub-goals must be set up and integrated into the overall effort; delays, tangents and false starts proliferate. Initial sketches, rough drafts and early notebooks play a crucial role in shaping and guiding projects. For example, Picasso's famous painting *Guernica* began as a sketch which underwent successive elaborations and transformations over a month to yield the final product (Arnheim, 1962). Often, the creative individual has a network of related projects, some of which are relatively active and some relatively dormant at any one time. These interrelated projects influence each other and can offer useful analogies from one project to another and general linking themes. For example, Darwin worked on geological, zoological, psychological and botanical projects; a linking theme which he developed in all areas was that of *gradualism* ('nature makes no jumps'). Gruber and Davis (1988) also argue that multiple projects enable the creative individual to continue good work even when experiencing a blockage on one project; an alternative project is taken up until perhaps an accidental stimulus offers a way of dealing with the impasse in the first project. Finally, intrinsic motivation to work in the domain concerned for its own sake seems to be essential and underlies the high activity levels of creative individuals.

C. The information-processing approach

1 Simon: creativity and search

Simon (1966) indicated how the information-processing approach might tackle the topic of creativity in science. He pointed out that high-level creativity in science is a rare event and that scientific discovery is a very slow process (as Gruber has also argued). A theory of scientific creativity therefore should account not only for the occurrence of major conceptual advances but also for their rarity of occurrence.

Simon proposed that the information-processing theory of small-scale problem solving can be applied usefully to highly creative scientific thinking. The information-processing theory of problem solving is basically that outlined in Chapters 2 and 3 of this book. Thinking is seen as a hierarchical organization of elementary processes carried out one at a time. Considerable search is postulated, limited by selective heuristics, such as means–end analysis.

Scientific biographies generally reveal considerable trial-and-error search through a vast space of alternative hypotheses before breakthroughs occur. Persistence and strong motivation are marked characteristics of successful scientists. Some scientists apparently have better heuristics than others and can reach solutions more rapidly on that account. A prime source of heuristics are good representational or observational methods. For instance, many advances followed the inventions of telescopes and microscopes. These devices presumably helped in formulating the nature of the relevant problems more clearly and in ruling out possible alternative hypotheses more decisively than had been possible previously.

Simon's outline of how scientific discovery might be accounted for in information-processing terms has been vindicated by the development of computer program models capable of inducing laws such as Kepler's Third Law of planetary motion, (Langley et al., 1987). The program BACON, reported by Langley et al., uses simple heuristics to search through the space of possible laws that might interrelate quantitative data. For example, consider Kepler's Third Law. This says that the cube of a planet's distance from the sun is proportional to the square of its period.

Symbolically, the Law can be expressed as $D^3/P^2 = c$, where D is the distance, P the period and c a constant. Three heuristics aid in discovering such laws:

(1) If the values of a term are constant, then infer that the term always has that value.
(2) If the values of two numerical terms increase together, then consider their ratio.
(3) If the values of one term increase as those of another decrease, then consider their product.

Suppose data are available for three planets, as follows:

	P	D
Planet A	1.0	1.0
Planet B	8.0	4.0
Planet C	27.0	9.0

Heuristic 2 can be applied; since D increases with P, consider their ratio and call it Term 1. Applying the heuristic gives the following data:

	P	D	Term 1
Planet A	1.0	1.0	1.0
Planet B	8.0	4.0	0.5
Planet C	27.0	9.0	0.333

Now, D increases as Term 1 decreases. Thus, Heuristic 3 applies. Take the product of D and Term 1 and define it as Term 2 $[D(D/P) = D^2/P]$. Carrying out Heuristic 3 we now have the following:

	P	D	Term 1	Term 2 (D^2/P)
Planet A	1.0	1.0	1.0	1.0
Planet B	8.0	4.0	0.5	2.0
Planet C	27.0	9.0	0.333	3.0

Since Term 1 increases as Term 2 decreases, Heuristic 3 applies again. Define Term 3 as the product of Term 1 and Term 2 $[(D/P)(D^2/P) = D^3/P^2]$. The data are now as follows:

	P	D	Term 1	Term 2	Term 3 (D^3/P^2)
Planet A	1.0	1.0	1.0	1.0	1.0
Planet B	8.0	4.0	0.5	2.0	1.0
Planet C	27.0	9.0	0.333	3.0	1.0

Term 3 is constant, so Heuristic 1 applies and we assert $D^3/P^2 = c$, which is Kepler's Third Law. Using the types of heuristics outlined in this example, Langley *et al.*'s discovery program, BACON, was able to discover a number of quantitative laws starting from tables of 'raw' data (e.g. Ohm's Law, Coulomb's Law). Furthermore, Qin and Simon (1990) found that subjects given access to Kepler's data proposed similar rules to those of Kepler and that their heuristic methods were similar to those of the BACON program. Thus, BACON has merit as a simulation in addition to its merits as artificial intelligence program.

What of incubation and possible unconscious processes in discovery and invention? Simon (1966) argued that incubation and inspiration phenomena could be explained in terms of two mechanisms he labelled *familiarization* and *selective forgetting*. Familiarization is a slow process of building up a representation of the problem and relevant data in long-term memory. It is assumed that, in seeking information, the person is guided by a goal tree that is stored and developed in working memory. In the course of pursuing goals, information is obtained and added to the long-term memory. This information in turn is used in constructing new goals and sub-goals. Thus there is a continuous interaction between goal information in working memory and problem information in the long-term memory. When the problem is set aside, the goal information is lost and has to be reconstructed again. However, when the problem is taken up again, there is more information about the task in the long-term memory than there was before, so a different set of goals and sub-goals will likely be erected and these may lead to a quick solution where the previous goals did not.

There is no need for parallel processing in this theory. Inspiration would be explained by a switch of attention to the problem, followed by rapid solution. Attention switching could be accomplished by a time-sharing scheme that checked on outstanding goals or tasks at regular intervals and decided whether the current task should continue to occupy attention or whether to switch for a while to a different task. Such systems are common in computer installations and ensure that all outstanding claims on processing time get a fair share of attention. Further discussion of this topic will be found in Chapter 11, where the issue of parallel *v.* serial thought processes is considered in the general context of research on thinking.

To sum up, Simon's (1966) analysis foreshadowed detailed computer models such as BACON which show concretely how the information-processing approach can tackle creative processes in science and which appear to simulate some examples of human rule induction (Qin and Simon, 1990).

2 The Geneplore model

Finke and colleagues (Finke, 1990; Finke *et al.*, 1992) have (creatively) invented a new term 'geneplore' to label their cognitive model of creativity. 'Geneplore' is a selective combination of the words 'generate' and 'explore' and indicates that these processes are central to their theory. They postulate two distinct phases in creative activity: (a) a generative phase in which mental representations called preinventive structures are constructed and (b) an exploratory phase in which the preinventive structures are interpreted for possible meanings and uses. The process typically involves a number of cycles where either new preinventive structures are formed or initial preinventive structures are elaborated toward useful solutions. Goal or product constraints may apply to either or both main phases and bias generation or exploration and interpretation.

Support for this model has been drawn from experiments on creative invention (Finke, 1990) that utilize laboratory analogues of invention. In such experiments subjects were first shown a set of 15 basic object parts, e.g. sphere, half-sphere, tube, bracket, hook and cross. Three different parts were presented by name on each trial and subjects were to imagine combining the parts to make a practical object or device. All three parts had to be used but subjects could vary the size, position or orientation of any part. Objects had to belong to one of eight general categories, such as furniture, transportation, tools and utensils, etc. Three main experimental conditions were explored: (1) subjects were given a category at random but could choose the three parts, (2) the parts were assigned at random but the subjects could choose the category and (3) both the parts and the category were assigned at random. Examples of objects produced are: a shoe-string unlacer, a hip exerciser and a novel hamburger patty maker. The highest rate of products judged creative (i.e. practical and original) was found with randomly assigned categories and parts, suggesting that subjects' habitual tendencies and sets may have reduced creativity when free choice of objects or categories was allowed. Retrospective reports indicated that subjects tended to use an exploratory strategy in which they began by constructing interesting (prein-ventive) forms and then tried to interpret these forms rather than starting with the function or category and trying to generate objects to fit. In a further study, subjects were asked simply to combine three randomly chosen shapes into interesting forms without any intended object category being given in advance. After a shape had been generated, subjects were asked to interpret the form as a practical object or device within a randomly chosen category. In other conditions, subjects chose the category in advance or were given a random category in advance of generation. Rate of creative production was highest in the case where no category was specified in advance but was given at random after generation.

The results can be interpreted in terms of the geneplore model as reflecting the separation of generation and exploration and the benefits of not invoking product or goal constraints too early. The separation of generation and exploration is remin-iscent of the separation of idea generation and evaluation in brainstorming, and the condition in which no goal is given represents an extreme form of such a separation. Notions similar to that of preinventive form have also been invoked by Simonton (1988) in his idea of initial chance configurations which require elaboration, and by Gruber and Davis (1988) in their idea of the 'initial sketch' that guides creative work. From the practical point of view, the finding that preinventive forms can be useful when produced with no specific goal in mind suggests that inventors could benefit from a playful initial approach in which elements are combined without strong goal constraint. Given a form, often it can be reinterpreted in many ways (as furniture, as tool, as toy, and so on); or, as Finke (1993) has put it, "function follows form" rather than the more frequently cited "form follows function" in creative invention.

3 Boden: improbabilist and impossibilist creativity

Boden (1990, 1994) has argued that there are two broad types of creativity which she labels 'improbabilist' and 'impossibilist'. These in turn can both be divided into psychological–personal and historical creativity. *Improbabilist* creativity involves generating new and valued products while working within an established rule system which defines a conceptual space of possibilities; *impossibilist* creativity involves the transformation of conceptual spaces so that new ideas arise that were impossible within pre-transformation spaces. Psychological–personal creativity involves the production of ideas new to the individual (although they may have been produced by many others), whereas historical creativity involves producing ideas that have never been produced by anyone before. Boden points out that historical creativity is a subset of psychological–personal creativity and she focuses on impossibilist psychological–personal creativity. To transform a conceptual space Boden argues that one must be able to map and explore the space. She points to developmental evidence that children become ever more flexible by using 'representational rede-scriptions' of lower-level skills (Karmiloff-Smith, 1993). Initially, children develop basic schemas for drawing a person. These schemas are quite rigid and 4 year olds cannot spontaneously draw a one-legged person because that is outside the schema (or conceptual space). They have difficulty copying out-of-schema figures also. By 10 years of age most children can distort, repeat and omit parts, and have greatly transformed their earlier schemas. These transformations develop in a fixed order. Generally, children can change the size or shape of an arm before they can insert an extra arm, and well before they can draw a person with wings instead of arms.

Larger-scale examples may be found in the history of music and mathematics. Post-Renaissance music in the West involved explorations of tonal harmony. Atonal music (Schoenberg) represents a marked transformation of the original tonal space into the atonal space. The transformation fundamentally consisted of dropping the requirement that a piece of music must have a 'home key' from which it starts and must return. Schoenberg dropped this constraint and added new ones (e.g. using every note in the chromatic scale.) A similar case of dropping constraints to develop a new space is found in the move from Euclidean to non-Euclidean geometry, which arose from dropping Euclid's fifth axiom.

What type of cognitive architecture might support impossibilist creativity? Boden suggests a hybrid serial–parallel architecture. On this view, long-term knowledge is stored in a connectionist network which can throw up unusual associations, com-binations and analogies, while the serial part steadily searches through problem spaces. The network may suggest new problem spaces through associations and analogies retrieved in reponse to the task. For example, Duncker's X-ray task might elicit the 'fort' analogy in suitably primed subjects (Cheng and Holyoak, 1985), and this would define a new problem space within which the problem could be tackled. There are echoes here of the traditional view that the unconscious (the network) is the source of inspiration and that the conscious (the serial system) carries out the more routine work of preparation and verification (Wallas, 1926).

V. SUMMARY AND CONCLUDING COMMENTS

This chapter has been concerned with the kinds of thinking involved in generating creative products, where a creative product was defined as being both novel and valuable, in some way. Studies of individuals acknowledged to be creative (i.e. to have a tendency to make creative products) noted tendencies towards dominance, radicalism and high intelligence as conventionally measured (Cattell and Drevdahl, 1955). In the sciences, creative individuals tended to be first-born or only sons (Roe, 1952). Aggression was not far below the surface, especially in connection with rival scientists. However, aggressive tendencies usually did not show up in projective test responses, probably because such tests were not congenial to the scientists' preferred 'convergent' style of thinking (Hudson, 1966; Mitroff, 1974). Artists and writers do seem to display higher than average rates of manic depression and depression than the general population (Jamison, 1995). Aspects of manic thought promote rapid work and unusual associations which may be beneficial.

Personal accounts by scientists and artists suggested four broad phases in creative work that Wallas (1926) labelled 'preparation', 'incubation', 'illumination' and 'verification'. Patrick's (1935, 1937) laboratory studies indicated some support, at least, for the conscious phases or stages of preparation, illumination and verification. Her results on incubation were less clear, perhaps because the problems were too small scale in terms of the times involved. Incubation has largely resisted capture in the laboratory, although Murray and Denny (1969) and Fulgosi and Guilford (1968) did find some beneficial effects of incubation opportunities. Even if incubation opportunities do facilitate later solution, the mechanisms involved are not clear. Unconscious work, selective forgetting and spreading activation (Yaniv and Meyer, 1987) are viable explanatory candidates and will remain so until the appropriate experiments have been devised.

Various schemes for increasing idea production have been promoted. Many studies have focused on Osborn's brainstorming method, which involves deferment of idea evaluation until after a period of free-wheeling idea production. Brainstorming seems to be beneficial on many problems and appears to work for both groups and individuals. However, from many experiments it seems that the group version of the method is inhibiting compared with individual brainstorming (Stein, 1975). Other individual-oriented techniques, such as short idea-spurring checklists and Zwicky's (1969) morphological synthesis, appear to be useful (Warren and Davis, 1969). Although they have been widely adopted in practice, there has been little experimental evaluation of Gordon's (1961) synectics techniques, which are based on using various forms of analogy (personal, direct, symbolic and fantasy). Bouchard (1972) did find results in favour of using the personal analogies technique in brainstorming sessions. Some support has been reported for de Bono's (1983) lateral-thinking programme.

A number of theoretical approaches were considered. Associative theory, as developed by Mednick (1962), gained some empirical support from the apparent validity of the Remote Associates Test, which was constructed on the basis of the theory. However, perhaps because of a general disenchantment with associative theories of thinking, this approach has not been further developed. Koestler's (1964) bisociative theory allows more complexity to mental organization than Mednick's associative theory, and postulates 'associative contexts' or 'frames of reference'. He proposed that normal, non-creative, thought proceeds *within* particular contexts or frames and that the creative act involves linking together previously unconnected frames. Although Koestler's ideas are attractive, they remain unexplored in the laboratory or by computer modelling. Simonton (1988) has developed associative notions further and explored the mathematical consequences of chance permutation of ideas. Broadly, Simonton's results match data on age trends and on links between productivity and creative eminence. Like Koestler, Gruber (1980; Gruber and Davis, 1988) has based his analysis on case studies. He has focused especially on Darwin's development of the theory of evolution. Using piagetian notions, such as assimilation and accommodation, Gruber shows how Darwin's system of ideas changed very slowly over a period of many years. 'Moments of insight', in Gruber's analysis, were the culminations of slow long-term processes. If this approach is accepted, laboratory analysis of high-level creativity would seem to be ruled out in favour of meticulous case studies.

Finally, the information-processing approach, as represented by Simon (1966) and Langley *et al.* (1987), was considered. Simon indicates how the apparent phenomena of incubation and inspiration could be explained in information-processing terms by using the notions of 'familiarization' and 'selective forgetting'. No parallel processing is required by Simon's scheme. He points out the importance of good problem representations, both to ensure search is in an appropriate problem space and to aid in developing heuristic evaluations of possible research directions. As Simon notes, many advances in science have followed improved representational technology (e.g. microscopes and telescopes). Also, he reminds us that the rate of progress in science is generally slow, and this fact fits well with the information-processing notion of the thinker as a limited capacity, serial system slowly searching for solutions in a vast space of possibilities. The work of Langley *et al.* (1987) demonstrates how such search processes, realized in computer programs, can indeed discover many basic laws of science from tables of raw data. Finke (1990) has extended the information-processing approach into laboratory studies of creative combination of images and has shown the importance of an exploratory approach where forms are devised before functions are considered ('function follows form' rather than 'form follows function'). Boden (1990, 1994) has stressed the importance of restructuring the problem space in creative work to develop new genres and paradigms in the arts and sciences.

VI. FURTHER READING

Boden, M. (1990). *The creative mind: myths and mechanisms.* London: Cardinal. A very accessible presentation of Boden's information-processing theory of high-level creativity.
Finke, R.A., Ward, T.B. and Smith, S.M. (1992). *Creative cognition: theory, research and applications.* Cambridge, MA: MIT Press. A clear exposition of the geneplore model of creative cognition.

11

Thinking: theoretical overview, progress and prospects

In this book thinking has been taken to be a form of information processing and, on this view, models of thinking should relate to more general frameworks for understanding human information processing. A number of broad frameworks have been proposed, and until the early 1980s certain assumptions were widely accepted by different theorists [from Broadbent (1958) to Anderson (1983)]. These common assumptions formed an important part of what has been referred to as the 'standard model' for thinking (Simon and Kaplan, 1989). According to the standard model, individuals have a vast long-term memory and a small-capacity working memory. These two memories are supplemented in the overall system by high-capacity but short-lived sensory memories (e.g. Sperling, 1960), which are not usually regarded as very important for thinking and may be ignored for our present purposes. In the standard model, thinking is seen as the manipulation of symbols both within working memory and between long-term and working memory. 'Manipulations' of symbols are viewed as consisting of elementary information-processing operations such as comparing symbols, copying symbols, deleting and adding symbols (Newell and Simon, 1972); appropriate combinations of elementary operations may form complex manipulations. The manipulations are assumed to be in accord with rules stored in long-term memory. At a given time, the rule selected from long-term memory for application will depend on which goals are current and on the content of the working memory. It is assumed that only one thinking step occurs at a time (the *seriality* assumption). This standard model of thinking, as rule-governed symbol manipulation, is consistent with many broader frameworks for the whole human information-processing system. However, more recently, associationist approaches have gained fresh life in the form of the 'new connectionism' (Quinlan, 1991) in which the seriality assumption is abandoned and the role of rule-governed symbol manipulation is called into question. Somewhat 'in between' positions have also been promoted in which rule-governed symbol manipulation is assumed although strict seriality is abandoned and parallel rule applications permitted. These non-standard approaches will be considered shortly. But first, it is still worth asking: "How well does the standard model of thinking cope with the experimental data?".

We will then consider a second question: "What implications do developments in our general understanding of human information processing have for models of thinking?".

In addition to these questions, this chapter will also suggest likely research trends in the thinking area.

I. STANDARD MODEL ASSUMPTIONS

A. Memory and symbol manipulation

First, the memory assumptions of the standard model do not appear to be directly challenged by the data. Quite sharp limits on mental search were indicated by the data from problem solving, reasoning and decision making. Working memory can sustain only a limited size of symbol structure representing sequences of possible actions. These working memory limitations probably underlie the preference for depth-first searches, in which memory load grows slowly, compared with breadth-first searches. The 'progressive deepening' strategy observed in chess play (De Groot, 1965) may reflect a familiarization process that builds up a structure in long-term memory to represent explored paths (Simon, 1966). Through a process of 'chunking', ultimately quite long paths can be represented by single symbols in working memory. Ericsson (1985) has shown that practice in chunking can lead to very large digit spans. Presumably experts could similarly increase their effective memory span, e.g. for chess-move sequences. Ericsson and Kintsch (1995) have also indicated how experts could use long-term memory to augment normal working memory. Differences in long-term memory contents between individuals are important in explaining skill differences in many areas of problem solving. For example, the data from studies of expertise indicate that the experts' advantage in many areas resides in vast collections of familiar patterns in long-term memory rather than in any quantitative superiority in working memory capacity beyond average levels. It was very notable that De Groot's (1965) chess masters searched to about the same depth as did less skilled players, and this result suggests essentially equal working memory capacities in both groups. The greater effectiveness of the master players' mental explorations reflected the superior structuring they imposed on the initial problem configuration, compared with that of the good, but amateur, players. Similar results have been found with experts in other domains, such as physics problem solving (Chi *et al.*, 1982).

The notion that thinking is goal directed is non-controversial, at least in the case of problem solving. However, difficulties for the standard model do arise in connection with goal scheduling and with urgent interruptions to single-minded goal seeking, that demand attention in real time (Simon, 1967; Neisser, 1963b). These questions relate to the serial *v.* parallel thinking issue and will be discussed in the next section. Even the apparently undirected thoughts involved in daydreaming are in fact often related to goals (or 'current concerns'), although the thought sequence is not constrained by higher level goals of 'keeping to the topic' or 'consider only practical possibilities'. However, the occurrence of 'intrusive thoughts', reported in the daydreaming literature, is a possible problem for the standard serial model, in that such thoughts suggest parallel processes 'breaking through' into consciousness.

The view of thinking as symbol manipulation is fundamental to the information-processing approach and is not directly challenged by the research results that have been reviewed here. However, the assumption that thinking can be fully described as symbol manipulation according to rules has been questioned on philosophical grounds by John Searle (1984, 1990). Searle has argued that since thought is meaningful and meaning cannot reside merely in symbols, then thinking cannot be fully understood simply as symbol manipulation. In Searle's view, then, a robot equipped with an impeccable natural language understanding program would not truly "understand" language because it would only be manipulating symbols. The argument is bolstered by inviting the reader (assumed not to know Chinese) to consider him or herself hand-simulating such a program to deal with Chinese language inputs and produce acceptable Chinese language outputs. Would the hand-simulator truly understand Chinese? Intuitively, it would seem not. However, a counter argument is that the broader context of processing must be considered, in that symbols relate to sensory inputs and motor outputs, as well as to each other. Meaning, it may be argued, resides in systems as wholes not in surgically isolated symbols or symbol strings.

Assuming that thinking is symbol manipulating, the further specification of the standard model that manipulations are either within working memory (e.g. re-arranging letters in a short anagram) or between working memory and long-term memory (e.g. in mental arithmetic, retrieving an intermediate sum from long-term memory and copying it to working memory) discounts manipulations occurring purely within long-term memory. On this point, the standard model clashes with notions of spontaneous activity within long-term memory as proposed by Freud (1900), Neisser (1963b), Singer (1975a) and Gestalt memory theorists (see Baddeley, 1976, Ch. 4), among others. Theorists who have postulated activity within long-term memory have usually also considered that this activity could occur in parallel with the main stream of conscious thinking. Since the notion of within long-term memory activity thus also clashes (potentially at least) with the seriality assumption, this matter will be discussed more fully in a later section on the issue of parallelism.

From this brief survey, then, the assumption of serial processing emerges as a problematic aspect of the standard model. Hence, the seriality issue will now be considered in more detail.

B. Serial or parallel thought processes?

This question is very important for modelling thought in that the answer chosen influences the model maker's treatment of many other topics, e.g. interpretation of 'incubation' data, daydreaming (especially intrusive thoughts), goal scheduling and goal interruptions. This issue also impinges on the utility of verbal reports. If all thinking is serial, then verbal reports could give a good view of, at least, that large portion of thought which is in a verbal code or readily translatable into verbal terms

(Ericsson and Simon, 1980, 1984, 1993). However, if parallel streams of thought exist and people can report only on that stream going through working memory, then much thought could not be reported and less direct methods would be needed to tap the 'underground' thought streams. Of course, the seriality assumption is simpler, more parsimonious and more testable than the alternative and has the advantage of leading to models for particular tasks that can be readily explored on existing computer systems, which are completely serial devices. So, there is much to be said for adopting the seriality assumption as an initial hypothesis. Also, as Newell has argued (1962), an awkward possibility arises when parallel activities are permitted, in that information processing may become like an "Alice in Wonderland croquet game, with porcupine balls unrolling themselves and wandering off, and flamingo mallets asking questions at inopportune times" (p. 398). Newell is here pointing to the chaotic possibilities of parallel systems; however, other theorists have not been so deterred, and although some have willingly embraced chaos (e.g. as a potential source of novel ideas), yet others have striven to show how order and parallel activity can coexist within a single system. Consideration of some of these proposals and of the 'serialist' treatment of the relevant data is now in order.

1 Neisser and Simon on the 'multiplicity' of thought

In a paper entitled 'The imitation of man by machine', Neisser (1963a) argued that thought is intimately linked with emotions and usually serves more than one goal at a time. He charged that information-processing models cast in the form of computer programs lack any representation of emotion and are overly single minded in seeking relentlessly for a single top-level goal. Simon (1967) replied with suggestions for incorporating some emotional phenomena and for dealing with multiple goals. In the case of emotion, Simon proposed that emotion is associated with interruption of the current activity sequence by an urgent stimulus demanding real-time attention (e.g. shouts of 'Fire' while working on an algebra problem). However, to handle 'interruptions' Simon did allow that a low-level monitoring process may take place along with the main stream of thought. In his own words:

> A certain amount of processing must go on continuously or almost continuously, to enable the system to *notice* when conditions have arisen that require ongoing programs to be interrupted. The noticing processes will be substantially in parallel with the ongoing goal attaining program of the total system, although this parallelism may be realized in fact, by the high frequency time sharing of a single serial processor (1967 p. 34, Simon's italics)

Thus, Simon raised the possibility of parallel 'noticing' processes that scan for 'danger' signals, but he kept open the serialist option of 'time sharing'. The notion of 'time sharing' is simply that the system rapidly switches from one program to another and so gives the appearance of doing two things at once without true simultaneity. Time sharing requires a higher-level program to determine which lower-level program should take over next and for how long. Time sharing is one way in which real computer systems allocate processing to the various jobs that come in and queue for attention. So, it is a method of known utility for serial systems.

Neisser's point about humans having multiple goals and being other than single minded is more easily tackled without parallelism. Simon showed that multiple goals can be readily generated in computer game playing, for instance, and that current goals can be set aside for other goals on the basis of time – and effort – limits put on the search for goal states.

Thus Neisser's anti-serialist points in the 1963a paper were acknowledged and largely 'defused' by Simon, but in a second paper in the same year Neisser (1963b) espoused the radical notion of multiple simultaneous thought processes, and this concept cannot be accommodated within a serial framework.

Neisser proposed that a number of more or less independent trains of thought co-occur but that there is a 'main sequence' corresponding to the ordinary flow of consciousness. The main sequence, except perhaps in pathological cases, has control of motor activity. It was suggested that the unconscious trains of thought might generally follow the rules of Freud's primary process thinking and interact together in a chaotic way. However, when the main sequence is not too demanding, the unconscious sequences may attain high degrees of complexity and do useful 'unconscious work' – the results of which can later be made available to consciousness. Accounts of incubation and inspiration in creative thinking were taken by Neisser as supporting these ideas. Serialist rejoinders (Simon, 1966; Ericsson and Simon, 1980, 1984, 1993; Ohlsson, 1992) have tended (a) to play down the solidity of reports of incubation, and (b) to propose alternative explanations for any apparently well-founded claims of incubation phenomena. So, for instance, Ericsson and Simon pointed out that reports of incubation have frequently been given many years after the supposed events occurred. It could be that the scientists, inventors or artists concerned did start consciously to muse on their problems but, on the critical occasion of 'inspiration', rapidly solved, forgot the details of their own thought processes and then reported the event as one of sudden insight occurring without warning (Woodworth and Schlosberg, 1954). The occurrence of a rapid solution on trial $n + 1$ after n failures may be attributed (Simon, 1966) to beneficial forgetting of misleading sub-goals in the rest period between trial n and $n + 1$. The topic of 'incubation' is clearly very important for theories of thinking, but unfortunately the supposed phenomenon has proven difficult to capture in the laboratory. Apart from a few published experimental studies (e.g. Patrick, 1937; Fulgosi and Guilford, 1968; Murray and Denny, 1969; Dominowski and Jenrick, 1972; Olton and Johnson, 1976), there are only anecdotal data on which to rely. Of course, if incubation is a real phenomenon but is associated only with high-level creativity, psychologists are unlikely to be able to observe it with the usual laboratory tools of small-scale, often artificial, puzzles presented to normal subjects for short periods. Intuitively, incubation does seem to play a role in less exalted, more everyday, forms of problem solving, and it may yet be possible to get leads on this elusive process, either in laboratory settings or perhaps through naturalistic 'diary' studies using more ordinary people than those whose recollections fill the anthologies on creative thinking experiences (e.g. Ghiselin, 1952). However, at present, the very existence of the phenomenon, let alone its explanation, is uncertain.

The question of 'intrusive' thoughts also arises in connection with the 'parallelism' issue. Becker *et al.* (1973) and Antrobus *et al.* (1966) found that unwelcome thoughts appear to intrude into consciousness following exposure to disturbing information. This phenomenon is certainly consistent with Neisser's multiple thinking scheme. The rival serial position could propose, along with Simon's (1967) reply to Neisser (1963a), that goals of "assimilating the disturbing information" are set up and given high priority. Thus, a time-sharing system could switch from external task goals to the 'intrusive' goals quite frequently. It is conceivable that a long-standing high-level goal is to process disturbing information, even if it is painful, and that this goal is not easily ignored. An alternative proposal by Wegner (1994) is that the goal of avoiding disturbing thoughts unavoidably becomes conscious from time to time and thus produces the very thoughts it is intended to suppress. This proposal is consistent with either a limited degree of parallelism or with time sharing.

2 Dissociations between verbal reports and behaviour

If the important thought processes involved in problem solving are serial, then it is reasonable to hope that verbal reports could be informative about the course of those processes. On the other hand, if parallel thought streams are importantly involved, the best verbal reports can only be very incomplete, being restricted to the main conscious stream. Thus, the status of verbal reports on mental processes is relevant to the serial *v.* parallel issue.

The question of the accuracy of verbal reports of mental activity has generated considerable controversy, since the era of the introspectionists until the present time. A major critique of verbal reports as a source of information on cognitive processes was presented by Nisbett and Wilson (1977) and this article stimulated replies from Ericsson and Simon (1980, 1984, 1993), who attempted to detail the circumstances under which the 'standard model' of thinking would expect verbal reports to be valid [see also, White (1988) for a critique of Nisbett and Wilson's assumptions].

Nisbett and Wilson (1977) reviewed a large collection of studies, mainly from the social psychological literature, which involved such varied topics as subjects changing their opinions (Goethals and Leckmann, 1973), coming to eat grasshoppers (Zimbardo *et al.*, 1969b), taking electric shocks (Zimbardo *et al.*, 1969a) and selecting which of four pairs of stockings they preferred. When subjects in these various studies were asked about the cognitive processes that had led them to make their responses, their verbal reports did not refer to the stimuli that the experimenters could demonstrate to be influencing their behaviour. In view of the very low accuracy of the verbal reports in these studies, Nisbett and Wilson concluded that reports on cognitive processes are not based on genuine 'privileged' information of a type available only to introspection but, rather, are based on implicit and widely held causal theories of which stimuli could cause given responses. This latter point draws its support from studies in which control subjects are asked to say which factors they think will be effective in particular experiments. Control groups' predictive judgements of the effectiveness of experimental variables were highly correlated with experimental subjects' judgements – but both sets of judgements were equally inaccurate. Nisbett and Wilson qualify their condemnation of verbal reports and allow that such reports may be accurate if confined to mental *contents* (e.g. contents of focal attention, current sensations, plans, etc.), but they maintain that verbal reports will be woefully inaccurate regarding mental *processes*. Thus, they are claiming that the most important processes underlying behaviour in a variety of tasks are unavailable to consciousness and that the conscious thought stream is largely epiphenomenal.

Even if Nisbett and Wilson's conclusions are accepted, a serial model could still be tenable, if the unreportable processes could be seen as not using working memory but as being run off in a 'ballistic' or 'compiled' mode, such as has been postulated for highly practised actions (e.g. Anderson, 1983). However, this explanatory escape route seems implausible, in view of the unfamiliar nature of many of the tasks in which inaccurate verbal reporting has been claimed. Ericsson and Simon (1980, 1984, 1993) take a different tack and, on the basis of the standard serial model, they propose conditions under which accurate verbal reports should and should not occur. In particular they suggest that verbalization can be expected to be accurate only to the degree that the report is made *concurrently* with the task-related cognitive activity. Furthermore, for maximum validity the report should be made in a free manner, i.e. in the subject's own words, not confined to some experimenter-set categories which may not match the subject's own representational schemes. The basic notion put forward by Ericsson and Simon is that only information in focal attention can be verbalized. This principle limits 'verbalizable' information to that in working memory and, further, it predicts that information about the inputs and outputs of current processes will receive priority in free concurrent verbal reports. Ericsson and Simon point out that almost all the studies discussed by Nisbett and Wilson involved retrospective reports, often some considerable time after the behaviour concerned had occurred. The serial standard model would not predict accurate reports in such circumstances since the contents of working memory during processing are very transitory, and so subjects asked to give retrospective reports have to fall back on inferences based on their implicit causal theories of behaviour. Under more favourable conditions, such as in Newell and Simon's (1972) study of cryptarithmetic problem solving, Ericsson's (1975) studies of 8-puzzle performance and De Groot's (1965) studies of chess play, concurrent verbal reports appear quite consistent with behaviour and lead to coherent models of underlying processes.

From Ericsson and Simon's analysis, it follows that processes not using working memory will not be reportable. This would be true for highly practised sequences of operations. Beginners at writing, say, would perhaps be able to report how they wrote a 't', at least to the level of 'draw vertical' then 'put cross bar through vertical', whereas skilled writers would probably not be able to say with confidence which operation had been carried out first. Highly practised motor sequences become 'automatic' and seem to run off as wholes without reference to working memory. Of course, this is a generally useful development, although it can contribute to accidents since intermediate steps are not monitored and may be based on assumptions that no longer hold [see, for instance, Reason (1979) and Norman (1981) on behavioural slips and accidents]. On this view, the depth of detail with which processes can be verbally reported will depend on their degree of automaticity. Where sub-processes have not been 'compiled' or automatized into larger wholes, extensive detail would be expected. A further point of contention lies in Nisbett and Wilson's claim that, although mental processes can never be reported, mental *contents* sometimes can. This may be disputed. For example, if we set people the task of multiplying 11 × 15 while thinking aloud, the labels of various processes are likely to be mentioned, e.g. '*multiply* 5 × 11' or '*add* 15 to 150'. Reports will tend to mention inputs, outputs and process labels. Admittedly, if we ask 'how did you multiply 5 by 11' the answer will likely be 'I don't know how – I just know it's 55'. The relevant 'look up' or retrieval process from long-term memory is automatized in the practised numerate person. It seems that processes *can* be reported, down to the level of those component sub-processes that have been automatized.

Overall, then, it seems that much information on mental contents and processes can be reported accurately, in the proper conditions, up to the point at which automatized sub-processes come into play. The proper conditions include those of both the main task and of the verbalization task. For accurate reports the task must not be too highly practised and free concurrent verbalization should be used since this is much more likely to yield valid introspective reports than delayed retrospections to vague or inappropriate probes.

Thus, on the issue of serial *v.* parallel processing, it appears that the data from studies of subjective report validity are not absolutely decisive. In certain circumstances, detailed by Ericsson and Simon, and summarized above, valid reports of working memory contents, including process labels, can be given in accord with the serialist position. A parallel model would interpret cases of valid verbal reporting to mean that, in the appropriate circumstances, behaviour is controlled by the introspectible main sequence. What of inaccurate verbal reports? The serialist position could account for many of these cases in terms of delays in reporting short-lived working memory contents, leading to retrospective rationalizations rather than to valid introspections, since the relevant information may have been lost before the query was made. Also, failures to report accurately may be due to the relevant processes being automatized and so not using working memory. The parallel alternative would propose that the effective processes were unconscious in the cases of inaccurate verbal reports and so were never available, even for concurrent reports. In the face of the controversy over verbal report accuracy, it may be noted that an obvious research possibility is to carry out the relevant experiments reported by Nisbett and Wilson, but to obtain verbal reports in accord with the conditions that Ericsson and Simon deem ideal for valid introspective reports. If the results remained as before (i.e. inaccurate reports), then the view that important thought processes can be unconscious and parallel to the conscious stream would be upheld. A relevant study is that of White (1989) in which it was found that immediate retrospective reports of reasons given for liking or disliking imaginary characters, presented by questionnaire, were more accurate than delayed retrospections, as the standard model would predict. (The materials in White's study were arranged with the imaginary characters' attributes varied in such a way that inferences could be made of which attributes affected liking and disliking, so that accuracy of self-report could be assessed.)

Perhaps further resolution of the serial *v.* parallel issue might be obtained by looking at the broader context of human information processing? Within this wider area, a number of theorists have proposed schemes that incorporate parallel processes, yet still possess a degree of orderliness. The serialist position in thinking has generally derided the parallel alternative as being a recipe for chaos, while the opposite insult is that serial models are mechanistically single minded. In conflicts like this, compromise positions are worth exploring and I will next consider some possible mergers of parallel and serial views.

3 Hierarchical parallelism

A popular analogy for an orderly parallel system is that of the hierarchical bureaucracy. In such systems, upper levels decide on broad forms of action while lower levels attend to the details. The various levels intercommunicate information and instructions. Most interestingly, the sub-systems at each level can work simultaneously and largely independently of each other.

So, while the chief executive of a large company is pondering the next 5-year plan, numerous shop-floor workers, clerks and intermediate-level managers pursue their own functions. The levels must interact, of course, to avoid chaos developing. Thus, the upper levels have to monitor lower-level performance, send instructions down the line and receive information from below. Instructions from above are only as detailed as need be since they can be unpacked by lower-level specialists. So, if the top level decrees "increase production of Brand Y and phase out Brand X", lower-level specialists will attend to the details of, say, increasing orders of some raw materials and reducing others, shifting workers and changing equipment, etc.

Indeed, the upper levels do not need to know how the lower levels actually execute their orders ('principle of executive ignorance'; Becker, 1975). Similarly, on this type of model, within an individual person an upper-level process may initiate an action sequence (e.g. picking up a cup), but no information about the lower-level, detailed sensorimotor processes that execute the sequence is available to the upper levels. Johnson-Laird (1983) has developed a computational model, incorporating hierarchical parallel processes. This is similar to the 'bureaucratic' model but without the homuncular overtones. The top level of his system is identified with computer-operating systems that govern the behaviour of sub-processes rather than with human executives.

The motivation for hierarchical or multi-level parallel models of human information processing becomes more apparent if one steps back from the 'thinking' domain and looks more broadly at human behaviour. The 'thinker', after all, may be driving a car, walking or carrying out any other routine activity at the same time as mentally exploring a chess problem. The ability to carry out two or more tasks simultaneously can be readily explained in terms of different levels and types of processing which can proceed simultaneously as long as they do not require the same input and output channels. The multi-level approach explains why some task combinations are easier than others (i.e. those not requiring the same input and output channels) and also helps to explain why drugs and stress may have un-expected effects, e.g. depressants, such as alcohol, may knock out an upper level and lead to increased activity by lower-level processes normally controlled by the upper level [see Broadbent (1977) for relevant general discussion], producing the apparent paradox of a depressant drug increasing overt activity rather than decreasing it. These points about task compatibility and differential (and unexpected) effects of drugs, stress, fatigue, brain damage, and so on, do not seem to be so readily met by the thorough-going serialist proposal that all appearances of parallel activity are due to the 'time sharing' of a single central processor.

4 Parallel production systems

Approaching the question from the neuropsychological angle, a number of theorists have put forward possible schemes of parallel neural activity (e.g. Arbib, 1972; Shallice, 1972, 1978). The brain, of which thought is a product, appears to be highly parallel in its operations, and Allport (1980a) has argued strongly in favour of the view that processing is distributed throughout the brain. On the basis of neurological data, experiments on divided attention (e.g. Spelke *et al.*, 1976) and production systems notions in AI, Allport proposes that the human information-processing system can best be represented by a highly parallel model in which productions can 'fire' independently and simultaneously. On this scheme no central processor is required. A 'withering away' of the executive is attractive in view of the unfortunate homuncular properties of the 'central processor/executive' in most previous models. Conflicts between productions calling for the same output systems could be handled by means of other productions that are triggered by conflict states and that specialize in resolving conflicts. Thus a special executive or decision maker does not need to be postulated, since the decision-making functions can be taken over by production rules identical in form to all the other production rules stored in long-term memory. [Many of these ideas have been developed, apparently independently, in Holland *et al.*'s (1986) model for induction, and in Newell's (1990) SOAR model, which are discussed in Chapter 4.]

What limits might there be on parallel mental activity? Allport (1980b) suggests that various forms of inter-process interference impose limitations. Physically in-compatible actions cannot occur simultaneously and so must be 'queued' or alternated. Slightly more subtly, on the production system approach, if two activities have similar conditions, there is a grave risk of 'cross-talk', such that the stimuli meant to be dealt with by activity 1 actually elicit activity 2, and vice versa. Such 'data-specific' limitations would clearly restrict the degree to which the activities concerned could be carried out effectively in parallel with each other.

How might these limitations affect thinking? In the case of problem solving, it may well be that data-specific limitations would restrict parallel mental exploration of alternative courses of action within a single problem. If parallel exploration was attempted, then the productions involved in generating and assessing the different alternatives would be in danger of calling on similar data (i.e. the task definitions) and so interfere with one another. So simultaneous exploration of different lines of attack on the same problem seems unlikely. However, when a problem has been familiarized thoroughly and can be explored mentally without references to outside sensory channels or to external memories, and the mainstream of thought is concerned with some other goal, it is possible that some processing could take place on the familiarized problem in parallel with the mainstream. These conditions for successful parallel streams of thought are essentially those reported for successful incubation. So, although this particular parallel processing approach does not predict simultaneous thought streams on the same problem, it would be compatible with some parallel processing on different problems. Thus, it seems that a broad range of data favours a parallel or distributed processing approach to human information handling in general, but there are severe limits on the degree of parallelism in thinking. Thus, in many cases, especially of directed thinking, a serial model will be consistent with the data.

5 The connectionist approach

Connectionist approaches differ from the parallel models discussed so far in that they postulate massively parallel processing carried out by simple units passing activating or inhibiting signals to each other throughout an extensive network. In contrast, Holland *et al.*'s (1986) model, for example (discussed in Chapter 4), proposes a relatively modest degree of parallel activity at the symbolic level of production rules. Connectionist theorists argue that production systems lack psychological reality and that, although such systems may summarize mental processes in a rather approximate way, a more accurate characterization of mental processes will be given by analyses in terms of densely interconnected units that fluctuate in activation level and pass excitatory and inhibitory signals among themselves. The units can be interpreted either sub-symbolically or symbolically. In the sub-symbolic case the units are taken to represent micro-features. For example, recognition of the symbol 'A' would be interpreted as due to the response of a network of micro-featural units which respond maximally to the constituent features of the graphemic input 'A', while other networks do not respond so strongly to this input. An example of symbolic interpretation may be found in Gluck and Bower's (1988) study of a learning task akin to medical diagnosis. In their model, symptoms were represented as the input nodes (one node corresponding to one symptom) and disease categories were represented by output nodes (again, one node to one disease category). Each input node was linked to every output node and the model learned appropriate weights on the links between inputs and outputs so that the appropriate disease would be maximally activated by an input symptom pattern.

Connectionist models have proved fruitful in studies of letter and word recognition (Rumelhart and McClelland, 1982), associative learning (McClelland and Rumelhart, 1986), in learning past tenses of verbs (Rumelhart and McClelland, 1986) and in analogy solving (Holyoak and Thagard, 1990). The models are readily computable (even on strictly serial machines) and often deliver surprisingly human-like performance. For many years cognitive models have been guided by the '(serial) computer metaphor'; the connectionist approach offers an alternative, 'brain metaphor' [Rumelhart et al., 1986a; see also Quinlan (1991) for a detailed overview and evaluation of the connectionist approach].

At first sight, the notion of massively parallel activity in simple units would not appear to be applicable to sequential thinking. However, Rumelhart et al. (1986c) and Smolensky (1986) have indicated possible applications. Rumelhart et al. suggested that thinking involves a succession of states of consciousness in which the stable states last about 500 milliseconds (ms) and the transitions require on the order of 100 ms. They then argue that the stable states of consciousness reflect stable states of activation in the underlying network of sub-symbolic units and that about 100 ms is a reasonable estimate of the time required for a new activation pattern to become established. Since the network can be in only one state at any one time, an appearance of seriality holds when the time-scale of study is in terms of seconds or minutes, as is usually the case in studies of problem solving, for example. With shorter time-scales, up to 100 ms or so, parallel processes of interpretation emerge into theoretical view. Rumelhart et al. further proposed that much problem solving involves a cyclical process of creating a representation (i.e. a stable state of the network), processing that state to produce a new representation (network state), and so on, until a goal state is recognized. This account has plausibility for routine types of problem solving such as mental arithmetic in adults. Rumelhart et al. also indicated how their approach could lead to a model for playing the game known as tic-tac-toe in the US and as noughts-and-crosses in Britain. The model incorporates a representation of both the player and his or her opponent, and essentially 'imagines' a whole game of moves and counter-moves. Although Rumelhart et al. did not discuss the notion of a working memory in their treatment of thinking, some such notion seems necessary for those cases where a subject thinks ahead through a tree of alternative moves before selecting one [Holding (1985) reports considerable relevant data on search in chess, for example]. However, McClelland (1986) describes a 'programmable blackboard model' which offers a possible treatment of working memory in a connectionist scheme. So perhaps this aspect of thinking will also be dealt with in later developments of the theory.

However, although connectionist models are impressive in accounting for the acquisition of specific, contingent, input-output associations, they do not readily represent abstract rules with necessary consequences for specific cases. Thus, a connectionist model accounts readily for the acquisition of knowledge of contingent symptom–disease links from a collection of cases but accounts less readily for logical inference or the acquisition of logically necessary rules.

People, and indeed crows and rooks but not pigeons (Mackintosh, 1988), can apparently acquire and apply quite abstract rules with little training (e.g. 'pick the odd one out of a set' in discrimination learning). People acquire very general, abstract rules implicitly in language learning (Fodor and Pylyshyn, 1988) and explicitly in many domains. Linguistic rules are involved in verbal thinking and so verbal thought must have the properties of linguistic systems such as *productivity* and *systematicity*. Productivity is the capacity to generate an indefinite number of grammatical sentences given a relatively few rules, and systematicity refers to the ability to understand related sentences; for example, if someone understands "Joe loves Mary", they will also understand "Mary loves Joe" and all other such sentences with different person names substituted. Connectionist schemes do not naturally handle productivity and systematicity, which are important features of language and hence of thought.

Since rule-following is a critical issue for connectionist approaches, it is important to establish criteria for rule-following and to assess behaviour against these criteria. Smith *et al.* (1992) proposed eight useful criteria for explicit rule-following. These are:

(1) Performance on rule-governed items is as accurate with unfamiliar as with familiar material.

(2) Performance on rule-governed items is as accurate with abstract as with concrete material.

(3) Early in acquisition, a rule may be applied to an exception (the rule is overextended).

(4) Performance on a rule-governed item or problem deteriorates as a function of the number of rules that are required for solving the problem.

(5) Performance on a rule-governed item is facilitated when preceded by another item based on the same rule (application of a rule primes its subsequent use).

(6) A rule, or components of it, may be mentioned in a verbal protocol.

(7) Performance on a specific rule-governed problem is improved by training on abstract versions of the rule.

(8) Performance on problems in a particular domain is improved as much by training on problems outside the domain as on problems within it, as long as the problems are based on the same rule.

Most of the above criteria have been investigated for the following rules: Modus Ponens, Modus Tollens, Contracts, Causal rules, and the Law of Large Numbers (i.e. that sample statistics approach population parameters as the sample size increases and population variance decreases (see Nisbett *et al.*, 1983.) In general, all the rules listed, except Modus Tollens, largely meet the criteria for rule following according to studies reviewed by Smith *et al.* (1992).

Given that rule-following is psychologically real, but that connectionist systems do not readily capture rule-following, it appears that the connectionist approach cannot fully explain thinking, although it may help with part of the story (e.g. pattern recognition as part of problem encoding).

Norman (1986) suggested that a dual model, with a connectionist approach to lower-level cognition and a serial approach to higher-level cognition, may be a good theoretical combination, and a model of this type has been applied successfully to physics problem solving (Lamberts, 1990).

II. THEORETICAL PROGRESS?

Has the information-processing approach to thinking led to genuine progress in our understanding of thought? Certainly, within the framework of the standard model, Simon and his colleagues at Carnegie-Mellon University have succeeded in interpreting an ever-widening range of thinking tasks over the past 30 years or so. Their task analyses have ranged from symbolic logic (Newell *et al.* 1958), cryptarithmetic, chess (Newell and Simon, 1972), understanding task instructions (Simon and Hayes, 1976) and the accuracy of introspective data (Ericsson and Simon, 1980, 1984) to scientific discovery (Langley *et al.*, 1987; Qin and Simon, 1990; Dunbar, 1993). Therefore, it would seem that steady progress has been demonstrated by this research team. However, as indicated in the previous sections of this chapter, there is some dissatisfaction with the limited, rather one-dimensional, perspective of the standard model. Richer models are under development, but it seems likely that the serial model will survive as a component of a broader scheme which also includes a degree of distributed processing.

Despite the good example of the Carnegie-Mellon group, it must be admitted that the thinking field of research could still be accused, with some justice, of being excessively 'phenomenon-driven' and not sufficiently concerned with general theory [as Newell (1973) charged of cognitive psychology in general]. It is quite easy to list a string of phenomena that have attracted research e.g. 'state–action problems', 'expert and novice memory', 'intermediate effect', 'atmosphere effect', 'matching bias', 'verification set', 'intrusive thoughts', 'incubation', 'brain storming', 'introspective accuracy', 'conjunction effect', 'base rate neglect' and 'analogy use', among many others. Unfortunately, a truly general theory that would tie all these topics together convincingly is lacking. Although some theoretical progress has been made, particularly by the Carnegie-Mellon group, and parallel distributed processing notions look promising as part of the answer at least, the overall problem of accounting for thought in all its manifestations still stands as a challenge to future researchers and theorists.

III. RESEARCH TRENDS

Will future research be essentially 'more of the same'? Since the early 1980s research has shown a change in emphasis away from laboratory settings toward more real-life tasks [e.g. Isenberg's (1987) study of senior managers' thinking]. This trend is likely to continue.

It is notable that many of the earlier studies reviewed in this book used very artificial tasks (e.g. missionaries and cannibals; Wason's four-card task). Arguments for using simple artificial materials were generally in terms of equating subjects' prior task experience and helping to ensure uniform interpretations of task materials. Of course, experimenters hoped that the artificial tasks would reflect aspects of real-life problem solving such as 'looking ahead' or 'testing hypotheses'. In Neisser's (1976) terminology, 'ecological validity' was hoped for – but rarely demonstrated. A recent research trend has been to focus on real-life skills (expertise), although often in a reduced form suitable for the laboratory. To complement laboratory studies, it is worthwhile to examine cases of real-life problem solving. For instance, Mitroff's (1974) study of moon scientists indicated that 'verification' tendencies were by no means limited to artificial laboratory conditions. This study also helped explain why verification tendencies arise in view of the positive, motivating functions of a personal commitment to a hypothesis. Furthermore, Mitroff highlighted the long-term and social dimensions of much real-life problem solving – factors that are generally still ignored in laboratory investigations. More detailed studies of group problem-solving processes would be useful in taking the field beyond its present focus on individual processes to consider processes distributed across individuals; this movement has begun in developmental studies (Resnick *et al.* 1990), if not in adult research.

Csikszentmihalyi's (1975) research on the experience of self-motivated problem solving suggests other reasons for studying real-life problem solving. Csikszent-mihalyi found that people reported very enjoyable 'flow' experiences when totally absorbed in self-set problems that matched their skill levels. So, the mountaineer, the chess player and the surgeon, for instance, find enormous satisfaction when they are working on problems just within their skill limits. If the problems are too easy boredom results, and if they are too difficult anxiety is produced. A better under-standing of motivation for problem solving may come from such out-of-the-laboratory studies. In the laboratory, the motivation is supplied by an outside agent, the experimenter. It may be that the levels of performance obtained (e.g. depth of look-ahead) would be much greater with self-motivation and when the problem is enjoyed for its own sake. That problem solving is often enjoyable is evident from the reports cited by Csikszentmihalyi and also from the high circulation figures of puzzle magazines, the enduring popularity of crossword puzzles, and the successes of Rubik's cube and its derivatives and descendants.

IV. CONCLUDING COMMENTS

I will finish by summarizing briefly my conclusions about the recent past and the possible future of studies of thinking. Although the standard serial model of human thinking has coped with a wide range of data, there are some anomalies (e.g. incubation, intrusive thoughts) that tax the purely serial scheme. Equally, highly parallel connectionist schemes have difficulty with rule-governed processing. These points suggest that there will be an increasing trend toward hybrid models with serial and parallel components. In terms of research techniques, more out-of-laboratory studies and more emphasis on problem solving distributed over a number of participants seem likely, and will be useful complements to existing methods.

V. FURTHER READING

Quinlan, P. (1991). *Connectionism and psychology: a psychological perspective on the new connectionist research*. Hemel Hempstead: Harvester–Wheatsheaf. A clear account of the strengths and problems of connectionism, with particular reference to higher mental processes.

Eysenck, M.W. and Keane, M.T. (1995). *Cognitive psychology: a student's handbook*, 3rd edn. Hove: Lawrence Erlbaum Associates. A useful overview of cognitive psychology to help place thinking within the broad picture of mental activity.

References

Adamson, R.E. and Taylor, D.W. (1954). Functional fixedness as related to elapsed time and set. *Journal of Experimental Psychology* **147**, 122–126.

Adelson, B. (1981). Problem solving and the development of abstract categories in programming languages. *Memory and Cognition* **9**, 422–433.

Alba, J.W. and Marmorstein, H. (1987). The effects of frequency knowledge on consumer decision making. *Journal of Consumer Research* **14**, 14–26.

Albert, R.S. (1975). Toward a behavioral definition of genius. *American Psychologist* **30**, 140–151.

Allport, D.A. (1980a). Patterns and actions: cognitive mechanisms are content-specific. In G. Claxton (Ed.), *Cognitive psychology*. London: Routledge and Kegan Paul.

Allport, D.A. (1980b). Attention and performance. In G.Claxton (Ed.), *Cognitive psychology*. London: Routledge and Kegan Paul.

Anderson, J.R. (1978). Arguments concerning representations for mental imagery. *Psychological Review* **86**, 249–277.

Anderson, J.R. (1983). *The architecture of cognition*. Cambridge, MA: Harvard University Press.

Anderson, J.R. (1991). Is human cognition adaptive? *Behavioral and Brain Sciences* **14**, 471–517.

Andreasen, N.C. (1987). Creativity and mental illness: prevalence rates in writers and their first degree relatives. *American Journal of Psychiatry* **144**, 1288–1292.

Antonietti, A. (1991). Why does mental visualization facilitate problem solving? In R.H. Logie and M. Denis (Eds), *Mental images in human cognition*. Amsterdam: North-Holland Press.

Antrobus, J.S., Singer, J.L. and Greenberg, S. (1966). Studies in the stream of consciousness: experimental enhancement and suppression of spontaneous cognitive process. *Perceptual and Motor Skills* **23**, 399–417.

Antrobus, J.S., Coleman, R. and Singer, J.L. (1967). Signal detection performance by subjects differing in predisposition to daydreaming. *Journal of Consulting Psychology* **31**, 487–491.

Anzai, Y. (1991). Learning and use of representations for physics expertise. In K.A. Ericsson and J. Smith (Eds), *Towards a general theory of expertise*. Cambridge: Cambridge University Press.

Anzai, Y. and Simon, H.A. (1979). The theory of learning by doing. *Psychological Review* **86**, 124–140.

Arbib, M. (1972). *The metaphorical brain*. New York: John Wiley.

Arnheim, R. (1962). *Picasso's Guernica: the genesis of a painting*. Berkeley: University of California Press.

261

Atkinson, R.C. and Shiffrin, R.M. (1968). Human memory: a proposed system and its control process. In K.W. Spence and J.T. Spence (Eds), *The psychology of learning and motivation*, Vol. 2. New York: Academic Press.

Atwood, M.E. and Polson, P.G. (1976). A process model for water jug problems. *Cognitive Psychology* **8**, 191–216.

Atwood, M.E., Masson, M.E.J. and Polson, P.G. (1980). Further exploration with a process model for water jug problems. *Memory and Cognition* **8**, 182–192.

Baddeley, A.D. (1976). *The psychology of memory*. New York: Basic Books.

Baddeley, A.D. (1986). *Working Memory*. Oxford: Oxford University Press.

Baddeley, A.D. (1992). Is working memory working? *Quarterly Journal of Experimental Psychology* **44A**, 1–33.

Baddeley, A.D. and Hitch, G.J. (1974). Working memory. In G. Bower (Ed.), *The psychology of learning and motivation*, Vol. VIII. New York: Academic Press.

Balla, J.I., Biggs, J.B., Gibson, M. and Chang, A.M. (1990). The application of basic science concepts to clinical problem solving. *Medical Education* **24**, 117–123.

Baron, J. (1994). Nonconsequentialist decisions. *Behavioral and Brain Sciences* **17**, 1–42.

Baron, J. and Jurney, J. (1993). Norms against voting for coerced reform. *Journal of Personality and Social Psychology* **64**, 347–355.

Baron, J. and Ritov, I. (1993). Intuitions about penalties and compensation in the context of tort law. *Journal of Risk and Uncertainty* **7**, 17–33.

Baron, J., Gowda, R. and Kunreuther, A. (1993). Attitudes towards managing hazardous waste: what should be cleaned up and who should pay for it? *Risk Analysis* **13**, 183–192.

Barron, F. (1955). The disposition toward originality. *Journal of Abnormal and Social Psychology* **51**, 478–485.

Bassok, M. (1990). Transfer of domain-specific problem-solving procedures. *Journal of Experimental Psychology: Learning, Memory and Cognition* **16**, 522–533.

Baylor, G.W. and Gascon, J. (1974). An information processing theory of aspects of the development of weight seriation in children. *Cognitive Psychology* **6**, 1–40.

Beattie, J. and Baron, J. (1988). Confirmation and matching biases in hypothesis testing. *Quarterly Journal of Experimental Psychology* **40A**, 269–297.

Beattie, J. and Baron, J. (1991). Investigating the effect of stimulus range on attribute weight. *Journal of Experimental Psychology: Human Perception and Performance* **17**, 571–585.

Becker, J.D. (1975). The formal representation of behavior. In D.G. Bobrow and A. Collins (Eds), *Representation and understanding*. New York: Academic Press.

Becker, S., Horowitz, M. and Campbell, L. (1973). Cognitive responses to stress: effects of changes in demand and sex. *Journal of Abnormal Psychology* **82**, 519–522.

Begg, I. and Denny, J.P. (1969). Empirical reconciliation of atmosphere and conversion interpretations of syllogistic reasoning errors. *Journal of Experimental Psychology* **81**, 351–354.

Begg, I. and Harris, G. (1982). On the interpretation of syllogisms. *Journal of Verbal Learning and Verbal Behaviour* **21**, 595–620.

Bell, A.G. (1978). *The machine plays chess?* Oxford: Pergamon Press.

Bennet, W. (1980). Providing for posterity. *Harvard Magazine*, **82**(3), 13–16.

Berkowitz, J. (1969). *The roots of aggression*. New York: Lieber-Atherton.

Berlyne, D.E. (1965). *Structure and direction in thinking*. New York: John Wiley.

Bernoulli, D. (1954). Exposition of a new theory on the measurement of risk. *Econometrika* **22**, 23–26 (originally published, 1738).

Bettman, J.R., Johnson, E.J. and Payne, J.W. (1990). A componential analysis of cognitive effort in choice. *Organizational Behavior and Human Decision Processes* **45**, 111–139.

Bhaskhar, R. and Simon, H.A. (1977). Problem solving in semantically rich domains: an example from engineering thermodynamics. *Cognitive Science* **1**, 193–215.

Birch, H.G. (1945). The relation of previous experience to insightful problem solving. *Journal of Comparative Psychology* **38**, 367–383.

Birch, H.G. and Rabinowitz, H.S. (1951). The negative effect of previous experience on productive thinking. *Journal of Experimental Psychology* **41**, 122–126.

Boden, M.A. (1990). *The creative mind*. London: Weidenfeld and Nicolson.

Boden, M.A. (1994). Précis of *The creative mind*: myths and mechanisms. *Behavioral and Brain Sciences* **17**, 519–570.

Bonatti, L. (1994). Propositional reasoning by model? *Psychological Review* **101**, 725–733.

Boshuizen, H.P.A., Schmidt, H.G. and Coughlin, L.D. (1987). *On-line representation of a clinical case and the development of expertise*. Paper presented at the American Educational Research Association Conference, Washington.

Bouchard, T.J., Jr. (1972). A comparison of two group brainstorming procedures. *Journal of Applied Psychology* **56**, 418–421.

Bouchard, T.J., Jr. and Hare, M. (1970). Size, performance, and potential in brainstorming groups. *Journal of Applied Psychology* **54**, 51–55.

Bourne, L.E. (1966). *Human conceptual behavior*. Boston, MA: Allyn and Bacon.

Bracewell, R.J. (1974). *Interpretation factors in the four card selection task*. Paper presented at the Selection Task Conference, Trento, Italy, 17–19 April 1974.

Bracewell, R.J. and Hidi, S.E. (1974). The solution of an inferential problem as a function of stimulus materials. *Quarterly Journal of Experimental Psychology* **26**, 480–488.

Bradley, A., Hudson, S., Robbins, T. and Baddeley, A. (1987). *Working memory and chess*. Cambridge: Medical Research Council Applied Psychology Unit (unpublished report).

Braine, M.D.S. (1978). On the relation between the natural logic of reasoning and standard logic. *Psychological Review* **85**, 1–21.

Braine, M.D.S. (1990). The 'natural logic' approach to reasoning. In W.F. Overton (Ed.), *Reasoning, necessity and logic: developmental perspectives*. Hillsdale, NJ: Erlbaum.

Braine, M.D.S., Reiser, B.J. and Rumain, B. (1984). Some empirical justification for a theory of natural propositional logic. In G.H. Bower (Ed.), *The psychology of learning and motivation*. Vol. 18. New York: Academic Press.

Brilhart, J.K. and Jochem, E.M. (1964). Effects of different patterns on outcomes of problem solving discussions. *Journal of Applied Psychology* **48**, 175–179.

Broadbent, D.E. (1958). *Perception and communication*. Oxford: Pergamon Press.

Broadbent, D.E. (1977). Levels, hierarchies, and the locus of control. *Quarterly Journal of Experimental Psychology* **29**, 181–201.

Broadbent, D. (1993). Comparison with human experiments. In D. Broadbent (Ed.), *The simulation of human intelligence*. Oxford: Blackwell.

Brown, J. (1958). Some tests of the decay theory of immediate memory. *Quarterly Journal of Experimental Psychology* **10**, 12–21.

Brown, R. (1973). *A first language*. Cambridge, MA: Harvard University Press.

Bruner, J.S. (1957). On going beyond the information given. In *Contemporary approaches to cognition*. Cambridge, MA: Harvard University Press.

Bruner, J.S., Goodnow, J.J. and Austin, G.A. (1956). *A study of thinking*. New York: John Wiley.

Burnham, C.A. and Davis, K.G. (1969). The 9-dot problem – beyond perceptual organization. *Psychonomic Science* **17**, 321–323.

Byrne, R.M.J. (1989). Suppressing valid inferences with conditionals. *Cognition* **31**, 61–63.

Campbell, D. (1960). Blind variation and selective retention in creative thought as in other knowledge processes. *Psychological Review* **67**, 380–400.

Card, S.K. (1992). Reframing the problem of intelligent behavior. *Behavioral and Brain Sciences* **15**, 438–439.

Carlson, R.A. and Detweiler, M. (1992). A unified theory for psychologists? *Behavioral and Brain Sciences* **15**, 440.

Casscells, W., Schoenberger, A. and Grayboys, T. (1978). Interpretation by physicians of clinical laboratory results. *New England Journal of Medicine* **299**, 999–1000.

Cattell, R.N. (1959). The personality and motivation of the researcher from measurements of contemporaries and from biography. In C.W. Taylor (Ed.), *The 1959 University of Utah Research Conference on the Identification of Creative Scientific Talent.* Salt Lake City: University of Utah Press.

Cattell, R.B. and Drevdahl, J.E. (1955). A comparison of the personality profile (16PF) of eminent researchers with that of eminent teachers and administrators, and of the general population. *British Journal of Psychology* **46**, 248–261.

Ceraso, J. and Provitera, A. (1971). Sources of error in syllogistic reasoning. *Cognitive Psychology* **2**, 400–410.

Chalmers, A.F. (1978). *What is this thing called science?* Milton Keynes: Open University Press.

Chapman, J.L. and Chapman, J.P. (1959). Atmosphere effect re-examined. *Journal of Experimental Psychology* **58**, 220–226.

Charness, N. (1976). Memory for chess positions: resistance to interference. *Journal of Experimental Psychology: Human Learning and Memory* **2**, 641–653.

Charness, N. (1979). Components of skills in bridge. *Canadian Journal of Psychology* **33**, 1–16.

Charness, N. (1981a). Aging and skilled problem solving. *Journal of Experimental Psychology: General* **110**, 21–38.

Charness, N. (1981b). Search in chess: age and skill differences. *Journal of Experimental Psychology: Human Perception and Performance* **7**, 467–476.

Charness, N. (1981c). Visual short term memory and aging in chess players. *Journal of Gerontology* **36**, 615–619.

Charness, N. (1989). Expertise in chess and bridge. In D. Klahr and K. Kotovsky (Eds), *Complex information processing: the impact of H.A. Simon.* Hillsdale, NJ: Lawrence Erlbaum Associates.

Charness, N. and Reingold, E. (1992). Eye movement studies of problem solving in chess. *International Journal of Psychology* **27**, 149-150.

Chase, W.G. and Ericsson, K.A. (1981). Skilled memory. In J.R. Anderson (Ed.), *Cognitive skills and their acquisition.* Hillsdale, NJ: Lawrence Erlbaum Associates.

Chase, W.G. and Ericsson, K.A. (1982). Skill and working memory. In G.H. Bower (Ed.), *The psychology of learning and motivation*, Vol. 16. San Diego, CA: Academic Press.

Chase, W.G. and Simon, H.A. (1973a). Perception in chess. *Cognitive Psychology* **4**, 55–81.

Chase, W.G. and Simon, H.A. (1973b). The mind's eye in chess. In W.G. Chase (Ed.), *Visual information processing.* New York: Academic Press.

Cheng, P.W. and Holyoak, K.J. (1985). Pragmatic reasoning schemas. *Cognitive Psychology* **17**, 391–416.

Chi, M.T.H., Feltovich, P.J. and Glaser, R. (1981). Categorisation and represention of physics problems by experts and novices. *Cognitive Science* **5**, 121–152.

Chi, M.T.H., Glaser, R. and Rees, E. (1982). Expertise inproblem solving. In R.J. Sternberg (Ed.), *Advances in the psychology of human intelligence*, Vol. 1. Hillsdale, NJ: Lawrence Erlbaum Associates.

Chi, M.T.H., Bassok, M., Lewis, M., Reimann, P. and Glaser, R. (1989). Self-explanations: how students study and use examples in learning to solve problems. *Cognitive Science* **13**, 145–182.

Chipman, S.F. (1992). Re-membering cognition. *Behavioral and Brain Sciences* **15**, 441–442.

Claessen, H.F. and Boshuizen, H.P.A. (1985). Recall of medical information by students and doctors. *Medical Education* **19**, 61–67.

Clement, J. (1982). *Analogical reasoning patterns in expert problem solving.* Paper presented to the 4th Annual Conference of the Cognitive Science Society, August 1982.

Cohen, L.J. (1981). Can human irrationality be experimentally demonstrated? *Behavioral and Brain Sciences* **4**, 317–331.

Collins, A.M. and Loftus, E.F. (1975). A spreading activation theory of semantic processing. *Psychological Review* **82**, 407–428.

Collins, A.M. and Quillian, M.K. (1969). Retrieval time from semantic memory. *Journal of Verbal Learning and Verbal Behavior* **8**, 240–247.

Copi, I. (1954). *Symbolic logic.* New York: Macmillan.

Cosmides, L. (1989). The logic of social exchange: has natural selection shaped how humans reason? Studies with the Wason selection task. *Cognition* **31**, 187–276.

Cosmides, L. and Tooby, J. (in press). Are humans good intuitive statisticians after all? Rethinking some conclusions from the literature on judgment under uncertainty.

Craik, K.J.W. (1943). *The nature of explanation.* Cambridge: Cambridge University Press.

Czikszentmihalyi, M. (1975). *Beyond boredom and anxiety.* San Francisco: Jossey-Bass.

Dawes, R.H. (1979). The robust beauty of improper linear models in decision making. *American Psychologist* **34**, 571–582.

De Bono, E. (1976). *Teaching thinking.* London: Temple Smith.

De Bono, E. (1983). The Cognitive Research Trust (CoRT) thinking program. In W. Maxwell (Ed.), *Thinking: the expanding frontier.* Philadelphia, PA: The Franklin Institute Press.

De Groot, A.D. (1965). *Thought and choice in chess.* The Hague: Mouton.

De Paulo, B., LeMay, C.S. and Epstein, J. (1991). Effects of importance of success and expectations of success on effectiveness at deceiving. *Personality and Social Psychology Bulletin* **17**, 14–24.

De Sanchez, M.A. and Astorga, M. (1983). *Projecto aprendar a pensor.* Caracas: Ministerio de Educacion.

Dennis, W. (1955). Variations in productivity among creative workers. *Scientific Monthly* **80**, 277–278.

Dickstein, L.S. (1978). The effect of figure on syllogistic reasoning. *Memory and Cognition* **6**, 76–83.

Dillon, P.C., Graham, W.K. and Aidells, A.L. (1972). Brainstorming on a 'hot' problem: effects of training and practice on individual and group performance. *Journal of Applied Psychology* **56**, 487–490.

Djakow, I.N., Petrowski, N.W. and Rudik, P.A. (1927). *Psychologie des Schachspiels (The psychology of chess).* Berlin: de Gruyter.

Dominowski, R.L. (1981). Comment on an examination of the alleged role of 'fixation' in the solution of several insight problems by Weisberg and Alba. *Journal of Experimental Psychology: General* **110**, 193–198.

Dominowski, R.L. and Jenrick, R. (1972). Effects of hints and interpolated activity on solution of an insight problem. *Psychonomic Science* **26**, 335–338.

Doran, J.W. and Michie, D. (1966). Experiments with the graph traverser program. *Proceedings of the Royal Society (A)* **294**, 235–259.

Drevdahl, J.E. and Cattell, R.N. (1958). Personality and creativity in artists and writers. *Journal of Clinical Psychology* **14**, 107–111.

Dunbar, K. (1993). Concept discovery in a scientific domain. *Cognitive Science* **17**, 397–434.

Duncker, K. (1945). On problem solving. *Psychological Monographs* **58**, 1–113.

Dunnette, M.D., Campbell, J. and Jaastad, K. (1963). The effects of group participation on brain-storming effectiveness for two industrial samples. *Journal of Applied Psychology* **47**, 10–37.

Edwards, J. and Baldauf, R.B. (1983). Teaching thinking in secondary science. In W. Maxwell (Ed.), *Thinking: the expanding frontier.* Philadelphia, PA: The Franklin Institute Press.

Edwards, W. (1977). Use of multiattribute utility measurement for social decision making. In D.F. Bell, R.L. Keeney and H. Raiffa (Eds), *Conflicting objectives in decisions.* Chichester, UK: John Wiley.

Egan, D.W. and Greeno, J.G. (1974). Theories of rule induction: knowledge acquired in concept learning, serial pattern learning, and problem solving. In L.W. Gregg, (Ed.), *Knowledge and cognition.* New York: John Wiley.

Ehrlich, K. and Soloway, E. (1984). An empirical investigation of tacit plan knowledge in programming. In J.C. Thomas and M.L. Schneider (Eds), *Human factors in computing systems.* Norwood, NJ: Ablex.

Einhorn, H.J. and Hogarth, R.M. (1975). Unit weighting schemes for decision making. *Organisational Behaviour and Human Performance* **13**, 171–192.

Eisenstadt, M. and Kareev, Y. (1977). Perception in game playing. In P.N. Johnson-Laird and P.C. Wason (Eds), *Thinking*. Cambridge: Cambridge University Press.

Ellen, P. (1982). Direction, past experience and hints in creative problem solving: reply to Weisberg and Alba. *Journal of Experimental Psychology: General* **111**, 316–325.

Elstein, A.S., Shulman, L.S. and Sprafka, S.A. (1978). *Medical problem solving: an analysis of clinical reasoning*. Cambridge, MA: Harvard University Press.

Engle, R.W. and Bukstel, L. (1978). Memory processes among bridge players of differing expertise. *American Journal of Psychology* **91**, 673–689.

Erickson, J.R. (1974). A set analysis theory of behavior in formal syllogistic reasoning tasks. In R. Solson (Ed.), *Theories of cognitive psychology: The Loyola Symposium*. New Jersey: Lawrence Erlbaum Associates.

Erickson, J.R. (1978). Research in syllogistic reasoning. In R. Revlin and R.E. Meyer (Eds), *Human reasoning*. Washington, DC: Winston.

Ericsson, K.A. (1975). *Instruction to verbalize as a means to study problem solving processes with the 8-puzzle: a preliminary study*. Report No. 458, Department of Psychology, The University of Stockholm, Stockholm.

Ericsson, K.A. (1985). Memory skill. *Canadian Journal of Psychology* **39**, 158–231.

Ericsson, K.A. and Kintsch, W. (1995). Long-term working memory. *Psychological Review* **102**, 211–245.

Ericsson, K.A. and Pennington, N. (1993). The structure of memory performance in experts: implications for memory in everyday life. In G.M. Davies and R.H. Logie (Eds), *Memory in everyday life*. Amsterdam: Elsevier.

Ericsson, K.A. and Polson, P.G. (1988a). An experimental analysis of a memory skill for dinner orders. *Journal of Experimental Psychology: Learning, Memory and Cognition* **14**, 305–316.

Ericsson, K.A. and Polson, P.G. (1988b). Memory for restaurant orders. In M. Chi, R. Glaser and M. Farr (Eds), *The nature of expertise*. Hillsdale, NJ: Lawrence Erlbaum Associates.

Ericsson, K.A. and Simon, H.A. (1980). Verbal reports as data. *Psychological Review* **87**, 215–251.

Ericsson, K.A. and Simon, H.A. (1984). *Protocol analysis*. Cambridge MA: MIT Press.

Ericsson, K.A. and Simon, H.A. (1993). *Protocol analysis: verbal reports as data*. Cambridge MA: MIT Press.

Ericsson, K.A. and Smith, J. (1991). Prospects and limits of the empirical study of expertise: an introduction. In K.A. Ericsson and J. Smith (Eds), *Towards a general theory of expertise*. Cambridge: Cambridge University Press.

Ericsson, K.A., Krampe, R.T., and Tesch-Rohmer, C. (1993). The role of deliberate practice. *Psychological Review* **100**, 363–406.

Ernst, G.W. and Newell, A. (1969). *GPS: a case study in generality and problem solving*. New York: Academic Press.

Evans, J.St.B.T. (1977). Linguistic factors in reasoning. *Quarterly Journal of Experimental Psychology* **29**, 297–306.

Evans, J.St.B.T. (1980a). Current issues in the psychology of reasoning. *British Journal of Psychology* **71**, 227–239.

Evans, J.St.B.T. (1982). *The psychology of deductive reasoning*. London: Routledge and Kegan Paul.

Evans, J.St.B.T. (1984). Heuristic and analytic processes in reasoning. *British Journal of Psychology* **75**, 451–458.

Evans, J.St.B.T. (1989). *Bias in human reasoning: causes and consequences*. Hove, UK: Lawrence Erlbaum Associates.

Evans, J.St.B.T. (1992). Reasoning with bounded rationality. *Theory and Psychology* **2**, 237–242.

Evans, J St.B.T. (1995). Relevance and reasoning. In S.E. Newstead and J.St.B.T. Evans (Eds), *Current directions in thinking and reasoning*. Hove, UK: Lawrence Erlbaum Associates.

Evans, J.St.B.T. and Lynch, J.S. (1973). Matching bias in the selection task. *British Journal of Psychology* **64**, 391–397.

Evans, J.St.B.T. and Wason, P.C. (1976). Rationalization in a reasoning task. *British Journal of Psychology* **67**, 479–486.

Evans, J.St.B.T., Ball, L.J. and Brooks, P.G. (1987). Attentional bias and decision order in a reasoning task. *British Journal of Psychology* **78**, 385–394.

Evans, J.St.B.T., Newstead, S.E. and Byrne, R.M.J. (1993). *Human reasoning: psychology of deduction*. Hove, UK: Lawrence Erlbaum Associates.

Falkenhainer, B., Forbus, K.D. and Gentner, D. (1986). Structure mapping engine. *Proceedings of the Annual Conference of the American Association for Artificial Intelligence*. Los Altos: Morgan Kaufmann.

Farris, H. and Revlin, R. (1989). The discovery process: a counterfactual strategy. *Social Studies of Science* **19**, 497–513.

Feltovich, P.J. and Barrows, H.S. (1984). Issues of generality in medical problem solving. In H.G. Schmidt and M.L. de Volder (Eds), *Tutorials in problem-based learning*. Assen, The Netherlands: Van Gorcum.

Feltovich, P.J., Johnson, P.E., Moller, J.H. and Swanson, D.B. (1984). LCS: the role and development of medical knowledge in diagnostic expertise. In W.J. Clancey and E.H. Shortcliffe (Eds), *Readings in medical artificial intelligence*. Reading, MA: Addison Wesley.

Fiedler, K. (1988). The dependence of the conjunction fallacy on subtle linguistic factors. *Psychological Research* **50**, 123–129.

Fillenbaum, S. (1993). Deductive reasoning: what are taken to be the premises and how are they interpreted? *Behavioral and Brain Sciences* **16**, 348–349.

Findler, N. (1978). Computer poker. *Scientific American* **239**, 112–119.

Finke, R.A. (1990). *Creative imagery: discoveries and inventions in visualization*. Hillsdale, NJ: Lawrence Erlbaum Associates.

Finke, R.A. (1993). Mental imagery and creative discovery. In B. Roskos-Ewoldson, M.J. Injons-Peterson and R.E. Anderson (Eds), *Imagery, creativity and discovery*. Amsterdam: Elsevier.

Finke, R.A., Ward, T.B. and Smith, S.M. (1992). *Creative cognition: theory, research, applications*. Cambridge, MA: MIT Press.

Fodor, J.A. and Pylyshyn, Z.W. (1988). Connectionism, and cognitive architecture: a critical analysis. *Cognition* **28**, 3–71.

Ford, M. (1995). Two modes of mental representation and problem solution in syllogistic reasoning. *Cognition* **54**, 1–71.

Frensch, P.A. and Sternberg, R.J. (1989). Skill related differences in game playing. In R.J. Sternberg and P.A. Frensch (Eds), *Complex problem solving: principles and mechanisms*. Hillsdale, NJ: Lawrence Erlbaum Associates.

Freud, S. (1900). The interpretation of dreams. In *Standard Edition*, Vols IV and V. London: Hogarth Press, 1953 (first German edition 1900).

Frey, P.W. and Adesman, P. (1976). Recall memory for visually presented chess positions. *Memory and Cognition* **4**, 541–547.

Frijda, N.H. and De Groot, A.D. (1981). *Otto Selz: his contribution to psychology*. The Hague: Mouton.

Fulgosi, A. and Guilford, J.P. (1968). Short term incubation in divergent production. *American Journal of Psychology* **81**, 241–246.

Gale, J. and Marsden, P. (1983). *Medical diagnosis: from student to clinician*. Oxford: Oxford University Press.

Galotti, K.M., Baron, J. and Sabini, J.P. (1986). Individual differences in syllogistic reasoning: deduction rules or mental models? *Journal of Experimental Psychology: General* **115**, 16–25.

Gardner, H. (1985). *The mind's new science.* New York: Basic Books.

Garnham, A. (1993). A number of questions about a question of number. *Behavioral and Brain Sciences* **16**, 350–351.

Garnham, A. and Oakhill, J. (1994). *Thinking and reasoning.* Oxford: Blackwell.

Gentner, D. (1980). The structure of analogical models in science. *Bolt Beranck & Newman Technical Reports.* No. 4454.

Gentner, D. (1983). Structure-mapping: a theoretical framework for analogy. *Cognitive Science* **7**, 155–170.

Gentner, D. and Gentner, D.R. (1983). Flowing waters and teeming crowds: mental models of electricity. In D. Gentner and A.L. Stevens (Eds), *Mental models.* Hillsdale, NJ: Lawrence Erlbaum Associates.

Ghiselin, B. (1952). *The creative process.* Berkeley, CA: University of California Press.

Gick, M.L. (1986). Problem solving strategies. *Educational Psychologist* **21**, 99–120.

Gick, M.L. and Holyoak, K.J. (1980). Analogical problem solving. *Cognitive Psychology* **12**, 306–355.

Gick, M.L. and Holyoak, K.J. (1983). Schema induction in analogical transfer. *Cognitive Psychology* **15**, 1–38.

Gick, M.L. and McGarry, S.J. (1992). Learning from mistakes: inducing analogous solution failures to a source problem produces later successes in analogical transfer. *Journal of Experimental Psychology: Learning, Memory and Cognition* **18**, 623–639.

Gigerenzer, G. (1993). The bounded rationality of probabilistic mental models. In K.I. Manktelow and D.E. Over (Eds), *Rationality: psychological and philosophical perspectives.* London: Routledge.

Gigerenzer, G. and Hug, K. (1992). Domain-specific reasoning: social contracts, cheating and perspective change. *Cognition* **43**, 127–171.

Gilhooly, K.J. (1988). *Thinking: directed, undirected and creative.* 2nd Edition. London: Academic Press.

Gilhooly, K.J. and Falconer, W. (1974). Concrete and abstract terms and relations in testing a rule. *Quarterly Journal of Experimental Psychology* **26**, 355–359.

Gilhooly, K.J., Logie, R.H., Wetherick, N.E. and Wynn, V. (1993). Working memory and strategies in syllogistic reasoning tasks. *Memory and Cognition* **21**, 115–124.

Gluck, M.A. and Bower, G.H. (1988). Evaluating an adaptive network model of human learning. *Journal of Memory and Language* **27**, 166–195.

Glucksberg, S. and Danks, J.H. (1968). Effects of discriminative labels. *Journal of Verbal Learning and Verbal Behaviour* **7**, 72–76.

Glucksberg, S. and Weisberg, R.W. (1968). Verbal behavior and problem solving. *Journal of Experimental Psychology* **71**, 659–664.

Goethals, G.R. and Leckmann, R.F. (1973). The perception of consistency in attitudes. *Journal of Experimental Psychology* **9**, 491–501.

Golding, W. (1955). *The inheritors.* London: Faber and Faber.

Goldstein, W.M. (1990). Judgements of relative importance in decision making: global *vs.* local interpretation of subjective weight. *Organisational Behaviour and Human Decision Processes* **47**, 313–336.

Goodwin, R.Q. and Wason, P.C. (1972). Degrees of insight. *British Journal of Psychology* **63**, 205–212.

Gordon, W.J.J. (1961). *Synectics.* New York: Harper.

Gorman, M.E. (1986). How the possibility of error affects falsification on a task that models scientific problem solving. *British Journal of Psychology* **77**, 85–96.

Gorman, M.E. (1992). Experimental simulations of falsification. In M.T. Keane and K.J. Gilhooly (Eds), *Advances in the psychology of thinking.* London: Harvester Wheatsheaf.

Gorman, M.E. and Gorman, M.E. (1984). A comparison of disconfirmation, confirmation and control strategy on Wason's 2–4–6 task. *Quarterly Journal of Experimental Psychology* **36A**, 629–648.

Gorman, M.E., Gorman, M.E., Latta, R.M. and Cunningham, G. (1984). How discon-
firmatory, confirmatary and combined strategies affect group problem solving. *British Journal of Psychology* **75**, 65–80.

Gorman, M.E., Stafford, A. and Gorman, M.E. (1987). Disconfirmation and dual hypotheses on a more difficult version of Wason's 2, 4, 6 task. *Quarterly Journal of Experimental Psychology* **39A**, 1–28.

Grant, J. (1989). Clinical decision making: rational principles, clinical intuition or clinical thinking. In J.I. Balla, M. Gibson and A.M. Chang (Eds), *Learning in medical school: a model for the clinical professions*. Hong Kong: Hong Kong University Press.

Green, A.J.K. and Gilhooly, K.J. (1990). Individual differences and effective learning procedures: the case of statistical computing. *International Journal of Man–Machine Studies* **33**, 97–119.

Grice, H.P. (1975). Logic and conversation. In P. Cole and J.L. Morgan (Eds), *Syntax and semantics*, Vol. III. New York: Academic Press.

Griggs, R.A. and Cox, J.R. (1982). The elusive thematic-materials effect in Wason's selection task. *British Journal of Psychology* **73**, 407–420.

Griggs, R.A. and Cox, J.R. (1983). The effects of problem content and negation on Wason's selection task. *Quarterly Journal of Experimental Psychology* **35A**, 519–534.

Griggs, R.A. and Warner, S.A. (1982). Processing artificial set inclusion relations: educing the appropriate schema. *Journal Experimental Psychology: Learning, Memory and Cognition* **7**, 51–65.

Gruber, H.E. (1980). *Darwin on man: a psychological study of scientific creativity*, 2nd edn, Chicago: University of Chicago Press.

Gruber, H.E. and Davis, S. (1988). Inching our way up Mount Olympus: the evolving systems approach to creative thinking. In R.J. Sternberg (Ed.), *The nature of creativity: contemporary psychological perspectives*. Cambridge: Cambridge University Press.

Gustin, W.C. (1985). The development of exceptional research mathematicians. In B.S. Bloom (Ed.), *Developing talent in young people*. New York: Ballantine Books.

Guyote, M.J. and Sternberg, K.J. (1981). A transitive-chain theory of syllogistic reasoning. *Cognitive Psychology* **13**, 461–525.

Hayes, J.R. and Simon, H.A. (1974). Understanding written problem instructions. In L.W. Gregg (Ed.), *Knowledge and cognition*. Hillsdale, NJ: Lawrence Erlbaum Associates.

Hayes, J.R. and Simon, H.A. (1977). Psychological differences among problem isomorphs. In N.J. Castellan, D.B. Pisoni and G.R. Potts (Eds), *Cognitive theory*, Vol. 2. Hillsdale, NJ: Lawrence Erlbaum Associates.

Hearst, E. (1977). Man and machine: chess achievements and chess thinking. In P.W. Frey (Ed.), *Chess skill in man and machine*. New York: Springer.

Hegarty, M. (1991). Knowledge and processes in mechanical problem solving. In R.J. Sternberg and P.A. Frensch (Eds), *Complex problem solving: principles and mechanisms*. Hillsdale, NJ: Lawrence Erlbaum Associates.

Henle, M. (1962). On the relation between logic and thinking. *Psychological Review* **69**, 366–378.

Henle, M. (1978). Foreword. In R. Revlin and R.E. Mayer (Eds), *Human reasoning*. New York: John Wiley.

Hesse, M. (1975). Bayesian methods and the initial probabilities of theories. In G. Maxwell and R.M. Anderson, Jr. (Eds), *Induction, probability and confirmation*. Minneapolis, MI: University of Minnesota Press.

Hilgard, E.R. (1962). Impulsive *versus* realistic thinking: an examination of the distinction between primary and secondary processes in thought. *Psychological Bulletin* **59**, 477–489.

Hobbes, T. (1651). *Leviathan*, 1919 edn. London: J.M. Dent.

Hobus, P.P.M., Schmidt, H.G., Boshuizen, H.P.A. and Patel, V.L. (1987). Contextual factors in the activation of first diagnostic hypotheses: expert–novice differences. *Medical Education* **21**, 471–476.

Hobus, P.P.M., Boshuizen, H.P.A. and Schmidt, H.G. (1989). *Mental representation of proto-typical patients: expert–novice differences.* Paper presented at First European Congress of Psychology, Amsterdam, The Netherlands 1989.

Hoelscher, T.J., Klinger, E. and Barta, S.G. (1981). Incorporation of concern and nonconcern related verbal stimuli into dream content. *Journal of Abnormal Psychology* **90**, 88–91.

Holding, D.H. (1979). The evaluation of chess positions. *Simulation and Games* **10**, 207–221.

Holding, D.H. (1985). *The psychology of chess.* Hillsdale, NJ: Lawrence Erlbaum Associates.

Holding, D.H. (1989). Adversary problem solving by humans. In K.J. Gilhooly (Ed.), *Human and machine problem solving.* New York, NY: Plenum Press.

Holding, D.H. and Reynolds, J.R. (1982). Recall or evaluation of chess positions as determinants of chess skill. *Memory and Cognition* **10**, 237–242.

Holland, J.H., Holyoak, K.J., Nisbett, R.E. and Thagard, R.R. (1986). *Induction: processes of inference, learning and discovery.* Cambridge, MA: MIT Press

Holyoak, K.J. (1984). Mental models in problem solving. In J.R. Anderson (Ed.), *Tutorials in learning and memory.* San Francisco, CA: W.H. Freeman.

Holyoak, K.J. and Koh, K. (1987). Surface and structural similarity in analogical transfer. *Memory and Cognition* **15**, 332–340.

Holyoak, K.J. and Thagard, P. (1989). Analogical mapping by constraint satisfaction. *Cognitive Science* **13**, 295–355.

Holyoak, K.J. and Thagard, P. (1990). A constraint satisfaction approach to analogical mapping and retrieval. In K.J. Gilhooly, M.T. Keane, R. Logie and G. Erdos (Eds), *Lines of thinking: reflections in the psychology of thought*, Vol. 1. Chichester, UK: John Wiley.

Hsu F., Anantharam, T., Campbell, M. and Nowatzyk, A. (1990). A grandmaster chess machine. *Scientific American* **263**, 18–24.

Hudson, L. (1966). *Contrary imaginations.* London: Methuen.

Hull, C.L. (1934). The concept of the habit-family hierarchy and maze-learning. *Psychological Review* **41**, 33–52, 134–152.

Humphreys, P.C. and Humphreys, A.R. (1975). An investigation of subjective preference orderings for multi-attributed alternatives. In D. Wendt and C. Vlek (Eds), *Utility, probability and human decision making.* Dordrecht: Reidel.

Isenberg, D.J. (1987). Inside the mind of the senior manager. In D.N. Perkins, J. Lochhead and J.C. Bishop (Eds), *Thinking.* Hillsdale, NJ: Lawrence Erlbaum Associates.

Israel, R.A. *et al.* (Eds) (1980). *International classification of diseases*, 9th revision, *clinical modification*, 2nd edn. US Department of Health and Human Services, Public Health Service, Health Care Financing Administration. Washington, DC: US Government Printing Office.

Jacob, F. and Monod, J. (1961). Genetic regulatory mechanisms in the synthesis of proteins. *Journal of Molecular Biology* **3**, 318–356.

James, W. (1890). *The principles of psychology.* New York: Henry Holt.

Jamison, K.R. (1995). Manic-depressive illness and creativity. *Scientific American* **272**, 46–51.

Jeffries, R., Polson, P.G., Razran, L. and Attwood, M.E. (1977). A process model for missionaries–cannibals and other river crossing problems. *Cognitive Psychology* **9**, 412–420.

Jeffries, R., Turner, A., Polson, P. and Atwood, M. (1981). The processes involved in designing software. In J.R. Anderson (Ed.), *Cognitive skills and their acquisition.* Hillsdale, NJ: Lawrence Erlbaum Associates

Johnson, P.E., Duran, A.S., Hassebrock, F., Moller, J., Prietula, M., Feltovich, P.J. and Swanson, D.B. (1981). Expertise and error in diagnostic reasoning. *Cognitive Science* **5**, 235–283.

Johnson-Laird, P.N. (1975). Models of deduction. In R.C. Falmagne (Ed.), *Reasoning: representation and process.* Hillsdale, NJ: Lawrence Erlbaum Associates.

Johnson-Laird, P.N. (1983). *Mental models.* Cambridge, UK: Cambridge University Press.

Johnson-Laird, P.N. (1993). *Human and machine thinking*. Hillsdale, NJ: Lawrence Erlbaum Associates.

Johnson-Laird, P.N. and Bara, B.G. (1984). Syllogistic inference. *Cognition* **16**, 1–61.

Johnson-Laird, P.N. and Byrne, R.M.J. (1991). *Deduction*. Hove, UK: Lawrence Erlbaum Associates.

Johnson-Laird, P.N. and Byrne, R.M.J. (1993). Precis of *Deduction*. *Behavioral and Brain Sciences* **16**, 323–380.

Johnson-Laird, P.N. and Steedman, M. (1978). The psychology of syllogisms. *Cognitive Psychology* **10**, 64–99.

Johnson-Laird, P.N. and Tagart, J. (1969). How implication is understood. *American Journal of Psychology* **2**, 367–373.

Johnson-Laird, P.N. and Wason, P.C. (1970). A theoretical analysis of insight into a reasoning task. *Cognitive Psychology* **1**, 134–148.

Johnson-Laird, P.N., Byrne, R.M.J. and Schaeken, W. (1992). Propositional reasoning by model. *Psychological Review* **90**, 418–439.

Johnson-Laird, P.N., Legrenzi, P. and Legrenzi, M.S. (1972). Reasoning and a sense of reality. *British Journal of Psychology* **63**, 395–400.

Johnson-Laird, P.N., Byrne, R.M.J. and Schaeken, W. (1994). Why models rather than rules give a better account of propositional reasoning: a reply to Bonatti and to O'Brien, Braine and Yang. *Psychological Review* **101**, 734–739.

Jones, E. (1961). *The life and work of Sigmund Freud*. L. Trilling and S. Marcus, Eds. London: Hogarth.

Kahneman, D. and Tversky, A. (1984). Choices, values and frames. *American Psychologist* **39**, 341–350.

Kaplan, G.A. and Simon, H.A. (1990). In search of insight. *Cognitive Psychology* **22**, 374–419.

Karat, J. (1982). A model of problem-solving with incomplete constraint knowledge. *Cognitive Psychology* **14**, 538–559.

Karmiloff-Smith, A. (1993). Is creativity domain-specific or domain-general? Clues from normal and abnormal development. *Artificial Intelligence and Simulation of Behavior Quarterly*, August, 1993.

Keane, M. (1988). *Analogical problem solving*. Chichester, UK: Ellis Horwood.

Keane, M.T. and Brayshaw, M. (1988). The incremental analogy machine: a computational model of analogy. In D. Sleeman (Ed.), *Third European Working Session on Learning*. London: Pitman.

Keane, M.T., Ledgeway, T. and Duff, S. (1994). Constraints on analogical mapping: a comparison of 3 models. *Cognitive Science* **18**, 287–334.

Kirby, K.N. (1994). Probabilities and utilities of fictional outcomes in Wason's four-card selection task. *Cognition* **51**, 1–28.

Klayman, J. (1985). Children's decision strategies and their adaptation to task characteristics. *Organizational Behavior and Human Decision Processes* **35**, 179–201.

Klayman, J. and Ha, Y.-W. (1987). Confirmation, disconfirmation and information in hypothesis testing. *Psychological Review* **94**, 211–228.

Klayman, J. and Ha, Y.-W. (1989). Hypothesis testing in rule discovery: strategy, structure and content. *Journal of Experimental Psychology: Learning, Memory and Cognition* **15**, 596–604.

Klinger, E. (1971). *Structure and function of fantasy*. New York: John Wiley.

Klinger, E. (1974). Utterances to evaluate steps and control attention distinguish operant from respondent thought while thinking out loud. *Bulletin of the Psychonomic Society* **4**, 44–45.

Klinger, E. (1978). Modes of normal conscious flow. In K.S. Pope and J.L. Singer (Eds), *The stream of consciousness*. New York: John Wiley.

Klinger, E., Barta, S.G. and Maxeimer, M.E. (1980). Motivational correlates of thought content frequency and commitment. *Journal of Personality and Social Psychology* **39**, 1222–1237.

Klinger, E. and Cox, W.M. (1988). Dimensions of thought flow in everyday life. *Imagination, Cognition and Personality* **7**, 105–128.

Kochen, M. and Badre, A.N. (1974). Questions and shifts of representation in problem solving. *American Journal of Psychology* **87**, 369–383.

Koehler, J.J. (in press). The base rate fallacy reconsidered: descriptive, normative and methodological challenges. *Behavioral and Brain Sciences*.

Koestler, A. (1964). *The act of creation*. London: Hutchinson.

Kohler, W. (1925). *The mentality of apes*. New York: Harcourt Brace.

Kosslyn, S.M. (1981). The medium and the message in mental imagery: a theory. *Psychological Review* **88**, 46–66.

Kosslyn, S.M. and Pomerantz, J.R. (1977). Imagery, propositions, and the form of internal representations. *Cognitive Psychology* **9**, 52–76.

Krechevsky, I. (1935). Brain mechanisms and 'hypotheses'. *Journal of Comparative Psychology* **19**, 425–462.

Kripke, D.F. and Sonnenschein, D. (1978). A biologic rythm in waking fantasy. In K.S. Pope and J.L. Singer (Eds), *The stream of consciousness*. New York: John Wiley.

Kuhn, T. (1970). *The structure of scientific revolutions*, 2nd edn. Chicago: University of Chicago Press.

Lachman, R. (1973). Uncertainly effects on time taken to access the internal lexicon. *Journal of Experimental Psychology* **99**, 199–208.

Lakatos, I. (1970). Falsification and the methodology of scientific research programmes. In I. Lakatos and A. Musgrave (Eds), *Criticism and the growth of knowledge*. London: Cambridge University Press.

Lamberts, K. (1990). A hybrid model of learning to solve physics problems. *European Journal of Cognitive Psychology* **2**, 151–170.

Langley, P., Simon, H.A., Bradshaw, G.L. and Zytkow, J.M. (1987). *Scientific discovery: computational explorations of the creative process*. Cambridge, MA: MIT Press.

Larkin, J.H. (1978). Problem solving in physics: structure, process and learning. In J.M. Scandura and C.J. Brainerd (Eds), *Structural/process models of complex human behavior*. The Hague, Netherlands: Sijthoff and Noordhoff.

Larkin, J.H. (1979). Information processing models and science instruction. In J. Lochhead and J. Clement (Eds), *Cognitive process instruction*. Philadelphia, PA: Franklin Institute Press.

Larkin, J.H. (1983). The role of problem representation in physics. In D. Gentner and A.L. Stevens (Eds), *Mental models*. Hillsdale, NJ: Lawrence Erlbaum Associates.

Larkin, J.H. and Simon, H.A. (1987). Why a diagram is (sometimes) worth ten thousand words. *Cognitive Science* **11**, 65–100.

Larkin, J.H., McDermott, J., Simon, D.P. and Simon, H.A. (1980). Models of competence in solving physics problems. *Cognitive Science* **4**, 317–345.

Laughlin, P.R., Doherty, M.A. and Dunn, R.F. (1968). Intentional and incidental concept formation as a function of motivation, creativity, intelligence and sex. *Journal of Personality and Social Psychology* **8**, 401–409.

Legrenzi, P. (1971). Discovery as a means to understanding. *Quarterly Journal of Experimental Psychology* **23**, 417–422.

Lehman, H.C. (1953). *Age and achievement*. Princeton, NJ: Princeton University Press.

Lesgold, A.M. (1984). Acquiring expertise. In J.R. Anderson (Ed.), *Tutorials in learning and memory*. San Francisco, CA: W.H. Freeman.

Lesgold, A.M., Rubinson, H., Feltovich, P., Glaser, R. and Klopfer, D. (1988). Expertise in complex skills: diagnosing X-ray pictures. In M. Chi, R. Glaser and M. Farr (Eds), *The nature of expertise*, Hillsdale, NJ: Lawrence Erlbaum Associates.

Levy, D. (1978). Computers are now chess masters. *New Scientist* 27 July, pp. 256–258.

Lewandowsky, S. (1992). Unified cognitive theory: having one's apple pie and eating it. *Behavioral and Brain Sciences* **15**, 449–450.

Lewis, C. (1981). Skill in algebra. In J.R. Anderson (Ed.), *Cognitive skills and their acquisition*. Hillsdale, NJ: Lawrence Erlbaum Associates.

Lichtenstein, S., Slovic, P., Fischhoff, B., Layman, M. and Coombes, B. (1978). Judged frequency of lethal events. *Journal of Experimental Psychology: Human Learning and Memory* **4**, 551–578.

Logie, R.H. (1986). Visuo-spatial processing in working memory. *Quarterly Journal of Experimental Psychology* **38A**, 229–247.

Logie, R.H., Gilhooly, K.J. and Wynn, V. (1994). Counting on working memory in arithmetic problem solving. *Memory and Cognition* **22**, 395–410.

Lopes, L. (1976). Model based decision and inference in stud poker. *Journal of Experimental Psychology: General* **105**, 217–239.

Luchins, A.W. (1942). Mechanization in problem solving: the effect of Einstellung. *Psychological Monographs* **54**, 000–000.

Ludwig, A.M. (1992). Creative achievement and psychopathology: comparison among professions. *Journal of Psychotherapy* **46**, 330–356.

Luger, G.F. (1976). The use of the state-space to record the behavioural effects of subproblems and symmetries on the Tower of Hanoi problem. *International Journal of Man–Machine Studies* **8**, 411–421.

Lung, C.T. and Dominowski, R.C. (1985). Effects of strategy instructions and practice on nine-dot problem solving. *Journal of Experimental Psychology: Learning, Memory and Cognition* **11**, 804–811.

MacKintosh, N.J. (1988). Approaches to the study of animal intelligence. *British Journal of Psychology* **79**, 509–525.

McClelland, J.L. (1986). The programmable blackboard model of reading. In J.L. McClelland, D.E. Rumelhart and the PDP Research Group (Eds), *Parallel distributed processing*, Vol. 2. Cambridge, MA: MIT Press.

McClelland, J.L. and Rumelhart, D.E. (1985). Distributed memory and the representation of general and specific information. *Journal of Experimental Psychology: General* **114**, 159–188.

McClelland, J.L. and Rumelhart, D.E. (1986). A distributed model of human learning and memory. In J.L. McClelland, D.E. Rumelhart and the PDP Research Group (Eds), *Parallel distributed processing*, Vol. 2. Cambridge, MA: MIT Press.

McClelland, J.L., Rumelhart, D.E. and Hinton, G.E. (1986). The appeal of parallel distributed processing. In J.L. McClelland, D.E. Rumelhart and the PDP Research Group (Eds), *Parallel distributed processing*, Vol. 1. Cambridge, MA: MIT Press.

McCloskey, M. (1983). Intuitive physics. *Scientific American* **24**, 122–130.

McCloskey, M. and Kaiser, M.K. (1984). Children's intuitive physics. *The Sciences* **24**, 40–45.

MacDonald, R.R. (1986). Credible conceptions and implausible probabilities. *British Journal of Mathematical and Statistical Psychology* **39**, 15–27.

McGuire, C.H. (1985). Medical problem solving: a critique of the literature. *Journal of Medical Education* **60**, 587–595.

McKeithen, K.B., Reitman, J.S., Rueter, H.H. and Hirtle, S.C. (1981). Knowledge organization and skill differences in computer programmers. *Cognitive Psychology* **13**, 307–325.

McKeller, P. (1957). *Imagination and thinking*. New York, Basic Books.

MacKinnon, D.W. (1962). The personality correlates of creativity: a study of American architects. In *Proceedings of the 14th Congress of Applied Psychology*, Vol. 2. Munksgaard. Excerpts reprinted in P.E. Vernon (Ed.), *Creativity*. Harmondsworth: Penguin Books, 1970.

McLelland, D.C. (1962). On the dynamics of creative physical scientists. In H.E. Gruber *et al.* (Eds), *Contemporary approaches to creative thinking*. New York: Atherton.

Macnamara, J. (1986). *A border dispute: the place of logic in psychology*. Cambridge, MA: Bradford Books/MIT Press.

Maltzman, I. (1955). Thinking: from a behavioristic point of view. *Psychological Review* **62**, 275–286.

Manktelow, K.I. and Evans, J.St.B.T. (1979). Facilitation of reasoning by realism: effect or non-effect? *British Journal of Psychology* **70**, 477–488.

Manktelow, K.I. and Over, D.E. (1991). Social roles and utilities in reasoning with deontic conditionals. *Cognition* **39**, 85–105.

Marcus, S.L. (1982). Recall of logical argument lines. *Journal of Verbal Reasoning and Verbal Behaviour* **21**, 549–562.

Marcus, S.L. and Rips, L.J. (1979). Conditional reasoning. *Journal of Verbal Reasoning and Verbal Behaviour* **18**, 199–233.

Markovits, H. (1988). Conditional reasoning, representation, empirical evidence on a concrete task. *Quarterly Journal of Experimental Psychology* **45A**, 133–148.

Mawer, R.F. and Sweller, J. (1982). Effects of subgoal density and location on learning during problem solving. *Journal of Experimental Psychology: Learning, Memory and Cognition* **8**, 252–259.

Meadow, A., Parnes, S.J. and Reese, H. (1959). Influence of brainstorming instruction and problem sequence on a creative problem solving test. *Journal of Applied Psychology* **43**, 413–416.

Mednick, S.A. (1962). The associative basis of the creative process. *Psychological Review* **69**, 431–436.

Mendelsohn, G.A. and Griswold, B.B. (1964). Differential use of incidental stimuli in problem solving as a function of creativity. *Journal of Abnormal and Social Psychology* **68**, 431–436.

Meskin, B.B. and Singer, J.L. (1974). Daydreaming, reflective thought and laterality of eye movements. *Journal of Personality and Social Psychology* **30**, 64–71.

Metcalfe, J. (1986a). Feeling of knowing in memory and problem solving. *Journal of Experimental Psychology: Learning, Memory and Cognition* **12**, 288–294.

Metcalfe, J. (1986b). Premonitions of error predict impending insight. *Journal of Experimental Psychology: Learning, Memory and Cognition* **12**, 623–634.

Metcalfe, J. and Weibe, D. (1987). Intuition in insight and noninsight problem solving. *Memory and Cognition* **15**, 238–246.

Meyer, B.J.F. (1975). *The organisation of prose and its effects on memory*. Amsterdam: North-Holland.

Mill, J.S. (1875/1967). *A system of logic*. London: Longmans.

Millenson, J.R. (1967). *Principles of behavioral analysis*. New York: MacMillan.

Miller, G.A. (1956). The magical number seven, plus or minus two: some limits on our capacity for processing information. *Psychological Review* **63**, 81–87.

Miller, G.A. (1960). *Psychology: the science of mental life*. Harmondsworth: Penguin.

Miller, G.A., Galanter, E.H. and Pribram, H.H. (1960). *Plans and the structure of behavior*. New York: Holt.

Mitroff, I.I. (1974). *The subjective side of science*. Amsterdam: Elsevier.

Moore, O.K. and Anderson, S.B. (1954a). Modern logic and tasks for experiments on problem solving behavior. *Journal of Psychology* **38**, 151–160.

Moore, O.K. and Anderson, S.B. (1954b). Search behavior in individual and group problem solving. *American Sociological Review* **19**, 702–714.

Murray, H.G. and Denny, J.P. (1969). Interaction of ability level and interpolated activity in human problem solving. *Psychological Reports* **24**, 271–276.

Mynatt, C.R., Doherty, M.E. and Tweney, R.D. (1977). Confirmation bias in a simulated research environment: an experimental study of scientific inference. *Quarterly Journal of Experimental Psychology* **29**, 85–95.

Mynatt, C.R., Doherty, M.E. and Tweney, R.D. (1978). Consequences of confirmation and disconfirmation in a simulated research environment. *Quarterly Journal of Experimental Psychology* **30**, 395–406.

Neisser, U. (1963a). The imitation of man by machine. *Science* **139**, 193–197.

Neisser, U. (1963b). The multiplicity of thought. *British Journal of Psychology* **54**, 1–14.

Neisser, U. (1976). *Cognition and reality*. San Francisco, CA: Freeman.

Newell, A. (1962). Some problems of basic organization in problem solving programs. In M.C. Yovits, G.T. Jacobi and G.D. Goldstein (Eds), *Self organizing systems*. Washington, DC: Spartan Books.

Newell, A. (1973). You can't play 20 questions with nature and win. In W.G. Chase (Ed.), *Visual information processing*. New York: Academic Press.

Newell, A. (1990). *Unified theories of cognition*. Cambridge, MA: Harvard University Press.

Newell, A (1992). Précis of *Unified Theories of Cognition*. *Behavioral and Brain Sciences* **15**, 425–492.

Newell, A. and Rosenbloom, P.S. (1981). Mechanisms of skill acquisition and the law of practice. In J.R. Anderson (Ed.), *Cognitive skills and their acquisition*. Hillsdale, NJ: Lawrence Erlbaum Associates.

Newell, A. and Simon, H.A. (1972). *Human Problem Solving*. Englewood Cliffs, NJ: Prentice Hall.

Newell, A., Shaw, J.C. and Simon, H.A.(1958). Elements of a theory of human problem solving. *Psychological Review* **65**, 151–166.

Newell, A., Shaw, J.C. and Simon, H.A. (1962). The processes of creative thinking. In H.E. Gruber, G. Terrell and M. Wertheimer (Eds), *Contemporary approaches to creative thinking*. New York: Atherton.

Newman, J.P., Wolff, W.T. and Hearst, E. (1980). The feature-positive effect in adult human subjects. *Journal of Experimental Psychology: Human Learning, Memory and Cognition* **6**, 630–650.

Newstead, S.E. (1989). Interpretational errors in syllogistic reasoning. *Journal of Memory and Language* **28**, 78–91.

Newstead, S.E. and Griggs, R.A. (1983). Drawing inferences from quantified statements: a study of the square of opposition. *Journal of Verbal Learning and Verbal Behaviour* **22**, 535–546.

Nidditch, P.H. (1962). *The development of mathematical logic*. London: Routledge and Kegan Paul.

Nilsson, N.J. (1971). *Problem solving methods in artificial intelligence*. New York: McGraw-Hill.

Nisbett, R.E. and Borgida, D. (1975). Attribution and the psychology of prediction. *Journal of Personal and Social Psychology* **32**, 932–943.

Nisbett, R.E. and Wilson, T.D. (1977). Telling more than we can know: verbal reports on mental processes. *Psychological Review* **84**, 231–259.

Nisbett, R.E., Krantz, D.H., Jepson, D. and Kunda, Z. (1983). The use of statistical heuristics in everyday reasoning. *Psychological Review* **90**, 339–363.

Norman, D.A. (1981). Categorization of action slips. *Psychological Review* **88**, 1–15.

Norman, D.A. (1986). Reflections on cognition and parallel distributed processing. In D.E. Rumelhart, J.L. McClelland and the PDP Research Group (Eds), *Parallel distributed processing*, Vol. 2. Cambridge: MA: MIT Press.

Norman, G.R. (1988). Problem solving skills, solving problems and problem based learning. *Medical Education* **22**, 279–286.

Norman, G.R., Rosenthal, D., Brooks, L.R., Allen, S.W. and Muzzin, L.J. (1989). The development of expertise in dermatology. *Archives of Dermatology* **125**, 1063–1068.

O'Brien, D.P. (1993). Mental logic and human irrationality: we can put a man on the moon, so why can't we solve those logical-reasoning problems? In K.E. Manktelow and D.E. Over (Eds), *Rationality: psychological and philosophical perspectives*. London: Routledge.

O'Brien, D.P., Braine, M.D.S. and Yang, Y. (1994). Propositional reasoning by mental models? Simple to refute in principle and in practice. *Psychological Review* **101**, 701–704.

Oaksford, M. and Chater, N. (1994). A rational analysis of the selection task as optimal data selection. *Psychological Review* **101**, 608–631.

Oldfield, R.C. (1966). Things, words and the brain. *Quarterly Journal of Experimental Psychology* **18**, 340–353.

Ohlsson, S. (1984). Restructuring revisited. II. An information processing theory of restructuring and insight. *Scandinavian Journal of Psychology* **25**, 117–129.

Ohlsson, S. (1990). The mechanism of restructuring in geometry. *Proceedings of the Twelfth Annual Conference of the Cognitive Science Society*. Hillsdale, NJ: Lawrence Erlbaum Associates.

Ohlsson, S. (1992). Information processing explanations of insight and related phenomena. In M.T. Keane and K.J. Gilhooly (Eds), *Advances in the psychology of thinking*. London: Harvester Wheatsheaf.

Olton, R.M. and Johnson, D.M. (1976). Mechanisms of incubation in creative problem solving. *American Journal of Psychology* **7**, 617–630.

Osborn, A.F. (1953). *Applied imagination*. New York: Scribners.

Osherson, D. (1975). Logic and models of logical thinking. In R.J. Falmagne (Ed.), *Reasoning: representation and process in children and adults*. Hillsdale, NJ: Lawrence Erlbaum Associates.

Over, D.E. and Manktelow, K.I. (1993). Rationality, utility and deontic reasoning. In K.I. Manktelow and D.E. Over (Eds) *Rationality: psychological and philosophical perspectives*. London: Routledge.

Parnes, S.J. and Meadow, A. (1963). Development of individual creative talent. In C.W. Taylor and F. Barron (Eds), *Scientific creativity: its recognition and development*. New York: John Wiley.

Patel, V.L. and Groen, G.J. (1986a). Knowledge-based solution strategies in medical reasoning. *Cognitive Science* **10**, 91–116.

Patel, V.L. and Groen, G.J. (1986b). Non-monotonicity in novice–intermediate-expert comparisons. *Proceedings of the 27th Annual Meeting of the Psychonomic Society*, New Orleans, LA.

Patel, V.L. and Medley-Mark, V. (1985). Knowledge, integration from clinical texts, use of factual, inferential and integrative questions. *Proceedings of the 24th Annual Conference of Research in Medical Education*, Washington, DC.

Patel, V.L., Arocha, J.F. and Groen, G.J. (1986a). Strategy selection and degree of expertise in medical reasoning. *Proceedings of the Eighth Annual Conference of the Cognitive Science Society*. Hillsdale NJ: Lawrence Erlbaum Associates.

Patel, V.L., Groen, G.J. and Frederiksen, C.H. (1986b). Differences between students and physicians in memory for clinical cases. *Medical Education* **20**, 3–9.

Patel, V.L., Evans, D.A. and Chawla, A.S. (1987). Predictive versus diagnostic reasoning in the application of biomedical knowledge. *Proceedings of the Eighth Annual Conference of the Cognitive Science Society*. Hillsdale, NJ: Lawrence Erlbaum Associates.

Patel, V.L., Groen, G.J. and Scott, H.M. (1988). Biomedical knowledge in explanations of clinical problems by medical students. *Medical Education* **22**, 398–406.

Patel, V.L., Evans, D.A. and Groen, G.J. (1989a). Biomedical knowledge and clinical reasoning. In D.A. Evans and V.L. Patel (Eds), *Cognitive science in medicine*. Cambridge, MA: MIT Press.

Patel, V.L., Evans, D.A. and Kaufman, D.R. (1989b). *Reasoning strategies and the use of biomedical knowledge by medical students*. McGill University pre-publication Manuscript, Technical Report No. CME89 CS14.

Patel, V.L., Groen, G.J. and Arocha, J.F. (1990). Medical expertise as a function of task difficulty. *Memory and Cognition* **18**, 394–406.

Patrick, C. (1935). Creative thought in poets. *Archives of Psychology* **26**, 73.

Patrick, C. (1937). Creative thought in artists. *Journal of Psychology* **4**, 35–73.

Payne, J. (1976). Task complexity and contingent processing in decision making: an information search and protocol analysis. *Organizational Behavior and Human Performance* **16**, 366–387.

Payne, J.W., Bettman, J.R. and Johnson, E.J. (1993). *The adaptive decision maker.* Cambridge: Cambridge University Press.

Payne, J.W., Bettman, J.R. and Johnson, E.J. (1988). Adaptive strategy selection in decision making. *Journal of Experimental Psychology: Learning, memory and cognition* **14**, 534–552.

Pearl, J. (1983). On the nature of pathology in game searching. *Artificial Intelligence* **20**, 427–453.

Perkins, D. (1981). *The mind's best work.* Cambridge, MA: Harvard University Press.

Peterson, C.R. and Peterson, M.J. (1959). Short-term retention of individual verbal items. *Journal of Experimental Psychology* **58**, 193–198.

Pfau, H.D. and Murphy, M.D. (1988). The role of verbal knowledge in chess skill. *American Journal of Psychology* **98**, 271–282.

Platt, J.R. (1964). Strong inference. *Science* **146**, 347–353.

Poincaré, H. (1908). *Science et méthode.* Paris: Flammarion.

Politzer, G. and Nguyen-Xuan, A. (1992). Reasoning about conditional promises and warnings: darwinian algorithms, mental models, relevance judgements or pragmatic schemas? *Quarterly Journal of Experimental Psychology* **44**, 401–412.

Pollard, P. and Evans, J.St.B.T. (1981). The effects of prior beliefs in reasoning: an associational interpretation. *British Journal of Psychology* **72**, 73–82. Cambridge, MA: Harvard University Press.

Polson, P.G. and Jeffries, R. (1982). Problem solving as search and understanding. In R.J. Sternberg (Ed.), *Advances in the psychology of human intelligence.* Hillsdale, NJ: Lawrence Erlbaum Associates.

Polya, G. (1957). *How to solve it.* Princeton, NJ: Princeton University Press.

Pope, K.S. and Singer, J.L. (1978). Regulation of the stream of consciousness: toward a theory of ongoing thought. In G.E. Schwartz and D. Shapiro (Eds), *Consciousness and self-regulation,* Vol. 2. New York: John Wiley.

Pople, H.E. (1982). Heuristic methods for imposing structure on ill structured problems: the structuring of medical diagnostics. In P. Szolovits (Ed.), *Artificial intelligence in medicine.* Boulder, CO: Westview Press.

Popper, K.R. (1959). *The logic of scientific discovery.* London: Hutchinson.

Pylyshyn, Z.W. (1973). What the mind's eye tells the mind's brain: a critique of mental imagery. *Psychological Bulletin* **80**, 1–24.

Pylyshyn, Z.W. (1981). The imagery debate: analogue media versus tacit knowledge. *Psychological Review* **88**, 16–45.

Qin, Y. and Simon, H.A. (1990). Laboratory replication of scientific discovery process. *Cognitive Science* **14**, 281–312.

Quillian, M.R. (1968). Semantic memory. In M. Minsky (Ed.), *Semantic information processing.* Cambridge, MA: MIT Press.

Quinlan, P. (1991). *Connectionism and psychology: a psychological perspective on new connectionist research.* Hemel Hempstead, UK: Harvester-Wheatsheaf.

Raphael, B. (1976). *The thinking computer.* San Francisco, CA: Freeman.

Reason, J. (1979). Actions not as planned: the price of automatization. In G. Underwood and K. Stevens (Eds), *Aspects of consciousness,* Vol. 1. London: Academic Press.

Reed, S.K., Dempster, A. and Ettinger, M. (1985). Usefulness of analogous solutions for solving algebra word problems. *Journal of Experimental Psychology: Learning, Memory and Cognition* **11**, 106–125.

Reitman, J. (1976). Skilled perception in Go: deducing memory structures from interresponse times. *Cognitive Psychology* **8**, 336–356.

Reitman, W.R. (1965). *Cognition and thought.* New York: John Wiley.

Remington, R.W., Shafto, M.G. and Seifert, C.M. (1992). How human is SOAR? *Behavioral and Brain Sciences* **15**, 455.

Resnick, L.B., Levine, J.M. and Teasly, S.D. (Eds), (1990). *Socially shared cognition.* Washington, DC: American Psychological Association.

Restle, F. and Davis, J.H. (1962). Success and speed of problem solving by individuals and groups. *Psychological Review* **69**, 520–536.

Rips, L.J. (1983). Cognitive processes in propositional reasoning. *Psychological Review* **90**, 38–71.

Rips, L.J. (1994). *The psychology of proof: deductive reasoning in human thinking.* Cambridge, MA: MIT Press.

Ritov, I. and Baron, J. (1990). Reluctance to vaccinate: omission bias and ambiguity. *Journal of Behavioral Decision Making* **3**, 263–277.

Robinson, J.A. (1965). A machine oriented logic based on the resolution principle. *Journal of the Association for Computing Machinery* **12**, 25–41.

Roe, A. (1952). A psychologist examines sixty-four eminent scientists. *Scientific American* **187**, 21–25.

Rosch, E. (1978). Principles of categorization. In *Cognition and categorization.* Hillsdale, NJ: Lawrence Erlbaum Associates.

Ross, B.H. (1984). Remindings and their effects learning a cognitive skill. *Cognitive Psychology* **16**, 371–416.

Ross, B.H. (1989). Distinguishing types of superficial similarities: different effects on the access and use of earlier problems. *Journal of Experimental Psychology: Learning, Memory and Cognition* **15**, 456–468.

Ross, B.H. and Kennedy, P.T. (1990). Generalizing from the use of earlier examples in problem solving. *Journal of Experimental Psychology: Learning, Memory and Cognition* **16**, 42–55.

Ruger, H. (1910). The psychology of efficiency. *Archives of Psychology (New York)* **15**.

Rumain, B., Connell, J. and Braine, M.D.S. (1983). Conversational comprehension processes are responsible for reasoning fallacies in children as well as adults. *Developmental Psychology* **19**, 471–481.

Rumelhart, D.E. (1980). Schemata: the building blocks of cognition. In R.J. Spiro, B.C. Bruce and W.F. Brewer (Eds), *Theoretical issues in reading comprehension.* Hillsdale, NJ: Lawrence Erlbaum Associates.

Rumelhart, D.E. and McClelland, J.L. (1982). An interactive activation model of context effects in letter perception: Part 2. The contextual enhancement effect and some tests and extensions of the model. *Psychological Review* **89**, 60–94.

Rumelhart, D.E. and McClelland, J.L. (1986). On learning the past tenses of English verbs. In J.L. McClelland, D.E. Rumelhart and the PDP Research Group (Eds), *Parallel distributed processing*, Vol. 2. Cambridge, MA: MIT Press.

Rumelhart, D.E., Hinton, G.E. and McClelland, J.L. (1986a). A general framework for parallel distributed processing. In D.E. Rumelhart, J.L. McClelland and the PDP Research Group (Eds), *Parallel distributed processing*, Vol. 1. Cambridge, MA: MIT Press.

Rumelhart, D.E., McClelland, J.L. and the PDP Research Group (Eds) (1986b). *Parallel distributed processing*, Vol. 1. Cambridge, MA: MIT Press.

Rumelhart, D.E., Smolensky, P., McClelland, J.L. and Hinton, G.E. (1986c). Schemata and sequential thought processes in PDP models. In J.L. McClelland, D.E. Rumelhart and the PDP Research Group (Eds), *Parallel distributed processing*, Vol. 2. Cambridge, MA: MIT Press.

Russo, J.E. and Dosher, B.A. (1983). Strategies for multiattribute binary choice. *Journal of Experimental Psychology: Learning, Memory and Cognition* **9**, 676–696.

Saariluoma, P. (1984). Coding problem spaces in chess. *Commentationes scientarium socialium*, Vol. 23. Turku: Societas Scientiarum Fennica.

Saariluoma, P. (1985). Chess players' intake of task relevant cues. *Memory and Cognition* **13**, 385–391.

Saariluoma, P. (1990a). Chess players search for task relevant cues: are chunks relevant? In D. Brogan (Ed.), *Visual search.* London: Taylor and Francis.

Saariluoma, P. (1990b). Apperception and restructuring in chess players' problem solving. In

K.J. Gilhooly, M.T.G. Keane, R.H. Logie and G. Erdos (Eds), *Lines of thought: reflections on the psychology of thinking*, Vol. 2. Chichester, UK: J. Wiley.

Saariluoma, P. (1991a). Visuo-spatial interference and apperception in chess. In M. Denis and R.H. Logie (Eds), *Mental images in human cognition*. Amsterdam: Elsevier.

Saariluoma, P. (1991b). Aspects of skilled memory in blindfold chess. *Acta Psychologica* **77**, 65–89.

Saariluoma, P. (1992). Visuo-spatial and articulatory interference in chess players' information intake. *Applied Cognitive Psychology* **6**, 77–89.

Samuelson, W. and Zeckhauser, R. (1988). Status-quo bias in decision making. *Journal of Risk and Uncertainty* **1**, 7–59.

Savage, L.J. (1954). *The foundation of statistics*. New York: J. Wiley.

Schacter, S. (1968). Obesity and eating. *Science* **161**, 751–756.

Scheerer, M. (1963). Problem-solving. *Scientific American* **208**, 118–128.

Schmidt, H.G. and Boshuizen, H.P.A. (1993). On the origin of intermediate effects in clinical case recall. *Memory and Cognition* **21**, 338–351.

Schmidt, H.G., Boshuizen, H.P.A. and Hobus, P.P.M. (1988). Transitory stages in the development of medical expertise: the intermediate effect in clinical case representation studies. Paper at 10th Annual Conference of Cognitive Science Society, Montreal, Canada.

Schmidt, H.G. and Norman, G.R. (1988). *On the development of expertise in medicine: evidence from case-representation studies*. Technical Report No.123, University of Limburg, Maastricht, The Netherlands.

Schoenfeld, A.H. (1983). Episodes and executive decisions in mathematical problem solving. In R. Lesh and M. Landau (Eds), *Acquisition of mathematical concepts and processes*. New York: Academic Press.

Schoenfeld, A.H. and Hermann, D.J. (1982). Problem perception and knowledge structure in expert and novice mathematical problem solvers. *Journal of Experimental Psychology: Learning, Memory and Cognition* **8**, 484–494.

Searle, J. (1984). *Minds, brains and science*. London: British Broadcasting Corporation.

Searle, J. (1990). Is the brain's mind a computer program? *Scientific American* **262**, 20–25.

Sells, S.B. (1936). The atmosphere effect: an experimental study of reasoning. *Archives of Psychology* **200**, 1–72.

Sells, S.B. and Koob, H.F. (1937). A classroom demonstration of 'atmosphere effect' in reasoning. *Journal of Educational Psychology* **72**, 197–200.

Shallice, T. (1972). Dual functions of consciousness. *Psychological Review* **79**, 383–393.

Shallice, T. (1978). The dominant action system: an information-processing approach to consciousness. In K.S. Pope and J.L. Singer (Eds), *The stream of consciousness*. New York: John Wiley.

Shannon, C. (1950). Programming a computer to play chess. *Philosophy Magazine* **41**, 256–275.

Shapiro, D. (1971). 'Representativeness', structure and content in a reasoning problem. *Bulletin of the British Psychological Society* **24**, 43–44.

Shepard, R.N. and Metzler, J. (1971). Mental rotation of three-dimensional objects. *Science* **171**, 701–703.

Simon, H.A. (1957). *Models of man: social and rational*. New York: John Wiley.

Simon, H.A. (1966). Scientific discovery and the psychology of problem solving. In R.G. Colodny (Ed.), *Mind and cosmos: essays in contemporary science and philosophy*. Pittsburgh: University of Pittsburgh Press.

Simon, H.A. (1967). Motivational and emotional controls of cognition. *Psychological Review* **74**, 29–39.

Simon, H.A. (1975). The functional equivalence of problem solving skills. *Cognitive Psychology* **7**, 268–288.

Simon, H.A. (1978). Rationality as process and product of thought. *American Economic Association* **68**, 1–16.

Simon, H. and Barenfeld, M. (1969). Information-processing analysis of perceptual processes in problem-solving. *Psychological Review* **76**, 473–483.

Simon, H.A. and Chase, W.G. (1973). Skill in chess. *American Scientist* **61**, 394–403.

Simon, H. and Gilmartin, K. (1973). A simulation of memory for chess positions. *Cognitive Psychology* **8**, 165–190.

Simon, H.A. and Hayes, J.R. (1976). The understanding process: problem isomorphs. *Cognitive Psychology* **8**, 165–190.

Simon, H.A. and Kaplan, C.A. (1989). Foundations of cognitive science. In M.I. Posner (Ed.), *Foundations of cognitive science*. Cambridge, MA: MIT Press.

Simon, H.A. and Reed, S.K. (1976). Modelling strategy shifts on a problem solving task. *Cognitive Psychology* **8**, 86–97.

Simonton, D.K. (1977). Creative productivity, age and stress: A biographical time-series analysis of 10 classical composers. *Journal of Personality and Social Psychology* **35**, 791–804.

Simonton, D.K. (1984). Creative productivity and age: a mathematical model based on a 2-step cognitive process. *Developmental Review* **4**, 77–111.

Simonton, D.K. (1988). Creativity, leadership and chance. In R.J. Sternberg (Ed.), *The nature of creativity*. Cambridge: Cambridge University Press.

Singer, J.L. (1975a). Navigating the stream of daydreaming and related inner experience. *American Psychologist* **30**, 727–738.

Singer, J.L. (1975b). *Daydreaming and fantasy*. London: Allen and Unwin.

Singer, J.L. (1978). Studies of daydreaming. In K.S. Pope and J.L. Singer (Eds), *The stream of consciousness*. New York: J. Wiley.

Singer, J.L. and Antrobus, J.S. (1972). Daydreaming, imaginal processes, and personality: a normative study. In P. Sheehan (Ed.), *The function and nature of imagery*. New York: Academic Press.

Singer, J.L. and McCraven, V. (1961). Some characteristics of adult daydreaming. *Journal of Psychology* **51**, 151–164.

Skinner, B.F. (1985). Cognitive science and behaviourism. *British Journal of Psychology* **76**, 291–301.

Slate, D.J. and Atkin, C.R. (1977). Chess 4.5. The Northwestern University chess program. In P.W. Frey (Ed.), *Chess skill in man and machine*. New York: Springer.

Slovic, P., Fischhoff, B. and Lichtenstein, S. (1982). Response mode, framing, and information processing effects in risk assessment. In R. Hogarth (Ed.), *New directions for methodology of social and behavioral science: question framing and response consistency*. San Francisco, CA: Jossey-Bass.

Smalley, N.S. (1974). Evaluating a rule against possible instances. *British Journal of Psychology* **65**, 293–304.

Smith, E.E., Langston, C. and Nisbett, R.E. (1992). The case for rules in reasoning. *Cognitive Science* **16**, 99–102.

Smolensky, P. (1986). Information processing in dynamical systems: foundations of harmony theory. In D.E. Rumelhart, J.L. McClelland and the PDP Research Group (Eds), *Parallel distributed processing*, Vol. 1. Cambridge, MA: MIT Press.

Soloway, E., Adelson, B. and Ehrlich, K. (1988). Knowledge and process in the comprehension of computer programs. In M.T.H. Chi, R. Glaser and M.J. Farr (Eds) *The nature of expertise*, Hillsdale, NJ: Lawrence Erlbaum Associates.

Sosniak, L.A. (1985). Learning to be a concert pianist. In B.S. Bloom (Ed.), *Developing talent in young people*. New York: Ballantine Books.

Spelke, E., Hirst, W. and Neisser, U. (1976). Skills of divided attention. *Cognition* **4**, 215–230.

Spence, K.W. (1936). The nature of discrimination learning in animals. *Psychological Review* **43**, 427–449.

Sperling, G.A. (1960). The information available in brief visual presentation. *Psychological Monographs* **74**, No. 498.

Spranca, M., Minsk, E. and Baron, J. (1991). Omission and commission in judgment and choice. *Journal of Experimental Psychology* **27**, 76–105.

Stein, M. (1974). *Stimulating creativity*, Vol. 1. New York: Academic Press.

Stein, M. (1975). *Stimulating creativity*, Vol. 2. New York: Academic Press.

Sternberg, R. (1987). Coping with novelty and human intelligence. In P. Morris (Ed.), *Modelling cognition*. Chichester, UK: John Wiley.

Sternberg, R.J. and Davidson, J.E. (1982). Componential analysis and componential theory. *Behavioral and Brain Sciences* **53**, 352–353.

Swanson, D.B. (1987). A measurement performance for performance-based tests. In I. Hart and R. Harden (Eds), *Further developments in assessing clinical competence*. Montreal: Heal.

Swanson, D.B. and Stillman, P.L. (1990). Use of standardized patients for teaching and assessing clinical skills. *Evaluation and the Health Professions* **13**, 79–103.

Sweller, J. and Levine, M. (1982). Effects of goal specificity on means–ends analysis and learning. *Journal of Experimental Psychology: Learning, Memory and Cognition* **8**, 463–474.

Sweller, J., Mawer, R.F. and Ward, M.R. (1983). Development of expertise in mathematical problem-solving. *Journal of Experimental Psychology: General* **112**, 639–661.

Taplin, J.E. (1971). Reasoning with conditional sentences. *Journal of Verbal Learning and Verbal Behaviour* **10**, 219–225.

Taylor, D.W., Berry, P.C. and Block, C.H. (1958). Does group participating when using brainstorming facilitate or inhibit creative thinking? *Administrative Science Quarterly* **3**, 23–47.

Teasdale, J.D. (1989). Daydreaming, depression and distraction. *The Psychologist* **2**, 189–190 (Abstract).

Teasdale, J.D. and Barnard, P.J. (1993). *Affect, cognition and change: re-modelling depressive thought*. Hove, UK: Lawrence Erlbaum Associates.

Thomas, J.C., Jr. (1974). An analysis of behavior in the hobbits–orcs problem. *Cognitive Psychology* **6**, 257–269.

Thorndike, E.L. (1898). *Animal intelligence*. New York: Macmillan.

Thouless, R.H. (1953). *Straight and crooked thinking*. London: Pan Books.

Tikhomirov, O.K. and Poznyanskaya, E.D. (1966). An investigation of visual search as a means of analysing heuristics. *Soviet Psychology* **5**, 3–15.

Tikhomirov, O.K. and Terekhov, V.A. (1967). Evristiki cheloveka (human heuristics). *Voprosy Psikhologii* **13**, 26–41.

Tolkien, J.R.R. (1966). *The hobbit*, 3rd edn. London: Allen and Unwin.

Tulving, E.C. (1983). *Elements of episodic memory*. Oxford: Oxford University Press.

Tukey, D.D. (1986). A philosophical and empirical analysis of subject's modes of inquiry in Wason's 2–4–6 task. *Quarterly Journal of Experimental Psychology* **38A**, 5–34.

Tversky, A. (1969). Intransitivity of preferences. *Psychological Review* **76**, 31–48.

Tversky, A. (1972). Elimination by aspects: a theory of choice. *Psychological Review* **79**, 281–299.

Tversky, A. and Kahneman, D. (1974). Judgment under uncertainty: heuristic and biases. *Science* **125**, 1124–1131.

Tversky, A. and Kahneman, D. (1980). Causal schemata in judgements under uncertainty. In M. Fishbein (Ed.), *Progress in social psychology*. Hillsdale, NJ: Lawrence Erlbaum Associates.

Tversky, A. and Kahneman, D. (1981). The framing of decisions and the psychology of choice. *Science* **211**, 453–458.

Tversky, A. and Kahneman, D. (1983). Extensional *vs.* intuitive reasoning: the conjunction fallacy in probability judgement. *Psychological Review* **90**, 293–315.

Tweney, R.D. (1985). Faraday's discovery of induction: a cognitive approach. In D. Gooding and F. James (Eds), *Faraday rediscovered: essays on the life and work of Michael Faraday, 1771–1867*. New York: Stockton Press.

Tweney, R.D., Doherty, M.E., Warner, W.J., Pliske, D.B., Mynatt, C.R., Gross, K.A. and Arkkezin, D.L. (1980). Strategies of rule discovery in an inference task. *Quarterly Journal of Experimental Psychology* **32**, 109–124.

Van Duyne, P.C. (1974). Realism and linguistic complexity in reasoning. *British Journal of Psychology* **65**, 59–67.

Van Duyne, P.C. (1976). Necessity and contingency in reasoning. *Acta Psychologica* **40**, 85–101.

Varendonck, J. (1921). *The psychology of daydreams*. New York: Macmillan.

Vernon, P.E. (1970). *Creativity*. Harmondsworth, UK: Penguin Books.

Vincente, K.J. and Brewer, W.F. (1993). Reconstructive remembering of the scientific literature. *Cognition* **46**, 101–128.

Vincente, K.J. and de Groot, A.D. (1990). The memory recall paradigm: straightening out the historical record. *American Psychologist* **45**, 285–297.

Von Neumann, T. and Morgenstern, O. (1944). *Theory of games and economic behavior*. Princeton, NJ: Princeton University Press.

Voss, J.F., Greene, T.R., Post, T.A. and Penner, B.C. (1983). Problem solving skill in the social sciences. In G. Bower (Ed.), *The psychology of learning and motivation*, Vol. 17. New York: Academic Press.

Voss, J.F., Wolfe, C.R., Lawrence, J.A. and Engle, R.A. (1991). From representation to decision: an analysis of problem solving in international relations. In R.J. Sternberg and P.A. Frensch (Eds), *Complex problem solving: principles and mechanisms*. Hillsdale, NJ: Lawrence Erlbaum Associates.

Wagner, D.A. and Scurrah, M.J. (1971). Some characteristics of human problem solving in chess. *Cognitive Psychology* **2**, 451–478.

Wallas, G. (1926). *The art of thought*. London: Jonathan Cape.

Warren, T.F. and Davis, G.A. (1969). Techniques for creative thinking: an empirical comparison of three methods. *Psychological Reports* **25**, 207–214.

Wason, P.C. (1960). On the failure to eliminate hypotheses in a conceptual task. *Quarterly Journal of Experimental Psychology* **12**, 129–140.

Wason, P.C. (1966). Reasoning. In B.M. Foss (Ed.), *New horizons in psychology*. Harmondsworth: Penguin.

Wason, P.C. (1968). Reasoning about a rule. *Quarterly Journal of Experimental Psychology* **20**, 273–281.

Wason, P.C. (1969). Regression in reasoning? *British Journal of Psychology* **60**, 471–480.

Wason, P.C. and Evans, J.St.B.T. (1975). Dual processes in reasoning? *Cognition* **3**, 141–154.

Wason, P.C. and Johnson-Laird, P.N. (1970). A conflict between selecting and evaluating information in an inferential task. *British Journal of Psychology* **61**, 509–515.

Wason, P.C. and Johnson-Laird, P.N. (1972). *Psychology of reasoning: structure and content*. London: Batsford.

Wason, P.C. and Shapiro, D. (1971). Natural and contrived experience in a reasoning problem. *Quarterly Journal of Experimental Psychology* **23**, 63–71.

Watson, J.B. (1913). Psychology as the behaviorist views it. *Psychological Review* **20**, 158–177.

Wegner, D.M. (1994). Ironic processes of mental control. *Psychological Review* **101**, 34–52.

Wegner, D.M. and Erber, R. (1992). The hyperaccessibility of suppressed thoughts. *Journal of Personality and Social Psychology* **63**, 903–912.

Wegner, D.M., Schneider, D.J., Carter, S. and White, L. (1987). Paradoxical effects of thought suppression. *Journal of Personality and Social Psychology* **53**, 5–13.

Wegner, D.M., Shortt, J.W., Blake, A.W. and Page, M.S. (1990). The suppression of exciting thoughts. *Journal of Personality and Social Psychology* **58**, 408–418.

Wegner, D.M., Erber, R. and Bowman, R.E. (1993a). *On trying not to be sexist* (unpublished manuscript).

Wegner, D.M., Erber, R. and Zanakos, S. (1993b). Ironic processes in the mental control of mood and mood-related thought. *Journal of Personality and Social Psychology* **65**, 1093–1104.

Weisberg, R.W. (1986). Creativity: genius and other myths. San Francisco, CA: W.H. Freeman.

Weisberg, R.W. (1988). Problem solving and creativity. In R.J. Sternberg (Ed.), *The nature of creativity: contemporary psychological perspectives*. Cambridge: Cambridge University Press.

Weisberg, R.W. and Alba, J.W. (1981a). An examination of the alleged role of 'fixation' in the solution of several 'insight' problems. *Journal of Experimental Psychology: General* **110**, 169–192.

Weisberg, R.W. and Alba, J.W. (1981b). Gestalt theory, insight and past experience: reply to Dominowski. *Journal of Experimental Psychology: General* **110**, 193–198.

Weisberg, R.W. and Alba, J.W. (1982). Problem solving is not like perception: more on Gestalt theory. *Journal of Experimental Psychology: General* **111**, 326–330.

Wertheimer, M. (1945). *Productive thinking*. New York: Harper and Row.

Wetherick, N.E. (1962). Eliminative and enumerative behaviour in a conceptual task. *Quarterly Journal of Experimental Psychology* **14**, 246–249.

Wetherick, N.E. (1970). On the representativeness of some experiments in cognition. *Bulletin of the British Psychological Society* **23**, 213–214.

Wetherick, N.E. (1971). 'Representativeness' in a reasoning problem: a reply to Shapiro. *Bulletin of the British Psychological Society* **24**, 213–214.

Wetherick, N.E. (1979). The foundations of psychology. In N. Bolton (Ed.), *Philosophical problems in psychology*, pp. 89–100. London: Methuen.

Wetherick, N.E. (1989). Psychology and syllogistic reasoning. *Philosophical Psychology* **2**, 111–124.

Wetherick, N.E. (1993). More models just means more difficulty. *Behavioral and Brain Sciences* **16**, 367–368.

Wetherick, N.E. and Gilhooly, K.J. (1990). Syllogistic reasoning: effects of premise order. In K. Gilhooly, M.T.G. Keane, R. Logie and G. Erdos (Eds), *Lines of thought: reflections in the psychology of thinking*, Vol. 1. London: John Wiley.

Wetherick, N.E. and Gilhooly, K.J. (1995). Atmosphere, matching and logic in syllogistic reasoning. *Current Psychology*, **14**(3), 000–000.

Wharton, C.M., Cheng, P.W. and Wickens, T. D. (1993). Hypothesis testing strategies: why two goals are better than one. *Quarterly Journal of Experimental Psychology* **46A**, 743–758.

White, P.A. (1988). Knowing more about what we can tell: 'Introspective access' and causal report accuracy 10 years later. *British Journal of Psychology* **79**, 13–46.

White, P.A. (1989). Evidence for the use of information about internal events to improve the accuracy of causal reports. *British Journal of Psychology* **80**, 375–382.

Wickelgren, W. (1974). *How to solve problems*. San Francisco, CA: W.H. Freeman.

Wilkins, M. (1928). The effect of changed material on ability to do formal syllogistic reasoning. *Archives of Psychology* **16**, 83.

Winston, P.H. (1984). *Artificial intelligence*, 2nd edn. New York: Addison-Wesley.

Woodworth, R.S. and Schosberg, H. (1954). *Experimental psychology*, 3rd edn. London: Methuen.

Woodworth, R.S. and Sells, S.B. (1935). An atmosphere effect in formal syllogistic reasoning. *Journal of Experimental Psychology* **18**, 451–460.

Wright, G. (1984). *Behavioural decision theory*. Harmondsworth: Penguin Books.

Young, R. (1974). Production systems as models of cognitive development. *Bionics Research Reports*, No. 22. Bionics Research Laboratory, School of Artificial Intelligence, University of Edinburgh, Edinburgh.

Yaniv, I. and Meyer, D.E. (1987). Activation and metacognition of inaccessible stored information: potential bases for incubation effects in problem solving. *Journal of Experimental Psychology: Learning, Motivation and Cognition* **13**, 187–205.

Zakay, D. (1985). Post-decisional confidence and conflict experienced in a choice process. *Acta Psychologica* **58**, 75–80.

Zangwill, O.L. (1980). Kenneth Craik: the man and his work. *British Journal of Psychology* **71**, 1–16.

Zimbardo, P.G., Cohen, A., Weisenberg, M., Dworkin, L. and Firestone, I. (1969a). The control of experimental pain. In P.G. Zimbardo (Ed.), *The cognitive control of motivation.* Glenview, IL: Scott, Foresman.

Zimbardo, P.G., Weisenberg, M., Firestone, I. and Levy, B. (1969b). Changing appetites for eating fried grasshoppers with cognitive dissonance. In P.G. Zimbardo (Ed.), *The cognitive control of motivation.* Glenview, IL: Scott, Foresman.

Zwicky, F. (1969). *Discovery, invention, research.* New York: Macmillan.

Author Index

Subject Index